Theorizing Emotions

Debra Hopkins is a researcher at Aberdeen University and vice coordinator of the Sociology of Emotions Network. *Jochen Kleres* is currently finishing his PhD at the University of Leipzig. *Helena Flam* is professor of sociology at the University of Leipzig. *Helmut Kuzmics* is professor of sociology at the University of Graz.

Debra Hopkins, Jochen Kleres,
Helena Flam, Helmut Kuzmics (eds.)

Theorizing Emotions

Sociological Explorations and Applications

Campus Verlag
Frankfurt/New York

Bibliographic Information published by the Deutsche Nationalbibliothek.
Die Deutsche Nationalbibliothek lists this publication in the Deutsche Nationalbibliografie;
detailed bibliographic data are available in the Internet at http://dnb.d-nb.de.
ISBN 978-3-593-38972-1

Printed on acid free paper.
Printed in the United States of America

For further information:
www.campus.de
www.press.uchicago.edu

Contents

Preface: Notes on the Sociology of Emotions in Europe

Jochen Kleres

This volume opens a book series that will reflect a collective effort of the Emotions Network within the European Sociological Association. It is dedicated to theoretical developments in the sociology of emotions and captures the diversity of advances made by members of the network. Thus there is no overarching theoretical frame. Rather, contributions range from historical analyses and explorations in classical sociology to discourse and postmodern approaches. Finally, a number of chapters combine theoretical concerns with empirical research.

While this volume focuses on theoretical issues, future titles will cover emotions in organizations, methodology and politics/civil society. As a whole, the series is intended to display the most recent developments, contributions and achievements of the network. The diversity of theoretical approaches and subject matters in this volume as well as the thematic scope of the planned series testify to a constitutive premise of the sociology of emotions: the fundamental relevance of emotions to all aspects of social life and hence to sociology in general. As many academic fields are witnessing a so-called emotional turn, chances to promote this premise have considerably increased. Our endeavor is arguably bolstered by the other turns in our own and cognate disciplines, notably the biographical and the narrative turn.

The Emergence of the ESA Emotions Network

While some other sociological associations have over two decades old sections for emotion research (e.g. ASA, BSA, see Barbalet 2001, 21), the Emotions Network within the European Sociological Association (ESA) was established in 2004 after Jack Barbalet, a well-known theorist, organized a research stream devoted to emotions at the bi-annual ESA-conference in Murcia, Spain in 2003. This was preceded by a mini-conference in Leipzig, Germany, organized by Helena Flam, informal networks between a number of Europe-based scholars, such as Helena Flam, Jack Barbalet, Charlotte Bloch, and a collected volume edited by Jack Barbalet (2002). These focused efforts represent a distinct point of departure from the rather scattered state in which the sociology of emotions found itself in Europe for many years. Prior to the network's inception, sociological emotion research was mainly a project of individual scholars who stood more or less isolated within their national research communities or who blended in with other, related but distinct, research niches. In many ways, the sociology of emotions, in Europe, developed from the margins.

In German speaking countries, for instance, Jürgen Gerhards (1988), Brigitta Nedelmann (e.g. 1983; 1988) or Helmut Kuzmics (e.g. 1986; 1991; 1994; 1997; Kuzmics and Axtmann 2007) were among the first sociologists to take up emotions but remained isolated and later the first two moved away from the field. However, a few years later Helena Flam (1990a; 1990b) published a two-part article in *International Sociology* that made the American sociology of emotions widely visible to a broad audience in Germany and abroad. While she remained committed to research on emotions, she too was relatively isolated in Germany as were also such scholars as Sieghard Neckel (e.g. 1991; 1996). In sum, there was a handful of sociologists working on emotions, but they lacked a connecting framework and a critical mass. It took another decade before the sociology of emotions began to really take off as a distinguishable field. With this change in recent years, however, emotional issues have begun to receive increasing attention by sociologists in German speaking countries and a diverse group of academics is dealing with emotions, as perhaps recurring emotion-related sessions during national sociology conferences and an increasing number of publications demonstrate (e.g. Flam 2002; Schützeichel 2006; Scherke forthcoming; 2008a; Vandekerckhove et al. 2008). Indeed, the nineties, in the German speaking context, signify a decade during which sociological research on emotions managed to slowly establish itself (Scherke 2008b, 6).

The UK stands proud here as it arguably featured the strongest development of social science research on emotions in Europe. A series of collected volumes testifies to this development (Harré 1986; Fineman 1993; Harré and Parrott 1996; Bendelow and Williams 1998; see also Flam 2002, 118). The British Sociological Association established a section on emotions already in 1990. While Jack Barbalet worked in the UK for a few years before returning to Australia, as a key representative of the British sociology of emotions, together with Helena Flam, he was instrumental in initiating ESA's Emotions Network.

Another stronghold of the sociology of emotions in Europe developed in the Scandinavian countries, partly in the context of the fledgling European network. In Copenhagen Charlotte Bloch and in Karlstad, Sweden, Bengt Starrin, Gerd Lindgren and Åsa Wettergren were key figures in this process. Charlotte Bloch was one of the two initial vice-coordinators of the network and Åsa Wettergren its second convenor. Karlstad University organized a Scandinavian workshop on emotions, and later on, hosted the network's midterm conference in October 2006. Its interactive and rather informal form, along with the participation of Tom Scheff, no doubt accounted for its ability to attract already established Scandinavian emotion researchers, and also accounts for the presence of hitherto uninitiated mostly Scandinavian scholars. This midterm conference created the momentum for a sociology of emotions in these Scandinavian countries. Karlstad University also stands as an important nurturer of transatlantic and European relations.

Another foundation from which the present network emerged in Europe is Elias' figuration sociology, or rather civilization theory. Elias can indeed be seen as an important reference point for a sociology of emotions within classical social theory (cf. e.g. Neckel 1991 for an example that utilizes Elias without applying his framework of figuration sociology). Proponents of an Elias-inspired sociology have for years formed their own academic community. With a couple of exceptions, inasmuch as they dealt with emotions, they tended to do so under the heading of figuration sociology or civilization theory, rather than from the perspective of a more general sociology of emotion. This may be one reason why the contributions of Eliasian research to a sociology of emotions had not crossed the confines of this niche. The network came to function as a bridge into this research community as well, since some Elias' disciples now form an integral part of the network. Most notably, this goes for Helmut Kuzmics and Cas Wouters, both of whom are acclaimed Elias-experts. Both have long since contributed to the development of the burgeoning sociology of emotions. Kuzmics (1986; 1991), for example, offered an emotion-focused comparison of Goffman and Elias, while Wouters (1989; 1990) critically engaged with Hochschild's work and also traced the emergence of a sociology of emotions (Wouters 1992). There have also been some personal contacts, such as that between Helmut Kuzmics and Thomas Scheff, who had appreciated Elias' work prior to this contact. These examples suggest that the actual lack of transnational contacts may also have been conditioned by the reluctance of the burgeoning sociology of emotions to take on also an Eliasian approach to emotions.

As the contributions to this volume indicate, however, the network is not limited to a few UK-based, Scandinavian, Dutch or German speaking scholars. It reaches beyond Europe and includes, for instance, scientists from Israel, Australia, New Zealand and the US, reflecting the fact that the sociology of emotions in Europe has often been inspired and further promoted by contacts and exchange with leading academics from outside Europe.

It seems then that a number of scholars had been dealing with emotions long before the network was started. Their work had predated what has come to be known as the emotional turn. However, the logic of geographic and institutional boundaries, and of scholarly appetites, determined that these scholars were working alone or within other research niches. Today, however, and arguably due to the European character of the network under the auspices of the ESA, comprising a host of different scholarly traditions, the network is rapidly expanding. At the midterm workshop, hosted by the International Institute of Sociology at its congress in Budapest in 2008, the network received a large number of abstracts for consideration for the five sessions that we were granted. For the approaching ESA conference in Lisbon, more than 75 abstracts were submitted, many coming from France, Spain and Portugal. The number of members is now over 150.

As part of the so-called emotional turn in a host of academic disciplines, research on emotions is now greatly diversified beyond the immediate scope of the emotion network. Thus, the network has developed in the context of larger intellectual currents. It is to some of these trends that the next section will turn.

Some Notes on the Sociology of Emotions and the Themes in This Volume

Classical Sociology

The sociology of emotions can now look back on more than three decades of theorizing starting with a number of seminal publications in the mid-seventies (see Kemper 1990b, 3–4). This is sometimes described as part of a wider so-called emotional turn that spans across many academic disciplines, which is, however, a discourse of more recent origin than the sociology of emotions (cf. Greco and Stenner 2008b, 9). The sociology of emotions as a distinct sub-discipline is not only older than this recent turn, it can and should in fact draw on much older lines of theorizing emotions that go back to classical sociology. Modern sociology has been largely mute on emotions and remains hesitant to acknowledge their fundamental relevance to all social life. This explains the continuing status of the sociology of emotions as a specialized sub-discipline (on the expulsion of emotion from modern social theory see Barbalet 2001, 13–20). Classical sociology, in contrast, has often, albeit to varying degrees, included emotions in its theorizing (see e.g. Flam 2002; Shilling 2002; Barbalet 2001; Kuzmics 1986; 1991). Consider, for instance, Simmel, Durkheim, Weber, Cooley, Elias, Goffman or Garfinkel etc.—all of whom have included emotions in their theorizing. Arlie Hochschild (in this volume) points out that in this sense the sociology of emotions had existed for a long time before its name was coined. However, as also evidenced by some recent overviews of the field (e.g. Turner and Stets 2005; Stets and Turner 2006; Greco and Stenner 2008a), the role of emotions in classical sociology remains an under-researched niche (Flam 2002, 16; Shilling 2002), although prominent contemporary emotion theorists draw extensively upon classical sociology. For example, Goffman or Durkheim are central to the work of Hochschild (1979; 1983), Collins (1975) and Scheff (in this volume).

In many ways, this volume demonstrates the relevance of sociological classics to the study of emotions and hence the fundamental relevance of emotions to social theory and social life. Arlie Hochschild in her introductory reflections on her path-breaking intellectual journey describes the importance of classical sociology for her theorizing. She draws a line starting from her early inspiration by classics to her ongoing research on emotional labor in the globalized world that focuses on the interface between self and deep commodification. Indeed, as Hochschild concludes, this interface goes to the heart of the age in which we live. Helena Flam's contribution addresses the classics most directly by focusing on one of the central problems of sociology—that of social order. In her survey of the classics' answers to this problem she aptly demonstrates how these theorists view emotions as intimately intertwined with social order. By juxtaposing different theories, she can differentiate a number of ways in which the significance of emotions to social order can be theorized: while some classics view social order as pacifying negative emotions, an alternative view grants them a central role in constituting society. With her analysis, Flam makes a case for the sociology of emotions to move beyond the culture vs. social structure debate and to consider emotions not only as outcomes, but also to theorize about them as causes, generating new structures, institutions or cultural codes.

Other contributors also rely on classical sociology. Katrin Döveling, for instance, derives an emotion theory of group and community formation/reproduction from the works of Durkheim, Simmel and Collins which she then links to the influence of mass media. Cas Wouters has contributed an Eliasian analysis of informalization processes that followed earlier phases of formalization. The classics also lend themselves to meta-analyses, as Helmut Kuzmics' contribution illustrates. He views their texts as narratives that are emotionally structured and indicative of specific emotional approaches to the social world. Patrick Becker scrutinizes the classics' and other theorists' positions on emotions in his consideration of emotions as being a part of a discourse of modernity in his analysis of the genealogy and contemporary changes of the emotion-reason divide.

In sum, as the contributions to this volume testify and amply demonstrate, classical sociology forms a powerful reminder of the centrality of a systematic analysis of emotions to the overall sociological ambition. The chapters also show how classical sociology can inspire new research: while Wouters demonstrates in great detail the significance and potential of one classical approach, Flam stands back one step as she juxtaposes a number of theorists in order to push for overarching theoretical progress. Kuzmics and Becker adopt yet another take by assuming a narrative or discursive perspective on classical and some contemporary sociology.

Sociology and Biology

With the dominance of the cognitive in social theory, emotions as a unit of academic interest have been relegated to the spheres of the biological and the psychological. It was thus left to the emerging sociology of emotions, and indeed constitutive of its quintessence, that it wrestles emotions free from the grip of both of these academic disciplines in order to advance a distinctly sociological take on emotions. However, while developing and spreading this perspective on emotions within social sciences, it has not managed to upset a naturalizing view of emotions. The status of emotions has remained ambivalent—"natural," "neurological," "psychological," or "neuropsychological"—to other academic fields, including general sociology. This is even so within the sociology of emotions itself, where emotions became torn between a positivist-naturalizing camp that acknowledged some debt to biology (Kemper 1990a), and a constructivist-symbolic interactionist camp (Hochschild 1983; see also Thoits 1989, 320–1) that more or less rejected any recourse to biological conceptions.

It is in this split-view context that more recent theoretical trends within the emotional turn have developed. This is particularly true for advances in the neurosciences, presenting a part of the multidisciplinary turn to emotions. As Greco and Stenner (2008b, 9) note, there is a "renewed dominance and cultural presence of biology" contributing to the emotional turn. This seems to operate, among other things, on the basis of Western notions of the mind-body split and corresponding biological-corporeal renditions of emotions, i.e. notions which have retained their dominance when the sociology of emotions remained a marginal endeavor. It may be for this reason that renewed biological conceptions of emotions are sometimes quite readily incorporated into sociological thinking, as indicated by some recent handbooks in the sociology of emotions (Stets and Turner 2006; Turner and Stets 2005). The question of the nature of emotions in terms of academic disciplines is thus posed anew. Greco and Stenner (2008b, 9–10) interpret interest in emotions as a reaction against the exclusive theoretical focus on text and discourse as promoted by the textual turn. They argue for a post-deconstructive deepening of constructivism, a reconciliation between the natural and social sciences. Williams' chapter in this volume is in line with this recent trend of sociologists to take interest in biology. He surveys neurobiological research to identify a number of key areas where sociology and neurobiology could profitably communicate with each other.

This leads him to criticize some constructivist thinking while at the same time arguing for its reconciliation with biology.

While interdisciplinary communication is undoubtedly a laudable cause, a few words of reflection and caution seem necessary in this context. Surely, the sociology of emotions can receive new ideas and stimulating theoretical inputs from other academic disciplines, as Williams' contribution aptly shows (see also Barbalet and Becker, in this volume). It is curious, however, that the call for greater sociological openness to biology comes at a time when sociology at large has only started to come to terms with emotions, and when exploring emotions is yet to establish the strong position in social theory and empirical research that it deserves. This circumstance is so significant for the future of a sociology of emotions that I will afford myself some editorial license here in order to address the "lure of neurosciences."

While the positivist-constructivist debate has occupied the sociology of emotions for many years, the field has certainly not come to a point where its potential for generic sociological development has been fully exploited.[1] In this context, the operation of larger social processes that stimulate the turn towards biology should not be glossed over but taken into critical consideration instead. The social science take on emotions, still far from maturity and self-certainty, competes with the neurosciences' lure—with its promise of hard truths about human matters. Sociologists in turn, may feel inclined to line up with the neurosciences as these can bestow the appeal of "objective" and "real" on their research on emotions. As philosophers, such as Susanne Lettow (2009b; 2009a; 2006) have argued, there may be a tendency in a recent turn towards biology of (implicitly) adopting a naturalist paradigm, that is a rendering of natural sciences as absolute and as a fundamental basis for other disciplines, premised on the assumption that the "methods of natural science provide the only avenue to truth" (Thompson quoted in Keil and Schnädelbach 2000, 12). This may result in the attitude: "[w]here science will lead I will follow" (Keil and Schnädelbach 2000, 22). The primacy granted to natural sciences immunizes these disciplines against the need for any critical reflection, and precludes reflec-

---

1 See, for example, Helena Flam's call in this volume for theoretical comparison and moving beyond existing background assumptions and approaches; see also Jack Katz (1999) for an innovative, genuinely sociological approach that goes beyond a merely textual take on emotions, and his call to take seriously emotions' embodiedness and to combine interview techniques with observation and visual methods.

tions about epistemology (Lettow 2009a, 94). As Lettow (2009a, 88; 2009b) further argues, this stance and its assumption of omni-historical rationality ignores the fact that all human knowledge (including biology) is constructed and that construction processes are socio-culturally situated and intertwined with other historical, cultural and social practices. Attention should be focused on the applications to which a didactic biology, with its dual nature of natural science and socially normative knowledge, may be put—surely of major concern to sociologists. Perhaps an honorable ambition for a sociology of emotions is to continue to harness and develop new approaches to emotions, while keeping a keen eye on the role of epistemology and a keen sense for ideology's tendency to masquerade as science. As critics we should examine particular trends and hot spots in the scientific landscape—the Human Genome Project would be one, another would be the manufacturing and rise of the neurochemical self (Rose 2003). One key topic is their relationship to the ongoing struggle in the polity and academia as to how we should as a civilized society approach difference. The emphasis on the internal logic of the scientific method—objectivity, the dispassionate operator—fails to convince when one considers that emotions are not reducible to neurochemicals, but are only real in the sense that they are experienced within the context of sociality and more specifically of unfolding lives. Further, the uses to which biology and biotechnology are put involve the most fundamental evaluations of what a good, bad or better life may be—certainly a task that is perhaps a bit too much for and should not be allowed to be monopolized by these disciplines.

Fighting the Specter of Irrationality

At its outset the sociology of emotions not only departed from purely psycho-biological renditions of the matter, but also rejected the alleged irrationality attributed to all things emotional. Indeed, a key challenge was to develop the idea of an emotional self in sociologically fruitful ways, as Hochschild (in this volume) describes. In her seminal book Hochschild (1983) argued that emotions—rather than being irrational—function as cues or markers that form a necessary orientation system fundamentally enabling perception of reality and, ultimately, forms of rationality. In this vein Helena Flam (1990a; 1990b) elaborated the model of an "emotional man" contrasting it with its rational and normative—non-emotional—

predecessors. More specifically and fundamentally, the issue of the relation between emotions and rationality was addressed by Jack Barbalet (2001, 29–61) who argued, relying largely on William James' work, for an interlacing of rationality and emotion. Calling to mind Keynes' ideas on the role of confidence in investment decisions, he showed that in a key fortress of rationality emotion reigns supreme. Similarly, the idea of social science as a rational, objective endeavor devoid of emotions or any emotional register was challenged. Some critics, for instance, pointed out that explanatory strategies in the social sciences have specific feeling rules inscribed into them, some of which may smuggle in sympathy and understanding, others indifference and hostility towards the objects of investigation (Flam and Kleres 2008). Not only sociologists, but also, for example, linguists have shown how scientific texts are inextricably emotionally structured (Jahr 2000).

Indeed, a number of contributions in this volume testify to the long-standing centrality of these issues to the sociology of emotions: Jack Barbalet's chapter—reprinted here because of its exemplary theorizing on this matter—discusses the role of emotions in science. He traces how the expulsion of emotions from scientific self-awareness, starting in the 17th century, has developed. This enables him to show that emotions are in fact central to key aspects of scientific activities—commonly, but fallaciously, conceived of as reigned over by pure rationality. This raises a number of important questions about consciousness and emotions and leads him to conceptualize unconscious emotions. Crucially, he argues, the emotions relevant to science, like aesthetic pleasure, personal striving, altruistic impulses, filled as it is with the pains, joys and disappointments of the struggle, and the unrelenting and undeniable propulsion to understand and wonder at the world, remain unconscious. Helmut Kuzmics explores related issues, but employs an entirely different approach. While much sociological thinking has been at pains to emulate the natural sciences' ideal of objectivity, his analysis of classical sociological texts as narratives shows how they are interwoven with specific emotional approaches to social reality. The very emotionality of the classics, he argues, constitutes a fundamental precondition for their thirst for and gaining knowledge about the social world. Again, Patrick Becker's text, as a genealogy of the discourse of modernity, shows how the separation between emotionality and rationality has developed, so that despite a revalorization of emotions, these remain trapped in this conceptual divide. Crucially, he identifies recent trends towards emotionalization of societies that can be interpreted as indicating both a revival of romantic notions of emotionality and of a scientific disenchantment with emotions. These parallel developments converge in a new understanding of emotions that departs from the opposition between rationality and emotions.

It can thus be argued that social sciences and humanities have developed a generic line of research that has for some time advanced less dichotomous conceptions of the relationship between emotion and reason (see also Fischer and Jansz 1995, 59). Yet, the very same discourses tend to be overshadowed by the new attempts to root the sociology of emotions in biology. Thus, while less dichotomous conceptions have become more acknowledged and respectable, they sometimes tend to be advanced by employing neurobiological findings without much recourse to social science research (e.g. Turner and Stets 2005, 21–2, 284–6, 309–12, 314; Franks 2006). Given this bias, the recent debate about alternative, non-dichotomous emotion-reason-conceptions fallaciously appears as an exclusive invention of the hard sciences. To be sure, biology can arguably provide impulses and additional evidence in this and other respects, ensuring theoretical progress of interest to sociologists, as Williams (in this volume) demonstrates. There is, however, no need to jettison existing lines of thought advanced by the social sciences and humanities in order to exclusively seek redemption in biology. In the end, it is rather ironic that conceptualizations that stress the interlacing of reason and emotion manage to gain valence in the current emotional turn only via the so-called hard, supposedly objective and emotion-stripped sciences. Current appreciation of emotions is predicated upon presenting them in de-emotionalized scientific frames. Indeed it is a worthy sociological ambition to consider this paradox.

Historicity of Emotions

While historians have also turned to emotions independently of sociological theorizing, within sociology the grounds for a historical take on emotions have most impressively been laid out by Norbert Elias. When some recent overviews of the field ignore historical approaches, this may in part be due to the somewhat loose connections between Elias' paradigm and the sociology of emotions (see above). However, it is perhaps telling that

Elias' approach—which after all addresses human beings from the biological, socio-psychological and historical perspectives—is glossed over when a case is made for connecting with neurobiological research (see Stets and Turner 2006; Turner and Stets 2005; in contrast see Greco and Stenner 2008a). The sociological significance of paying attention to history and focusing on changes over time as providing a powerful testimony to the fundamental social malleability of emotions and the emotional underpinnings of sociability is thus ignored.[2]

Temporal changes in societies' predominant modes of emotionality—as manifested in dominant cultural codes or manners—are focal to Cas Wouters' chapter. He employs an Eliasian approach to explore the changing directions of the civilizing process. Presenting findings from his recent comparative project (Wouters 2004; 2007), he describes how and why manners and the emotionality inscribed into them have become increasingly informal in recent history. The informalization followed a time of intense formalization of manners which called for avoidance, repression and denial of many emotions. The trend towards informalization can be characterized as an emancipation of emotions in the sense that previously repressed emotions can now increasingly be acknowledged and lived out. This, however, should not be taken at face value as a simple reversal of earlier formalization of manners with its strict regime of emotion control. Rather, there is a shift from a guilt-culture to a shame-culture: while emotions are increasingly acknowledged and in this sense emancipated, control over oneself is at the same time increased and sustained. A controlled decontrolling of previously repressed emotions takes place. Emotions can be expressed—yet controls over emotionality are retained, albeit in more subtle self-steered ways. The explanatory power and sociological significance of Wouters' chapter rests in the attention he draws to the manifold macro-level changes that condition these processes, ranging from the rise of capitalism to shifting patterns of social stratification. Wouters' encompassing and structural explanatory framework aptly demonstrates that emotion research should and can in fact fruitfully link micro and macro. Speaking in Elias' terms, it can link psychogenetic and sociogenetic processes. To date this remains an under-attended yet acutely necessary theoretical concern.

---

2 As Keil and Schnädelbach (2000, 13-15) argue, historical (and cultural) approaches have functioned as counterparts of naturalism.

Specific Emotions: Love and Shame

A cultural perspective is employed in Eva Illouz' and Eitan Wilf's chapter. They reject a Jamesian view of emotions as physiological reactions that are universal invariants in order to posit them as shaped by cultural meanings and particularly by cultural conceptions of the person. Emotions are thus conceived of as activated by cultural knowledge. It is to this knowledge that the authors turn when analyzing love or rather the romantic code in Israel. They aim their argument at feminist discourses that identify liberalism as a key source of the marginalization of women and that imply lesser degrees of marginalization of women where the private-public-divide is less pronounced. Their exploration of the cultural matrix of Israeli romantic love shows how the weak private-public-divide allows for greater participation of women in public life. But this is conditional on confining their possible contributions to the community to family care, and their roles to that of wives and procreative mothers. The army is discussed as a passage into (amorous) adult life, which, however, reinforces womanhood's organization around hegemonic masculinity. Hence, the dominant Israeli code of love emerges as one that is not much differentiated from the public sphere inasmuch that it is less indebted to ideologies of romantic love. This, however, does not engender or reveal more egalitarian gender structures.

Thomas Scheff's chapter, a reprint of one of his seminal articles, also focuses on one specific emotion—shame. But, unlike that of Illouz and Wilf, his interest is in advancing a universal theory of this emotion as he theorizes shame and pride as pivotal mechanisms of social control. Drawing on Cooley and others, he conceptualizes shame as self's perception of the evaluation of self by others. Shame is thus posited as *the* social emotion. A key insight pertains to a riddle: if the significance of shame as a mechanism of social control is so fundamental, why then is it so rarely visible? A central condition for this is the recursive character of shame: it is usually shameful to be ashamed, which makes for a strong motivation to hide one's shame. This leads Scheff to adopt Helen Lewis' distinction between overt and bypassed shame. His text is thus an earlier, genuinely sociological formulation of the notion of unconscious emotions, which Barbalet (in this volume) elaborates for emotions in general (see also Williams, in this volume).

Emotions and Their Mediatization

The contributors discussed thus far have highlighted a host of actors, in-stitutions and cultural codes that shape emotions in given societies. This volume, however, focuses on two more key societal platforms of emotion-ality, one of which is "the media." While the emotional turn has attracted the attention of communication and media research, this research tends to promote a critical stance towards media's impact on how people feel—often diagnosed as "new forms of psychological depthlessness" (Greco and Stenner 2008a, 321) in particular in response to mediatized represen-tations of other people's suffering. The question is raised if this response induces political action or instead passivity. This volume departs in two ways from this dominant research focus on emotions and media.

First, Nicolas Demertzis arrives at a more nuanced perspective on the media's impact on how people relate to the suffering of others. He argues that media representations can either lead to quasi-emotional experience, or alternatively to a "thin morality" with a potential for social and political action. His point of departure is a conceptualization of social-cultural trauma, which he develops and defines, in contrast to psychological trauma, as a collectively held memory of horrendous events impacting in fundamental ways on people's identities. From this perspective, media emerge as pivotal collective mnemotechnical apparatuses. Crucially, Demertzis also explores the larger societal context which entails the cen-trality of trauma to contemporary risk societies.

Katrin Döveling's investigation also deviates from this dominant focus in emotion-media research and focuses instead on conceptualizing media's offers of emotionality and their link to social processes—an often ne-glected issue in the debate on emotions and the media. Specifically, she focuses on the role of media's emotional agenda in community building. This allows her to demonstrate and theorize the far reaching effects of media's emotional communication and associated strategies of emotionali-zation. Döveling proposes an encompassing interdisciplinary approach. Sociological theories ranging from Durkheim and Simmel to Collins allow her to conceptualize the role of emotions in the processes of building and maintaining community. Approaches from communication studies, in turn, help her theorize ways in which media communicate emotions and try to influence how recipients feel. For this she coins the term "emotional agenda." She applies her framework to an empirical case, the visits of Pope

John Paul II to the US and Germany, showing how they were covered by print media relevant to the religious communities in these two countries.

Together, both media-related chapters open up new perspectives for media research, while testifying to the crucial role the media play in shaping fundamental conditions of emotionality in specific societies. By conceptualizing this link they also demonstrate the larger relevance of emotion-media research for social analysis.

Emotions in Social Movements and Civil Society

Social movements constitute another important agent shaping the emotional configuration of societies. Social movement research has recently proven to be particularly open to analyzing emotions (see e.g. Flam and King 2005; Aminzade and McAdam 2002; Goodwin et al. 2001; Stets and Turner 2006). Interestingly, it was in the seventies when social movement research began to struggle to exclude "irrational emotions" from its theorizing in order to get rid of the stigma of irrationality hitherto attached to protest, that, more or less, the American sociology of emotions took off. Is this merely a happy coincidence? Flam (2005b, 2) argues that social movement research first returned to emotions in the nineties at a point when theoretical advances could only become possible by opening up to new concepts and conceptual frameworks.

Indeed, as Flam (2005a) has argued, social movements struggle to change the standard distribution of emotions in a given society. They promote liberation from emotions cementing structures of domination, and propose subversive counter-emotions. From this analytical perspective, social movements not only press for immediate political change but also for new ways of thinking and feeling. This renders them key sites where society's emotionality is (re-)configured.

This is also apparent in James Goodman's analysis of transnational mobilization around issues of refugee solidarity in Australia. Rather than viewing emotions as either cause or outcome of mobilization, he focuses on their dynamic interaction with ideological, organizational and action frameworks. Emotions then emerge as both cause and outcome of mobilization. Contrary to the widespread focus on anger in movement research (for a critique see Flam 2004) and much very diffuse talk about solidarity, Goodman focuses on different forms of solidarity showing how each entails specific other, moral emotions and divergent strategies. Crucially, he traces how different branches of one movement and their respective forms of solidarity relate to dominant discourses of nationalism. He thus shows how transnational solidarity may challenge nationalist policies or remain instead intertwined with nationalist premises.

Jochen Kleres also traces dominant emotional structures when he discusses a related yet distinct kind of civic action: volunteerism. Contrasting his case of buddies, i.e. volunteers who provide personal one-on-one care for people with HIV and/or AIDS, with existing theorizing he conceptualizes this form of relational civic engagement as emotional, meaningful and fundamentally organizationally embedded: buddy-volunteerism emerges from his analysis as constituted by a number of discourses and their implied feeling rules, e.g. friendship, family, professionalism and volunteerism, but also the general AIDS discourses that construct the epidemic. These discourses and their feeling rules are mediated by the organizational context. This kind of analysis opens up to perspectives on a positive conceptualization of volunteerism and allows the development of such definitions in relation to other civic identities, such as activism—a distinction that remains blurred in social research. It can serve as a basis for assessing the respective civic potential of such identities.

Conclusion: Book-Editing as Lived Scholarship

Editing a collected volume like this is very much an emotional endeavor in itself, one that can be described in terms of "lived scholarship" to adapt the title of Fonow's and Cook's edited volume (1991). Their aim was a transformation of the research process in the context of "limitations and strictures" of a malestream academe and the wider world that are placed on feminist scholars personally and professionally. Despite the different premises and objectives our endeavors are related.

Not only do both the sociology of emotions and feminism continue to operate under adverse institutional conditions: a hierarchical academe with its primacy of rationalism, excluding preference for certain types of evidence, the worship of "objectivity," and certain selected constructions of truth and reality, as indicated in this volume. More to the point both feminism and sociology of emotions are often met with cynicism, circumspection, and mistrust.

Despite these and other similarities,[3] there is also a stark difference between both volumes in terms of epistemology and empirical analyses. Emotions are quintessential to the research process—as expressed in four principles (Fonow and Cook 1991): reflexivity, action research, attention to the *affective* components of the research *act* (my emphasis), and use of the situation at hand. In other words, the emotions of the scholars and their relationship to their emotional register as it is experienced and calibrated through their scholarship is as much a legitimate field of enquiry as their "official" or external one. Could we set about explaining for instance, the apparent contradiction that emotions scholars for the most part tend to leave out their emotional registers from their emotions scholarship? Do we fear the challenge that we are indulging in scholastic affectation? Are we operating more than we might like to think under those same "limitations and strictures" which Fonow and Cook identify and refuse to accept?

During the emotional journey, that is implied in editing a volume like this, these principles took on a greater significance. For instance, as first time editor the journey has been marked out by a myriad of emotions: gratitude to the senior researchers who invited the junior editors to take up the challenge, and to the gracious disposition of the contributors who received our sometimes fledgling comments and suggestions, and gratitude also to the co-editors. Alongside the privilege of editing this volume comes a great deal of self-doubt that finds its experiential grip in emotional form—fear, and fear of embarrassment and humiliation, the heightening of emotions as experienced through the blanket of tiredness and in some cases boredom and irritation (how long can someone reasonably be expected to stay enthusiastic about paying exquisite attention to the exact location of full stops, the relative merits of a comma as opposed to a dash, in a thirty page text?), wonder, admiration and appreciation, anger. At every level, every judgment that has been made, every response to the written word and all that is beyond the limitations of the written word, are

---

3 This pertains e.g. to our similar leanings in terms of how we come at the world, and towards a kind of analysis that draws its breath from challenging the malestream with its rationalist and objectivist truth and knowledge claims; the fact that our respective empirical fields of enquiry often coincide, so that for instance in this volume, as in that of Fonow and Cook, the family, the media, objectivity and truth, race, gender and the workplace all appear, and all with a critical perspective.

not possible without our ability to emote and to calibrate our emotions. All of this without any doubt is invested in our scholarship, and in our human existence.

Acknowledgements

I would like to thank my co-editors Debra Hopkins, Helena Flam, and Helmut Kuzmics for their valuable feedback on and contributions to earlier drafts of this preface. The first section on *The Emergence of the ESA Emotions Network* is based on personal communication with Helena Flam, Helmut Kuzmics, Åsa Wettergren, and Cas Wouters. I wish to thank them for sharing their experience and insights. In the name of all four editors, I would like to thank all contributors for their co-operation and their willingness to respond to our ideas and feedback. A number of people and institutions helped to secure the resources that were necessary for producing this volume. Helmut Kuzmics made this publication possible. The present book appears with the support of the ESA's Emotions Network. We would like to thank Cas Wouters for his strong commitment to this project. We are very grateful to all. Our gratitude also goes to Eron Witzel who was often at hand to offer sound advice on tricky language issues. Finally, Joachim Fischer and Petra Zimlich of Campus have been a great source of support especially during the final phases of manuscript preparation.

References

Aminzade, Ron, and Doug McAdam (eds.). (2002). Special Issue on Emotions and Contentious Politics, *Mobilization: An International Journal*, 7 (2).

Barbalet, Jack M. (2001). *Emotion, Social Theory, and Social Structure: A Macrosociological Approach*. Cambridge, New York, Melbourne, Madrid, Cape Town, Singapore, Sao Paulo: Cambridge University Press.

— (2002). *Emotions and Sociology*. Oxford, Malden: Blackwell Publishers.

Bendelow, Gillian, and Simon J. Williams (eds.). (1998). *Emotions in Social Life: Critical Themes and Contemporary Issues*. London, New York: Routledge.

Collins, Randall (1975). *Conflict Sociology: Toward an Explanatory Science.* New York: Academic Press.

Fineman, Stephen (ed.). (1993). *Emotion in Organizations.* London, Newbury Park: Sage Publications.

Fischer, Agneta H., and Jeroen Jansz (1995). Reconciling Emotions with Western Personhood. *Journal for the Theory of Social Behaviour*, 25 (1), 59–80.

Flam, Helena (1990a). Emotional "Man": I. The Emotional "Man" and the Problem of Collective Action. *International Sociology*, 5 (1), 39–56.

— (1990b). Emotional "Man": II. Corporate Actors as Emotion-Motivated Emotion Managers. *International Sociology*, 5 (2), 225–34.

— (2002). *Soziologie der Emotionen. Eine Einführung.* Konstanz: UVK Verlagsgesellschaft (UTB für Wissenschaft).

— (2004). Anger in Repressive Regimes. A Footnote to Domination and the Arts of Resistance by James Scott. *European Journal of Social Theory*, 7 (2), 171–88.

— (2005a). Emotions' Map. A Research Agenda. In Helena Flam and Debra King (eds.). *Emotions and Social Movements*, 19–40. London, New York: Routledge.

— (2005b). Introduction. In Helena Flam and Debra King (eds.). *Emotions and Social Movements*, 1–18. London, New York: Routledge.

Flam, Helena, and Debra King (eds.). (2005). *Emotions and Social Movements.* London, New York: Routledge.

Flam, Helena, and Jochen Kleres (2008). Ungleichheit und Vorurteil. Deutsche SozialwissenschaftlerInnen als ProduzentInnen von Gefühlsregeln. *Österreichische Zeitschrift für Soziologie*, 33 (2), 63–81.

Fonow, Mary, M., and Judith A. Cook (1991). Introduction. In Mary Margaret Fonow and Judith A. Cook (eds.). *Beyond Methodology: Feminist Scholarship As Lived Research*, 1–11. Bloomington, Indianapolis: Indiana University Press.

Franks, David D. (2006). The Neuroscience of Emotions. In Jan E. Stets and Jonathan H. Turner (eds.). *Handbook of the Sociology of Emotions*, 38–62. New York: Springer.

Gerhards, Jürgen (1988). *Soziologie der Emotionen. Fragestellungen, Systematik und Perspektiven.* Weinheim, München: Juventa Verlag.

Goodwin, Jeff, James M. Jasper, and Francesca Polletta (eds.). (2001). *Passionate Politics. Emotions and Social Movements.* Chicago, London: The University of Chicago Press.

Greco, Monica, and Paul Stenner (eds.). (2008a). *Emotions: A Social Science Reader.* London, New York: Routledge.

— (2008b). Introduction: Emotion and Social Science. In Monica Greco and Paul Stenner (eds.). *Emotions: A Social Science Reader*, 1–21. London, New York: Routledge.

Harré, Rom (ed.). (1986.) *The Social Construction of Emotions.* Oxford, New York: Blackwell Publishers.

Harré, Rom, and W. Gerrod Parrott (eds.). (1996). *The Emotions: Social, Cultural and Biological Dimensions.* London, Thousand Oaks: Sage Publications.

Hochschild, Arlie R. (1979). Emotion Work, Feeling Rules, and Social Structure. *American Journal of Sociology*, 85 (3), 551–75.

— (1983). *The Managed Heart: Commercialization of Human Feeling.* Berkeley: University of California Press.

Jahr, Silke (2000). *Emotionen und Emotionsstrukturen in Sachtexten.* Berlin, New York: de Gruyter.

Keil, Geert, and Herbert Schnädelbach (2000). Naturalismus. In Geert Keil and Herbert Schnädelbach (eds.). *Naturalismus. Philosophische Beiträge*, 7–45. Frankfurt am Main: Suhrkamp.

Kemper, Theodore D. (1990a). Social Relations and Emotions: A Structural Approach. In Theodore D. Kemper (ed.). *Research Agendas in the Sociology of Emotions*, 207–37. Albany: State University of New York Press.

— (1990b). Themes and Variations in the Sociology of Emotions. In Theodore D. Kemper (ed.). *Research Agendas in the Sociology of Emotions*, 3–23. Albany: State University of New York Press.

Kuzmics, Helmut (1986). Verlegenheit und Zivilisation. Zu einigen Gemeinsamkeiten und Unterschieden im Werk von E. Goffman und N. Elias. *Soziale Welt*, 37 (4), 465–86.

— (1991). Embarrassment and Civilization: On Some Similarities and Differences in the Work of Goffman and Elias. *Theory, Culture & Society*, 8 (2), 1–30.

— (1994). Power and Work: The Development of Work as a Civilizing Process in Examples of Fictional Literature. *Sociological Perspectives*, 37 (1), 119–54.

— (1997). Von der Habsburgermonarchie zu "Österreich". Reichspatriotismus, "habsburgischer Mythos" und Nationalismus in den Romanen von Joseph Roth. *Archiv für Kulturgeschichte*, 79 (1), 105–22.

Kuzmics, Helmut, and Roland Axtmann (2007). *Authority, State and National Character: The Civilizing Process in Austria and England, 1700–1900.* Aldershot, Burlington: Ashgate.

Lettow, Susanne (2006). *Biophilosophien. Die Life Sciences in der philosophischen Diskussion.* Vienna: Institut für die Wissenschaft vom Menschen.

— (2009a). Biophilosophien. Philosophische Strategien und die politisch-ethische Formierung von Biowissenschaften. In Astrid Deuber-Mankowski, Christoph F. E. Holzhey, and Anja Michaelsen (eds.). *Der Einsatz des Lebens. Lebensweisen, Medialisierung, Geschlecht*, 87–100. Berlin: b-books Verlag.

— (2009b). Die Wahrheit der Biologisten. *Tagesspiegel*, 2 April 2009, 28.

Neckel, Sieghard (1991). *Status und Scham. Zur symbolischen Reproduktion sozialer Ungleichheit.* Frankfurt am Main, New York: Campus Verlag.

— (1996). Inferiority: From Collective Status to Deficient Individuality. *Sociological Review*, 44 (1), 17–34.

Nedelmann, Brigitta (1983). Georg Simmel – Emotion und Wechselwirkung in intimen Gruppen. *Kölner Zeitschrift für Soziologie und Sozialpsychologie*, Sonderheft (25), 174–209.

— (1988). "Psychologismus" oder Soziologie der Emotionen? Max Webers Kritik an der Soziologie Georg Simmels. In Otthein Rammstedt (ed.). *Simmel und die frühen Soziologen. Nähe und Distanz zu Durkheim, Tönnies und Max Weber,* 11–35. Frankfurt am Main: Suhrkamp.

Rose, Nikolas (2003). Neurochemical Selves. *Society,* 41 (1), 46–59.

Scherke, Katharina (ed.). (2008a). Special Issue on Sociology of Emotions. *Österreichische Zeitschrift für Soziologie,* 33 (2).

— (2008b). Editorial: Soziologie der Emotionen. *Österreichische Zeitschrift für Soziologie,* 33 (2), 3–18.

— (forthcoming). *Emotionen als Forschungsgegenstand in der deutschsprachigen Soziologie.* Wiesbaden: VS Verlag.

Schützeichel, Rainer (2006). *Emotionen und Sozialtheorie. Disziplinäre Ansätze.* Frankfurt am Main, New York: Campus Verlag.

Shilling, Chris (2002). The two Traditions in the Sociology of Emotions." In Jack Barbalet (ed.). *Emotions and Sociology,* 10–32. Oxford, Malden: Blackwell Publishing.

Stets, Jan E., and Jonathan H. Turner (eds.). (2006). *Handbook of the Sociology of Emotions.* New York: Springer.

Thoits, Peggy A. (1989). The Sociology of Emotions. *Annual Review of Sociology,* 15 (1), 317–42.

Turner, Jonathan H., and Jan E. Stets (2005). *The Sociology of Emotions.* Cambridge, New York, Melbourne, Madrid, Cape Town, Singapore, Sao Paulo: Cambridge University Press.

Vandekerckhove, Marie, Christian von Scheve, Sven Ismer, Susanne Jung, and Stefanie Kronast (eds.). (2008). *Regulating Emotions: Culture, Social Necessity, and Biological Inheritance.* Malden: Blackwell Publishing.

Wouters, Cas (1989). The Sociology of Emotions and Flight Attendants: Hochschild's Managed Heart. *Theory, Culture & Society,* 6 (1), 95–123.

— (1990). *Van Minnen en Sterven. Omgangsvormen Rond Seks en Dood in de Twintigste Eeuw.* Amsterdam: Uitgeverij Bert Bakker.

— (1992). On Status Competition and Emotion Management: The Study of Emotions as a New Field. *Theory, Culture & Society,* 9 (1), 229.

— (2004). *Sex and Manners: Female Emancipation in the West, 1890–2000.* London, Thousand Oaks, New Delhi: Sage Publications.

— (2007). *Informalization: Manners and Emotions Since 1890.* London, Thousand Oaks, New Delhi: Sage Publications.

Introduction: An Emotions Lens on the World

Arlie Russell Hochschild

Major 19th century thinkers who took on the big questions of their age—Karl Marx, Emile Durkheim, Max Weber and Sigmund Freud—all touched on emotion. In the *Economic and Philosophic Manuscripts* (1986), Marx spoke of the 19th century factory worker's alienation from the things he made and from the work he did to make them. The worker had lost pride and joy that come with the idea "I made that." In the *Elementary Forms of Religious Life* (1995), Emile Durkheim studied the religious rituals of Australian aborigines because he wanted to discover the conditions which inspired self-transcendent rapture. In the *Protestant Ethic and the Spirit of Capitalism* (2001), Max Weber singled out fear and desire for love and approval—feelings an early Protestant believer felt toward God—for in these he detected the motivational source of the Protestant work ethic. To Freud (1960), emotion, especially anxiety, was central to his entire enormous corpus of work, although for him emotion was hard to distinguish from instinct and underwent many transformations with the development of his theory of the ego and superego. To all of these 19th century thinkers, we sociologists of emotion owe a great debt.

Indeed, the field of sociology of emotion might be said to have existed for a long time without the name. But during the 19th and first part of the 20th century, it was a confusing warren of conceptual tunnels and fascinating empirical observations without a sustained focus on emotion as something in and of itself. I first came to use the term "sociology of emotion" in an 1975 essay entitled *The Sociology of Feeling and Emotion; Selected Possibilities*—while part of the early feminist movement and inspired by it to rethink the premises of sociology with the simple question: what would sociology look like if women had an equal presence in it? In popular culture of what was the recent past in 1975, women were stereotyped as "over emotional," "irrational" and focused on domestic relationships. In this way, women were portrayed as unfit for public life and cast to the margins of it.

Feelings and emotions were, meanwhile, covertly linked to irrationality and talk about these was associated with triviality, gossip, private life. But it began to strike me that it was not that *women were not* emotional, it was that *men are*. If either appeared as "unemotional" in stressful situations, it may be that they are doing some form of "emotion work" to sustain that appearance to others and to themselves. This, then, was my point of entrance into the sociology of emotion (Hochschild 1973; 1975, 2–3; 1983).

The first challenge was to conceptualize the image of a feelingful self. At that time, sociology seemed to me caught between two images of self— one in which emotion was the instinctual engine that motivates us to act (this from Freud) and the other in which emotion is that which we outwardly show (this from Goffman). But, what seemed to me to be missing was a model of the emotional self, a self beneath display—a self capable of feeling Marx's (1986) pride, Durkheim's (1995) rapture, Foster's (1972) envy (see *The Capacity to Feel* in Hochschild 2003, 75–86).

In trying to develop this model, there were many contemporary works, in addition to those of the great masters, on which I could draw. I include them in the references here as gems from the fields of phenomenology, anthropology, psychology, psycho-history,[1] and of special importance to me, and almost a field in himself, Erving Goffman. The anthropologists George Foster (1972) on envy, Robert Levy (1973) on the depressive emotions, the sociologists Kingsley Davis (1936) on jealousy, and William Goode (1964) on love, F. Gross and G. Stone (1964) on embarrassment, the psychoanalyst Geoffrey Gorer (1964) on grief, and the philosopher Sartre (1948) on the nature of emotion—all these helped clear the way for a sociology of emotions.

The premise they all suggest is this: joy, sadness, anger, elation, jealousy, envy, despair, anguish, grief—all these feelings are partly social. They are influenced by cultural ideas and images, and refracted through roles and relationships. Erving Goffman once wrote, "When they issue uniforms, they issue skins" (personal communication 1979). And, we can add, two inches of flesh. We enact a new role (put on a new uniform) let's say, and

---

1 Apthorpe (1972); Averill (1968); Block (1957); Blum and McHugh (1971); Bugenthal, et al. (1971); Coser (1960); Davitz (1969); Dollard et al. (1939); Erikson (1950); Gurr and Ruttenberg (1967); Jones et al. (1972); Kephart (1967); Lewis (1959); Malinowski (1927); Marcuse (1955); Mead (1949); Modigliani (1968); Moller (1958); Parsons (1968); Rapaport (1942); Rubin (1973); Schachter (1964); Schachter and Wheeler (1962); Schoeck (1966); Seeley (1967); Simmel (1950, 1971); Walters (1966); Wikler (1974).

so speak with more authority, we change our emotive appearance. That's what Goffman meant by "skin." But, we ourselves engage our deep feelings in new ways—that's what I mean by "two inches of flesh." The "social" goes far deeper than our current images of self lead us to suppose. Social roles and relations do not simply reflect patterns of thought and action, leaving the realm of emotion untouched, timeless and universal. No, there are social patterns to feeling *itself* (Hochschild 2003, 86).

So just how is feeling social? For one thing, feeling is elicited by interactions that we experience, remember, or imagine having with people in our lives. For another thing, each culture provides prototypes of feeling, which, like differently tuned keys on a piano, allows us to hear different inner notes. For example, the Tahitians have one word—sick—for what in other cultures might correspond to ennui, depression, grief, or sadness. According to the Czech novelist Milan Kundera (1992), the Czech word *litost*, refers to an indefinable longing, mixed with remorse and grief, which has no equivalent in any other language.

Cultures lay out the possibilities for emotion and in that way guide the act of recognizing a feeling. Apart from what we think a feeling is, we also have ideas about what it *should* be. We say, "you should be thrilled at winning the prize" or "you should be furious that he cheated you." We evaluate the fit between a particular feeling and context in light of what I call "feeling rules," which are themselves rooted in culture.

Given such feeling rules, we may then try to manage our feelings. We try to be happy at a party, or grief-stricken at a funeral. In short, it is through our perception of an interaction, our definition of feeling, our appraisal of feeling and our management of feeling that feeling is social. If, as C. Wright Mills (1963; 1967) said, the job of sociology is to trace the links between private troubles and public issues, the sociology of emotion lies at the very heart of sociology.

This approach to feeling offers us a way of looking at all spheres of life, including work. When paid to do certain jobs, we do what I call "emotional labor"—the effort to *seem* to feel and to *try* to *really* feel the "right" feeling for the job, and to try to induce the "right" feeling in certain others. For example, the flight attendant is trained to manage fear at turbulence, and anger at cranky or abusive passengers. A bill collector is trained to manage compassion for debtors. Wedding planners (one of the sort of para-familial service workers I'm interviewing these days) often try to help clients find tangible symbols for the special moment of falling in love, as well as deal with jealous mothers, quarreling sets of parents, or what one planner called "grooms' jitters." Hospice workers, as the Japanese scholar Haruo Sakiyama finds, undo the taboo on death, opening up people's right to feel whatever they feel.[2] Alcoholics Anonymous meanwhile creates a taboo, not felt before, on the desire to drink. Not all jobs that deal with feeling call for emotional labor, and not all emotional labor is stressful. But we are wise to put questions of emotional labor and its human cost on the table.

Over the last 40 years, the number of service sector jobs has rapidly grown all over the world. By my estimate, some six out of ten of those service jobs in the United States call for substantial amounts of emotional labor. This work falls unequally on men and women; only a quarter of men, but half of women work in jobs heavy in emotional labor—as elementary school teachers, nurses, social workers, child and elder care workers. Emotional labor has rewards but also hidden costs, and given their different upbringings, both form a larger part of female experience than male.

Emotional labor is going more and more global. Increasingly, we've seen what I call a South-to-North "heart transplant" (Ehrenreich and Hochschild 2003). A growing number of care workers leave the young and elderly of their families and communities in the poor South to take up paid jobs "giving their hearts to" the young and elderly in families and communities in the affluent North. Such jobs often call on workers to manage grief, depression, and anguish vis-à-vis their own children, spouses, and parents, even as they genuinely feel—and try to feel—joyful attachment to the children and elders they daily care for in the North.

Emotional labor crosses borders in other ways as well. Through telephone and email, service providers in Bangalore, India, for example, tutor California children with math homework, make long-distance purchases of personal gifts, and even scan romantic dating service Internet sites for busy professionals. The growth of medical tourism in India has also expanded the number of poor women who "rent their wombs" to bear babies conceived from the egg and sperm of couples in the North. This service calls for the ultimate in emotional labor—the effort to remain detached from the baby given up.

---

2 Personal communication. Haruo Sakiyama, College of Social Sciences, Ritsumeikan University, Kyoto, Japan.

Emotional labor has become more central to First World economies. After jobs in the industrial and administrative sectors are outsourced to such countries as India, China, Mexico, service jobs calling for face-to-face interaction are a higher proportion of those jobs that remain. Estimates of job loss vary greatly. High estimates predict that from 2003 to 2013, some six million manufacturing and non-interface service jobs may be lost from the U.S., while low estimates give the figure of 850,000.[3] Primary among jobs that remain are those in what I call the *emotional economy*—i.e. jobs that offer face-to-face personal service and call for emotional labor.

This important trend opens up an entirely new area of inquiry within the sociology of emotions—the emotional dimension of commodification. I do a favor for you; I engage in an activity—and it is likely that after a while you will do a favor for me, or if not you will wish me well, and this is the pre-market "gift exchange." I sell a service to you; my service becomes a commodity. As the market extends farther around the globe and deeper into our personal lives, more and more of the activities of the "life world" as Habermas (1985) called it, move into the "system world." Life moves out of the unpaid realm of home and community into the paid realm of economy and state. Emotional labor—as fact, and idea—forms a bridge between these two worlds.

Commodification, as Marx (1983), Polanyi (1957), Lukacs (2000) and others conceived of it, was a unitary phenomenon. For Marx, you commodified a thing or activity if you produced and sold it for the market. That was it.

But emotionally speaking, there is actually a *surface* commodification, and a *deep* commodification. In surface commodification, the client pays the childcare worker, the birthday party planner, the wedding planner, the life coach. The emotion worker is paid. Money changes hands.

But at a deep level, much else goes on as well—much that accounts for the powerful draw—conscious and unconscious—of the market. A customer may have an empty marriage and precarious job, but at the mall, at least for a period, s(he) can bask in the aura that "The customer is king." The customer may even derive a sense of constancy, trustworthiness, loyalty that s(he) seeks in real life in the things s(he) buys and service providers s(he) hires. S(he) may work three jobs, have two lovers, but the restaurant always serves the same menu, the hotel has the same color rug. Stan-

---

3 National Academy of Public Administration (2006). Table 4-2. The high estimate is based on research by Goldman Sachs, and the low estimate based on research by Deloitte.

dardization is, we often say, de-humanizing, but it can also provide a curious constancy in an ever changing world. This need for a trusting relationship to a good or service is, of course, what advertisers increasingly aim for. As Marc Gobé explains in his book, *Emotional Branding* (2001), the aim of advertising is to form an emotional bond with a relationship-seeking customer.

In addition, the market world of goods and services presents itself as amazing. As she walks the aisles of San Francisco's Macy's or Nordstroms, or cruises through the multifold glass shops of the Frankfurt airport, the consumer may feel dazzled, awestruck, as believers once felt in the great cathedrals and palaces of Europe. These are feelings sellers hope to inspire. In a parallel way, service-providers draw on an awesome world of knowledge. Expert providers know more than we do about how to name, potty-train, educate, exercise and socialize our child. They know more than we do, it can seem, about "romantic chemistry" or about what makes us love or resent our spouse. They can get along well with our elderly relatives, and help us relate to them in a better way, too.

In the post-seventies era, personal life has become difficult in a strange way. The era of the long term career is receding. Up until 2008, most Americans could get a job; they just didn't know if they could keep it, while now jobs themselves are harder to find. For increasingly jobs come and go with the rise and fall in supply and demand, unprotected by union or government constraint. Increasingly at work, people feel commodified.

Paradoxically, one thing service providers do, for a fee, is to help the client feel special, unique, de-commodified. A wedding planner, or life coach, may help a client feel "one of a kind." One wedding planner, for example, asked her young clients to tell her how they decided to marry. In a casual way, the groom described how he'd asked his girlfriend what it would take to induce her to move from New York to California. "I'd move if I had a lemon tree," she'd replied. So the young man sent her a lemon tree. The wedding planner then exclaimed, "Ah. *That* was the moment of your commitment!" She made out cards, set at the place of each guest at the wedding luncheon, describing "the legend" of the lemon tree. To the delighted couple, this act heightened—indeed created—the towering symbol of their union. A customer pays the planner a fee; that's surface commodification. But at a deeper level, this wedding planner was using the exchange of money for service to render the clients' marriage incomparable to any other, to de-commodify it. Insofar as we associate commodification with standardization, the wedding planner was in the surface sense, commodifying the wedding planning, but in the deep sense de-commodifying it.

On the other hand, a life coach may also help the client don the emotional armor needed to take the hard knocks of the marketplace. S(he) may teach a client to think of oneself as a brand, expect to bargain hard, to detach, and stay focused on the best market value in oneself, and others. ("I am a brand. I want high return on investment. I am the C.E.O. of my love life.") The customer is helped to put herself on the market while trying to avoid feeling hurt, lost or estranged.

All in all, the sociologist stands before an ever more important interface, between the self and commodification. In what ways, we can ask, do we try to embrace, absorb or resist the subtle and complex array of meanings hidden within deep commodification? I believe these issues—the social shape of feeling, emotional labor, commodification—go to the heart of the age in which we live and that, as a perspective, we can help lead the way in figuring out how to see them.

Acknowledgements

Parts of this chapter are based on Hochschild (2008).

References

Apthorpe, R. J. (1972). Comments (On Foster, 1972). *Current Anthropology*, 13, 203–4.

Averill, J. (1968). Grief. *Psychological Bulletin*, 70, 721–48.

Block, Jack (1957). Studies in the Phenomenology of Emotions. *Journal of Abnormal and Social Psychology*, 54 (3), 358–63.

Blum, A. F., and P. McHugh (1971). The Social Ascription of Motives. *American Sociological Review*, 36, 98–109.

Bugental, D., L. Love, and R. Gianetto (1971). Perfidious Feminine Faces. *Journal of Personality and Social Psychology*, 17, 314–8.

Coser, R. L. (1960). Laughter Among Colleagues. *Psychiatry*, 23, 81–95.

Davis, Kingsley (1936). Jealousy and Sexual Property. *Social Forces*, 14, 395–410.

Davitz, J. (1969). *The Language of Emotion*. New York: Academic Press.

Dollard, J., L. W. Doob, N. E. Miller, O. H. Mowrer, and R. R. Sears (1939). *Frustration and Aggression*. New Haven, Conn.: Yale University Press.

Durkheim, Emile (1995). *The Elementary Forms of Religious Life*. New York: The Free Press. [first published in 1912]

Ehrenreich, Barbara, and Arlie R. Hochschild (2003). *Global Woman: Nannies, Maids and Sex Workers in the New Economy*. New York: Metropolitan Press.

Erikson, Erik H. (1950). *Childhood and Society*. New York: W. W. Norton.

Foster, George M. (1972). The Anatomy of Envy. *Current Anthropology*, 13, 165–202.

Freud, Sigmund (1960). *The Ego and the Id (The Standard Edition of the Complete Psychological Works of Sigmund Freud by James Strachey)*. New York: W. W. Norton and Co.

Gobé, Marc (2001). *Emotional Branding: The New Paradigm for Connecting Brands to People*. New York: Allworth Press.

Goode, William (1964). The Theoretical Importance of Love. In R. Coser (ed.). *The Family*, 143–56. New York: St. Martin's Press.

Gorer, Geoffrey (1964). *The American People*. New York: W. W. Norton.

Gross, F., and G. Stone. (1964). Embarrassment and the Analysis of Role Requirements. *American Journal of Sociology*, 80, 1–15.

Gurr, T., and C. Ruttenberg (1967). *The Conditions of Civil Violence*. Princeton, N.J.: Center of International Studies, Princeton University.

Habermas, Jürgen (1985). The Theory of Communicative Action. Boston: Beacon Press.

Hochschild, Arlie R. (1973). *The Unexpected Community*. Englewood Cliffs, N.J.: Prentice-Hall.

— (1975). The Sociology of Feeling and Emotion; Selected Possibilities. *Sociological Inquiry*, 45 (2–3), 280–307.

— (1983). *The Managed Heart: The Commercialization of Human Feeling*. Berkeley, Los Angeles: University of California Press.

— (2003). *The Commercialization of Intimate Life: Notes from Work and Home*. Berkeley and Los Angeles: University of California Press.

— (2008). Feeling in Sociology and the World. *Sociologisk Forskning*, 45 (2).

Jones, L. E. et al. (1972). *Attribution*. Morristown, N.J.: General Learning Press.

Kephart, W. (1967). Some Correlates of Romantic Love. *Journal of Marriage and the Family*, 29, 470–4.

Kundera, Milan (1992). *The Book of Laughter and Forgetting*. London: Faber and Faber.

Levy, Robert I. (1973). *Tahitians*. Chicago: University of Chicago Press.

Lewis, C. S. (1959). *The Allegory of Love*. New York: Oxford University Press.

Lukacs, György (2000). *A Defence of History and Class Consciousness: Tailism and the Dialectic*. London, New York: Verso.

Malinowski, Bronislaw (1927). *Sex and Repression in Savage Society*. New York: Harcourt, Brace.

Marcuse, Herbert (1955). *Eros and Civilization*. New York: Vintage.

Marx, Karl (1983). *Letters on "Capital"*. London: New Park Publications.

— (1986). *The Economic and Philosophic Manuscripts*. New York: International Publishers. [first published in 1844]

Mead, Margaret (1949). *Male and Female*. New York: Morrow.

Mills, C. Wright (1963). *Power, Politics and People: The Collected Essays of C. Wright Mills*. New York: Oxford University Press.

— (1967). *The Sociological Imagination*. New York: Oxford University Press.

Modigliani, A. (1968). Embarrassment and Embarrassability. *Sociometry*, 31, 313–26.

Moller, H. (1958). The Social Causation of the Courtly Love Complex. *International Quarterly*, 1, 137–63.

National Academy of Public Administration (2006). *A Report For the U.S. Congress and the Bureau of Economic Analysis*, http://www.napawash.org/pubs/-ff-shoring-1-2006.htm.

Parsons, Talcott (1968). On the Concept of Value-Commitments. *Sociological Inquiry*, 38, 135–60.

Polanyi, Karl (1957). *The Great Transformation*. Boston: Beacon Press.

Rapaport, D. (1942). *Emotions and Memory*. Baltimore, Md.: Williams and Wilkins.

Rubin, Z. (1973). *Liking and Loving*. New York: Holt, Rinehart & Winston.

Sartre, Jean-Paul (1948). *The Emotions*. New York: Philosophical Library.

Schachter, S. (1964). The Interaction of Cognitive and Physiological Determinants of Emotional States. In P. Leidertnan and D. Shapiro (eds.). *Psychobiological Approaches to Social Behavior*, 138–73. Stanford, Calif.: Stanford University Press.

Schachter, S., and L. Wheeler (1962). Epinephrine, Chlorpromazine, and Amusement. *Journal of Abnormal and Social Psychology*, 65, 121–8.

Schoeck, Helmut (1966). *Envy: A Theory of Social Behavior*. New York: Harcourt, Brace & World.

Seeley, J. R. (1967). *The Americanization of the Unconscious*. New York: International Science Press.

Simmel, Georg (1950). *The Sociology of Georg Simmel*. Trans. and ed. K. Wolff. Glencoe, Ill.: The Free Press.

— (1971). Passionate Love. In B. L. Murstein (ed.) *Theories of Attraction and Love*, 85–99. New York: Springer.

Walters, R. H. (1966). Implications of Laboratory Studies of Aggression for the Control and Regulation of Violence. *Annals of the American Academy of Political and Social Science*, 364, 60–72.

Weber, Max (2001). *The Protestant Ethic and the Spirit of Capitalism*. London: Routledge Publishers. [first published in 1930]

Wikler, N. (1974). *Sexism in the Classroom*. Unpublished manuscript, Sociology Department, University of California at Santa Cruz.

Consciousness, Emotions, and Science

Jack Barbalet

Introduction

Consciousness is rather like time, as Augustine described it: You know what it is until you try to explain it. The ease of intuitive grasp of consciousness, coupled with the difficulty of intelligible exposition, offer clues to its nature. Because it is a necessary aspect of experience, we correctly *feel* that we know what consciousness is. At the same time, we struggle to articulate what is *meant* by consciousness because it is not external to our mental processes, but is a part of them. Consciousness, then, is not readily conceived as an object, in that sense, which would facilitate intellectual apprehension of it. Also, the mental processes in question are inherently complex and, possibly as a result of this complexity, paradoxically, are not adequately captured by self-awareness. With regard to the complexity of consciousness, William James, for instance, remarked that a purely cognitive description of it would leave consciousness dry and without purpose, a situation corrected by appreciating the importance of emotion to consciousness (James 1890a, 141–2). Even more counter-intuitive, it can be fairly asked whether persons are necessarily aware of their consciousness, are they necessarily conscious of being conscious? These are the focal questions—the consciousness of things emotions can provide, and the possibility of lack of awareness of such consciousness—when considering the role of emotions in science, which this paper shall address.

Before discussing emotions in science it is appropriate to change key and subject, and briefly consider the science of consciousness. For most of the 20th century suggestion of a science of consciousness would have provoked derision. Psychology studied behavior not mind, and rejected introspection as a method of inquiry when it was the most accessible means to consciousness. Neurology was simply uninterested in such ethereal and nebulous things as consciousness, which had no meaning for science. Since the nineties, however, consciousness has been rehabilitated and is not only now respectable for psychologist and neurologist to study, but highly topical for them to do so. This sea change is a result of developments in technologies, especially those that delineate and provide functional imaging of the electrical correlates of neurological activity. Such technologies reveal a correspondence between neural processes and aspects of conscious experience.

The social sciences, with the possible exception of anthropology, have been left out of the current concentration of scientific interest in consciousness. It is ironic that this too is reversal of an earlier trend. In a 26-page review of developments in the scientific study of consciousness, for instance, half a page only discusses "social theories," and of the 6 items cited in that short space, none is written by a social scientist (Zeman 2001, 1281–2). No doubt the majority of social scientists today share the image presented here, of a lack of interest in consciousness amongst them. And yet Marx's treatment of class-consciousness, for instance, defined his account of capitalist society; Durkheim's discussion of collective consciousness similarly captured his approach to social solidarity. The importance of consciousness to the sociology of Weber, Mannheim, Simmel, Cooley and Mead, to name only the most obvious, cannot go unremarked. While the causes of the tendency for sociology's disengagement from consciousness require careful consideration, reference to its recent "cultural turn" indicates a shift from a concern with social actor's apprehension of a world to which they relate, to a concern with a shaping spirit to which subjects without agency yield. In such realignment, consciousness is lost.

A sociological interest in emotions raises questions concerning consciousness. While the issues treated in such an inquiry will not be the same as those promoted by recent neurological and psychological research, drawing on the findings of such research will enrich sociological discussion. The broad concern of the following discussion is the role of emotions in science. This may at first seem remote from a concern with consciousness. Nevertheless, as we shall see, this enquiry unavoidably raises the question of emotional consciousness and aspects of the nature of consciousness itself. From the point of view of prevailing conventions emotions have only a disrupting or distorting role in science. Science practitioners, science educators and philosophers of science have long insisted that science can only proceed when emotion is expelled. But as emotions are pervasive in giving direction to and energizing human activity, it is a fair working hypothesis that some emotions will have a supporting role in science. Indeed, the significance of emotions in motivation to science is frequently acknowledged. Nevertheless, that emotions may have a positive role in core scientific activities is an idea that continues to attract skepticism. One reason for this, it will be argued, is that the emotions involved operate below the threshold of awareness, which is to say that scientists are typically not conscious of the emotions central to their activities. This idea, that emotions may be non-consciously experienced, also frequently meets resistance and will also be discussed below.

Part 1: Science and Emotions

Science is arguably the defining social institution of western societies, at least since the 17th century. The importance of science is not simply in its direct output of reliable knowledge, or even only in its contribution to technological development and the consequent expansion of economic production. The significance of these aspects of science is enormous, of course. But in addition to the direct yield of science is another element of its significance that makes it a pervasively dominating institution, namely that its form has tended to be replicated by all other social institutions including those associated with cultural production. There are broad imitative tendencies in areas outside of science to adopt its form. Under the aegis of science practically all areas of human endeavor tend to favor analysis rather than synthesis, for example, measurement rather than rule-of-thumb, and validation rather than enchantment. There is additionally a prevalent suspicion of emotion, exemplified in science and sometimes regarded as a leading if not defining feature of it. Any evidence of a recent weakening of the residual cultural suspicion of emotion may be explained in terms of the declining status of science in contemporary western cultures, as much as any other factor.

While not able to pursue all of the above themes in the present paper, the following discussion will focus on the relationship between science and emotion. The supposed antipathy between science and emotion is typically associated with Cartesian origins (Toulmin 1990, 113–5). The 17th century mathematician and philosopher, René Descartes, famously held that mind and body are radically different substances as it is possible, he argued, to doubt the existence of all physical objects, including one's own body, but impossible to doubt the existence of oneself as a thinking being. Passions, being of the body, are by hypothesis fundamentally distinct from mind. It follows, then, that science as a mental activity can only be disrupted by influence of the emotions. This extrapolation, that emotions disrupt science, while frequently attributed to Descartes, is not a complete representation of his position, as we shall see below. It is necessary to be clear, in any event, that concern here is the impossibility of emotion in the intrinsic activities of science. Yet this was not the original basis on which science and emotion were held to be opposed.

Passion in the Performance of Science but not the Communication of Science

When the Royal Society was founded in 1662, according to Thomas Sprat's *History of the Royal Society* (1667), eloquence in language was abolished because it is contrary to reason and abets passion (quoted in Jones 1953, 85). The underlying assumption seems to be that passion or emotions undermine science. Yet this is a curious conclusion to draw because the scientists who constituted the movement of this period, now known as the Scientific Revolution, frequently referred to the emotions they believed were necessary to their scientific activities.

William Harvey, for instance, writing about his research on mammalian hearts and circulation of blood in 1628, refers to emotional turmoil caused by the puzzlement he experienced in distinguishing systole and diastole. He explains how his "mind was therefore greatly unsettled," and how this emotional discomfort was resolved through experiment and observation, when "I had attained to the truth, that I should extricate myself and escape from this labyrinth" (Harvey 1952, 273). Isaac Newton, writing in 1672, indicates different emotions but imputes similar importance to them when referring to his response to light shone through a prism:

"It was at first a pleasing divertissement to view the vivid and intense colors produced thereby; but after a while applying myself to consider them more circumspectly, I became surprised to see them in an oblong form; which, according to the received laws of refraction, I expected should have been circular [...] Comparing the length of this colored spectrum with its breadth, I found it about five times greater, a disproportion so extravagant that it excited me to a more than ordinary curiosity of examining from whence it might proceed" (quoted in Daston and Park 2001, 303).

A century after Newton, Joseph Priestley reports his discovery of oxygen, when burning a candle in "air" extracted from mercuric oxide, in terms of the same emotions:

"But what surprised me more than I can well express, was, that a candle burned in this air with a remarkably vigorous flame [...] but as I had got nothing like this remarkable appearance from any kind of air besides this particular modification of nitrous air [nitric oxide], and I knew no nitrous acid was used in the preparation of *mercurius calcinatus* [mercuric oxide], I was utterly at a loss how to account for it" (Priestley 1965, 142).

After more detailed description of activity and reaction, following this passage, Priestley goes on to say: "I wish my reader be not quite tired with the frequent repetition of the word surprise, and others of similar import; but I must go on in that style a little longer" (Priestley 1965, 146).

The appreciation of the importance of emotion to science during this period has been noted by Lorraine Daston and Katherine Park when they wrote that "[m]using admiration, startled wonder, then bustling curiosity—these were the successive moments of seventeenth-century *clichés* describing how the passions impelled and guided natural philosophical investigations" (Daston and Park 2001, 303). Even Descartes gave a place in science to wonder, which he calls "the first of all the passions" (Descartes 1955, 358). This is because the only object of wonder is "the knowledge of the thing that we wonder at" (Descartes 1955, 363) and it therefore "disposes us for the acquisition of the sciences" (Descartes 1955, 365). Too much wonder, though, Descartes warns, can lead to pursuit of triviality and therefore in spite of its positive attributes he continues to regard it cautiously (Descartes 1955, 365).

What concerned the Royal Society was not passion in science but the dangers of passion in persuasion, a fear of distortion in scientific communication through emotion in eloquence. The source of this concern was the 17th century revival of classical rhetoric. Rhetoric is the study and discipline of persuasion. Aristotle's *Rhetoric*, which established the field, included a consideration of means of persuasion through the structure of argument and forms of speech. It also included a lengthy discussion of the emotions, "the nature and character of each, its origin, and the manner in which it is produced" (Aristotle 1926, 19). Aristotle wrote extensively on emotions in his *Rhetoric* because he believed that the success of persuasive efforts depends in part on the emotional dispositions of the audience. During the 16th century in England, however, works on rhetoric largely focused on linguistic form and neglected the emotions. This was corrected during the 17th century, through a return to the tradition of Aristotle (Sloan 1971, xxxii–xxxvi). This is best exemplified in Thomas Wright, *The Passions of the Minde in Generall*, a highly influential work of the time which went through 5 editions from 1601, when it was first published, to 1630, when the last edition appeared. If persuasive effort depends on the emotional dispositions of the audience, then the emotional manipulation of the audience became a further tool of persuasion. It was this latter prospect that led the Royal Society to caution concerning the role of emotion in artful persuasion.

Since the 17th century, concern regarding the place of emotions in science has tended to generalize from distortion in science communication to distortion in the practice of science itself. We shall see, though, that within this latter concern are a number of qualifications giving rise to quite different specific appraisals of the relationship between science and emotions. Indeed, the 17th century situation was more complex than described above, for against the Royal Society's concern with the possibility of distortion of science communications through emotions, and Harvey's and Newton's acceptance of emotional guidance in scientific investigation, there is Francis Bacon's position that:

"The human understanding is no dry light, but receives an infusion from the will and affections; whence proceed sciences which may be called 'sciences as one would' [...] Numberless [...] are the ways, and sometimes imperceptible, in which the affections colour and infect the understanding" (Bacon 1905, 267).

Bacon's statement resonates with the view that became dominant from the late 18th century, namely that for science to precede emotion must be expelled.

The convention from the 18th century, captured by the quotation from Bacon above, and frequently summarized as "Cartesian," holds that as science is to provide knowledge of the world external to the scientific observer, then science must adequately represent that world, and thus it must be independent of the scientific observer. According to this position, then, scientific knowledge is necessarily *impersonal*. Representation of the impersonality of science is typically achieved by characterizing science in terms of its formal properties, especially those associated with its methods, rather than in terms of its human attributes, including the scientist's emotions.

The exclusion of emotion from science by virtue of its impersonality is in fact compatible with emotions having a role in two aspects of scientific activity, namely the motivation of the scientist's investigation and commitment of the scientist to the social institution of science.

Emotion and Scientific Motivation

The motivation of scientists, like that of human agents in general, can be characterized emotionally. The emotions that Newton, Harvey, and Priestley refer to, quoted above, are the affective base of their motivation for scientific investigation. The joy of discovery, for instance, is frequently mentioned as a continuing emotional incentive to engage in scientific work: the "joy of discovery is a very real incentive to research, despite the rareness of its realization" (Baker 1942, 17; see also Feuer 1963, 1, 7, 13). Baker, who was a British zoologist, goes on to show that the emotionality of the scientist's motivation can coexist with the impersonality of science:

"It is an error to suppose that the scientist is unemotional, or could succeed if he were. The error has arisen through a misconception. The absolute necessity that a scientist's findings shall not be changed from objective truth in response to emotional urges of any kind does not result in his becoming a particularly unemotional person: whether a discoverer or anyone else is pleased with a discovery has no effect on its validity" (Baker 1942, 17–8).

Writing at the same time as Baker, the American sociologist Robert Merton shifted the focus away from individual motives to institutional control.

The individual or personal motives of scientists are necessarily diverse, as Merton says, and may include, among a host of possibilities, a "passion for knowledge, idle curiosity, altruistic concern with the benefit to humanity" (Merton 1968b, 613) and so on. Against these individual or "distinctive motives" Merton posits the "distinctive pattern of institutional control of a wide range of motives which characterize the behavior of scientists" (Merton 1968b, 613). As he indicated in an earlier article, institutional control does not operate to the exclusion of emotions but refers to a sociologically significant emotional attachment to institutional norms: "The institution of science itself involves emotional adherence to certain values" (Merton 1968a, 601). Merton makes his point in terms similar to Baker's on individual motivation:

"Although it is customary to think of the scientist as a dispassionate, impersonal individual—and this may not be inaccurate as far as his technical activity is concerned—it must be remembered that the scientist […] has a large emotional investment in his way of life, defined by the institutional norms that govern his activity" (Merton 1968a, 596).

Thus emotions can operate at the level of both the scientist's individual motivation and commitment to institutional norms, without undermining the essential impersonality of what Merton calls the "technical activity" of science.

In these accounts, then, emotions are confined to the motivational framework of science and not its interior. The sustaining institutional controls of science summarized by Merton as the "ethos of science" and represented as four sets of institutional imperatives, namely universalism, communism, disinterestedness, and organized skepticism, are infused with emotion. Indeed, Merton refers to the ethos of science variously as "an emotionally toned complex of rules, prescriptions, mores, beliefs, values and presuppositions" (Merton 1968a, 595, note 16), and, with greater succinctness and increased neutrality, as "that affectively toned complex of values and norms" (Merton 1968b, 605). In each case, though, the emotional element is pronounced. And yet, the ethos of science is "one limited aspect of science as an institution" namely its "cultural structure," and must be distinguished from both the "set of characteristic methods by means of which knowledge is certified […] [and the] stock of accumulated knowledge" (Merton 1968b, 605). Thus in this representation the interior of science remains free of emotions.

Merton's account of the norms of science has been frequently challenged (Barnes and Dolby 1970; Kuhn 1977, 330–9). Even more serious, Merton's norms have been transgressed without undermining the scientific enterprise but with the effect of enhancing it. In a study based on interviews with 42 eminent scientists who worked on the Apollo moon rocks, for instance, it was shown that rather than open-mindedness among scientists it was frequently dogged commitment and "even bias" that proved to be the "strongest sustaining forces both for discovery of scientific ideas and for their subsequent testing" (Mitroff 1974, 73). Such emotional attachment to ideas and assessments idiosyncratically held and possibly contrary to existing evidence contravenes in various ways the entirety of the ethos of science as Merton conceives it. Nevertheless, such commitments proved necessary for the advancement of science in this case, and were elements in the practice of scientific rationality (Mitroff 1974, 249). While this brief account may undermine the Mertonian ethos, it leaves intact Merton's view that emotions are in the framework of science but not its interior. Commitment and bias are given to the findings of investigation and are not interior to investigation itself.

In a quite different assessment Lorraine Daston (1995) has shown that because of their implicit metaphysical grounding Merton's norms are un fortunately impervious to historical variation and cultural modification. In place of this rigid ethos of science Daston posits a "moral economy of science" which is "a web of affect saturated values that stand and function in well-defined relationship to one another [...] a balanced system of emotional forces, with equilibrium points and constraints" (Daston 1995, 4). Through a discussion of the significance of moral economies in the generation and operations of quantification, empiricism, and objectivity, Daston demonstrates the role of the emotions and values of historically situated scientists in the formation of scientific rationality: "By examining in a new light just those ways of knowing once thought to exempt science from the realm of emotions and values, a study of moral economies may illuminate the nature of the rationality that seemed to exclude them" (Daston 1995, 24). While rightly criticizing Merton's insensitivity to developments of custom and practice, Daston fails to go beyond his relegation of emotion to the framework of science and leaves unexplored the emotional components of the practical activities of science.

Emotions Within Science

Michael Polanyi (1974) presents a very different approach to the role of emotions in science than Merton's. He says:

"The outbreak of such emotions [as elation] in the course of discovery is well known, but they are not thought to affect the outcome of discovery. Science is regarded as objectively established in spite of its passionate origins [...] I dissent from that belief [...] and want to deal explicitly with passions *in* science [...] [S]cientific passions are no mere psychological by-product, but have a logical function which contributes an indispensable element to science" (Polanyi 1974, 134).

The function of scientific passion, according to Polanyi, "is that of distinguishing between demonstrable facts which are of scientific interest, and those which are not [...] [and] also as a guide in the assessment of what is of higher and what of lesser interest" (Polanyi 1974, 135). In addition to this selective function Polanyi identifies two further functions of scientific passion, the heuristic function and the persuasive function. The latter is self-explanatory. The heuristic passion, which Polanyi says is the main-spring of originality, "the force which impels us to abandon an accepted framework of interpretation and commit ourselves, by the closing of a logical gap, to the use of a new framework," serves as a guide to enquiry as it "links our appreciation of scientific value to a vision of reality" (Polanyi 1974, 159). Whereas Merton excludes emotions from the method and substance of science, Polanyi says that they are indispensable within it.

Polanyi trained as a scientist and was for many years Professor of physical chemistry at the University of Manchester in England. His state-ment of the importance of scientific passions therefore can be regarded as a conclusion of participant observation. And yet his account deals only with the functional aspects of scientific passions and lacks a description of the particular emotions involved. Indeed, the scientific passions that he refers to have the form and character of postulated entities rather than of empirical phenomena, more like quarks in quantum chromodynamics than DNA in molecular biology. Another scientist, whose writings have also attracted a philosophical and sociological readership, Ludwik Fleck, also advocated the functional importance of emotions for scientific work. Fleck's discussion complements Polanyi's and suggests why description of emotions in science may be so difficult.

Fleck insists that "emotionless thinking is meaningless" (Fleck 1979, 49) when arguing against the German sociologist Wilhelm Jerusalem, writ-ing in 1924, that the appropriately trained "individual acquires the ability to state facts purely objectively and thus learns to think theoretically, that is, free from emotion" (quoted in Fleck 1979, 49). In countering the notion that there is thinking free from emotion Fleck argues that emotion is only either noticed or not noticed, and when not noticed it may be thought to be absent:

"There is only agreement or difference between feelings, and the uniform agree-ment in the emotions of a society is, in its context, called freedom from emotions. This permits a type of thinking that is formal and schematic, and that can be couched in words and sentences and hence communicated without major defor-mation" (Fleck 1979, 49).

The society Fleck refers to is the "thought collective" constitutive of a particular scientific community, and the agreement of feelings he postulates derives from the shared "thought style" that characterizes the stock of knowledge and level of culture of a scientific community (Fleck 1979, 39).

According to Fleck, the emotional basis of science is pervasive (see Barbalet 2002, 140–4). He shows that it is in the structure of the thought collective (Fleck 1979, 105–12), in the epistemological modeling of a "discovery" into a "fact" (Fleck 1979, 86, 119, 144), and in the sense of certainty surrounding "factual" knowledge (Fleck 1979, 117, 145) Given that pattern recognition has such a central role in the observations that are at the heart of scientific research (Ziman 1978, 43–53), it is appropriate to focus on the affective dimension of this aspect of Fleck's account of scientific discovery. It is here that Polanyi's first function of scientific passion is to be located, that of "distinguishing [...] facts that are of scientific interest" (Polanyi 1974, 135).

Fleck indicates, firstly, that scientific observation can occur only after a period of scientific training has been undertaken (Fleck 1979, 48). He immediately goes on to say that the role of training is to generate appropriate experience in the trainee. Experience is so important because it is the basis of emotional sensibility, as we shall see. Through possession of appropriate experience the trainee thereby qualifies for membership in the thought collective. This experience and its consequences therefore provide access to observations consonant with the correlative thought collective: "Direct perception of form requires being experienced in the relevant field of thought [...] At the same time, of course, we lose the ability to see something that contradicts the form" (Fleck 1979, 92). The epistemological importance of experience referred to here is in the fact that scientific experience or training produces particular expectations and therefore provides an appropriate focus of attention.

Attention is the property of cognition that selects only a portion of the vast range of sensory involvement for conscious awareness. Fleck gives the example of the selection of different bacterial colonies from over a hundred different cultures. The observations are not "pure," he says, but "anticipate" differences (Fleck 1979, 90). Expectancy or anticipation is an affective element of a number of particular emotions. It is the fundamental emotional basis of all vision and observation. Because they are not given social representation these emotions are not culturally labeled, and are therefore without names. Thus, scientists are seldom conscious of experiencing them, even though they underpin the conscious awareness of pattern recognition that is central to scientific observation.

Given the significance of emotions in Fleck's characterization of thought collective it is important to appreciate the consistency of his account of thought style. According to Fleck, truth and facts derive their meaning from particular thought styles. A thought style, Fleck says, "consists of a certain mood and of the performance by which it is realized." He continues by saying that a "mood has two closely connected aspects: readiness both for selective feelings and for correspondingly directed action" (Fleck 1979, 99). As "mood" changes, so does meaning (Fleck 1979, 110). The link indicated here between emotions and meaning has been observed in a number of contexts, including empirical observation and theory formation (see James 1890b, 312–7; 1958, 128–9). Again, while conscious awareness of meaning is taken for granted, the underlying emotional basis is typically not experienced consciously.

To summarize discussion to this point: Fleck demonstrates the functions of emotion in science that Polanyi similarly points to. The emotions involved remain unnamed by the scientists who experience them, and it is highly probable that scientists are not consciously aware of the emotions involved. While the emotions in question are central to selection of the relevant facts connected with scientific pattern recognition and observation in general, and consciousness of those facts, scientists are not conscious of the underlying emotions. Even the more externally apparent Mertonian emotions essential for motivation and the institutional framework of science are frequently not consciously experienced by the scientists subject to them, judging by the continuing denial by numbers of scientists of emotional involvement in scientific activity.

Part 2: Emotions – Conscious and Unconscious

The conclusion of the previous section, that key emotions in science are experienced non-consciously, is unacceptable to a body of literature. Other relevant literatures, though, in different ways, acknowledge the possibility of non-conscious emotional experiences. The present section of the paper will review arguments concerning this aspect of emotions.

Emotions as Conscious States

The question whether emotions can be non-consciously experienced was asked in a recent state-of-the-art summary of current findings of emotions research (Ekman and Davidson 1994). A psychologist (Clore 1994) and a neuroscientist (LeDoux 1994) each answered explicitly that it was not possible for emotions to be non-conscious. A third emotions scientist, a psychologist (Zajonc 1994), was less explicit in so far as his answer to the question seemed to move from non-conscious emotion to non-conscious influence on emotion, things which Clore and LeDoux appropriately distinguished. The arguments of Clore and LeDoux are essentially identical.

Clore holds that "while the cognitive processing that causes the emotion is unconscious, the informational and motivational effects of emotion depend on conscious experience in order to capture the attention of the experiencer" (Clore 1994, 285). He goes on to explain that the feeling component of emotion is necessary, and that it is the fact that the emotion is felt that makes it conscious (Clore 1994, 286–7). These same elements of the argument feature in LeDoux's account: while unconscious processes underlie emotions, emotional feeling—the fact that emotions are "affectively charged"—means that emotions are conscious states (LeDoux 1994, 291). It is almost a matter of definition, then, that emotions are conscious states, and that they cannot, therefore, be experienced non-consciously.

Against these conclusions an important contribution to the sociology of emotions has demonstrated that certain emotions, at least, can be experienced without being felt. By combining aspects of the work of sociologist Charles Horton Cooley (1964) and psychologist Helen Block Lewis (1971), Thomas Scheff, for instance, has been able to demonstrate that adult humans typically experience pride and shame with "such low-visibility that [they] do not notice it" (Scheff 1988, 399). It is possible to conclude from Scheff's argument, therefore, that when the feeling component of the emotion is "bypassed" a person may experience shame without being conscious of the emotion.

Scheff argued that it is possible to indicate an incidence of shame, through presentation of behavioral evidence, even though subjects may fail to report experience of shame. He did this by drawing upon Lewis' analysis of a large number of clinical encounters, which showed that while participants were not conscious of the majority of shame episodes that they experienced, non-verbal or behavioral shame-markers were nevertheless manifest (Scheff 1988, 401). Scheff went on to confirm Lewis' conclusions through a re-analysis of Solomon Asch's celebrated conformity experiments. He shows that Asch's subjects who unreasonably conformed to a group norm did so under the pressure of unacknowledged and unrecognized shame (Scheff 1988, 402–5). In this manner Scheff shows that a key mechanism of social organization, namely conformity, functionally depends on experiences of shame that occur below the threshold of awareness, that is to say, non-consciously.

Juxtaposing the conclusions of Clore and LeDoux on the one hand and Scheff on the other raises a number of issues, for both sets of conclusions cannot be correct. One question is the significance and role of feelings in emotions and in consciousness. Not all approaches to emotion accept the primacy of feeling in emotional experience that Clore and LeDoux assume. According to one philosophical theory of emotions, cognitivism, individuals subjectively infer their emotions not from the feelings associated with them but through the beliefs inculcated by the emotions. Cognitivism need not be understood to claim that feeling is not necessary to emotion, only that it is not sufficient. The issue here is not the truth or otherwise of cognitivism, but the question of the status of feeling in emotional experience. Scheff, for one, points to conforming behavior that the subject may subjectively explain in terms of beliefs, without being aware of a feeling of shame. Another question: even if feeling is a sufficient element of emotional experience, does it follow that the feeling must be experienced consciously? Clore discredits an account that purports to show that fear can be experienced without the feeling component being consciously experienced (Clore 1994, 286–7). This question does not arise for Scheff when he argues that the feeling of an emotion may be "bypassed." We shall see that it is not unintelligible to hold that feeling might be experienced non-consciously.

Unconscious Emotion

When consciousness becomes an object of enquiry, the possibility of an alternative state, unconsciousness becomes a matter of interest. To this point of the discussion non-consciousness rather than unconsciousness has been mentioned because the former term carries less cultural baggage than the latter, as we shall see. We shall also see that under certain interpreta-

tions the terms are more or less equivalent, but not under all interpretations. To appreciate just how confusing the matter of unconsciousness is
we might consider Clore's remark, that "in agreement with Freud, I would
argue that it is not possible to have an unconscious emotion because emotion involves an experience, and one cannot have an experience that is not
experienced" (Clore 1994, 285). This is to ask: is it possible to have an
experience that the experiencing agent is not aware of?

Much routine experience, of course, involves activities of which the
subject is not necessarily conscious. Indeed, in "habitual action," as William
James observes, "mere sensation is sufficient guide, and the upper regions
of brain and mind are set comparatively free" (James 1890a, 115–6). Typical examples of this include the experience of driving a car or locking the
front door when leaving the house. These types of experience frequently
contain significant unconscious elements in so far as there is a lack of consciousness awareness of key facets of driving and locking the house on the
part of those engaged in such experiences. This occurs even though the
experience of driving involves tactile and practical awareness of the clutch
and accelerator, of the road, and so on; just as experience of leaving the
house involves experience of the door, the lock and the key. It is simply
that those persons having these experiences need not be consciously aware
of being aware of the things they engage when they drive or lock the door.
In philosophical terminology, there is an absence of second-order
awareness even though first-order awareness occurs. Could not emotional
experiences conform to this type of possibility?

It is implicit in the position of Clore and LeDoux that emotional experiences are different than non-emotional experiences insofar as emotions
are themselves a special type of awareness by virtue of the feeling component. This position invites closer consideration. Emotions provide those
experiencing them with awareness of both internal processes of arousal
and also external objects. Awareness of internal states and external objects
is linked by emotion through formation of intention, which is experienced
as an internal disposition but whose object is most frequently located in an
external environment or arena. It can be accepted that emotion is registered to the person experiencing it through its affective component or
dimension, through the feeling of the emotion. As we shall see below,
however, it is possible that the emoting subject may not be aware of being
aware of their internal arousal nor of an external body that is the object of
their emotion, any more than the driver who is aware of the road is neces-

sarily aware that they are aware of the road. The absence of second-order awareness is the condition of unconsciousness in this sense.

For Freud, however, whom Clore invokes in making his case, unconsciousness is not a lack of consciousness but a mental entity in its own right, parallel to consciousness, and possessing its own separate aspirations and concerns. This distinction, between unconsciousness as an absence of consciousness, and unconsciousness as a distinct mental entity, is crucial in addressing the question of consciousness. It is not always understood (Griffiths 1997, 151–5). According to Freud, personally painful and otherwise emotionally unacceptable memories and thoughts become integrated into a subject's unconscious through a process of repression. It is a matter of doctrine for Freud that the associated emotions loose their connection with the repressed material and are not themselves repressed (Zangwill 1987, 277). The entity Freud postulates as the unconscious, and the attendant notion that there are no unconscious emotions, simply offers nothing to an understanding of whether emoting subjects are aware of the emotions they experience.

William James, for instance, was aware of the problem of confusing unconscious as an absence and as a substance. Indeed, he developed a critique of pre-Freudian notions of unconscious substance (James 1890a, 164–76). He did not dismiss the importance of unconsciousness as an absence, however, for he observed the significance of experiences of which the subject is not aware. To describe these latter he explicitly rejected the "adjective 'unconscious,' being for many of them almost certainly a misnomer," replacing it with the "vaguer term 'subconscious' or 'subliminal'" (James 1958, 170). What James calls subliminal consciousness might be described, in light of preceding discussion, as first-order conscious, in which there is experiential awareness of objects by virtue of affective relations with them, but without attendant second-order consciousness of subject-awareness of first-order consciousness.

Terminological proliferation is not usually a source of clarity, but James does endeavor to avoid confusion when he distinguishes between "consciousness of the ordinary field" on the one hand, and a "consciousness existing beyond the field, or subliminally" on the other (James 1958, 188). Subliminal consciousness, the discovery of which James says is "the most important step forward that has occurred in psychology" during his lifetime (James 1958, 188), refers to "a set of memories, thoughts, and feelings which are extra-marginal and outside of the primary consciousness altogether, but yet must be classed as conscious facts of some sort, able to reveal their presence by unmistakable signs" (James 1958, 188). The context of this discussion is religious conversion, and James is here concerned with the consequences of "strongly developed" subliminal consciousness of religious innovators (James 1958, 189). The general significance of subliminal consciousness, however, is its universality (James 1958, 188). Indeed, experience of subliminal consciousness is held to be a "peculiarity in the constitution of human nature" (James 1958, 188).

The role of this peculiarity, as opposed to its incidence, can be readily demonstrated. To take an instance unconnected with James or religious conversion, the behavioral zoologist Niko Tinbergen, for example, discusses the study of posturing behavior in the Herring Gull:

"In a social species such as the Herring Gull, numerous movements of the individual are 'understood' by its companions, who react to them in special ways. Some of these movements and postures are not difficult even for the human observer to appreciate, though the detection of most of them requires careful study. There are a multitude of very slight movements, most, if not all, of them characteristic of a special state of the bird. The student of behaviour is to a high degree dependent on his ability to see and interpret such movements. In the beginning, he will notice them unconsciously. For instance, he will know very well on a particular occasion that a certain gull is alarmed, without realizing exactly how he knows it. Upon more conscious analysis of his own perception (an important element in behaviour study), he will notice that the alarmed gull has a long neck" (Tinbergen 1961, 7).

Here is an account of the progress of scientific knowledge and understanding in terms of a movement from subliminal consciousness to second-order consciousness. The first phase includes perceptual awareness of gull behavior in the absence of awareness of that concrete perception. This is knowing that the gull is alarmed without knowing how it is known. The second phase includes the observer's awareness of her perception, awareness of being aware of the extension of the gull's neck. This account is continuous with the discussion of pattern recognition in the treatment above of Fleck's contribution to our appreciation of the role of emotions in scientific observation.

Emotion and Core Consciousness

What James refers to and Tinbergen describes, modern neuroscience explains. Antonio Damasio, for instance, distinguishes "three stages of processing along a continuum: *a state of emotion,* which can be triggered and executed non-consciously; *a state of feeling,* which can be represented nonconsciously; and *a state of feeling made conscious,* i.e., known to the organism having both emotion and feeling" (Damasio 2000, 37; emphasis in original). According to Damasio, "feeling is a private, mental experience of an emotion," whereas emotion is understood as "the collection of responses, many of which are publicly observable" (Damasio 2000, 42). The distinction between feeling and emotion drawn by Damasio is curious insofar as these are not symmetrical elements of a frequently associated couple. More typically emotion is understood to comprise a number of elements or components of which feeling is one, the others being motor expression, motivation and behavioral tendencies, cognitive stimulus processing, and neurophysiological processes (see Scherer 1984). It is possible to say that these components are "indicators" of emotion and that no one of them singly or in combination comprises "the emotion," which remains a particular type of experience (Leventhal 1984, 271–2). The matter of interest in Damasio's account, however, is that the feeling state need not be registered consciously for it to be experienced.

Damasio demonstrates his claim with a clinical case study. A patient in Damasio's neurological clinic had 20 years previously suffered extensive damage to both temporal brain lobes that had profound consequences for his capacity to learn and remember. The patient, David, was as a result of his injuries physically incapable of recognizing or naming any of the persons with whom he interacted on a daily basis, and was incapable of ever remembering whether he had seen any of them before. And yet David nevertheless seemed to display consistent preferences and avoidances for certain persons. This apparent inconsistency between David's condition and his behavior was examined through an experiment designed by Damasio and a colleague (Damasio 2000, 43–4). The experiment consisted of David being subject to 3 distinct types of interaction over a period of time.

The first type of interaction, with an experimental "good guy," was pleasant, welcoming and rewarded; the second type, with a "neutral guy," was emotionally neutral and involved tasks that were neither pleasant nor unpleasant; the third type, with a "bad guy," was extremely tedious and boring. Subsequent to these encounters David was given 2 further tasks involving photographs of the 3 persons who had played the good, neutral and bad guys. It is important to appreciate that David was able to neither recognize the persons in the photographs nor remember whether he had ever encountered them before. Nevertheless, when asked to whom he would go if he needed help David consistently chose the good guy and consistently failed to choose the bad guy. Although he was unable to say that he knew anything about the persons in the photographs and could not remember ever seeing them before, when asked who was his friend he consistently chose the good guy (Damasio 2000, 45).

While nothing in David's consciousness could be responsible for his correct characterization of the good guy and the bad guy, his non-conscious preferences are to be explained in terms of the experimentally induced emotions in the different types of interactions he had been subjected to (Damasio 2000, 45–7). Damasio notes that "David's brain could generate actions commensurate with the emotional value of the original encounters" (Damasio 2000, 46). It is likely that David's emotions were accompanied by a feeling of those emotions, but in the "absence of an appropriately related set of images that would explain to him the cause of the reaction" the feelings remained isolated and disconnected from their antecedent conditions and from David's subsequent behavior (Damasio 2000, 46). David seemed to have no consciousness of his emotional feelings. Yet David's emotions provided him with a subliminal consciousness, to revert to James' terminology, of the good and bad guys. Damasio accounts for the differences indicated here in terms of the distinction between what he calls core consciousness and extended consciousness: David's core consciousness was intact, but his neurological damage prevented extended consciousness.

Core consciousness, according to Damasio, is essentially a self's consciousness of immediacy, of the here and now; whereas extended consciousness provides elaboration of each of the component parts of core consciousness to such a degree that it is qualitatively distinct, drawing upon quite different neurological structures and processes (Damasio 2000, 234–76). The sense of self, while rudimentary in core consciousness, is elaborate in terms of identity and personhood in extended consciousness. Extended consciousness goes well beyond the here and now of core consciousness and provides a rich awareness of both a lived past and anticipated future. Extended consciousness but not core consciousness comprises

second-order conscious experiences. This is because extended consciousness treats memories and other mental representations as objects, giving
rise to a sense of self-knowing. In Damasio's words extended consciousness is:

"the precise consequence of two enabling contributions: First, the ability to learn
and thus retain records of myriad experiences […] Second, the ability to reactivate
those records in such a way that, as objects, they, too, can generate 'a sense of self
knowing,' and thus be known" (Damasio 2000, 197).

It is now possible to state the relationship posited by Damasio between
emotion, feeling, and the two forms of consciousness, core and extended.
The relationship between emotions on the one hand and core consciousness on the other is necessary, they occur together or are absent together
because they require the same neural substrates (Damasio 2000, 100).
There is "no such functional relationship between emotional processing
and extended consciousness," continues Damasio, which is why "impair-
ments of extended consciousness are not accompanied by a breakdown of
emotion" (Damasio 2000, 101). Indeed, emotion is part of the mechanism
that drives core consciousness. In briefly describing this process, Damasio
suggests what is the relationship between feeling and consciousness when
he says that:

"Emotion has a truly dual status in relation to consciousness: the actual responses
whose consequences, as an ensemble, eventually produce an emotion are part of
the mechanism that drives core consciousness; a frame of time later, however, the
collections of responses which constitute a particular emotion can also be treated
as an object to be known. When the 'emotional' object is made conscious, it becomes a feeling of emotion" (Damasio 2000, 350).

Emotional feeling, then, gives representation to the emotion in thought,
introducing a possibility of mental regulation as well as enhanced self-
knowledge (Damasio 2000, 56). Emotional feeling, then, is an object of
extended consciousness, in which it has instrumental possibilities and
through which the emoting subject is aware of it and the emotion with
which it is associated. Emotional feeling is a necessary product or consequence of core consciousness, but not known to the emoting subject
through it.

Emotional Consciousness and Consciousness of Emotions

Damasio's account described above provides a means of overcoming the limitations of those that fail to distinguish between levels of consciousness. It is, however, in many ways similar to an earlier statement in the history of writing about emotion that it nonetheless fails to mention, namely Jean-Paul Sartre's phenomenological theory of emotion. Damasio's distinction between emotion as apprehension of the here and now in core consciousness, on the one hand, and the apprehension of emotional feeling as an object in extended consciousness on the other, has its analogue in Sartre's earlier statement of a distinction between emotion as a form of consciousness on the one hand, and consciousness of emotion on the other.

Sartre begins by describing emotion, in contradistinction to the usual psychological and psychoanalytic accounts, as an "indispensable structure of consciousness" (Sartre 1948, 15). The consciousness that pertains to emotion, however, is not consciousness *of* the emotion, but rather the emotion's consciousness of the world. Sartre says that: "Fear is not originally consciousness *of* being afraid [...] Emotional consciousness is, at first, unreflective [...] Emotional consciousness is, at first, consciousness of the world [...] the person who is afraid is afraid *of* something" (Sartre 1948, 50–1).

As emotion is necessarily conscious of its object, which is in "the world," Sartre insists that emotion is therefore never unconscious but only unreflective (Sartre 1948, 56–7). None of this departs from the position that has been developed in preceding sections of this discussion, even though there is a continuing absence of terminological consistency—which reflects the state of the literature and not the present writer—conceptual agreement is nevertheless achieved. Emotion is consciousness but unreflective in the sense that as an apprehension of the world, or at least objects in it, emotion entails first-order consciousness. Sartre insists that second-order consciousness of emotion is not required for emotional experience. This latter, for Sartre, is emotional apprehension of the world rather than the emoting subject's awareness of those emotions.

Here, then, Sartre's idea that emotions are never unconscious is merely terminological. An absence of consciousness of emotion is not an instance of non-conscious emotion because emotion itself is a form of consciousness as relating to an object in the world. Incidentally, Sartre also explicitly rejects the notion of unconscious substance, conducted in a slightly earlier work (Sartre 1957, 54–8). It is ironic, given his critique of William James' theory of emotion (Sartre 1948, 22–40), that Sartre's critique of unconscious substance is reminiscent of James' argument against unconscious substance, mentioned above.

In all of this Sartre says in a different way what has already been treated in discussion above. The real novelty of Sartre's account of emotions, however, that for our purposes is especially relevant for an understanding of the role of emotions in science, is his account of the transformative capacity of emotion. But what is of value in this notion has to be surgically extracted from Sartre's incomplete and misleading treatment of the magical nature of emotional transformation.

Sartre says that emotional consciousness, a consciousness of the world through emotion, is "a certain way of apprehending the world" in which "the affected subject and the affective object are bound in an indissoluble synthesis" (Sartre 1948, 52). The apprehension of the world through emotional consciousness, he goes on to say, is a "transformation of the world" (Sartre 1948, 58). Sartre explains:

"When the paths traced out become too difficult, or when there is no path, we can no longer live in so urgent and difficult a world. All the paths are barred. However, we must act [...] Before anything else [emotional consciousness] is the seizure of new connections and new exigencies [...] Thus, through a change of intention, as in a change of behaviour, we apprehend a new object, or an old object in a new way [...] The impossibility of finding a solution to the problem objectively apprehended as a quality of the world serves as motivation for the new unreflective consciousness [emotion] which now perceives the world otherwise and with a new aspect, and which requires a new behaviour—through which this aspect is perceived—and which serves as [material] for the new intention" (Sartre 1948, 58–60).

The characterization of emotional consciousness, as transformation of the world through seizure of new connections and the apprehension of a new object or an old object in a new way, is entirely equivalent to Adam Smith's (1980) account of scientific discovery in *The History of Astronomy*, to which we shall turn shortly. While Sartre is correct to insist that "emotion is [...] accompanied by belief [about the world]" (Sartre 1948, 73), his claim that such beliefs are necessarily false cannot be sustained.

Sartre is committed to untruth in emotion. He regards emotions as essentially magical not because he associates emotions with imagination but because he assumes that actors engage emotional consciousness only when they are impotent in facing a world hostile to their desires (Sartre 1948, 67).

Even joy is rationalized in this way when Sartre describes its expressions, dancing and singing, as "symbolically approximate behaviour, incantations" designed to "realize the possession of the desired object as instantaneous totality" (Sartre 1948, 69). The characterization of emotion as magical in transforming, indeed distorting, reality in order to match frustrated desire, leads Sartre to describe it as degraded consciousness (Sartre 1948, 75–7, 83). Inherently ineffective, according to this view, emotion is at best a form of coping behavior, for Sartre. And here is the flaw in Sartre's otherwise suggestive and potentially useful account of emotion: not all emotions are expressive, nor are they meaningfully describable as behavior, as Sartre argues (see Solomon 1981, 222). Indeed, the emotions central to science that manifest transformative powers of re-conceptualization of natural relationships are not behavioral and entirely non-conscious, or, in Sartre's terms, unreflective and not the objects themselves of consciousness. Before discussing further the transformative power of emotions, we shall briefly consider their truth value.

In the passage quoted above Sartre refers to the "impossibility of finding a solution to the problem objectively apprehended as a quality of the world [which] serves as motivation for the new unreflective consciousness [emotion] which now perceives the world otherwise and with a new aspect." The objective world is somehow unacceptable thus promoting a response that is an emotional apprehension that presents the world differently. There is a double error in Sartre's statement. First, what might be called an empiricist dogma that objectively ascribed qualities are timelessly true; and second, that emotional consciousness is necessarily false.

Sartre's archetypical emotional transformation is performed by Aesop's fox, who in his disappointment and frustration in failing to reach ripe grapes turns them sour (Sartre 1948, 61). This is one possibility, certainly. But it is not the only one. Compare Sigmund Freud's characteristically similar acknowledgment of the transformative power of emotion, when he refers to love, for example, as leading to "sexual-overestimation," to "idealization" that "falsifies judgment" (Freud 1957, 190), with James' treatment of love, in which special qualities of another, otherwise missed without the penetrating cognitive benefit of love, are apprehended through it (James 1899, 266–7). While there is no guarantee of truth in emotional experience, there is no necessity of untruth either. In the context of science, emotion is foundation to advancement of knowledge through its transformative capacity.

In a remarkable but neglected treatment of emotions in science, con-temporary with historically early scientific achievement, Adam Smith (1980), in a posthumously published essay, points to a transformative ca-pacity of emotions to which Sartre is blinded through magical incantation. Natural philosophers, says Smith, through training and disposition, are liable to "feel an interval betwixt two objects, which, to more careless ob-servers, seem very strictly conjoined" (Smith 1980, 45). The natural philo-sopher's experience of a thing's "dissimilitude with all the objects he had hitherto observed" has the consequence of producing in him "uncertainty and anxious curiosity" (Smith 1980, 40). These anxious and painful emo-tions that beset the scientist or natural philosopher are cured by scientific engagement:

"Philosophy, by representing the invisible chains which bind together all these disjointed objects, endeavours to introduce order into this chaos of jarring and discordant appearances, to allay this tumult of the imagination, and to restore it, when it surveys the great revolutions of the universe, to that tone of tranquillity and composure, which is most agreeable in itself, and most suitable to its nature" (Smith 1980, 45–6).

Science, then, relies on an emotional process of the anxious discomfort of perception of disjuncture leading to the construction of explanations—representations of "invisible chains"—that ease the pain, as "the repose and tranquility of the imagination is the ultimate end of [natural] philoso-phy," according to Smith (1980, 61). In Smith's account, then, a problem objectively apprehended promotes an emotional experience that leads, through the transformative capacity of emotion, to a new perception of objectively ascribed qualities of the world, which can be described as more appropriately, accurately or truthfully representing that world.

Part 3: Self-Transcending Emotions and Science

Self-Asserting and Self-Transcending Emotions

Rebuttal, above, of Sartre's supposition that emotional transformation necessarily leads to false constructions of reality was that such transforma-tions do not necessarily lead to false constructions. An understanding of the role of emotion in science requires more than so ambiguous a conclu-sion. The transformative capacity of emotions that Sartre focuses upon, and that Adam Smith also points to in his history of the progressive attainment of improved astronomical knowledge, is connected with emotional intentionality. There is broad agreement that emotions are not mere apprehensions of reality but interested apprehensions that lead those who experience them to particular dispositions.

A defining feature of emotions is that they perceive the world from the perspective of the emoting subject's needs or preferences. Few would disagree with the statement that: "One of the major functions of emotion consists of the constant evaluation of external and internal stimuli in terms of their relevance for the organism and the preparation of behavioural reactions which may be required as a response to those stimuli" (Scherer 1984, 296).

Different evaluations are entailed in different emotions. If the environment is experienced as unduly inhibiting, for instance, the "organism" will evaluate it as hostile and the accompanying emotion will be anger through which there is preparation to act against what is perceived as the constraining factor. Sartre's insight is to see that a person's inability to cope with changes in their circumstances may transform a notice from the bank, for instance, into the service manager's hostility. But this is not the only possibility. It is not the only possibility not just because different people see the world differently but also because there are different types of emotions, and the intentionality of some does not function to assert self-needs in this narrow sense.

When Scherer wrote the passage quoted above it is likely that he had in mind those emotions that are associated with the possibility of behavioral reaction, that typically have high expressivity and clear if not strong physiological correlates, such as anger, fear, love, disgust, shyness and so on. There are a number of ways in which emotions can be categorized; the most frequently cited being the distinction between basic or primary emotions and secondary emotions. The categorization that is most useful in understanding the role of emotions in science, however, is that which distinguishes self-asserting emotions on the one hand and self-transcending emotions on the other. This categorization can be traced back to the work of William James, and no doubt many other writers, and is explicitly stated by Arthur Koestler (1964). The emotions listed above, and that best fit the statement of function in the quotation from Scherer in the previous paragraph, are self-asserting emotions. Self-transcending emotions have a very different profile and serve quite different purposes.

Koestler noted that self-transcending emotions tend to be ignored by emotions researchers, who typically focus instead on self-asserting emotions (Koestler 1964, 285). The neglect of self-transcending emotions, which continues still, is a measure of their lack of salience but cannot be construed as an index of their lack of importance or infrequent incidence. Examples of self-transcending emotions identified by Koestler include grief, longing, worship, raptness, and aesthetic pleasure (Koestler 1964, 285). While all emotions are in principle delinked from action, self-asserting emotions entail characteristic dispositional programs in which the possibility of action consequent upon them is an element in their meaning. Experience of fear, for instance, does not necessarily lead to flight or fight, but the possibility of these associated behaviors is integral to what is meant by fear. A characteristic feature of self-transcending emotions, on the other hand, is the relative absence of behavioral concomitant. As Koestler says, "grief, longing, worship, raptness, aesthetic pleasure are emotions consummated not in overt but in internalized behaviour […] [that] induce passive contemplation, silent enjoyment" (Koestler 1964, 285). Here is the lack of salience or visibility in self-transcending emotions. But here also is a property of a type of emotion that would perform service to and is likely to be associated with science.

By its nature, science is a cognitively expansive set of practices, ever seeking new findings and new means for attaining new findings. Indeed, one concern of those fearful of the disruptive role of emotions is the way in which emotions may inappropriately narrow scientific focus through the introduction of self-interested goals. This was the issue mentioned above in Baker's expression of the concern that "a scientist's findings shall not be changed from objective truth in response to emotional urges" (Baker 1942 17–8). This possibility is a justifiable concern relating to self-asserting emotions because of their propensity to narrow the consciousness of those who experience them. Self-transcending emotions, on the other hand, partly because they share a participatory dimension, Koestler says, involve "an expansion of consciousness by identificatory processes of various kinds" (Koestler 1964, 286). This point can be demonstrated by considering one particular self-transcending emotion, aesthetic pleasure, and its role in science.

Aesthetic Emotion in Science

When a choice has to be made, regarding what particular direction would move scientific research forward, Thomas Kuhn notes that it is not infrequent that sound reasons exist for a number of different options or possibilities (Kuhn 1977, 328). Under such circumstances, closure cannot be achieved by appeal to the facts because alternative possibilities will each typically draw on factual support. Kuhn's resolution is an appeal to values. This approach, however, must be regarded at least incomplete, for Kuhn says that values "influence" but do not "determine" choice (Kuhn 1977, 331). It should be noted that scientists themselves frequently appeal not to values but to aesthetic pleasure in such circumstances, even though they seldom if ever report such emotions in scientific publications. One reason that aesthetic pleasure as a decision mechanism is not incorporated in research findings is the assumption that such feelings are entirely personal and therefore lack the qualities appropriate to sustain research. Nevertheless, implicit in the notion of a scientific community, for instance, is the possibility that experience of aesthetic pleasure is not merely private and idiosyncratic but rather an outcome of consistency of social milieu. Indeed, the importance of training and experience to scientific cognition, discussed above, further suggests a basis of convergence of aesthetic judgment in scientific communities and its possible application to scientific decision making.

Aesthetic experience has a number of elements, of which the emotional component is the most obvious. A second element, that reinforces the self-transcending nature of aesthetic pleasure, is the intellectual component of aesthetic experience. This aspect is inherent in aesthetic pleasure because such experiences are disinterested in the sense that they arise from focus on an object's appearance or structure. As a consequence of disinterested concentration the aesthetic object's instrumental or practical attributes, which relate more directly to the needs of self-assertion, are placed out of focus. In this way the intrinsic properties of objects are emotionally apprehended through aesthetic pleasure (see Maslow quoted in Kemper 1979, 305). This raises, then, the question of the phenomenal object of the emotional-intellectual pleasure that derives from aesthetic experience, to which we now turn.

The aesthetic object is never a thing in itself, but refers instead to an arrangement of things or parts, or to a perspective that permits a view of arrangements. At the heart of aesthetic experience, and the source of joy that accompanies it, is perception of characteristic organization or form in an apparent disconnection or even chaos of parts. Aesthetic experience, then, arises through perception of a particular type of organization of elements that realizes certain values. To this extent Kuhn is correct to point to the role of values in theory choice. The values integral to aesthetic experience have been identified by Maslow, for instance, as wholeness, uniqueness, and aliveness (quoted in Kemper 1979, 303). Within the context of a scientific community, the appreciation of such values will be inherent in the structure of the thought collective, to use Fleck's (1979) term, referred to above. Indeed, the experiential basis of scientific cognition, discussed above, necessarily includes a practical specification of precisely those values central to such aesthetic experience.

Aesthetic experience, then, is a response to the realization of the values characterized here as wholeness, uniqueness, and aliveness, in the circumstances of scientific research and decision-making. In other words, aesthetic experience is a response to a correspondence between these values of the scientific thought collective and the conditions encountered in a particular research episode. The attainment of correspondence between values and condition is the circumstance that evokes the emotions of joy, delight, and pleasure. Kuhn's reference to mere values is therefore insufficient in so far as the efficacy of values in scientific choice is through the role of emotions in signaling correspondence between values and conditions in aesthetic experiences.

The conditions have now been specified in which values can be regarded, as Kuhn suggests, as a guide for action through ambiguous situations. That a scientist realizes her values is a necessarily desirable event, in which satisfaction, indeed joy, is inherent. This is the point: the experience of joy, which is the affective force of all aesthetic experience, is the emotional expression of the realization of values, of attaining a correspondence between the values which guide a scientist's choice and the conditions that that scientist encounters and perceives. In signaling a perception of correspondence between values and conditions, joy is precipitated as a feeling of self-actualization and meaningfulness in a person's activities, indeed being (de Rivera 1977, 64). It can be noted, given the role of wonder in scientific discovery, that joy and wonder have been described as parallel emotions (de Rivera 1977, 66).

The aesthetic experience, then, in the context of scientific choice, is an emotional apprehension of one possibility of action or direction over others on the basis of a felt realization of pertinent values in one set of conditions or practices and their absence in alternative conditions or practices. That this is an emotional apprehension of choice reflects the nature of scientific choice. It must be emphasized that these latter arise when "there is always at least some good reasons for each possible choice" (Kuhn 1977, 328). The question of choice arises not because there is an absence of evidence for one finding or theory as against others, but because there is evidence for all, and therefore an absence of determining evidence. The necessity of aesthetic emotion or joy is therefore unavoidable in such circumstances in the development and progress of science. Because the emotions involved are self-transcending they direct first-order consciousness of the objects they apprehend that then becomes the object of second-order consciousness.

Through the emotions within scientific activity the scientist is aware of the objects the emotions bring to consciousness, even though the emotions do not draw attention to themselves. As archetypical self-transcending emotions they are experienced through the aesthetic objects they draw to the scientist's attention and are themselves experienced non-consciously. An extremely astute observer, the plant morphologist Agnes Arber, has captured something of this:

"It is not possible to offer strict scientific evidence for the idea that not only reason but emotion has a function in biological discovery [...] we can only point to slight indications which are at least compatible with its truth. It is recognized, for instance, that the moment at which a fruitful combination of ideas enters the awareness, is often charged with a particular feeling of joy, which precedes and seems independent of, the rational satisfaction of goal-attainment" (Arber 1954, 20–1).

The joy that Arber refers to is not the motivational joy exterior to science that comes with the satisfaction of any job well done. It is an emotional basis of activity interior to science. Neither is this joy register of the conclusion of a piece of scientific work, but the affective mechanism that allows it to continue toward its conclusion.

Conclusion

It has been shown that emotions are not only central to the sustaining framework of science but also necessary in its core activities. Emotions are able to discriminate between relevant and irrelevant objects of scientific concern, and underlie the scientist's consciousness of those objects. That such emotions are typically experienced non-consciously is a dimension of emotional experience deserving of further investigation. Indeed, it is likely that the incidence of an absence of full conscious awareness of emotional experience is not confined to science, and in the broad span of human activity is statistically very high. Study of science, then, in addition to its intrinsic interest is also in this regard a model for research of other social institutions where non-conscious emotional experience is to be found.

Acknowledgements

This chapter has been published previously as Barbalet (2004).

References

Arber, Agnes (1954). *The Mind and the Eye: A Study of the Biologist's Standpoint.* Cambridge: Cambridge University Press.

Aristotle (1926). *Art of Rhetoric. Loeb Classical Library.* Cambridge, MA: Harvard University Press. [originally written in 330BC]

Bacon, Francis (1905). Novum Organum. In J. M. Robertson (ed.). *The Philosophical Works of Francis Bacon,* 256–387. London: George Routledge and Sons. [first published in 1620]

Baker, John R. (1942). *The Scientific Life.* London: George Allen and Unwin.

Barbalet, Jack (2002). Science and Emotions. In Jack Barbalet (ed.). *Emotions and Sociology,* 132–50. Oxford: Blackwell.

— (2004). Consciousness, Emotions, and Science. *Advances in Group Processes: A Research Annual,* 21, 245-72.

Barnes, S. B., and R. G. A. Dolby (1970). The Scientific Ethos: A Deviant Viewpoint. *European Journal of Sociology,* 11, 3–25.

Clore, Gerald L. (1994). Why Emotions are Never Unconscious. In Paul Ekman and Richard J. Davidson (eds.). *The Nature of Emotion: Fundamental Questions*, 285–90. New York: Oxford University Press.

Cooley, Charles Horton (1964). *Human Nature and the Social Order*. New York: Schocken Books. [first published in 1922]

Damasio, Antonio (2000). *The Feeling of What Happens: Body and Emotion in the Making of Consciousness*. London: William Heinemann.

Daston, Lorraine (1995). The Moral Economy of Science. *OSIRIS*, 10, 3–24.

Daston, Lorraine, and Katherine Park (2001). *Wonders and the Order of Nature, 1150–1750*. New York: Zone Books.

Descartes, René (1955). The Passions of the Soul. In Elizabeth S. Haldane and G. R. T. Ross (eds.). *Philosophical Works of Descartes*, 329–427. New York: Dover Publications. [first published in 1649]

Ekman, Paul, and Richard J. Davidson (eds.). (1994). *The Nature of Emotion: Fundamental Questions*. New York: Oxford University Press.

Feuer, Lewis S. (1963). *The Scientific Intellectual: The Psychological and Sociological Origins of Modern Science*. New York: Basic Books.

Fleck, Ludwik (1979). *Genesis and Development of a Scientific Fact*. Chicago: University of Chicago Press. [first published in 1935]

Freud, Sigmund (1957). Group Psychology and the Analysis of the Ego. In John Rickman (ed.). *A General Selection from the Works of Sigmund Freud*, 169–209. Garden City, NY: Doubleday Anchor. [first published in 1921]

Griffiths, Paul E. (1997). *What Emotions Really Are: The Problem of Psychological Categories*. Chicago: University of Chicago Press.

Harvey, William (1952). An Anatomical Disquisition on the Motion of the Heart and Blood in Animals. In Robert Maynard Hutchins (ed.). *Great Books of the Western World, Volume 28: Gilbert, Galileo, Harvey*, 267–304. Chicago: Encyclopaedia Britannica. [first published in 1658]

James, William (1890a). *The Principles of Psychology, Volume 1*. New York: Henry Holt and Company.

— (1890b). *The Principles of Psychology, Volume 2*. New York: Henry Holt and Company.

— (1899). *Talks to Teachers on Psychology: and to Students on Some of Life's Ideals*. London: Longmans, Green and Co.

— (1958). *The Varieties of Religious Experience: A Study in Human* Nature. New York: Mentor Book. [first published in 1902]

Jones, Richard Foster (1953). *The Triumph of the English Language: A Survey of Opinions Concerning the Vernacular From the Introduction of Printing to the Restoration*. Stanford, CA: Stanford University Press.

Kemper, Theodore D. (1979). *A Social Interactional Theory of Emotions*. New York: Wiley.

Koestler, Arthur (1964). *The Act of Creation*. London: Hutcheson.

Kuhn, Thomas S. (1977). Objectivity, Value Judgment and Theory Choice. In Thomas S. Kuhn. *The Essential Tension: Selected Studies in Scientific Tradition and Change*, 320–39. Chicago: University of Chicago Press.

LeDoux, Joseph (1994). Emotional Processing, but not Emotions, Can Occur Unconsciously. In Paul Ekman and Richard J. Davidson (eds.). *The Nature of Emotion: Fundamental Questions*, 291–2. New York: Oxford University Press.

Leventhal, Howard (1984). A Perceptual Motor Theory of Emotion. In Klaus R. Scherer and Paul Ekman (eds.). *Approaches to Emotion*, 271–91. Hillsdale, NJ: Lawrence Erlbaum Associates.

Lewis, Helen Block (1971). *Shame and Guilt in Neurosis*. New York: International Universities Press.

Merton, Robert K. (1968a). Science and Social Order. In Robert K. Merton. *Social Theory and Social Structure. Enlarged Edition*, 591–603. New York: Free Press. [first published in 1938]

— (1968b). Science and Democratic Social Structure. In Robert K. Merton. *Social Theory and Social Structure. Enlarged Edition*, 604–15. New York: Free Press. [first published in 1942]

Mitroff, Ian I. (1974). *The Subjective Side of Science: A Philosophical Inquiry Into the Psychology of the Apollo Moon Scientists*. Amsterdam: Elsevier Scientific.

Polanyi, Michael (1974). *Personal Knowledge: Towards a Post-Critical Philosophy*. Chicago: The University of Chicago Press.

Priestley, Joseph (1965). The Discovery of Oxygen Abstracted From Experiments and Observations on Different Kinds of Air. In John A. Passmore (ed.). *Priestley's Writings on Philosophy, Science and Politics*, 139–50. New York: Collier Books. [first published in 1776]

Rivera, Joseph de (1977). *A Structural Theory of the Emotions*. New York: International Universities Press.

Sartre, Jean-Paul (1948). *The Emotions: Outline of a Theory*. New York: Philosophical Library. [first published in 1939]

— (1957). *The Transcendence of the Ego: An Existentialist Theory of Consciousness*. New York: The Noonday Press. [first published in 1936–1937]

Scheff, Thomas J. (1988). Shame and Conformity: The Deference-Emotion System. *American Sociological Review*, 53, 395–406.

Scherer, Klaus R. (1984). On the Nature and Function of Emotion: A Component Process Approach. In Klaus R. Scherer and Paul Ekman (eds.). *Approaches to Emotion*, 295–317. Hillsdale, NJ: Lawrence Erlbaum Associates.

Sloan, Thomas O. (1971). Introduction. In Thomas Wright. *The Passions of the Minde in Generall*, facsimile reprint of the 1630 edition, xi–lxiii. Urbana: University of Illinois Press.

Smith, Adam (1980). The History of Astronomy. In Adam Smith. *Essays on Philosophical Subjects*, 33–105. Oxford: Oxford University Press. [first published in 1795]

Solomon, Robert C. (1981). Sartre on Emotions. In Paul Arthus Schilpp (ed.). *The Philosophy of Jean-Paul Sartre*, 211–28. La Salle, IL: Open Court.

Tinbergen, Niko (1961). *The Herring Gull's World: A Study in the Social Behaviour of Birds*. New York: Basic Books.

Toulmin, Stephen (1990). *Cosmopolis: The Hidden Agenda of Modernity*. New York: Free Press.

Zajonc, Robert B. (1994). Evidence for Nonconscious Emotions. In Paul Ekman and Richard J. Davidson (eds.). *The Nature of Emotion: Fundamental Questions*, 293–7. New York: Oxford University Press.

Zangwill, Oliver (1987). Freud on Mental Structure. In Richard L. Gregory (ed.). *The Oxford Companion to the Mind*, 276–8. Oxford: Oxford University Press.

Zeman, Adam (2001). Consciousness. *Brain*, 124, 1263–89.

Ziman, John (1978). *Reliable Knowledge: An Exploration of the Grounds of Belief in Science*. Cambridge: Cambridge University Press.

Extreme Feelings and Feelings at Extremes

Helena Flam

The general aim of this chapter is to show that selected pre- and post-war classics of sociology interwove their discussions of the question of order with references to emotions. In fact they never left emotions out of their theorizing about social order. More specifically, I will demonstrate that some theorists believed that the social and political order constitutes an effective barrier to lurking, upsetting emotions, or even to life-and-limb threatening instincts and affects. Other theorists posited individuals as being both aware and wary of the painful emotions that threaten to surface when orderly interactions become upset. These theorists suggested that in order to prevent this from happening, individuals as social actors are willing to cooperate in sustaining social norms and conventional patterns of interactions. Taken together they surprise by their shared view that the social order and successful social interactions block negative emotions. More or less explicit in their writings is the idea that if we—as individuals and as social collectives—do not co-operate in sustaining political and social (interactive) order, we make each other and ourselves unhappy. Only a tiny minority among classical sociologists saw emotions as constitutive of the individual and the social order. They argued that emotions do "good works"—they help individuals to develop "social" selves that co-operate in creating and sustaining a "good" society. Also in contrast to those who saw social order as blocking negative emotions, more recently several theorists have argued that (the hierarchical) social order cannot *but* produce negative emotional outcomes. In all these ways, this text thus shows that the question of order has been, and remains, also about emotions.

Extreme Feelings at the Extremes – Unruly Times and Territories, System Breakdown, Disintegration

Let me start with a couple of rather well known, and therefore briefly presented examples. In Max Weber's reflections on charisma and in particular on the prophets, we find the first association between the breakdown of a social order and negative emotions (Flam 2002, 57–9). He proposed that when the law and rules break down and people find themselves in the situation of distress, they turn very emotional—desperate in fact, which makes them susceptible to various contenders for charismatic power. These, be it prophets, saviors, knights or political leaders, are all extremely emotional. Weber was impressed by the furious anger of prophets, and not only by their rationalizing reforms (Barbalet 2000), such as introducing taxes or bureaucracy. The feeling and thinking of the charismatic leaders transcends the realm of routine and everyday rules. Nothing short of intense *love* and devotion binds the followers to the charismatic leaders. The masses bow out of deference and *admiration* before their wisdom and fury. However, the leaders aspiring and wishing to consolidate their charismatic rule have repeatedly to prove themselves to their followers and to the masses. Should they fail, the deference and admiration of the masses turns into *hate*—the leaders risk being chased away. Since the breakdown is unique, it generates exceedingly strongly felt emotions: *despair, love, admiration* and *hate*. Very similar to that of Weber's, is Hannah Arendt's main thesis in *The Origins of Totalitarianism* (1973). In it she argues that a system breakdown frees the feelings of masses, turning them both desperate and "millennial," making it possible for the new—totalitarian—leaders to harness them to their goals. Writing about concrete historical cases, Arendt is specific about the elements of the breakdown. She refers to the failure of democratic institutions (political parties, parliament) and the Church to provide economic stability and orientation, in addition to the disintegration of the social classes that cease to be capable of capturing and regulating the lives of their members. In both Weber's and Arendt's analysis of the breakdown the deep *despair* of the masses, their own millennial and the leaders' transcendental aspirations and emotions come together to build the new social and political order.

Norbert Elias, quite explicitly, proposed that an orderly/ordinary nation-state constitutes a main prerequisite of civilized, mannerly conduct and everyday, routine emotions. He argued (Elias 1978, 134–42; Bartels

1995; Wouters 1998) that what he called the civilizing process did away with the original—natural, raw, extreme—*instincts* and *affects* which initially dictated the terms of human interaction. In dealing with each other and in competing for scarce goods, human beings resorted to aggression and violence. In the course of the civilizing process, a few centralizing (state) powers/rulers emerged in Western Europe from among thousands of competing political units. The central ruler became a monopolistic (more, rather than less legitimate) wielder of violence. Within pacified territories ruled by such violence-monopolizing rulers, it became both possible and necessary for the courtiers—dependent on the ruler for their access to, and for their positioning in the polite society—to compete for the royal attention and/or privileges. This was achieved through relying on peaceful means—good manners—rather than, as was the case earlier, through taking up of arms. It is to this constellation that Elias dated back the assertion and consolidation of the first strong, uniform rules constraining and regulating bodily and *emotional expression*. What started as a set of external controls in the form of monitoring, prohibitions and negative sanctions became internalized in the course of the civilizing process to constitute the pillar of individual self-control—the more or less conscious ability of individuals to monitor, suppress and regulate their own instincts and affect. The internalization process as such was predicated upon individuals' new ability to feel (i) *shame* [*Scham*] about one's own transgressions of the ever more sophisticated manners and (ii) painful *embarrassment* [*Peinlichkeit*] when witnessing the transgressions of the others.

The first key insight of Elias then is that it takes a complex, highly contingent constellation of forces to create a civilized society. At the core of this constellation stands a pacified territory ruled and administered by a centralized power that possesses a legitimate monopoly on the use of means of violence, a central administration, and a standing army. The second key insight is that inhabitants of this territory are tied to each other by the mutual dependence and asymmetries of power that compel them to follow the regulatory rules of conduct imposed from above. They accept these rules for *fear* of otherwise losing out in the ongoing competition for economic resources, status and power, but also because, in the meantime, the *others' embarrassment has turned into their shame and vice versa.*

These two insights imply the conditions under which the "civilized" manners lose their hold on the members of the polite society. By the same token they also suggest the conditions under which the fear of losing in the competition, and the fear of feeling shame and embarrassment, will lose their edge, and with it their capacity to restrain and regulate conduct. Specifically, these emotions lose their grip over the individuals when the central power's monopoly on violence and its control over administration diminish, and/or when the chains of mutual dependence among and power relations between people weaken. Elias envisioned not only the civilization process, but also occasional regression periods (see Elias 1994). In those, shame and embarrassment recede and lose their status as instruments of self- and other-control. Un-civilized aggressive, predatory instincts and primitive affects, such as *frustration, aggression, envy* or *hostility* re-emerge. Violence in dealing with each other re-surfaces.

Surprisingly, even Erving Goffman, in addressing the role of the state and its political system, conveyed a similar message: the state guarantees social order, this social order sustains our bodily and acting autonomy, thus keeping our negative emotions at bay. In his 1983 Presidential Address, Goffman (1983, 6) stressed that

"[t]he modern nation state, almost as a means of defining itself into existence, claims final authority for the control of hazard and threat to life, limb, and property throughout its territorial jurisdiction. Always in theory, and often in practice, the state provides stand-by arrangements for stepping in when local mechanisms of social control fail to keep break-downs of interaction order within certain limits. [...] To be sure, the interaction order prevailing even in the most public places is not a creation of the apparatus of the state. Certainly most of this order comes into being and is sustained from below, as it were [...] Nonetheless the state has effectively established legitimacy and priority here, monopolizing the use of heavy arms and militarily disciplined cadres as an ultimate sanction."

Much earlier, in his *Asylums*, Goffman referred explicitly to macro-level, in part political, conditions or context prerequisites that have to be in place before individuals can slide into their everyday social roles (Goffman 1991, 13–72). Among these we find: (i) peaceful, bourgeois-democratic societies with their basic citizen rights; (ii) respect for the "private sphere;" and (iii) segmented social controls which tend towards maximum on the "front stage" and tend towards nil on the "backstage." Goffman indicated that a free political order is a precondition for the emergence and reproduction of the mundane social order that we see as self-explanatory. It is, in fact, the freedom from oppression and our status as free citizens in a free country that allows us to take it for granted that (a) our bodies, which are in fact extremely "vulnerable to physical assault, sexual molestation, kidnapping, robbery and obstruction of movement" (Goffman 1983, 4, 17, 25, 27, 33, 35, 37) will neither become subject to (criminal or disciplinary) assault, nor dirtied, made unpresentable or inexpressive of our social status—so that we can make moral claims to the trust, respect and attention of others; (b) we will stay in control of the autobiographical stuff/props used for presentations of our selves in everyday life; (c) we will pattern the flow and rhythm of the non-working part of the day (relying on our rights and individual discretion), including controlling the timing, duration and style of the strenuous public encounters and of the withdrawal back into the "private sphere," where no authority or public are present; (d) we will use "private sphere" and segmentation of social controls to regenerate (in private or the backstage) our overall capacity to play official/public roles, etc.

These and similar prerequisites of everyday action are intimately interwoven with basic citizen rights and thus by implication constitute macro-level preconditions for routine self-presentations, whose further micro-level prerequisites will be discussed later. It is only when the macro-level prerequisites are present that Goffman's tacit acknowledgment and accreditation conspiracy can develop, making us all co-operate mannerly in sustaining the basic put-on-acts of our interaction partners. Only when these prerequisites are in place, can demeanor and deference be reciprocated, and *deep, paralyzing embarrassment* and/or *anxiety* be prevented, which surfaces when the desired role-performance cannot be carried out (see also Goffman 1967, 5–12, 22–3).

In *Asylums* Goffman (1991) argued at great length, providing very many examples, that a disciplinary order, such as we find in coercive-punitive social settings of prisons, coercion camps, mental asylums, etc., undermines the individual's capacity to engage in simple everyday playacting. These settings abolish not only our civic rights and deprive us of our autonomy. Importantly, they cause, at least initially and for some on a long-term basis, the inability to keep back the feelings of *utter helplessness, despair, extreme irritation, frustration, shame or anger* which necessarily emerge when the individual cannot assert his/her control over either the situation or their own self-presentation. Although Goffman's view on the role of emotions in social interactions is much more complex than I have sketched so far, this summary suffices for now. I will return to other elements of his theorizing later on.

Durkheim's approach to social reality, although de-politicized, transports a similar top-down view. He argued in *Suicide* (1951) and The *Division of Labor in Society* (1960) from a functionalist perspective that social institutions are necessary to shape and regulate individual instincts and desires. He also pointed out specific situations and contexts in which this is not the case. When institutions, such as the family, the Church or the society at large, lose their integrating and regulating powers, individuals become disoriented, their instincts and desires unhinged. The state is too distant to play an integrating role. For Durkheim then, social disintegration and "extreme," unregulated feelings go hand in hand. In aggregate, these individual feelings become visible in *collective disquiet, anxiety, melancholy or depression* (Flam 2002, 61–83).

In Durkheim's view, not only disintegrating social institutions, but also times of rapid economic change (industrial expansion, boom, decline) cause the normative and regulatory frame to lag behind the real developments. Its effects are especially keenly felt where capital and labor encounter each other—the immediate result is that their class egoisms collide and the resulting *hostility* between the classes is left completely unrestrained. Similarly, in cases of an economic crisis or a boom, occasioning rapid individual upward or downward mobility, a mismatch between norms and the real life situation of the individual develops: although the individual still adheres to old norms and rules, these no longer fit the new situation. That is why societal disintegration, rapid economic change or social mobility, by depriving individuals of appropriate moral guidance, make them more likely to feel emotionally *confused* and *disoriented*—in fact extremely so.

Following both classical philosophy and the psychology of his time, Durkheim proposed that *happiness* can only be felt when it is moderate and regulated—when its parameters are clearly and explicitly defined, albeit differently for each social stratum (Flam 2002, 70–5). Like Simmel (1999) writing on the money economy [*Geldwirtschaft*], he found that the industrial economy pushes individuals to want ever more, never to feel satiated or satisfied. This economy develops quicker than the new norms, leaving the individuals without much guidance as to how much it is appropriate to possess as a member of a specific stratum. Individuals' desires remain unbound and unmoderated—a major reason for *unhappiness*, in Durkheim's view.

Just as the *anxiety, depression* or *melancholy* as outcomes of de-regulation and a normative vacuum are extremely felt, so too is this new *unhappiness*—

the effect of the novel, incessantly desire-stimulating economic system left unembraced by norms. These emotions heighten the tendency to suicide. The link between missing regulation/integration and negative emotions in Durkheim's theorizing represents the reverse side of his familiar major thesis that individuals can only be *happy* in (moderately) regulated and integrated societies.

Although the sociologists presented so far greatly differed in how they saw society, they seemed to draw on the same few dichotomies. The first well-known dichotomy contrasts the state of nature with the civilized state. It loomed large in Durkheim's, Weber's and Elias' work. They saw human nature as mercilessly instinct-, desire-, impulse- and passion-ridden, and contrasted it with, respectively, the norm-guided/regulated, self-controlled and civilized human state. Durkheim saw society with its cognitive categories, collective norms and regulations as a precondition for human freedom from instincts, desire and passions. Weber ascribed the same liberating, self-control-augmenting role to the hard versions of Protestantism, and to emotion-suppressing, rationalizing bureaucracies of the enterprise and the modern state to which they had given rise (see, for example, Ritzer 1996, 99; Barbalet 1999, 34–8; Barbalet 2000). Elias, finally, stressed the contribution of the violence-monopolizing central ruler/state to the process that made civilized human beings out of drive-ridden, aggressive and shameless egoists. These classics also associated the state of nature with much unhappiness, but only Durkheim hoped that a reformed, orderly/regulated modern society would provide a base for moderate happiness. In contrast to Durkheim, Weber saw not only long-term, goal-oriented, that is, rationalized, passion but also disenchantment as looming large in a new world of "rational" self-control. For Elias it was shame and embarrassment, and in particular their avoidance, that played a dominant role in sustaining civilized society. In sum, these theorists agreed in their negative assessment of the state of nature, but they differed quite a bit in their view of the modern society, linking it with conduct-controlling emotions (Elias), emotion-regulating institutions (Durkheim) or emotion-disciplining rationalizing tendencies (Weber).

Behind Weber's and Arendt's ideas on the breakdown of a social and political order, which they both associated with mostly negative emotions, one discovers another important dichotomy. Both drew on, and at the same time, criticized the masses-elite theories of their time. These associated the masses with nature, wickedness, evil and danger, while they posited the elites as superior, responsible and rational. While Weber escaped this polarizing dichotomy, proposing instead despair as the main characteristics of the masses and showing that charismatic leaders combine *emotion* with *rationality*, Arendt stayed closer to these theories insofar as her "plebs" are, by definition, evil, while her "masses" end up being evil. However, the responsibility for the evil Arendt attributed in part to the elites spurring the plebs and the masses on, and in this respect at least she did not fall into the usual argumentative trap.

Weber, Arendt, Elias and Durkheim seem to have taken it for granted that strong emotions are innately threatening, but are either blocked, repressed, marginalized, hidden or kept at bay by the institutional, interactional or legal frameworks, and/or the violence-monopolizing ruler/state. Their accounts also imply that if these rules or frameworks break down, negative feelings will become unhinged, unregulated and threatening. In that sense, they also offer a kind of Hobbesian or Freudian imagery of "state-less," "unframed" or "unbound" emotions.

Only Goffman at first glance did not seem to work with a polarized worldview that associates emotions with nature, chaos, violence or evil, and social order with civility, peace and good. However, in his *Asylums* he replicated and expanded the Cold War discourses which praised democracy while condemning totalitarian political systems. Goffman's dichotomous worldview does not contrast the state of nature with the social and political order. It instead juxtaposes the evil totalitarian and the good, orderly and democratic form of life.

In the contemporary world, the "orderly-happy" reality is associated with Europe or the West, while the state of nature or "Hobbesian-unruly and unhappy" reality is associated with the rest of the world. As Billig argues in *Banal Nationalism* (2004), this, however, is a fundamentally false worldview. Our Western "orderly-happy" world is neither as orderly nor as happy as these theories seem to imply. In fact, another set of theories, focused on face-to-face interactions that are set against a background of social structures, helps us to reject such a naïve, simplistic view of ourselves. Their authors argue that Western societies, even when the political and social order does not break down, do not constitute an orderly paradise of happy individuals. This is so because inequality constitutes a constant irritant, and a source of much *unhappiness*.

"Real," "Stressful" and "Shameful" Emotions in Everyday Life

Next I will briefly present Theodore Kemper's (1978) theory of "real emotions" that is indebted to another important post-World War II discourse—that of (in)equality (see Porpora 2002, 44, 46, 56–7). I will then link his theory to a larger family of such theories that together present a compelling argument to the effect that inequality is an omnipresent source of social friction and much *unhappiness* in the West, looming large in remembered, present and anticipated social interactions.

According to inequality discourses, most individuals end up *frustrated* and/or *angry* when they receive too little autonomy, social recognition or power, and they see their interaction partner rather than themselves, as the agent/cause of this interaction outcome. In Kemper's view, they even feel bad when they catch themselves being stingy in granting power and autonomy to others. This implies that the West is not the oasis of happiness in a world-wide desert of unhappiness. Inequality—played out in endless social interactions—makes its inhabitants profoundly unhappy. Kemper's "real" yet "stressful" emotions emerge in ongoing, remembered or anticipated social encounters. His theory is that negations of one's own power and status in everyday interactions will always cause specific negative emotions, such as *frustration* or/and *anger*, if perceived as the fault of the interaction partner. In reverse, when one feels that one received social recognition/power in excess of the expected status or power, and that one is oneself to blame for this excess, one will feel *guilt* and *shame* (Kemper 1978, 33). Kemper calls the feelings that emerge out of such unequal interactions "real emotions." They are involuntary and should be seen as outcomes of social relations rather than as outcomes of culture and its feeling rules. In fact, one feels them *despite* feeling rules (see Hochschild 1979) that forbid them and their expression. They are an outcome of unequal social relations, and in particular their assertion.

Kemper is not alone in this argument. Also Thomas Scheff (1994) in the US, and Sighard Neckel (1991) or Axel Honneth (1998) in Germany argue that individuals only end up *happy* about their interactions when they grant equal respect and autonomy/power to each other. The implicit thesis in their respective arguments is that inequality—played out in unequal interactions—makes people deeply *unhappy*. It is a cause in fact of *shame, guilt, humiliation, frustration* and *anger*.

Randal Collins' (2004) concept of ritual interactions chains, which applies equally to interactions between two individuals as much as it does to those among large collectives, is also indebted to this same (in)equality discourse. According to Collins, while inequalities that are played out in interactions *upset*, rough equality in power and status is a key precondition for successful interactions (rituals). These make people feel *happy* (see also Goffman 1956, 270–1). Successful rituals generate effervescence that leads to, among other things, feelings of solidarity and positive emotional energy. It is perhaps worth noting that Collins' (2004) book devoted to the interaction conditions that make people happily energized is by far outnumbered by books focused on those social encounters that generate unhappiness.

(Extreme?) Emotions Behind Pattern-Variables and Action-Parameters

Apart from the question of relative status and power, in dealing with each other individuals have to decide *how* to approach each other. The American classic of sociology, Talcott Parsons, repeatedly returned to the question of how this is done. Not only Parsons, but Goffman and Elias too, posed this question, and in so doing drew attention to the role of painful emotions, such as *guilt, shame* or *embarrassment*, that accompany normative transgressions. Well-socialized individuals both feel intensively, and are apprehensive about experiencing these emotions. The very apprehension, the very fear of doing something that would cause these emotions to take hold of one, suffices to persuade most individuals to conform rather than risking nonconformity with its attendant painful emotions. In paying attention—however weakly—to such emotions, these theorists more or less explicitly argue that the macro-level social and political order is not enough to keep painful emotions at bay. It also takes recurrent resolution to conform. The daily, step-for-step, individual mini-resolutions, taken by each member of the society, constitute the micro-level guarantee of a functioning social and interactional order. Importantly, it is the anticipation of the *fear* of painful emotions that underwrites these resolutions.

In working out *the very first version* of his pattern variables,[1] Parsons proposed that in each social situation the individual decides according to which—if at all—pattern variables she or he will act (Flam 2002, 103). Surprising—given the mass of critical literature on how Parsons conceived of individuals as social puppets always following social norms—is his very statement that individuals can decide not to follow any of the pre-set action alternatives. He said that should they reject them, they would suffer *guilt* feelings—but that is all. If we expand his reasoning just a tiny bit, it implies that individuals' consent to follow social norms depends crucially on the extent to which they are capable in general and in specific situations to feel *guilt*.

Goffman also posed the "how"-question, but what puzzled him was the question why—given the temptation to use the opportunity to deceive created by the very *play*acting itself—most individuals stay honest. Perhaps again surprising, given the massive literature that emphasizes contrasts rather than similarities between Parsons and Goffman, it turns out that they thought similarly, about what one could call "controlling" emotions. Goffman argued that *guilt, fear* and *shame* keep individuals from deceptive playacting, since most of us are certainly capable of deception and often have good reasons to deceive (Goffman 2005, 55). In contrast to cynics, (social) critics and the naïve, the great majority of individuals bring to the social interaction their a) *guilt* about dishonesty; b) *fear* of disclosure and c) a fundamental capacity to feel *shamed* by disclosures. These emotions— guilt, fear and shame—make it possible for members of the public to switch into a trusting, honest and respectful mode that renders them ready to tolerate or oversee minor lapses (Goffman 2005, 65–6). *Guilt, fear* and *shame*, then, make for adhesion to social rules for playacting. They also chase away dishonesty, suspicion, skepticism and doubt.

Goffman was not alone in adopting parts of the Freudian and/or social anthropological discourses on the role of shame and guilt in sustaining the basic institutions of "primitive" and "complex" cultures/societies. Parsons

---

1 Parsons proposed several versions of pattern variables between 1951 and 1960 (Flam 2002, 107–10). These aimed at answering the question of how/according to which values a social actor defines and can act in any specific situation. Only in the first version did the actor have a choice of rejecting all dichotomous, patterned choices. In the later versions the actor no longer had this freedom and could only decide among and within patterned dichotomous variables, that is, whether or not to act oriented to self or a collectivity, particular or universal criteria, ascription or achievement, specific or diffuse criteria, affectivity or affective neutrality. Note that each version included a reference to emotions.

also directly referred to Freud when writing about guilt and socialization processes. Neither, however, became engaged in the debates about the steering role of shame and guilt in different cultures at any length (for an overview, see, for example, Neckel 1991, 41–58).

Goffman, however, did not stop at examining emotions that motivate individuals to offer honest playacting. He was also curious about the "emergent" emotions that surface during face-to-face encounters, at the micro-level, as it were. His thesis was that if and when one or more of the interaction prerequisites are missing or remain unconvincing, *strong, negative emotional reactions* would result. Individuals or props may be missing. Individuals—in part because their feelings intervene—may play incompetently: stumble or blunder. The public may refuse to offer *trust* and thus boycott the entire encounter (Goffman 2005, 8, 9, 11, 17, 19, 21, 26, 49–50, 54). This happens when the public finds the acting unconvincing since the actor seems disingenuous, or displays too much or too little *pride*, too much or too little *self-assurance*, puts too much or too little effort into acting, or because it has a good reason to feel *hostile* (when a class or political enemy speaks). This amounts to saying that at the micro-level Goffman identified the bad performance or failure at instantiation of the social order as a typical cause of enacted *emotional upset*.

In arraying the prerequisites for successful interactions, he simultaneously defined those that undermine believable performance and cause much upset: *cynicism* as a case of missing individual motivation, accidental blunders, a *disrespectful, distrustful* and thus uncooperative public, or unconvincing props. When, for any of these reasons, the performance collapses, all interaction participants suddenly face a situation in which they find it no longer possible to follow acting routines. When this happens, undesired emotional outcomes are to be expected: *embarrassment* and *confusion* take over (Goffman 2005, 15). Or the major actor feels *shamed*, while the members of the public feel *hostility, anxiety, shock, confusion*—in short anomie (Goffman 2005, 15). As is well known, Goffman pointed out that a myriad of response cries, such as "ah," "uh," "um," or "oops," "Ahh," "Whoops," both express that the interaction is in some kind of crisis, and are meant to bring redress to the playacting—and thus reconstitute the emotional balance of those involved (Goffman 1981, 101, 109). These remedies help to underscore how painful it is for interacting actors to see the interactions fail.

With Goffman's theorizing about the consequences of threatened or failed encounters, we come full circle. Similarly to those classical theorists which I addressed in the first part of this text, Goffman argued that when the routine interaction patterns fail to be sustained through the playacting actors, so that the actual performance disappoints, individual and collective feelings, most of them negative, surface. These have to be addressed, redressed and hidden again. In defining interaction prerequisites, Goffman simultaneously discovered the conditions under which interaction becomes threatened, disrupted or breaks down, and whereby unexpected, undesired emotions surface. Goffman's treatment of *guilt, fear, shame,* and *pain of embarrassment* as concepts renders them comparable to Elias' treatment of *shame* and *embarrassment.* In Goffman's writing, *embarrassment*—or more specifically the efforts of individuals to avoid it and its interaction-disrupting, and therefore even more embarrassing consequences—constitutes the very key emotion that steers most face-to-face encounters. Individuals know that *embarrassment* can bring their interactions to a stop, making everybody feel even more embarrassed than the initial display of embarrassment or the mishap that led to it. They therefore exert themselves to the limits to prevent embarrassing situations. If, for Elias, it was *shame* and *embarrassment* that carry the polite society with its rules of etiquette, for Goffman it was the *fear* of pain associated with embarrassment that motivates every well-orchestrated social encounter. Ultimately, one can perhaps argue that it is the *fear* of the pain, which embarrassment brings with it to all present, that keeps the interaction order going.

To reiterate, and by way of introducing the next section on the positive role of emotions in constructing and sustaining the social fabric, Goffman (and Garfinkel[2]) linked threatened and failed encounters to painful emotions. In addition, Goffman argued that in order to avoid these emotions individuals are ready to follow interaction rules. Durkheim, by contrast, stressed the positive role that extreme emotions, such as *hostility, moral outrage* or *shaming,* play in re-dressing normative transgressions of social and symbolic order. In Durkheim's well-known view, these emotions help to

---

2 For reasons of limited space, references to Garfinkel's (1964) work has been omitted, although his 'breaching experiments' demonstrated that when, even the simplest of rules regulating social interaction are not followed, strong, mostly negative, emotions surface. Individuals turn frustrated, aggressive, while friendships and family relationships suffer. Trust evaporates. An analogy between Garfinkel's micro- and Durkheim's macro-level statements to this effect has often been noted. As I just showed, also Goffman linked failed interactions to negative emotions.

mobilize the collectivity or the elites to impose a punishment on the guilty parties and so to re-instate strongly *felt* norms and collective representations to their previously sacred state. As the next section shows, Durkheim was not the only sociologist to stress the positive contribution of emotions to social order, although he—rather like Parsons, Elias or Goffman—paid attention to just a few extreme and negative emotions rather than, like Simmel or Cooley, taking on their entire range. Simmel and Cooley were also exceptional in that they posited emotions as constitutive of the society.

The Opposite View – (Not-Only-Extreme) Emotions and Their "Good Works"

Georg Simmel (1992; Flam 2002, 16–21), yet another classic of sociology, proposed that in the course of European history the development of the intellect and modern money economy took place at the expense of instincts, drives and affect, wherein their partial suppression was a precondition for the development of the first two. However, Simmel simultaneously held that what he called the *"primary emotions"* constitute the very fabric of society. Primary emotions, according to Simmel, are the very cause of social interactions, the very reason why social interactions emerge in the first place. To appreciate this thesis one has to know that by interactions (*Wechselwirkungen*) Simmel did not understand only short-lived encounters but also what we today call institutions. Primary emotions, such as *love*, are constitutive of friendship or marriage. *Gratitude*, which complements present-giving or (uneven) exchange processes, attaches those grateful to the giver of the present they received to the giver, and to the relation between them, much more than the mere exchange transaction ever could. To Simmel's mind, *gratitude* constitutes the very cement of every society, binding milliards of individuals permanently to each other. *"Secondary emotions"* in turn are an outcome of social interactions. For example, as Simmel argued, *love* may evaporate, but *loyalty*, which emerges in its stead, will keep a couple together long after love is over. Simmel did not see emotions as *per se* controlled or managed (although in case of hostility he drew attention to the rules and actor constellations that regulate and neutralize it). On the contrary, to him they are unpredictable, overwhelm and stay outside of individuals' control. They also display an own dynamic—some reinforce each other (as *love* and *respect*), others undermine or contradict each other (as *love* and *jealousy*), and yet others develop in a typical sequence, following one upon the other. In short, for Simmel, although he was not consistent in this, emotions as a matter of principle do not lose their *sui generis* ability to constitute the fabric of society, nor do they become more malleable, polite, controlled or regulated in the course of historical development. Whether negative or positive, they bond and introduce richness and unpredictability into our everyday relations. They and their (inter)actional consequences can only be disciplined when *shame*—a chief controlling emotion—enters the stage.

Cooley shared with Simmel a positive view of emotions: most importantly, he grounded the "healthy" self not only in the discerning, individuating mind but also in enthusiastic, world embracing loving emotions of which it is capable (1970, 188). Cooley argued that the feeling of *joyous, naive pride* (in self and its material and immaterial qualities and possessions) constitutes the self. While *love* helps this self to embrace the world, self-feeling helps it to direct and individuate the appropriation of selected slices of this world (Cooley 1970, 187). Should this *love* disappear, however, "the self contracts and hardens: the mind [...] busies itself more and more with self-feeling, which takes on narrow and disgusting forms, like avarice, arrogance, and fatuity" (Cooley 1970, 188). Cooley's famous *looking-glass self* implies frequent, emotion-laden comparisons with others that shape and spur on our own development. The imagined judgment of the other with whom we compare ourselves urges us on, and so plays a key role in socialization processes (Cooley 1970, 184). When the imagined appraisal of the other is positive, we feel confirmed and *proud* of our qualities and achievements, and therefore want to retain them, but when it is negative we question ourselves, feel *ashamed* or *mortified*, compelling us to consider how we can change for the better. In Cooley's view then, under ideal conditions emotions and (self-)appraisals help us blossom, and constitute the invisible hand that promotes a good society.[3]

---

3 Decades later, a pioneer in the Sociology of Emotions in the seventies, Arlie Hochschild (1979), subordinated emotions to special norms pertaining to them. Hochschild, explicated what, apart from Goffman, no other sociologist discussed so far made clear: individuals' spontaneous feelings are often not in tune with the situational requirements, demotivating them to playact as expected. But instead of positing guilt, fear, shame and embarrassment, as Goffman did, to explain why people often in the end act according to expectation, Hochschild pointed to the importance of general as well as more specific, managerial and gender ideologies with their attendant feeling rules situated in a speci-

Uwe Schimank, a contemporary German sociologist shares with Arlie Hochschild (1979) the basic conviction that social rules and emotions are involved in sustaining complex societies. He argues, however, that in our societies the division of labor (occupational specialization) and individual efforts at self-defining are so advanced that in many areas of life institutions do not provide any normative rules for acting. His identity-ascertaining individuals who, based on Flam (1990), he conceptualizes as three-dimensional, that is, rational, normative and emotional, have to fall back on their *feelings* and interests to figure out how to act in situations deprived of institutional guidance (Schimank 2000, 65). Schimank's argument is that contemporary individuals take over regulatory functions in situations where institutions fail to do so. They work to adjust differing (life sphere, institutional) demands to each other, just as they shape multifaceted identities for themselves. For our purposes, of key interest here is, however, that where the institutions and/or rules do not exist or do not suffice to provide guidance, individuals are also left to their own devices in the realm of feelings. Rather than having feelings imposed by society's prescriptions, the individual feels in order to find out how one should rightfully, or how one should best act. An interesting construct—instead of moving from a norm to a prescribed emotion, it moves from a feeling to morality or norm. It reminds a bit of the current trend in philosophy to load emotions with the capacity to provide moral guidance (see Archer 2000, and Flam 2008; 2009 for critique), but it goes further in attributing to emotions the capacity to build and sustain institutions.

---

fic—Western—culture. These ideologies and rules possess a normative force, compelling us most of the time to manage our emotions in order to conform. In many everyday situations and on festive occasions we motivate ourselves to conform to these rules out of consideration for our family, friends or acquaintances whose feelings we do not want to hurt. On the job, it is the external pressure and our own unwillingness to risk our jobs that instead make us conform. Hochschild's message about the state of individuals in our service sector and triple-burden (work, housework, childcare) societies is that, thanks to feeling rules and the willingness of at least some people to follow these, their employers, co-workers, clients, husbands, wives and children can hope to enjoy a modicum of (admittedly stressed or ambivalent) "happiness."

Conclusion

While some theorists, such as Durkheim, Weber and, later on, Arendt and Elias, attributed to social institutions the crucial capacity to keep—what they saw as—undesired, threatening, irrational, extreme emotions at bay, they also associated the breakdown of the social and political order and institutional failure with the surfacing of painful, confusing or threatening extreme emotions. Similarly, Goffman (and Garfinkel) pointed to the painful emotions that surface when threatened or failed interactions make their participants unhappy, while Kemper, Scheff, Honneth and Neckel attracted our attention to the emotional "ups and downs" resulting from structures of inequality turning daily, routine interactions into a battlefield on which struggles for social recognition and power take place. Only two of the theorists included here, who neither saw emotions as negative nor associated them with the state of nature, explicitly attributed a central role to emotions in constructing society. Simmel saw all emotions, whether positive or negative, as enriching, cementing and shaping the society by binding the individuals to each other. Similarly, Cooley posited them as constitutive of the healthy self and the good society. But even Durkheim stressed that they play a key role in reproducing society's sacred realms and here he was seconded by, for example, Parsons, Elias and Goffman who all saw the fear of painful emotions, such as embarrassment, shame or guilt, as both controlling individual conduct and motivating individuals to make a sustained effort to maintain the interactive and institutional order.

One key debate, which in fact can be said to have launched and kept the sociology of emotions going, has been about whether culture, or embodied social structures or situations, determine the emotions that individuals feel (Hochschild 1979; Shott 1979; Kemper 1978; 1981; Barbalet 1999, 23–8, 179–183; Collins 2004; 1992). This debate considers emotions as outcomes: the quarrel has been about what determines them. The present text suggests that the sociology of emotions does not have to confine itself to discussions of the ways in which institutions, social structures, culture and/or interactions generate emotions. This it achieves through demonstrating that some old, and some new classics of sociology, even if inadvertently, saw emotions as constitutive of society—both its micro-interactive and its macro-institutional order. It would also be interesting to reverse causality in order to investigate which emotions, when and how, generate (new elements of) the social order, culture, social structures or interaction patterns (cf. Barbalet 1999). The sociology of emotions could only benefit from a systematic effort to highlight the generative-causal role of emotions (see, for example, Flam 1990; 1996; 2005, 32–7; and Barbalet 1999 for such earlier attempts).

In this text, I have identified discourses to which various theorists— more or less explicitly—referred. I suggested that their theorizing about emotions was indebted to discourses on nature vs. society, civilization vs. the Hobbesian state of nature or Freudian instinct of aggression and destruction, masses vs. elites, totalitarianism vs. democracy, and on inequality, among others. Now that I have highlighted this, the question can be posed whether the discourses on which they drew, and which they developed, are still convincing today. We can ask, in addition, what our theorizing about emotions and social order would look like, if it were instead embedded in Rousseau's or Cooley's, or participatory-democratic, or eco-feminist discourse. Would we still make assumptions about evil human beings in a state of nature and the regulating and civilizing role of society and the state? Would we still adopt an evolutionary perspective? What diagnosis of today and prognosis for the future would we then formulate?

Following Elias, Goffman (and Garfinkel) I devoted some attention to the role that emotions, such as the fear of shame and embarrassment, play in making individuals in principle wish to conform to the expected social interaction patterns. I referred to Simmel's, Cooley's and Parsons' views that shame and guilt motivate self-control, self-improvement and overall conformity to social norms and ideals. Leaning on their research, I can now posit fear-driven, and shame, embarrassment and guilt-avoiding social actors. Alternatively, following Durkheim, Simmel, Cooley or Kemper, I could posit a *micro-actor* who is pursuing happiness, who is steered by feelings of pride and shame and who is cemented to the others by feelings ranging from love through hate to loyalty and gratitude. These can then join a "social actor parade" featuring, for example, Anthony Giddens' rule-instantiating, knowledgeable, angst-avoiding *ontological security-seekers*, and Collins' limited-cognition, information-reducing, lazy-conservative, *emotional energy-maximizing situationists* (both in Collins 1992, 87–95). These are followed by Kemper's *"real emotion"-feeling equality seekers*, Hochschild's rule-knowing, but at times rule-subverting *emotion-managers*, Flam's *emotional "men"* and Schimank's identity-ascertaining, interest-pursuing, *emotion-guided institution-builders*.

So far, Hochschild's *emotion managers* and Collins' *ee-maximizing situationists*, perhaps along with Kemper's *"real-emotion"-feeling equality seekers*, have dominated the research agenda of the sociology of emotions. Although there is probably some room for even more theorizing about social actors, their emotions, and the social (interactive) order, it is worth stressing that rather than creating additional micro-actor models we instead need more comparative, explicit discussions concerning their relative theoretical-empirical merits (cf. Collins 1992; see also Archer 2000).

These different attempts to think about the nature of the micro-actor contrast strongly with Jack Barbalet's (1999) determination to conceptualize and address the emotions of social actors not in abstract, but only after they have been situated—in place, time and a specific social category, such as business or political elite, or working class. In Barbalet's view, contextualization is necessary to show in what ways specific emotions determine social action. A discussion of what are the advantages and disadvantages of these two research methods is long overdue.

Acknowledgments

This text is dedicated to Jack Barbalet. I would like to thank Jochen Kleres and Debra Hopkins for their comments, and Manuela Beyer for reference-checking.

References and Consulted Sources

Archer, Margaret (2000). *Being Human: The Problem of Agency*. Cambridge: Cambridge University Press.

Arendt, Hannah (1973). *The Origins of Totalitarianism*. New York: Harcourt Brace Jovanovich. [first published in 1951]

Barbalet, Jack (1999). *Emotion, Social Theory, and Social Structure: A Macrosociological Approach*. Cambridge: Cambridge University Press. [first published in 1998]

— (2000). Beruf, Rationality, and Emotion in Max Weber's Sociology. *European Journal of Sociology*, 41 (2), 329–51.

Bartels, Hans Peter (ed.). (1995). *Ein Norbert Elias-Lesebuch*. Opladen: Leske+ Budrich.

Billig, Michael (2004). *Banal Nationalism*. London: Sage. [first published in 1995]

Bogner, Artur, and Cas Wouters (1990). Kolonialisierung der Herzen? Zu Arlie Hochschilds Grundlegung der Emotionssoziologie. *Leviathan*, 18 (2), 255–79.

Collins, Randall (1992). The Romanticism of Agency/Structure Versus the Analysis of Micro/Macro. *Current Sociology*, 40, 77–9.

— (2004). *Interaction Ritual Chains*. Princeton, N.J.: Princeton University Press.

Cooley, Charles Horton (1970). *Human Nature and the Social Order*. New York: Schocken Books.

Durkheim, Emile (1951). *Suicide*. New York: Free Press. [first published in 1897]

— (1960). *The Division of Labor*. Glencoe, IL: Free Press. [first published in 1893]

Elias, Norbert (1978). *The Civilizing Process*. New York: Urizen Books. [first published in 1939]

— (1994). *Studien über die Deutschen. Machtkämpfe und Habitusentwicklung im 19. und 20. Jahrhundert*. Frankfurt am Main: Suhrkamp.

Flam, Helena (1990). Emotional "Man": 1. The Emotional "Man" and the Problem of Collective Action. *International Sociology*, 5 (1), 39–56.

— (1996). Anxiety and the Successful Oppositional Construction of Societal Reality: The Case of KOR. *Mobilization*, 1 (1), 103–21.

— (2002). *Soziologie der Emotionen*. Konstanz: UVK.

— (2005). Emotions' Map: A Research Agenda. In Helena Flam and Debra King (eds.). *Emotions and Social Movements*, 19–40. London: Routledge.

— (2008). The Sentient "I": Emotions and Inner Conversation. *Theory. The Newsletter of the Research Committee on Sociological Theory of the International Sociological Association*, Spring/Summer 2008, 4–7.

— (2009). Authentic Emotions as Ethical Guides? A Case for Scepticism. In Mikko Salmela and Verena Mayer (eds.). *Emotions, Ethics, and Authenticity*. Amsterdam: John Benjamins Publishing, with the publisher.

Garfinkel, Harold (1964). Studies of the Routine Grounds of Everyday Activities. *Social Problems*, 2 (3), 225–50.

Goffman, Erving (1956). Embarrassment and Social Organization. *American Journal of Sociology*, 62 (3), 264–71.

— (1967). *Interaction Ritual*. New York: Pantheon Books.

— (1981). *Forms of Talk*. Philadelphia: University of Pennsylvania Press.

— (1983). The Interaction Order: American Sociological Association, 1982 Presidential Address. *American Sociological Review*, 48 (1), 1–17.

— (1991). *Asylums*. London: Penguin Books. [first published in 1961]

— (2005). *Wir alle spielen Theater*. München: Piper. [first published in 1959]

Hochschild, Arlie (1979). Emotion Work, Feeling Rules, and Social Structure. *American Journal of Sociology*, 85 (3), 551–75.

Honneth, Axel (1998). *Kampf um Anerkennung – zur moralischen Grammatik sozialer Konflikte*. Frankfurt am Main: Suhrkamp.

Kemper, Theodore D. (1978). Toward a Sociology of Emotions: Some Problems and Some Solutions. *The American Sociologist*, 13, 30–41.

— (1981). Social Constructionist and Positivist Approaches to the Sociology of Emotions. *American Journal of Sociology*, 87 (2), 336–62.

Kuzmics, Helmut (1986). Verlegenheit und Zivilisation. Zu einigen Gemeinsamkeiten und Unterschieden im Werk von E. Goffman und N. Elias. *Soziale Welt*, 37, 465–86.

— (1991). Embarrassment and Civilization: On Some Similarities and Differences in the Work of Goffman and Elias. *Theory, Culture & Society*, 8 (2), 1-30.

Neckel, Sighard (1991). *Status und Scham. Zur symbolischen Reproduktion sozialer Ungleichheit*. Frankfurt am Main: Campus.

Parsons, Talcott (1967). *Sociological Theory and Modern Society*. New York: Free Press.

Porpora, Douglas V. (2002). Social Structure: The Future of a Concept. In Sing C. Chew and J. David Knottnerus (eds.). *Structure, Culture and History: Recent Issues in Social Theory*, 43–59. New York: Rowman & Littlefield Publishers.

Ritzer, George (1996). *Sociological Theory*, fourth edition. New York: McGraw-Hill. [first published in 1983]

Scheff, Thomas J. (1994). *Microsociology: Discourse, Emotion, and Social Structure*. Chicago: University of Chicago School.

Schimank, Uwe (2000). *Handeln und Strukturen*. München: Juventa.

Shott, Susan (1979). Emotion and Social Life: A Symbolic Interactionist Analysis. *American Journal of Sociology*, 84 (6), 1317–34.

Simmel, Georg (1992). Zur Psychologie der Scham. In H.-J. Dahme and O. Rammstedt (eds.). *Schriften zur Soziologie*, 140–50. Frankfurt am Main: Suhrkamp.

— (1999). *Soziologie. Untersuchungen über die Formen der Vergesellschaftung*. Gesamtausgabe Band II. Ed. O. Rammstedt. Frankfurt am Main: Suhrkamp.

Weber, Max (1985). *Wirtschaft und Gesellschaft. Grundriß der verstehenden Soziologie*. Tübingen: Mohr.

Wouters, Cas (1998). How Strange to Ourselves Are our Feelings of Superiority and Inferiority. Notes on Fremde und Zivilisierung by Hans-Peter Waldhoff. *Theory, Culture & Society*, 15 (2), 131–150.

Sociology as Narrative: Examples of Sociological Language in "Classic" Texts

Helmut Kuzmics

Prefatory Remarks

According to Elias, if we want to achieve a deeper understanding of "human and social processes," particularly those social predicaments brought about by human beings and which in turn have an effect on them, we face a dilemma. We are seemingly limited to the choice between "models of a naïvely egocentric or magico-mythical kind, or else models from natural science" (Elias 1978, 17). The scientificization of thought, he asserted, has occurred primarily by means of "verbal and conceptual structures derived from the uncovering of physical and chemical structures." For Elias, these "have passed into the everyday stock of words and concepts of European society and taken root there" (Elias 1978, 17). This would not be a problem apart from the fact that they shut out ways of speaking and thinking that are more useful in explaining human figurations.

I believe this development includes a specific conception of scientific factuality and objectivity which can do no more than force social scientific statements into the most neutral, descriptive vocabulary possible. This makes it difficult or impossible to draw conclusions about individuals' emotional attitude to social reality, whether studied or observed, a reality which is perceived as non-cognitive.[1] This seems to me a gross foreshortening of the objectivity to which we should certainly aspire. It means that we would in principle approach human beings and human relations as we would the behavior of electrons or bacteria. In this case, we are not only prohibited from making jokes or spiteful remarks about them, but to do so would be scientifically meaningless. Yet in social reality this applies neither to the everyday nor to the scientific appraisal of the social world. From a

---

1 These traditions of thought may be described as "naturalistic," their particular form within the methodology of the social sciences characterized by the key terms operationalism, behaviorism and reductionism (see Zilian (1996, 1455).

particular, affectionately ironic distance, the Austrian bureaucracy looks quite different from, for example, its Prussian-German counterpart. If we ignore the narrative mode bound up with this ironic distance, a mode linked to its object, we are in fact unable to gain access to this specific difference. If one takes refuge in an entirely abstract and objective vocabulary, laden with statistics, one fails to capture a core dimension of reality.

Over the last few decades it has become fashionable within the human sciences to maintain a post-modern distance from all so-called "grand narratives"[2] of the Enlightenment, modernity and the triumph of rationalism. Often, acknowledging the plurality of narratives leads scholars to believe that all are fundamentally equal—all appear to be equally distant from an unattainable truth. I reject such a stance. Instead, I assume that, while a range of narrative types certainly exists, there is only one truth, which it is possible to approach if one takes into account the specific pragmatic context that emerges from the relationship between authors' and readers' position within society. This enables us to avoid the "ego-centrism" of mythical and magical ways of thinking about social reality, a topic which Elias addressed.

Here, we need to bear in mind that we may also view the rhetorical and generally narrative forms of the sociological text (Brown 1987, 172–220; White 1975, 133–264; Frye 1990, 131–239) as bound up with the author's emotional dispositions. The categories created by Hayden White (which draw upon literary scholarship, particularly the work of Northrop Frye), with their four forms of story (romance, satire, comedy and tragedy), thus correspond to certain emotional states generated among readers or viewers. If heroes who triumph over dark forces play a role, as in the epic romances,[3] this corresponds to a fundamentally optimistic prevailing mood —more or less the diametric opposite of Kafka's black despair (what

---

2 The most famous stance is that adopted by Lyotard who is equally dismissive of Enlightenment, idealism and historicism as meta-narratives with a claim to universality (see Lyotard 1979; Preglau 1998, 13–21).

3 As Frye puts it: "If superior in *degree* to other men and to his environment, the hero is the typical hero of *romance*, whose actions are marvellous but who is himself identified as a human being. The hero of romance moves in a world in which the ordinary laws of nature are slightly suspended: prodigies of courage and endurance, unnatural to us, are natural to him, and enchanted weapons, talking animals, terrifying ogres and witches, and talismans of miraculous power violate no rule of probability once the postulates of romance have been established" (Frye 1990, 33). There is no place for irony in this "Mythos of Summer," but there is for tragedy (at first) and comedy (at the end), on the model, for example, of a perilous journey that ends happily.

would a Kafkaesque sociology have looked like?). Tragedy inevitably features a bitter end which one is utterly unable to avoid;[4] this reflects a prevailing mood of gloom rooted in feelings of fear which may be overcome through varying degrees of emotional control, and through an attitude we might describe as courageous. Comedy, on the other hand, is generally even more cheerful than romance (a positive outcome is essential here) and is based on emotions to match;[5] the rational choice model, in which people can, in principle, appraise a given situation through rational consideration of means and ends, has comic traits and requires a correspondingly cheerful sociological disposition. Satire, with its vast potential for the expression of irony (rhetorical irony featuring a *reductio ad absurdum;* an "irony of forms" in which message and medium are out of sync; the "irony of events" which consists of the unintended or unexpected consequences of actions; and a "dramaturgical" or "dialectical" irony typical of novels and theatre) does have a cheerful component intended to make people laugh, yet the laughter often sticks in one's throat, as the outcome may be as bitter as in tragedy, and is thus, once again anchored in very dark emotions, such as sadness and fear. The thesis I wish to put forward here is that the emotions evoked by the various genres and narrative modes are not only of relevance to the addressees of literary or sociological writings, but may also be systematically bound up with the characteristics of those who produce them; that is, with emotions that constitute the starting point for what is written.[6] In general, sociological narratives may feature other pragmatic (illocutionary or perlocutionary[7]) elements. They may cry out in accusation and thus be the ex-

---

4 Here White, drawing on Frye, concludes: "In Tragedy, there are no festive occasions, except false and illusory ones; rather, there are intimations of states of division among men more terrible than that which incited the tragic agon at the beginning of the drama" (White 1975, 9).

5 For White, comedy's characteristic feature is its ultimately conciliatory nature—reconciliation between people and human reconciliation to the world or nature are inherent in it (White 1975, 9). Alongside the happy ending, there are other opportunities for laughter and merriment. For White, comedy has an affinity with conservative and organicist social thought (1975, 29).

6 This does not always apply of course; Shakespeare for instance, as is well known, wrote both tragedies and comedies, and it is anything but clear as to whether he was happy or depressive when he did so. In any event, it is impossible to make out a stable, lifelong emotional disposition underpinning his work.

7 Illocutionary speech acts refer to the intentions directed at certain actions by speech acts; these speech acts are classifiable according to certain criteria (such as Searle's representative—asserting, concluding; directive—requesting, ordering; commissive—promising, threatening; expressive or declarative). Perlocutionary effects (again, according to

pression of deep feelings of hostility and hatred; they may excuse, spur on, cast a shadow, fire enthusiasm and so on. Feelings of shorter or longer duration are also always present and constitute more or less stable behavioral dispositions. The present work is thus underpinned by a supposition rooted in the sociology of knowledge that must be backed up by plausible arguments.

In what follows I consider in turn just four key examples: Max Weber's tragic view of the development of Western society, Erving Goffman's satire, Norbert Elias' optimism, which—combined with rational skepticism—makes him seem like a "sage" to many, and the scientism of the Californian study on authoritarianism with its European roots and concealed emotional message. My intention is not to claim that there is no more to these four "classic" approaches than emotion and genre, but that it is highly informative to study them with these in mind.

Max Weber and Sociology as Tragedy

In the *Vorbemerkung* of his *Gesammelten Aufsätze zur Religionssoziologie* Max Weber expressed a clear view of the nature of scientific endeavor.

"Fashion and the zeal of the *literati* would have us think that the specialist can to-day be spared, or degraded to a position subordinate to that of the seer. Almost all sciences owe something to dilettantes, often very valuable view-points. But dilettantism as a leading principle would be the end of science. He who yearns for seeing should go to the cinema, though it will be offered to him copiously to-day in literary form in the present field of investigation also. Nothing is farther from the intent of these thoroughly serious studies than such an attitude. And, I might add, whoever wants a sermon should go to a conventicle. […] It is true that the path of human destiny cannot but appall him who surveys a section of it. But he will do well to keep his small commentaries to himself, as one does at the sight of the sea or of majestic mountains, unless he knows himself to be called and gifted to give them expression in artistic or prophetic form" (Weber 2003, 110–1).

Searle) refer mainly to the subsequent actions of listeners, while illocutionary effects—Ballmer states—tend to appeal to their understanding. See Ballmer (1979, 248) and Murgg (1993, 38–9), who deals with the indirect character of many illocutionary speech acts (as in irony or politeness).

This quotation, which—in its original German—is stylistically pleasing, also expresses two facts. First, Weber separates science out from art and prophecy. Second, he does so by using the very language that makes him more than an "ordinary" expert and which betrays deep emotional registers: *nüchtern* (sober), *streng* (serious, severe), *Schicksal* (Fate, destiny), *erschütternd* (deeply upsetting, better: heart-shattering), *brandet* (surging). It is, of course, impossible to sum up Weber's work which is complex, thousands of pages long, and includes painstaking nominal definitions of countless terms, within a single statement. It describes and explains from a comparative perspective that process of rationalization which today spans the globe, in which European science, the capitalist market, urban democracy, rational bureaucracy, etc. have come together to establish a qualitatively new form of society. Weber threw out a gigantic net of concepts which enabled him to comparatively analyze numerous individual empirical findings, and they are indeed often fundamentally corrective and falsifying.

Weber, though, also has a core message at hand without which we would not have attached such importance to his work. It is linked with the qualities addressed in the above quotation: it is the fundamental tragedy of this process that touches us to this day, and it is his study of the genesis of the capitalist spirit from a religiously ascetic attitude which provides us with a clear statement of this. A fully human existence is no longer possible if Puritan asceticism has created an economic order from which no one can escape:

"In Baxter's view the care for external goods should only lie on the shoulders of the 'saint like a light cloak, which can be thrown aside at any moment.' But fate decreed that the cloak should become an iron cage. Since asceticism undertook to remodel the world and to work out its ideals in the world, material goods have gained an increasing and finally an inexorable power over the lives of men as at no previous period in history" (Weber 2001, 123–4).

Weber's emphasis on the tragic character of this development (he cautiously lends his subsequent conclusions a hypothetical air) has become, for us, a very familiar way of thinking about the development of capitalism and administration.[8] It is thus worthwhile paying heed once again to the contrary position. On this view, triumphant capitalism is the marvel which will lead the entire globe towards prosperity and freedom (President George W.

---

8 Cf. also Breuer (2006, 49), who refers here, in particular, to the tragic consequences of the Protestant Ethic.

Bush used the word "freedom" more than forty times in his first official speech following re-election); free market theoreticians naturally tend towards this view. Weber, however, had other ideas:

"But victorious capitalism, since it rests on mechanical foundations, needs its support no longer. The rosy blush of its laughing heir, the Enlightenment, seems also to be irretrievably fading, and the idea of duty in one's calling prowls about in our lives like the ghost of dead religious beliefs" (2001, 124).

Capitalist competition ends either in sport or mechanized petrifaction; it is also possible that *ganz neue Propheten* will emerge or a renaissance of old ideals may occur.

Even in his comparative sociology of religion, Weber tended to suggest that the idea of an inevitable fate ending in death plays a central role in the religiosity of warrior societies—precisely, in other words, what we perceive as "tragedy." This, of course, consists of the fact that even the purest of intentions may end up pitted against each other due to prevailing circumstances, making it possible to be guilty yet innocent (a familiar motif, from the Iliad to the fall of the Nibelungs). What we know about Weber's life, his tremendous seriousness, sense of duty, personal readiness to practice self-denial as far as his sexuality was concerned,[9] and sense of honor (he was willing to engage in a duel to protect the honor of his wife), tells us a good deal about his basic emotional attitude, which reflects a sense of tragedy (see Marianne Weber's (1926) *Lebensbild* and Green's (1984) work on the *Richthofen sisters*). Weber expressed his understanding of a basic category of cultural life, even in advanced societies, in words that chimed with his "warrior ethic:"

---

9 Northrop Frye's characterization of the tragic hero seems made for Max Weber: "Tragic heroes are so much the highest points in their human landscape that they seem the inevitable conductors of the power about them, great trees more likely to be struck by lightning than a clump of grass" (Frye 1990, 207). The first account of Weber's life as a kind of heroic epic was provided by his wife Marianne (Weber 1926); his early interest in Thucydides is brought out by Hennis (2003, 20): "The strength of the boy's perception, his 'mind' is apparent in the fact that at the age of fourteen 'of all the writers he had read he liked Homer best;'" he had previously been very taken with Spain's Cid and the topic of fate in Homer. A description of the climate of sexual repression in which the Weber brothers grew up can be found in Green (1984); here, among other things, Green deals with his late relationship with Else, his disciple and lover. The most comprehensive and impressive Weber biography so far appeared recently, featuring a wealth of information, including some on Weber's nocturnal emissions (Radkau 2005, 273–311).

"For no form of civilised life can be without conflict. Its methods, its object, even its basic direction and the people involved in it can be altered, but it cannot be eliminated itself. It may take the form, not of an external struggle between enemies for external things, but of an internal struggle between friends for internal goods, and in the process external compulsion may be replaced by internal control (even in the form of devotion inspired by sexual or charitable feelings). It may, finally, mean an inner struggle of the individual with himself within his own soul. In whatever form, it is always with us. Often, it is all the more fraught with consequence the less it is noticed and the more it appears in the form of apathetic or easy-going tolerance or the illusions of self-deception, or takes the form of 'selection.' 'Peace' means nothing more than a shift in the forms of conflict or the parties to conflict or the objects of conflict or, finally, in the chances of selection" (Weber 1979, 92).

This is a truly gloomy way of looking at the world. Even love is to be seen as a battle and peace is a mere postponement of battle. In any event, this certainly allows us to escape the illusory notion which, as in numerous economic theories of the market, reduces the principle of competition merely to a formal mechanism for coordinating supply and demand. Weber took it for granted that competition is always a battle and thus produces winners and losers: this was obviously something he himself had experienced and which was accompanied by strong emotions on his part. As Hennis incisively puts it, for Weber the spirit of Thucydides came to determine his evaluation even of capitalism: as Hennis says, the Protestant Ethic is Weber's Peloponnesian War (Hennis 2003, 44).[10] On the other hand, the assumption of economic theory that suppliers and consumers simply respond in line with the harmless pleasures of utility and profit maximization betrays a naïve, optimistic conception of humanity, particularly if it also assumes that the market satisfies everyone in optimal fashion.

Weber was better able to grasp these things, and indeed could perceive them more clearly, *because* of his own psychological state. However, did he also perceive *other* things wrongly, precisely because of his disposition? Elias' attack on egocentrism may apply to Weber as well. Were Weber's evaluations of social facts very much anchored in his most personal experiences? Did this prevent him from producing a "decentered" conception of humanity which understands itself as part of a figuration and which is able to attribute quite different modes of experience to others because they too form part of the same figuration? Weber himself warned against

---

10 Hennis (2003, 44). I am grateful to Helena Flam for making me aware that Weber's attitude towards secularization and "disenchantment" as a whole can therefore be viewed from a similarly tragic perspective.

thinking of his conclusions as absolute. We should, of course, take Weber's emotional state into account when reading his work and contemplate contrary standpoints and modes of experience that have led to different conclusions. Nonetheless, we must acknowledge that Weber's poetic language, the expression of profound emotions, offers us insights into the functioning of social mechanisms which we would more or less lack otherwise. This language is, therefore, also justifiable and meaningful from a cognitive and descriptive point of view.

On 27 October 1916, as the world war raged around him, Weber gave a lecture that lays bare his sense of tragedy more clearly than ever:

"For *why* did we enter the spell of this power-political doom? Not because of vanity. But because of our *responsibility in the face of history*. Posterity will not call to account the Swiss, the Danes, the Dutch or Norwegians for their contribution in shaping the culture of this planet. It would not chastise them if the Western half of the globe were to know nothing but Anglo-Saxon convention or Russian bureaucracy. And rightly so. Since neither the Swiss nor the Dutch nor the Danes could prevent that. But, to be sure, we could. A nation of 70 millions, caught between such conquering world-powers, had the *duty* to be a power-state. We had to be a power-state and we had to risk war in order to have our say when the future of the planet had to be decided. We would even have had to do it ourselves if we had had to fear being overcome. *Since it would have brought disgrace in face of posterity and contemporaries* if we had shirked our duties cowardly and comfortably. The honor of our nationhood demanded it. It is *honor*, not changes of territorial maps or economic profit that the German war is fought for; we would not want to forget that" (Weber 1988, 176, own translation, Weber's emphasis).

The tragedy here is not the expectation of Germany's defeat, but being forced to make such a decision (Weber still firmly believed that Germany would triumph). It was surely statements such as these which made Weber seem an alarmingly nationalistic thinker to western European intellectuals such as Aron (1971, 234), and this assessment may have been reinforced in the light of subsequent National-Socialism. Weber did in fact speak unambiguously from a "we" rather than from a "you" perspective (Elias 1978, 125–8) which suggests greater distance, and appears to identify very strongly with the German cause. I have selected this passage not for this reason, but in order to shed light, through the particular context in which Weber argued here, on his general attitude to fate and honor, as well as to the tragic. It shows him to be a man of his time, a member of a German middle class characterized by thoroughgoing militarization, and a specific affective structure. This disposition molded both his language and social perception, a circumstance over which Weber did not draw a veil by deploying distant, physicalist concepts, or neutral clinical ones.

Erving Goffman and Sociology as Satire

In a footnote, Erving Goffman gives an example of a particular type of social exchange in which one of the parties to an interaction makes statements that put a stop to the original exchange by refusing to provide the ritual recognition of the first step in the interaction. The example is a series of four sketches by Charles Schulz, the creator of Peanuts:

"First frame: Schroeder is playing his piano and Lucy, elbow on other end, says, 'You don't like me, do you?'
Second frame: Schroeder says directly into Lucy's face. 'No, I never have liked you, and I doubt very much if I ever will like you!'
Third frame: Schroeder is back to playing the piano and Lucy is leaning on it, but no word is spoken.
Fourth frame: Lucy says, 'I can tell you don't like me.' Schroeder looks up nonplussed.
Lucy's fourth-frame response is what she would have said in the third frame had Schroeder said what was expected of him in the second, namely, some sort of denial of Lucy's self-disparagement. So necessary was it that the second frame be filled in this prefigured way that Lucy, after a moment's pause to gather her resources, must stubbornly act as if Schroeder had in fact done what the sequence demanded of him—for there is really nothing else she can do" (Goffman 1971, 213).

This example not only illustrates very well the formal qualities of a sequence of interactions, as Goffman intended it, but it also, in a certain sense, tells us something about his entire sociological oeuvre. It fits seamlessly into Goffman's language, which he used to sketch representational strategies and social exchanges within the context of everyday life, thus providing him with an endless supply of material. One element here is irony, primarily the "irony of events" (Brown 1987, 172–220), typically centered on the unintended and unexpected paradoxical consequences of action, but also the "irony of forms," in which message and medium contradict each other. According to R. H. Brown, irony, used sociologically, means either:

1. the exposure of a social fact whose relationship with the banal is made evident,
2. the mutual dependence of supposed opposites (A, although non-B, is more directly connected with B than anyone would suspect), or
3. the dialectical resolution of opposites (A, as counter-thesis to B, itself becomes B).

Because as a rule a "humorous contrast" which seems crucial to the joke is also produced in this way, the frequent use of irony takes us into the realm of satire. Frye calls satire the "Mythos of Winter" (Frye 1990, 223). For him, it is "militant irony." It is, however, possible, Frye asserts, for there to be irony but relatively little satire—mildly disorienting the readers who struggle to work out how they feel about the text.

In any event, satire is tied to humor: the presence of humor (from mild comedy to enjoyment of the grotesque) means that laughter rests upon an affective foundation, which may be due to pleasure, attempts to dominate, or relief from tension.[11] This inclination towards satire, but also simple irony, is an unmistakable feature of Goffman's most important writings. The basic thrust of his book *The Presentation of Self in Everyday Life* is a conception of the human being, regardless of historical era, as an actor who finds her/himself on a stage, may gather around her/himself an ensemble, and may have placed spies or hired applauders among the audience. Simply by attributing a performative component to every action, including instrumentally rational ones whose objective justification is more apparent than real, Goffman ascribed profoundly trivial but omnipresent underpinnings to even the most noble of motives; he often ended up "rubbishing" them. Here is Goffman on marriage:

"Thus in well-adjusted marriages, we expect that each partner may keep from the other secrets having to do with financial matters, past experiences, current flirtations, indulgencies in 'bad' or expensive habits, personal aspirations and worries, actions of children, true opinions held about relatives or mutual friends, etc." (Goffman 1969, 71).

---

11 See Berger (1997), for a thorough sociological analysis of humor; referring particularly to its tension-relieving effects, see pp. 48; on laughter and smiling among our primate forbears, see Argyle (1975, 33, 41). When analyzing emotions it is important to bear in mind that they feature both a somatic, emotion-oriented aspect and a behavior-oriented aspect (see, for example, Elias 1987a, 353–4). The latter aspect relates to visible expression, which has a special role within human group communication. Here, defensive self-irony must be clearly distinguished from aggressive mockery.

In this view, even for those with the best of intentions, marriage becomes a strategic theatrical production featuring highly trivial motives. It is robbed of its metaphysical sheen.

Everyone, according to Goffman, makes use at times of a highly elaborate stage set to create a specific expression, which in turn makes an impression on others. However, "It is only in exceptional circumstances that the setting follows along with the performers; we see this in the funeral cortège, the civic parade, and the dream-like processions that kings and queens are made of" (1969, 33).

Here we are compelled to dispense with the deeply felt sadness which is meant to surround funeral processions, enabling us to recognize what they have in common with military parades or royal processions, which of course inspire quite different feelings. In a similar vein, applying this approach to the Catholic procession robs it of some of its religious grandeur. There is no lack of ironical mockery, or self-irony, in Goffman's work—this last if we assume that Goffman identified with the weaker, the victims in the everyday life of society. Indeed, one of his main concerns was the unsparing analysis of awkward situations, and how otherwise socially competent actors may see their happy fortunes change through misjudging or mismanaging an awkward situation (Goffman 1972, 97–112).

The element of satire[12] is present in all his writings—in *Stigma* (Goffman 1968b), alongside heart-rending examples, even the stigmatized counter-strategies are ironized. The same also applies to *Asylums*, Goffman's analysis of prison-like settings in which the dignity and integrity of the "inmates" is constantly injured. By pointing out the formal similarities among "total institutions," Goffman played down the horrors of the concentration camp,[13] while casting a shadow over the image of the boarding school. His analysis of how public space is ordered invents the notion of individuals as "Vehicular Units" with a specific casing that varies in thickness, from that of human skin to that of the armor-plating on a submarine, and thus varying in the relative capacity to protect (Goffman 1971, 27). Individuals may thus be classified in line with their specific speed and po-

---

12 Scheff (2006, ix) characterizes Goffman's writing as follows: "It is brilliant, suggestive, and entertaining, but also playful and teasing, revealing and concealing."

13 See Goffman (1968a, 16): "A third type of total institution is organized to protect the community against what are felt to be intentional dangers to it, with the welfare of the persons thus sequestered not the immediate issue: jails, penitentiaries, P.O.W. camps, and concentration camps."

tential room for maneuver. Goffman, here and in general, did not moralize about lies and pretence, instead he analyzed their verbal and non-verbal forms of expression. This in itself causes the reader's moral compass to gyrate.[14]

Nonetheless, one may assume that Goffman was not unconcerned with the fate of those whose forms of expression and relationship he examined. On closer inspection, it emerges that Goffman was interested in something that is not always apparent—the dignity and integrity of people unable to defend themselves against others' thoughtlessness and disparagement. However, he was skeptical about attempts to locate the causes of these phenomena through the analysis of a "system" with an "internal logic." He seems to have rejected, with much cynicism, the critique of capitalism put forward by Marxist sociologist, Alvin Gouldner.[15] Indeed, to turn his analysis of the alienation characteristic of the social masquerade of modernity into a programme of political action *qua* Gouldner, would have appeared nonsensical to Goffman. Now, irony and self-irony may be understood both at the formal level of speech acts as well as in relation to emotions, which they—like humor generally—encourage. They are classed as indirect speech-acts (Groeben and Scheele 1986). They are among the forms of

---

14 Gary T. Marx, a follower of Goffman, described his impression of the latter as follows: "Goffman presented himself as a detached, hard-boiled intellectual cynic; the sociologist as fourties private eye. His was a hip, existential, cool, essentially apolitical (at least in terms of the prevailing ideologies) personal style. As a Canadian Jew of short stature working at the margins (or perhaps better, frontiers) of a marginal discipline, he was clearly an outsider. His brilliance and marginality meant an acute eye and a powerful imagination. He had a fascination with other people's chutzpah, weirdness and perhaps even degradation. He appreciated people who had a good thing going and those able to assert themselves in the face of what could be an oppressive social structure and culture. In a stodgy, timid, bureaucratic world the hustler has a certain freshness and perverse appeal. Goffman was drawn to disjunctive scenes. He had a voyeur's interest in the intimate details of other's lives, and a strong eye for the ironic and poignant. His humor was dry and indirect. A part of his appeal involved a fascination, like Simmel's, with the secret. There is a sense of self-importance and power that may come with the feeling that you were 'wise' or in the know. For persons feeling powerless, marginal and unsure of their place in the order of things, possession of such knowledge (or the belief that one has it) can be very attractive" (Marx 1984, 653; see also Treviño 2003, 3–6).

15 Gouldner states: "I remember one occasion after a long negotiating session with a publisher for whom Goffman and I are both editors. I turned to Goffman and said with some disgust, 'These fellows are treating us like commodities.' Goffman's reply was, 'That's all right, Al, so long as they treat us as expensive commodities'" (Gouldner 1971, 383).

"illocutionary speech" whose claim to efficacy is in reality constrained, such as in the case of politeness, where, instead of crystal clear assertions, demands, requests or accusations, it opts for modes of expression in which intentions become hypothetical and may be taken back. By way of further example, White attributed a liberal political concern to satire (White 1975, 29). However, alongside piercing satire, which provides an ideological accompaniment to the implementation of political interests, there also exist highly indirect forms in which the comical is bound up with conservatism and organicism in dealing with social inequality and domination.

The affective state of those who deploy irony, and whose weapon of choice is humor, can be highly complex. For example, Nestroy, the Austrian playwright, author of numerous comedies and actor, was a very inhibited individual who was unable to produce his theatrical mockery in interactions in a pub (Hannemann 1977, 152). To the extent that irony as a form of humor is intended to inspire laughter, it entails an element of pleasure and dominance.[16] However, as these impulses may be subject to a great deal of emotional inhibition, as in the case of cheerful contemplation, they will also be accompanied by social anxiety and shame. In the case of self-irony, this aspect is quite obvious: anyone who makes oneself smaller than one really is, wishes either to avoid leaving oneself open to attack or is counting on others present to bolster one's status (as in the ostensibly modest English understatement).

Goffman's sociology is thoughtful or, as we would say today, reflexive. It neither emphasizes action, nor does it conceive of the human being as replete with agency. It features dark aspects redolent of the tragic perspective. Here, the human being is anything but a soulless robot that simply executes system imperatives. Let us compare Goffman with a brief sample from Luhmann's systems theory:

"An overview of the distribution of the scarcity and elasticity of time given in the system can only be gained from a central position. This makes it necessary to deprive the individual actor of his mandate to decide on the points in time and the sequence of his action, if one wants to rationalize time-planning, and to manage

16 Scheff gives a vivid description of his own relationship with Goffman (as Goffman's former disciple and assistant). He stresses Goffman's strong impulse to haze and test his friends and colleagues, in sometimes very rude interactions, in which Scheff himself often fell victim to Goffman's partly humorous, partly hostile way. See Scheff (2006, 12): "What I saw was a quite small, dapper, boyish-looking male with a crew cut. […] Perhaps he defended against feelings resulting from my obliviousness and disconnection from him by hazing me. He was rejecting the rejecter."

these questions centrally, i.e. in the program of decision-making. This program will, then, as a goal-oriented program, not only fix causal and value-relations, but it must, at the same time, also determine action. Thereby, the complexity-potential of a system will increase, as will its own (inherent) complexity" (Luhmann 1973, 309–10, own translation).

In this sociology, unsurprisingly, both the tragic and the ironic are absent. Strictly speaking, so are people. Here, the sociologist becomes a kind of accountant, perhaps with a hobby such as collecting insects. Goffman was something else entirely. His collecting mania was not due to the need for administrative clarity. Rather, it facilitated the cataloguing of human striving and failure, with its frequently absurd outcomes. This perspective too narrows our vision to certain respects. Hebbel said of Nestroy that even a rose must have begun to stink when the latter had smelt it (Kahl 1970, 274). It is also true that Goffman tightly restricted the emotional spectrum of those he studied, and that "grand" emotions disappeared as a result. Yet irony, the "open act of violating the norm of sincerity" and the "dissociation of explicit affirmation und implicit denial" (Murgg 1993, 38–9), conveys insights that are otherwise inaccessible. This justifies their deployment in the language of sociology.

Norbert Elias and the Stance of the Optimistic Realist

The basic idea of Elias' civilization theory is that we can understand contemporary society with its rules and compulsions only if we know its past. For structural reasons, in this past (such as the European Middle Ages), life was highly insecure even for the upper classes. War was endemic, while famines and plagues bore witness to a comparatively limited capacity to dominate nature. People were, emotionally speaking, at the mercy of these uncertainties. Their emotional experience was characterized by fear of those stronger than them, and by feelings of dominance towards those weaker than them. Emotional experience was not comprehensive, and individuals had relatively weak affective control overall, including with respect to those affects with a highly physical basis, and when eating, drinking and giving full expression to so-called "natural" bodily functions. In line with this, societal institutions had not yet taken firm hold—particularly those which might discourage war and the direct physical expression of violence.

During the next half-millennium, up to the end of courtly society and the eve of the bourgeois and industrial revolution, monopolies on the control of violence were to take increasingly firm hold: absolutist princely states arose from unrestrained competition between landowning warlords capable of imposing and guaranteeing physical security—protection from attack by others—across a specific, now much larger area. In this process, complex, many-layered social formations developed with the princely "Court," the apex of society. The courts represented the centers of command and consumption of these aristocratically dominated societies, and they thus became the centers of taste refinement at the expense of growing inhibitions on the expression of emotion (the root of the German for "politeness," *Höflichkeit*, is *Hof* or "court"). Those at Court were, for the most part, also compelled to behave in a non-violent manner. The three dimensions of refinement, pacification and growing inhibition were joined by the art of observing the behavior of others (psychologization) and conscious self-control (courtly rationality). In sum, the concept of "civilization" arose, which Elias distilled and abstracted from another concept, namely the locality-bound and obviously ethnocentric understanding of the French upper classes, who wished to clearly set themselves apart from the peasantry and the "barbarians" of other continents when they talked of (using the French word) "civilisation" (Elias 2000, 31). Elias—after a) reconstructing the use of language from "*courtoisie*," "*civilité*" and "*civilisation*," and b) the self-understanding of its content by the French upper classes—goes on to develop c) a third, theoretical concept of "civilization," by defining and explaining socially typical affective states by means of a psychological and sociological model. "More civilized" now means that external and self-imposed constraints become more comprehensive and restrictive and that external constraints are, to some extent, converted into self-restraints. In this way, Elias wished to steer clear of the problem of passing judgment, that is, by assuming that "civilization" is better.

Large parts of Elias' work are in fact characterized by vigorous efforts to distance himself from emotive attempts to contrast a "wicked" or "fun" Middle Ages with a "good" or "insipid" modernity. He was equally keen to avoid presuming that England was "civilized" and Germany less so; he pointed out that the developmental paths of the two societies differed greatly (Elias 1996, 162–70). Yet some concern with normative matters persists: in the concluding remarks of his *Über den Prozeß der Zivilisation*, a "more genuine" civilization appears, if only as a utopia, which he felt struck a better balance between the satisfaction of drives and social structure. It was even more difficult for Elias to keep his distance from a normative understanding of civilization when he analyzed the "Breakdown of Civilization" characteristic of Nazi mass murder (in his late book on *The Germans*) (Elias 1996, 298–402). Here, the potential for pacification took on greater significance and was evaluated positively.

Elias' conception of civilization was, however, anything but naive. He neither suggested that social progress is inevitable, nor did he share the assessment of many cultural pessimists that everything is getting worse. While he felt that major civilizational disasters were far from unlikely (as late as the eighties he still put the likelihood that humanity would annihilate itself with nuclear weapons at 50 percent[17]), he was always of the opinion, whatever the setbacks, that the attempts of sociologists (and people in general) to imagine a form of society less senseless and contemptuous of life were worthwhile (Elias 1991, 224–5). His standpoint with respect to this is evident if we recall the example he used to illustrate the idea of the *Doppelbinderprozess*: E. A. Poe's tale of the fisherman caught in a maelstrom:

"One may remember that the fishermen, while they were slowly being drawn into the abyss of the whirlpool, for a while still floated, together with other pieces of wreckage, around the walls of its narrowing funnel. At first, both brothers—the youngest had been lost in the storm already—were too overcome by fear to think clearly and to observe accurately that was going on around them. After a time, however, one of the brothers, so Poe tells us, was able to shrug off his fears. While the elder brother cowered helplessly in the boat, paralysed by the approaching disaster, the younger man collected himself and began looking around with a certain curiosity. It was then, while taking it all in almost as if he were not involved, that he became aware of certain regularities in the movements of the pieces that were being driven around in circles together with the boat. In short, while observing and reflecting, he had an 'idea;' a connecting picture of the process in which he was involved, a 'theory,' began forming in his mind"[18] (Elias 1987b, 45).

---

17 Verbal communication with Artur Bogner, who was Elias' personal assistant in Bielefeld for a time in the early eighties. See also Elias (1985, 144) or Elias (1990, 31).

18 This metaphor also underlies the conclusion reached by Dennis Smith, who compares Elias' fundamental optimism with Foucault's tragic longing for liberation with the help of two key metaphors: that of the fisherman in the maelstrom and that of the prison. See Smith (2000, 158–9).

The younger man thus manages to save himself by tethering himself to a barrel which is being pulled down into the depths more slowly than his brother's boat; the latter drowns. This is what I propose to call "realistic optimism," a scholarly stance which imbues Elias' sociology time after time and which—I suggest—is due to a fundamental attitude to life. In Hayden White's terminology, narratives of this type are classified as "romances," a notion which seems to me not entirely fitting given the many shades of grey apparent in Elias' conception of civilization. In any event, however, Elias is miles away from Weberian tragedy and Goffman's absurdity. Imagine if Franz Kafka had tried his hand as a theoretician of civilization. Kafka, the author of the perpetually pending trial of K., would surely have emphasized different aspects from Elias, who was guided by a very positive fundamental feeling about life. Elias talked about this in a lengthy biographical interview:

"Perhaps if I express it in this way: just as astronomers have discovered that the whole universe is filled with the reverberations of the big bang, so humans carry a background-feeling with themselves which derives from their early childhood in family. I have a background feeling of great certainty that finally all will end well, and I credit this to the enormous emotional security that I, as a single child, experienced in the affection of my parents. I knew quite early what I wanted: I wanted to go to university, wanted to teach and to do research. This I knew from early on, and I worked towards that with perseverance, even though it seemed to be impossible sometimes" (Elias 1990, 22, own translation).

This species of certainty without doubt helped Elias cope better with the catastrophes of the century—wars, emigration and the traumatic loss of his parents—but it was in addition always a source of energy in his scholarly work, expressed in the style, choice of words, and the manner in which he defined the great issues he scrutinized. Elias' scientific language never became so different from that of everyday life that he had to seek refuge in purely invented words or fashionable jargon in English or German. However, no matter how realistic it is to speculate that Elias' analysis may be due to his existential optimism, making him a "sage"[19] for many readers and disciples, his emotional state also corresponds to a way of seeing the world which offers not only advantages but also limitations—if his optimism can be proved to be too bright. But be this as it may, reflection upon social setting and affective state (Elias 1987b, 7–73) fleshed out from a

---

19 For Elias, the image of the "torch-bearer," the "passing on of the torch" was a key metaphor from an early age: see Hackeschmidt (2000, 31).

sociology of knowledge perspective constitutes one valid and helpful way of coming to grips with Elias' work and person. It helps us steer clear of the risk of relativism, and to maintain our claim to truth.

The Authoritarian Personality – the Language of Variables with a Novelistic Subtext

In comparison with the very naïve *Autorität und Familie* which appeared in 1936 (Horkheimer 1936),[20] the study *The Authoritarian Personality* (Adorno et al. 1950) produced in Berkeley, California, was significantly more sophisticated methodologically and became vastly more influential. The immigrants from Frankfurt had brought with them an intellectual approach that integrated psychoanalysis and Marxism, and they were focused primarily on the issue of why exactly, despite the most promising of objective foundations, there was no proletarian revolution in Germany. Yet what they ultimately produced was the Berkeley-study which was scarcely Marxist in character. Fascist Germany was replaced by the arch-democratic United States. Rather than concentrating on the dearth of revolutionary workers, the study investigated the reasons for a latent or open anti-Semitism, which had merely been a marginal topic in Germany.

This operation, however, not only involved the loss of any reference to German society, but also, eventually, of any consideration of macro-level socio-political topics; this began when Adorno and Horkheimer were compelled to keep their Marxism under wraps (Samelson 1993). They attempted to survey the "potential fascism" in a society which, since the revolution of 1776 or even, perhaps since the ideology of the Pilgrim Fathers, had rebelled against all forms of official authority, as Tocqueville showed as early as the first third of the 19th century. The study's aim was to explore American society's susceptibility to fascism and anti-Semitism: any emergent sense of a country on trial is without doubt masked by a reserved, neutral stance evident in the authors' presentation. And yet even here, their partisanship is unmistakable in their formulation of certain key concepts; Roger Brown has analyzed this with great clarity by contrasting

---

20 The following analysis is an abridged version of a more lengthy treatment in Kuzmics and Mozetic (2003, 165-90).

the "J-Type" identified by Nazi psychologist Jaensch (1938) with the "authoritarian personality" in the Berkeley-study.

Those whom Jaensch considered strong, manly, reliable, unequivocal in their judgments and consistent in their behavior, were viewed by the authors of the Berkeley-study as rigid and incapable of dealing with ambiguity; as Brown says: "He was, more or less, Jaensch's J-Type, but J, who was a hero to Nazi social science, was a villain to American social science" (Brown 1966, 478). Authoritarian obsequiousness, authoritarian aggression, authoritarian submission, "a failure in super-ego internalization [...] due to weakness in the ego [...] inability to build up a consistent and enduring set of moral values within the personality" (Adorno et al. 1950, 234)—no one would like to be associated with such attributes.

Of course, not all of these terms inspire this response; "conventionalism," "anti-intraception" and "projectivity" sound like medical diagnoses or technical descriptions and evoke the image of researchers in white coats. The innumerable tables, featuring coefficients of correlation and abbreviations for variables such as TI and AS, trigger a particular kind of emotional anticlimax. This is a highly sublimated way of writing (and reading) about a problem with which the authors of the Berkeley-study were intensely concerned. The study's most important result was in providing evidence of significant potential for anti-democratic and authoritarian views within US society, whose founding myth, of course, entailed the exact opposite. The study combined qualitative and quantitative empirical research techniques—the latter in a substantially more mature form than its German predecessor. Its key conclusion, confirmed time and again in follow-up studies, was that there is an internal connection between anti-Semitic, ethnocentric and politically and economically conservative ideologies and "antidemocratic" postures, and that the lower the socio-economic status, IQ and educational level, the more these inclinations predominate. Below is a brief introduction to the main components of the famous "F-Scale" (Adorno et al. 1950, 228):

1. conventionalism
2. authoritarian submission (to the moral authority figures of an in-group; uncritical willingness to believe)
3. authoritarian aggression
4. anti-intraception (a tendency to reject more tactful, subjective and imaginative views)
5. superstition and stereotypy

6. power and "toughness;" identification with leader figures, etc.
7. destructiveness and cynicism
8. projectivity
9. sex; exaggerated concern about permissiveness in the field of sexual relations

The astonishing thing is that Heinrich Mann pre-empted significant elements of this concept in a novel as early as 1915 (*Der Untertan*, engl.: Mann 1998). From a young age, Diederich Heßling's family situation featured fear of the father and contempt for the mother, as well as fear of police and teachers. All of this is conveyed through scenes that indicate his tendency towards "authoritarian subservience." In addition, there are cases in which he felt superior to others weaker than himself, and humiliated them with the support of external authorities (teachers, the *Kaiser*). "Authoritarian aggression" is apparent in these figures and in Heßling's orientation towards the power-centered ideology of the dueling society, in how he dressed down bourgeois politicians and dignitaries; time and again he refused to identify with those weaker than him and dependent on him. His morality is revealed as highly conventionalist, geared more towards concepts of honor than of conscience. His Byzantine worship of imperial power is without doubt a core theme of the book.

Heinrich Mann wrote *Der Untertan* as a kind of political pamphlet; one year after the outbreak of war, he produced the following interpretation:

"Diederich Heßling—his name stands for that of a thousand others, who like him appeared in Germany one generation ago—had raised to the status of gospel the drive towards power, never acted according to another, either in little or on a grand scale, and had, to be sure, to do so finally and on the really grand scale. He had, long ago, known nothing but himself and what belonged to himself, nothing that was not predestined to be the prey of power—no other nation that he would not have regarded as decadent or barbarous, no other law that he would not have seen as inferior to his own, no human opinion that he would not have dismissed. He had looked through the deceptiveness and the non-committal contained in the concepts of democratic civility to which Europe and, before his own eyes, Germany, were attached. Freedom, justice, truth, humanity succumbed to his skepticism; only discipline, power, utility and mastery in the sense he had forged himself remained beyond any doubt. Autonomous in his judgment and undisturbed by all outer, foreign inducement, he recognized the shelling of London as a duty, like its companion, the shelling of Paris" (Mann quoted in: Deutsche Akademie der Künste 1971, 467–8, own translation).

Here we have, condensed in a few lines, the key components of what was called the "anti-democratic," "potentially fascist" or "authoritarian" personality in the Berkeley-study, though embedded in the specific situation of Germany and formulated as an accusation against its leader. It was surely aimed at those who Heinrich Mann considered to be fellow democrats, or potentially of like mind. What we have here, decades before empirical sociology and social psychology, is a critique of "authoritarian aggression," "destructiveness and cynicism," "anti-intraception" (refusal to identify with others, generally those weaker than oneself, opposition to the subjective, the imaginative, the tender-minded), "power and toughness," and this in the context of a concrete society and specific historical situation.

The central idea of the Berkeley-study rests on a model that links authoritarian aggression with authoritarian subservience, and presumes that dispositions towards both exist in early childhood. As Adorno summed it up in 1964:

"I may, perhaps, only remind that what psychoanalysis calls the Oedipal character is very often constituted by suppression, in particular, by violent, brutal paternal authority, which means that there are humans who are, on the one side, governed by repressed fury, and who, on the other, tend to identify themselves with that suppressing authority and who vent their suppressed and aggressive instincts on others, generally the weaker, because they have not been able to develop. The authority-bound, specifically anti-Semitic character is really the '*Untertan*,' as Heinrich Mann pictured it, or as one says plainly in good German, the '*Radfahrernatur*' [the cyclist's mentality]" (Adorno quoted in: Emmerich 1980, 154, own translation).

I shall now bring my reflections to a close. I showed that the subtext of the social scientific study which gives the appearance of being entirely scientific (on the model of the natural sciences) is in fact that of a novel, or at least novelistic representation. In the "scientific" text, minor gains in terms of standardization contrast with a substantial loss of close observation and contextual information. Heinrich Mann's portrayal of the lot of Heßling, an opportunist who kowtows to superiors while kicking underlings, is in many ways more plausible and verifiable than the operationalist and physicalist Berkeley-study. Through three examples I have attempted to demonstrate the closeness of social scientific language to various genres of novelistic narrative. The last example assumes that novelistic representation may also precede science, with the advantage of greater detail and innovative formation of concepts which anticipate later developments. In all four cases, the narrative style is also bound up with the authors' biographical experiences and their emotional structures. In both respects, sociology has much in common with literature. Does this mean that we must give up all claims to scientific objectivity and verifiable attempts to approach the truth? Quite the contrary! We would, however, be well advised to examine carefully both the literature present in sociology and the sociology in the novel, to explicate them and scrutinize their descriptive content within the process of communication between author and public. The novel and "scientificated" sociology may gradually differ. They will not, however, differ so fundamentally that they would ever become estranged from one another. This may not be a bad thing for either sociology or literature.

Acknowledgements

This chapter was translated by Alex Skinner, following a revised version of the article (Kuzmics 2006).

References

Adorno, Theodor W., Else Frenkel-Brunswik, Daniel J. Levinson, and R. Nevitt Sanford (1950). *The Authoritarian Personality*. New York: Harper & Row.

Argyle, Michael (1975). *Bodily Communication*. New York: International Universities Press.

Aron, Raymond (1971). *Hauptströmungen des soziologischen Denkens*. 2 vols. Cologne: Kiepenheuer und Witsch.

Ballmer, Thomas T. (1979). Probleme der Klassifikation von Sprechakten. In Günther Grewendorf (ed.). *Sprechakttheorie und Semantik*, 247–74. Frankfurt am Main: Suhrkamp.

Berger, Peter L. (1997). *Redeeming Laughter. The Comic Dimension of Human Experience*. Berlin, New York: Walter de Gruyter.

Breuer, Stefan (2006). *Max Webers tragische Soziologie. Aspekte und Perspektiven*. Tübingen: Mohr, Siebeck.

Brown, Richard Harvey (1987). *Society as Text. Essays on Rhetoric, Reason and Reality*. Chicago, London: University of Chicago Press.

Brown, Roger (1966). *Social Psychology*. New York, London: The Free Press/Collier-Macmillan Ltd.

Deutsche Akademie der Künste (ed.). (1971). *Heinrich Mann 1871–1950. Werk und Leben in Dokumenten und Bildern, mit unveröffentlichten Manuskripten und Briefen aus dem Nachlaß.* Berlin, Weimar: Aufbau-Verlag.

Elias, Norbert (1978). *What is Sociology?* Transl. Stephen Mennell and Grace Morrissey. With a Foreword from Reinhard Bendix. London: Hutchinson.

— (1985). *Humana Conditio – Beobachtungen zur Entwicklung der Menschheit am 40. Jahrestag eines Kriegsendes (8. Mai 1985).* Frankfurt am Main: Suhrkamp.

— (1987a). On Human Beings and Their Emotions. *Theory, Culture and Society,* 4 (2–3), 339–62.

— (1987b). *Involvement and Detachment.* Ed. Michael Schröter. Transl. Edmund Jephcott. Oxford: Blackwell.

— (1990). *Norbert Elias über sich selbst.* Frankfurt am Main: Suhrkamp.

— (1991). *The Symbol Theory.* London: Sage.

— (1996). *The Germans.* Ed. Michael Schröter. Transl. and with a preface by Eric Dunning and Stephen Mennell. Cambridge: Polity.

— (2000). *The Civilizing Process.* Oxford: Blackwell.

Emmerich, Wolfgang (1980). *Heinrich Mann: Der Untertan.* Munich: Fink.

Frye, Northrop (1990). *Anatomy of Criticism. Four Essays.* Princeton, NJ: Princeton University Press (tenth printing).

Goffman, Erving (1968a). *Asylums.* Essays on the Social Situation of Mental Patients and Other Inmates. Harmondsworth, Middlesex: Penguin.

— (1968b). *Stigma. Notes on the Management of Spoiled Identity.* Harmondsworth, Middlesex: Penguin.

— (1969). *The Presentation of Self in Everyday Life.* Harmondsworth, Middlesex: Penguin.

— (1971). *Relations in Public. Microstudies of the Public Order.* Harmondsworth, Middlesex: Penguin.

— (1972). *Interaction Ritual. Essays on Face-to-Face Behaviour.* Harmondsworth, Middlesex: Penguin.

Gouldner, Alvin W. (1971). *The Coming Crisis of Western Sociology.* London: Heinemann.

Green, Martin (1984). *Else und Frieda: Die Richthofen-Schwestern.* Munich: Deutscher Taschenbuch Verlag.

Groeben, Norbert, and Brigitte Scheele (1986). *Produktion und Rezeption von Ironie. Vol. 1: Pragmalinguistische Beschreibung und psycholinguistische Erklärungshypothesen.* Tübingen: Narr.

Hackeschmidt, Jörg (2000). Der Fackelläufer. Norbert Elias und das Problem der Generationen in der zionistischen Jugendbewegung 1918–1925. In Annette Treibel, Helmut Kuzmics, and Reinhard Blomert (eds.). *Zivilisationstheorie in der Bilanz. Beiträge zum 100. Geburtstag von Norbert Elias,* 19–34. Opladen: Leske und Budrich.

Hannemann, Bruno (1977). *Johann Nestroy. Nihilistisches Welttheater und verflixter Kerl. Zum Ende der Wiener Komödie.* Bonn: Bouvier.

Hennis, Wilhelm (2003). *Max Weber und Thukydides. Die hellenische Geisteskultur und die Ursprünge von Webers politischer Denkart*. Göttingen: Vandenhoeck & Ruprecht.

Horkheimer, Max (ed.). (1936). *Studien über Autorität und Familie*. Schriften des Instituts für Sozialforschung, vol. 5. Paris: Alcan.

Jaensch, Erich Rudolf (1938). *Der Gegentypus: psychologisch-anthropologische Grundlagen deutscher Kulturphilosophie, ausgehend von dem was wir überwinden wollen*. Leipzig: Barth.

Kahl, Kurt (1970). *Johann Nestroy oder der wienerische Shakespeare*. Vienna, Munich, Zürich: Molden.

Kuzmics, Helmut (2006). Soziologie als Erzählung. Die Sprache der Soziologie in "klassischen" Beispielen. In Reinhold Esterbauer, Elisabeth Pernkopf, Hans-Walter Ruckenbauer (eds.). *WortWechsel. Sprachprobleme in den Wissenschaften interdisziplinär auf den Begriff gebracht*, 51–72. Würzburg: Königshausen & Neumann.

Kuzmics, Helmut, and Gerald Mozetič (2003). *Literatur als Soziologie*. Zum Verhältnis von literarischer und gesellschaftlicher Wirklichkeit. Konstanz: UVK.

Luhmann, Niklas (1973). *Zweckbegriff und Systemrationalität*. Frankfurt am Main: Suhrkamp.

Lyotard, Jean-François (1979). *The Post-Modern Condition: A Report on Knowledge*. Minneapolis: University of Minnesota Press.

Mann, Heinrich (1998). *The Loyal Subject*. London, New York: Continuum Publishing Group. [German original: Heinrich Mann (1918). *Der Untertan*. Leipzig: Kurt Wolff Verlag]

Marx, Gary T. (1984). Role Models and Role Distance. A Remembrance of Erving Goffman. *Theory and Society*, 13, 649–62.

Murgg, Günter (1993). *Indirektheit und Mehrfachrealisierung illokutiver Funktionen*. PhD diss., Graz University.

Preglau, Max (1998). Einleitung. Zum Leitbegriff "Postmoderne". In Max Preglau and Rudolf Richter (eds.). *Postmodernes Österreich? Konturen des Wandels in Wirtschaft, Gesellschaft, Politik und Kultur*, 13–21. Vienna: Signum.

Radkau, Joachim (2005). *Max Weber. Die Leidenschaft des Denkens*. Munich: Hanser.

Samelson, Franz (1993). The Authoritarian Character From Berlin to Berkeley and Beyond: The Odyssey of a Problem. In William T. Stone, Gerda Lederer, and Richard Christie (eds.). *Strength and Weakness. The Authoritarian Personality Today*, 22–43. New York: Springer.

Scheff, Thomas J. (2006). *Goffman Unbound! A New Paradigm for Social Science*. Boulder, London: Paradigm Publishers.

Smith, Dennis (2000). The Prisoner and the Fisherman. In Annette Treibel, Helmut Kuzmics, and Reinhard Blomert (eds.). *Zivilisationstheorie in der Bilanz. Beiträge zum 100. Geburtstag von Norbert Elias*, 143–61. Opladen: Leske und Budrich.

Treviño, A. Javier (2003). Introduction. In A. Javier Treviño (ed.). *Goffman's Legacy*, 1–49. Lanham, MD: Rowman & Littlefield (=Legacies of social thought).

Weber, Marianne (1926). *Max Weber: Ein Lebensbild*. Tübingen: Mohr (Siebeck).

Weber, Max (1979). Value Judgements in Social Science. In Max Weber. *Selections in Translation*, 69–98. Ed. W. G. Runciman, transl. by E. Matthews. Cambridge: Cambridge University Press.

— (1988). *Gesammelte Politische Schriften.* Tübingen: Mohr.

— (2001). *The Protestant Ethic and the Spirit of Capitalism.* Transl. by Talcott Parsons, with an introduction by Anthony Giddens. London, New York: Routledge Classics.

— (2003). Prefatory Remarks to the Collected Essays in the Sociology of Religion. In Max Weber. *The Essential Weber. A Reader*, 101–12. Ed. Sam Whimster, London, New York: Routledge.

White, Hayden (1975). *Metahistory. The Historical Imagination in Nineteenth-Century Europe.* Baltimore, London: Johns Hopkins University Press.

Zilian, Hans Georg (1996). Sprachphilosophie in den Gesellschaftswissenschaften. In Marcelo Dascal, Dietfried Gerhardus, and Kuno Lorenz (eds.). *Sprachphilosophie. Philosophy of Language. La philosophie du langage*, 1454–69. Berlin, New York: Walter de Gruyter.

Hearts or Wombs? A Cultural Critique of Radical Feminist Critiques of Love

Eva Illouz and Eitan Wilf

General Introduction

Second wave feminism has profoundly transformed our understanding of the emotion of love.[1] Contrary to popular mythology, radical feminists argue, love is not the source of transcendence, happiness, and self-realization. Rather, romantic love is one of the main causes of the divide between men and women, as well as one of the cultural practices through which women are made to accept (and "love") their submission to men. For, when in love, men and women continue to perform the deep divisions that characterize their respective identities: in Simone de Beauvoir's famous words, even in love men retain their sovereignty, while women aim to abandon themselves (Beauvoir 1970). In her controversial *Dialectic of Sex*, Shulamith Firestone goes a step further: the source of men's social power and energy is the love women have provided and continue to provide for men, thus suggesting that love is the cement with which the edifice of male domination has been built (Firestone 1979). Romantic love not only hides a class and sex segregation, but also, in fact, makes it possible.

Feminist historians examining the constitution of the private and public spheres in the nineteenth century have reinforced these critiques. In organizing work and manufacture in factories, capitalism irrevocably destroyed domestic production and made invisible the work of women who supported the engine of capitalism, without being remunerated, and for that matter, without being even considered as workers. Having been barred from participating in the public sphere as citizens, women accepted their domestic work and roles as mothers and wives (Lystra 1989; Rothman 1984). The confinement of women in the private sphere—narrow, limiting, and disempowering—has in turn prevented women from acquiring self-

---

1 This paper deals with heterosexual love. Unless otherwise specified, our use of the term "love" should be understood in this sense.

mastery and political sovereignty (Douglas 1978; Landes 1998; MacKinnon 1989; Pateman 1989). As Michael Kimmel suggests, it is customary to see the nineteenth century as a period where women were "domestic prisoners, locked into the hole by an ideology of feminine domesticity and Christian piety and virtue" (Kimmel 1996, 157). Without a doubt, one of the emotional and ideological pillars supporting the edifice of the private sphere was romantic love. It is thus not surprising that romantic love—the fulcrum of the private sphere—has been viewed as an instrument of women's continued subordination to men. This also explains why radical feminist scholars have relentlessly attacked liberalism—as the theory that holds that the existence of a private sphere, free of the intervention of the state, is crucial for the exercise of personal freedom. Liberalism has been indicted as the political theory that, albeit premised on the family, has made it invisible, and has confined rather than liberated women by ascribing them to a social sphere and a corresponding cultural "essence" (MacKinnon 1989; Pateman 1989).

On a broad level, this paper hopes to achieve two tasks: the first is to argue that while radical feminist critiques of love presuppose that love is a historical ideology intertwined with institutions of male power, they have not undertaken to examine empirically how romantic love varies with different organizations of patriarchy. Ideologies of romantic love *vary* and do not reflect a fixed position of women in a structure of inequality. In particular, there has been no empirical attempt to compare the ways in which love is differently constructed in a communitarian, as opposed to a liberal polity. In this paper, our goal is to offer a cultural critique of the radical feminist critique of love by showing that the meaning of romantic love does not cover the same social and emotional meaning within two contrasted social organizations, the Israeli and the American. This makes possible an appreciation of how, when embedded in communitarian or liberal social organizations, these meanings in turn point to different modes of subjection of women by men.

The second goal of this paper is to argue that the liberal social organization, sharply dividing a (female) private sphere from a (male) public sphere, does not entail a greater subordination of women than a communitarian polity in which women are presumably more involved in the public sphere. As the Israeli case illustrates, women's greater involvement in the public sphere, far from granting them a higher status, makes them more dependent on hegemonic definitions of masculinity. The Israeli context in turn sheds a new light on the ideology of romantic love that has been central to the liberal ideology of the private sphere: romantic love may well have been a terrain on which men had to compromise with women, thus suggesting, perhaps counter intuitively, that through love, women have developed individual identity and autonomy. This paper hopes to make a contribution to a feminist theory of romantic love by suggesting that the model of romantic love that has been elaborated in "the shadowy realm of the interior"—to use Hannah Arendt's (1958) evocative, if derogatory, expression—has been an agent of individualization and autonomy for women. In rejecting the division between emotions and cognitions that has been at the center of western philosophy, we argue that romantic love contains the main cultural tropes of modernity—affirmation of the individual, autonomy of private choices, and democratization. The emotion of love has been an agent of equalization of gender relations inside the private sphere (Bailey 1993; Beck and Beck-Gernsheim 1995; Cancian 1987; Giddens 1992; Illouz 1997).

We will try to illustrate these claims by examining the cultural code of love in the Israeli context, a society that has been consistently characterized by its analysts as dominated by a strong communitarian ethos, and a devouring public sphere.

Cultural Codes and Emotions

To start addressing the broad theoretical questions raised here, we would like to inquire into the unique, that is, culturally specific (secular) conceptions of love at work in Israeli culture, and to integrate our findings within a broader understanding of the role of love in communitarian and liberal polities. It is obvious that there is a similarity between Israeli conceptions of romance on the one hand, and European and American conceptions on the other hand, and that there exist, too, multiple cultural codes of love in Israel. The article's analytic strategy is to bracket both the similarity between the American and Israeli conceptions of romance, and the diversity of romantic cultures inside Israel, in order to focus instead on the Israeli dominant romantic code—that is, that code which expresses most sharply the specificity of the Israeli context. Another reason for this analytic choice is that while there is a considerable scholarship on the European and

American romantic traditions (Bailey 1993; Beck and Beck-Gernsheim 1995; Cancian 1987; D'Emillio and Freedman 1988; Giddens 1992; Gillis 1988; Illouz 1997; Stone 1979), we know much less about the Israeli cultural specificity, especially with regards to its emotional fabric.

For the past two decades, the anthropology of emotions has consistently and successfully refuted the Jamesian view—hitherto dominant— that emotions are physiological responses to situations, which in turn make them universal invariants of human action. Indeed, numerous studies have showed repeatedly that emotions are shaped, through and through, by cultural meanings, and in particular by cultural conceptions of the person (Abu-Lughod 1986; Geertz 1973; Lutz 1988; M. Z. Rosaldo 1980; R. Rosaldo 1980; Stearns 1993; Vincent-Buffault 1991).

Emotional experience is embedded within cultural scripts, moral categories, and basic views of the person. These scripts and categories specify the degree of the person's autonomy *vis-à-vis* the group, the definition of rights and duties of individuals *vis-à-vis* their groups of membership, and the ways in which reciprocity and solidarity is established and negotiated in a particular cultural order. Through emotional experience one enacts, in an immediate and unreflective way, stored cultural knowledge pertaining to one's position within a given social environment.[2] Yet, even if emotions are activated by cultural knowledge, they are not equivalent to it (Barbalet 1998). As we illustrate further in the paper, emotions have a relative degree of autonomy from that very culture which gives them meaning.

More than other emotions, the emotion of love is embedded within public symbols and rituals (Alberoni 1983; Weitman 1998), and this because love is related to the most basic and essential institution of society, the family. Unlike other emotions, in love is at stake the central social institution of marriage, either because love threatens marriage or because it is claimed to be its foundation. Because marriage is the institution insuring both biological reproduction and economic survival, it is the object of close social control and scrutiny. This is why, ever since it has entertained an ambivalent relationship *vis-à-vis* marriage—claiming to be its rationale and yet threatening to dissolve its stability—, romantic love has been an endless object of discourse and representation (Illouz 1997). This also explains why, of all emotions, love is the most widely and relentlessly de-

---

2 Anger, for example, is an emotional reaction expressing cultural knowledge pertaining to the moral definition of a person, one's sense of entitlement, and signals to oneself where one stands in a particular social relationship.

picted in the cultural media, and the one about which there is the greatest amount of public cultural discussion.

Another characteristic which differentiates between love and other emotions is the fact that love is a narrative emotion, that is, it unfolds as a story, is conceived and felt in a story form and is intimately related to narratives of self. Most other emotions on the other hand, are lived as punctual events which may be told in stories, but do not have the capacity to provide an overall narrative of identity to the self. It is, for example, more difficult for us to think of anger as a sentiment through which one's life unfolds, while it is much easier for us to think of and summarize one's life through one's love or loves.[3] Thus, the emotion of love is a cultural narrative that points to larger cultural narratives of the self. Like other narratives, it is defined by the cultural codes it contains and enacts. As defined by K. Silverman,

"A cultural code can be defined as a conceptual system which is organized around key oppositions and equations, in which a term like 'woman' is defined in opposition to a term like 'man,' and in which each term is aligned with a cluster of symbolic attributes [...] Cultural codes provide the basis for connotation" (Silverman 1983, 36).

Through cultural codes, social reality is interpreted, shared, and acted upon. As post-structuralist historians and sociologists have suggested, meaning is conveyed through key paradigmatic oppositions, contrasts, and syntagmatic associations. Thus the US cultural code of love frequently contains such categories as "gentleness," "warmth," and "friendship," and is opposed to such meanings as "lust" or "violent passion." Cultural codes have a social basis. Networks of oppositions and associations are enacted through social institutions, organizations, and patterned processes. In the case of love, there are key institutional patterns that are likely to play a central role in the shaping of cultural codes: they are religion (Ozment 2001), strategies of economic survival (Cancian 1987; Shorter 1975; Stone 1979), the private/public divide (Demos 1997; Stearns and Stearns 1988; Zaretsky 1994), legislation (Nussbaum 1999), and the cultural complex within which sexual relations are organized, as in narratives of romantic love disseminated by the cultural genre of the novel (Giddens 1992; Luhmann 1986).

---

3 One can say, perhaps, that the emotion of revenge has the same characteristics that enable it to function as the center of a life story.

Methodology

Until the seventies the Israeli televised medium was underdeveloped (having only one public channel) and the media's orientation was directed to news more than to the display of life style (see Katz et al. 1997). It is reasonable then, to assume that at least until the end of the seventies, women's magazines played a significant cultural role in guiding, instructing, and exposing women to models and theories of love and femininity (modes of dress, makeup, behavior, etc.).

Another reason for analyzing women's magazines is that this literature is by definition a highly gendered one and is therefore highly informative on the cultural codes through which women are socialized to play and "do" their gender role through love. This is true of Israeli women as well as of women in the US, where, in the latter case, from the nineteenth-century onward, American women have been the object and target of advice by a vast number of social agents, such as clerics, secular moralists, psychologists, and physicians, who, through counseling and moral guidance, shaped and defined the role and duty of women as wives and mothers[4] (Ehrenreich and English 1978; Illouz 1991; Simonds 1992; Winship 1980). Because emotional life both in traditional and in modern world is deeply shaped and divided by gender (Abu-Lughod 1986; Lutz 1988; Smith-Rosenberg 1986; Stearns and Stearns 1988; Vincent-Buffault 1991), it is particularly useful to analyze a gendered cultural medium, such as women's magazines.

The following analysis is based on a sampled survey of a women's magazine, La'isha, from the inception of the state of Israel in 1948 until 1978.[5] A section of marital counseling and reports that dealt with love, marriage and sexuality were chosen for analysis. This thirty-year period was chosen because it corresponds to a period during which the state dominated the cultural and economic life of the country, thus providing a better illustration of a communitarian polity than that of the Israel of the nineteen eigh-

---

4 Although counseling literature was underdeveloped in the Israeli context in comparison to the American context, it still forms a convenient arena for sociological analysis, since by definition it makes explicit in a clear way the norms that are supposed to regulate behavior. By using a metaphor of Ann Swidler, this literature serves as the walls of a cave through the help of which a bat orients itself (Swidler 2001).

5 The following years and months were analyzed: 1948; 1953: January, June; 1958: January, June; 1963: January, June; 1968: January, June; 1973: January, June; 1978, January, June.

ties, which became far more liberal in its economic, cultural, and political orientation.

The magazine *La'isha* was chosen for three reasons. Firstly, it has enjoyed the highest circulation among Israeli women, from its first days until the present. For example, according to a survey conducted in 1980, 34 percent of the people who read periodicals chose *La'isha* as their preferred periodical (Rubin 1987, 38). Secondly, as already mentioned, this magazine was first published in 1947 and therefore serves as a suitable arena for a systematic analysis of romantic practices in the Israeli context starting from the first days of the state of Israel. Thirdly, *La'isha* forms a convenient arena for the analysis of patriarchy because from its first days it was edited and run by men. These men wrote almost all the articles of the magazine under different female pseudonyms. For example, in its first years, the advice, and sometimes the questions that were published in the advice column of the magazine, was written by the magazine's (male) first editor (Rubin 1987, 38, 41–2). The fact that *La'isha* is a highly gendered cultural medium makes it a convenient arena for the analysis of emotional life, as discussed above.

The Cultural Matrix of Israeli Romantic Love

The Division Between Private Sphere and Public Sphere

If the emergence of the American private sphere can be accounted for by the ways in which the capitalist economy divided male and female work, then we may also examine the relative weakness of the private sphere in Israel in reference to its economic organization.

Israeli founding myth and original social organization were such that the private and the public were not clearly, if at all, differentiated and can even be said to have been merged together. Much of Israel's present economic and political configuration has its origins in Zionist ideology operating in the pre-state period of the *Yishuv*. Social-Zionism, as propagated by the labor movement/the Mapai party, predominated Zionism both politically and symbolically for most of the *Yishuv* and the first decades of the state of Israel. As historian Zeev Sternhell claims, "the labor movement provided Israeli society with such a strong model of development that even after its fall from power in 1977 no real changes occurred in the economic, cultural, and social life of Israel" (Sternhell 1997, 4–5; see also Lissak 1995, 262).

One of the labor movement's basic ideological components was to establish a communal society that would be based on centralized supervision over the market and the society, and in which nationalization of private assets would bring forth equality in wages, consumption, and social status (Lissak 1995, 177–8).[6] The individual was expected to relinquish any private needs and aspirations if these did not match or merge with the collective needs of society. Various cooperative organizations were established as a way of implementing this vision, such as the *Kibbutz*, the *Moshav*, and several types of consumers' and producers' cooperatives in the cities. Free professionals such as physicians and lawyers were far less valued than in European countries, with the *Halutz* (the pioneer) taking the forefront of cultural and normative imagery. The pioneer—which combined images of agricultural hard work and fearless soldiers' spirit—was supposed to be moved by the needs of the community, primarily national.

Although the importance of the private sector to the development of the economy was acknowledged, the public sector won more economic and normative incentives (Lissak 1995, 252–3). The Israeli market was not guided, as was its American counterpart, by an ideology of rationality and efficiency but rather by ethno-religious and national considerations (Kimmerling 1982, 13–4).[7]

The articles in the magazine *La'isha* attest to the fact that the private is fully informed by the public. For one, one may observe that the theme of love as such is significantly less addressed than it is in equivalent American magazines. Instead, the bulk of the articles in the fifties address the importance of the family. In one article dated from 1948 the author tells about a conversation she had "overheard" between two civilian parents of two children and two soldiers.[8] In this overheard conversation, the soldiers suggested that, in times of distress and war, it is not appropriate to start a family and give birth to more children. This brings the mother's furious response: "we should not speak such words, let alone in times of war. Who

---

6 This, of course, was only one component of this movement's stated ideology. For a critical examination of Social-Zionism as a nationalist movement which had nothing to do with socialist concerns, see Sternhell (1997).

7 See the whole chapter, *The Model of Pioneering Economy* (Kimmerling 1982), for a discussion of the differences between the Zionist economy and Weber's model of rationalization in capitalism with reference to the Protestant ethic.

8 *La'isha*, 4 August 1948, 2, 4.

in your opinion will fill the places of the missing sons?" The soldier thus inquires about her comfort while she will be required to take care of her children, alone in her husband's absence, to which the woman responds, "comfortable, easy [...] these are the selfish terms! Please put them out of your vocabulary [...] We ought to turn every job and duty easy and comfortable in these days." The author of the article mentioned that in the end the woman convinced the soldiers. The idea of the family expressed here is similar to that of the republican ideal of the family. Rousseau best defined such an ideal, and his words would have been heartily endorsed by most writers of the period:

"Can devotion to the state exist apart from the love of those near and dear to us? Can patriotism thrive except in the soil of that miniature fatherland, the home? Is it not the good son, the good husband, the good father who makes the good citizen?" (Rousseau 1911, 326).

Rousseau excluded women from his view of citizenship, yet viewed the family as the indispensable soil on which the future citizen could and should grow. The family is in fact a micro political community, for in it, individuals are educated to care and sacrifice for the benefit of the greater community.

At face value, women are here made full participants in the project of nation-building, and are even made to prefer their public vocation to their private sentiments. Yet in the same way that the family was shot through by notions of collective good, women occupied the public sphere, by caring for men, in the position that had been traditional to women (Bernstein 1987, 22–3). In that way, we may say that the continuity between the private and public spheres was seamless.

Familism

It is thus not surprising that the ideal-typical woman posited by the magazine *La'isha* of the fifties, is one who has realized her self in motherhood, and who views this role as echoing her contribution to the community and the collective effort.[9] Family and motherhood define not only the good

---

9 We do not rule out *a priori* motherhood as a potentially liberating practice. Rather, we endorse Adrienne Riche's (1995) distinction between motherhood as experience and motherhood as institution. Thus, while Rich emphasizes the potential pleasure inherent

woman but also femininity at large. Let us take the example of an exchange between two women, presented by the magazine, as contrasted opposites. Such cultural oppositions and dichotomies are useful for the cultural analyst because, as structuralist anthropologists have repeatedly shown, these oppositions enact core cultural codes. One report titled *A Candid Letter From the 'Other Woman'*[10] presents a letter from a (single) woman to a married woman, with whose husband she is having an affair. It is thus a letter from the mistress to the wife. In this letter, the lover explains why it is right for the husband to be unfaithful to his wife. The main reason lies in the outward appearance of the wife: "Never, never will I look like you! [...] A woman who neglects her external appearance is stupid." In the following issue of the magazine, a reply is offered in which the wife explains that the neglect of her appearance was caused by the need to raise and maintain a family.[11] The wife wrote:

"I don't think that I didn't make it as a woman [...] we and women like us devoted our most beautiful years to starting a family. For other things outside marriage we have neither talent nor training. I don't agree that any other woman—that succeeded in maintaining her looks and lives her life in an atmosphere of beauty parlors, theatres and offices—has the right to take our husbands away from us."

Both the mistress' letter and the reply constitute a discussion on the definition of "good" femininity and are articulated through an opposition between the "feminine woman" and the mother. The feminine woman is construed here as an erotic creature, unconcerned with procreation and family. Both types of womanhood are similarly construed as ultimately subservient to the patriarchal order, yet the latter is nonetheless viewed as more commendable because it appears to be less individualistic and more oriented towards the needs of the community.

In Israel, personal welfare was largely defined by collective welfare, which in turn demanded high rates of fertility. The Israeli family was legitimated by a discourse of fertility. For example, another article entitled *The Birth Rate Decreasing*,[12] deals with the lack of organized and subsidized day-

---

in women's relationship to their powers of reproduction and to their children, she claims that in the current state of affairs superimposed on it are male control and patriarchal values. In the same vein, we claim that motherhood in Israel in the discussed years may be characterized as motherhood as institution.

10 *La'isha*, 2 June 1948, 1, 4.

11 *La'isha*, 10 June 1948, 1, 4.

12 *La'isha*, 1 December 1948, 1, 4.

care centers, and the influence it has on the possibility of women to fulfill themselves in the public sphere. If such centers are not made available, so the article holds, then women will have to give up the freedom they have achieved in order to protect the family, here equated with a large family. This article presented fertility as the obligatory task of men and women. Aside from emphasizing the importance of institutionalizing daycare centers, the reporter enumerated the actions needed in order to encourage births, such as building bigger apartments for larger families, since "every woman in Israel knows that we must increase the birth rate." It is interesting to notice that both men and women are defined in terms of their obligation to be fertile, with women however, having to bear alone the burdens of pregnancy, child-birth leave, and child rearing.

These findings are congruent with Sylvie Vogiel-Bijaoui's pioneering analysis of the contemporary Israeli family, in which she claims that Israeli society is less individualized and more oriented toward the family than its American or European counterparts: Israelis marry more, divorce less, and give birth to a higher number of children (Vogiel-Bijaoui 1999). This is attributed to the control of personal status laws by the religious clergy, whose conceptions of women, procreation and marriage permeate, so-to-speak, the general social fabric of marriage. Israel's pro-natalist legislation finds expression in the existence of different payments and allowances given as incentives for procreation, and in the large sums of money that the government invests in promoting the development and use of new reproductive technologies (Portuguese 1998).

State policy and religious laws combine with cultural schemas provided by the Jewish religious tradition to explain the remarkable naturalness with which Israelis complied with this specific model of the family. Indeed, as Baruch Kimmerling has shown (Kimmerling 1999), a significant part of Zionism's political decisions were embedded within the cultural tradition of Judaism (e.g., the decision on the territorial location of the Jewish people, the definition of who is a Jew, etc.).[13] A central ethos regarding sexuality and love operated throughout Jewish history, in which sexuality and Jewish identity were deeply associated with each other (Biale 1992, 13).

---

13 More generally, many sociologists, such as Weber and Durkheim, have emphasized the ability of modern secular culture to appropriate religious contents and behavior. As is well known, Weber showed how the Puritans' labor turned into the blind and compulsive rationality of modern capitalism. For Durkheim war is just a secular reenactment of religious rituals.

The result of the Jewish insistence on fertility, we would argue, was that it did not adopt as readily a model of romantic love, as it did an emotion and experience distinct from the dictates of the family. In general "what we call romantic love undergoes in the Midrash a relentless de-poetization" (Levinas 1963, 70). What this in turn suggests is that the tension between marriage and romantic love—which was at the heart of European conceptions of love, and which was bequeathed to the literary and cinematic imagination of modern Israelis—is less salient in the Jewish erotic imagination. The latter, in contrast to the European sensibility, viewed marriage positively and insisted on procreation as its main vocation. In Jewish culture, the family was defined and valued in reference to its role in preserving the ethnic boundaries of the group.[14]

Masculinity and Femininity: Opposites or Similar?

In the Israeli context, women are not viewed as the pure moral creatures whom men should strive to emulate. This is in contrast to the American context (Cott 1988; Elshtain 1995, 140–9). For example, in an article titled *Help Your Husband Be Faithful to You!*,[15] the author addresses the question of what women must do in order for their husbands to remain faithful to them. A woman must constantly monitor her husband's behavior, "perceive in time the warning signals," and act accordingly. A middle-aged man fears being old and needs constant reassurance. Therefore, his wife must be careful not to criticize or hurt him. "If the wife gives him this reassurance—he will not look for other women." Thus, although the report concludes with the remark that a woman is not the only one at blame for her husband's infidelity, this is the very conclusion the reader is forced to come up with at the end of the article. Here again we can offer an observation pertaining to the differences between the American and the Israeli context: in the US context, the male practice of "double standard" was precisely one of the moral battles that helped affirm the moral status of women, and from which women claimed equality to men. Through the Temperance

---

14 It is important to contrast this with the fact that the marriage of the aristocratic elite in Europe frequently crossed "national" borders (granting of course that "national" is a bit anachronistic as a word in this context). In contrast to Jewish culture, therefore, marriage was a source of mixing and blending in Europe.

15 *La'isha*, 3 March 1948, 1, 4.

Movement, and precisely using the moral leverage that had been bestowed on them in the private sphere, women organized moral crusades, in which they called upon men to reform the practice of double-standard, thus in fact claiming equality on the basis of the moral status they had been granted in the realm of love and sexuality. Toward the end of the nineteenth-century in the US, members of the clergy, moralists, and educators, praised women for having "all the milder virtues of humanity" and "a more exquisite sensibility than men [...] the god of heaven has more exquisitively [sic] attuned their [...] sensibility than men should to love, to sympathy and compassion" (quoted in Cott 1977, 23). Because they recognized women's superiority in the domestic sphere, they asked men to accommodate their behavior and personality to that of women.[16]

To provide another example of the ways in which Israeli women are not posited as having the moral superiority that was taken for granted in the US: three young women complain about the improper behavior of men while they are in their company. The counselor replies:

"You should know that these men are usually good men, serious, and clever. Their conduct toward women is dependent on her. She has to know how to put a guy in his place. Not by being overly strict, angry, or punitive. With laughter, a sharp word, with delicate firmness."[17]

While in the American context, men were the ones who had to watch their behavior carefully in order to meet the moral standards of women, here it is clearly the woman who had to adapt her conduct to that of the man, however violent and demeaning. Thus, one woman writes to the counseling section of *La'isha* that, because of her incapability to conceive children, she and her husband consider adoption. While she wants a girl, he wishes for a boy. The section advises the woman to give up and grant her husband his wish, in these words:

"you must understand your husband: every man instinctively wishes for the continuation of his name, lest it will be lost. A father to three beautiful and nice girls is never satisfied—even though he publicly declares that he doesn't wish for boys!

---

16 See Ann Douglas' different thesis in *The Feminization of American Culture* (Douglas 1978) which attributes the creation of a female sentimental culture in the nineteenth century to the decline of the influence of the church and of women (i.e. their exclusion from the public sphere), which resulted in the formation of an alliance between these two groups, see also Stearns and Stearns (1988).

17 *La'isha*, 2 June 1948, 3.

[...] Therefore in case you can't adopt two kids, my advice is that you adopt a son, a child is a child."[18]

The Army: A Gender Leveler?

While in the US romantic courtship and loss of virginity form important rites of passage into adulthood, in Israel it is one's duty service in the army which constitutes the major rite of passage into adulthood. The army service is a frequent occasion for men and women to explore their sexuality and romantic sentiments, but that exploration is subsumed under the military framework in which it takes place. The compulsory army service demands of men *and* women strong emotional control, endurance, overcoming of fear, and strong solidarity with their group of operation (Ben-Ari 2001). Thus, the image of a strong and muscular masculine body was central to the main codes and tropes of Israeli masculinity. What makes this muscular body masculine are its military feats, its ability to sacrifice itself to the collective, and to control fear and other negative emotions. In contradistinction to Western European masculinity, what defines Israeli masculinity is not the ability to please and flatter women, to bring them slowly into the complicated game of love and courtship, in short to engage in the infinitesimally complicated dynamic of distance and conquest, desire and longing. What does define it is rather its ability to withstand pressure, to be cool-headed, and to help other men in distress. In congruence with the general ethos of informality that has been dominant in the formation of the Israeli ethos, the Israeli man has traditionally shied away from the somewhat formal art of foreplay and elaborate rituals of courtship. This is because one of the main cultural and linguistic codes forged and conveyed by the army is that of the *Dugri* speech (Katriel 1986). *Dugri* speech—the dominant linguistic code regulating social interactions—is a form of speech in which directness is preferred to allusion, reference to concrete and practical matters preferred to the spiritual or emotional, and expression of familiarity is preferred to formal distance and deference. Such linguistic code, importantly, differs from the US romantic linguistic code, which

---

18 *La'isha*, 4 April 1948, 3. Many other articles deal with various "female faults" that cause men either to avoid, or to exploit them. See, for example, *Strictness or Lack of Sexual Maturity* (*La'isha*, 7 January 1953, 3) for the first case, and *An Amateur in Love* (*La'isha*, 2 January 1968, 20) for the second.

stresses indirectness, emotional expressivity, and male deference to the woman.

The powerful cultural influence of the army on women is felt in yet another way. The army enables two main modes of articulation of woman's identity. As Sasson-Levy showed, one mode is by making women adopt and imitate male identity (Sasson-Levy 2000). The second is by making them adopt the identity of the protective mother who takes care of the needs of men anyway (Martin and McCrate 1984). In that respect, we may say that the army reinforces the fact that womanhood is organized around and defined by hegemonic masculinity, either by playing the role of mothers (taking care of their sons) or by erasing gender differences altogether, that is, by aligning them around male masculinity. In the same way that the family is understood in terms of its contribution/participation to the body collective, the army often uses the rhetoric and roles shaped inside the family to make sense of gender relations.

Since the twenties, one of the main institutional sources for the codification of masculinity in the US has been the corporation and the market, which has entailed a strong individualization of masculinity through practices of competition and self-reliance. By contrast, the world of meaning of the Israeli male was not the firm and the business world, but rather the army and the community, both of which revolve around the key cultural code of solidarity. In the same way that the business world institutionalized US codes of manhood, the Israeli army has been the main institution providing codes of masculinity. This code included such values as courage, military prowess, readiness in sacrificing oneself, but also a certain informality in interpersonal relations, the ability to withstand pressure, and to show solidarity with other men. Because the American man perceives other men as competitors and as potential threats that can rob him of his masculinity and power, "his" woman is the "soothing" source from which he gets reassurance and strength—hence a strong cultural emphasis on a model of femininity defined by gentleness and compassion. On the other hand, the Israeli man is more likely to view other men as a source of strength and support, with the result that the Israeli woman is not posited and constructed as the beautiful soul who heals, soothes, and calms the wounds inflicted on (her) man by other men. The world of reference of the Israeli man is other men—he receives affection, solidarity, and brotherhood from other men. Interestingly enough, Israeli women were not posited and constructed as *opposed* to males, but rather as a replica of the very qualities men demanded from each other.

One interesting example that attests to the cultural importance of the army with reference to romantic practices in Israel is brought forth in an article titled *Four Sad Love-Relationships*,[19] which addresses the story of four women who married their partners after the male was handicapped due to war wounds. The reporter begins her article by stating that from time to time she reads in the newspapers about handicapped men, "all war heroes," who marry beautiful women. The purpose of the article is thus to find out what compels these women to marry handicapped men. Most revealing are the words of two of the women interviewed. One of them says that her future husband had no doubt that he would recuperate after his injury, for "he was a proud injured man. After all, this happened to him in the army, and not due to an accident."[20] In the same vein, in answering to the question whether she was embarrassed being seen in public with her one-legged partner, another woman stated that "when you are a girlfriend of an I.D.F.'s handicapped man, it is an honor. He is not handicapped as a result of a car-accident."[21] Indeed, in many ways, being married to an injured soldier in Israel is being married to a living symbol that stands for the core values of the community. The social prestige conferred to his war-made handicap attenuates the hardship of this relationship for the female partner.

Love: A Prison House for Women?

To summarize our claims up to this point, at face value, the Israeli code of romantic love should satisfy many of the criteria posited by some feminist critiques of liberalism. Marriage and family are continuous with the public sphere; a result of the fact that the private is located on a continuum leading to the public sphere—rather than opposed to it—entails a far lesser prominence of love. This accompanies the fact that in the Israeli context, the private sphere is not exalted as a feminine sphere. Femininity is organized around motherhood, which in turn, is directly connected to the na-

---

19 *La'isha*, 8 January 1973, 5–7, 83–6, 88–9.

20 *La'isha*, 8 January 1973, 6.

21 *La'isha*, 8 January 1973, 84.

tion. In the same way that the public political activities of women are often constructed and justified as an expansion of their role in the private sphere (Herzog 1999, 269; Rapoport et al. 1995), their role in the private sphere is mixed and continuous with their collective self-definition.

In the Israeli context, romantic love differs from its American counterpart in that the private sphere is less differentiated from the public sphere, and has not been the object of an intensive discourse of morality. The main institutional sources of such meanings are the emphasis put by Jewish religion and ritual on fertility, the aggressive state policy encouraging fertility, and the institutionalization of femininity and masculinity in the army. The upshot of the weak separation between private and public spheres is that the cultural divisions between men and women are less marked than in the American context. In the following section, we would like to discuss the implication that such findings have for our understanding of the role of love and the private sphere in a project of women's emancipation.

The Israeli case invites a revision or at least a nuancing of the radical feminist critique of liberalism, of the private sphere, and of love. Many of the attacks on the private sphere and on the emotion supposed to preside over the private sphere are part of a broader feminist rejection of liberalism. This is not surprising, for to a great extent, feminisms' self-proclaimed tasks have been to take women out of the isolation and confinement of the private sphere (Landes 1998), and to take issue with the most fundamental assumption of liberalism, namely that the private sphere is the realm free of external influence (mostly of the state), in order to, therefore, be the realm of creativity and self-realization. Instead, radical feminist critiques argue, the liberal ideal of the private sphere excludes women both in the public and private spheres, because it is in the private sphere that women have been most oppressed (McKinnon 1989; Moller-Okin 1991, Pateman 1989). Jean Bethke Elshtain who, more than most other feminists, has rehabilitated the private sphere, also distances herself from liberal feminism because it does not value the private sphere enough, and empties it from content by reducing motherhood to one formal role among others (Elshtain 1981). Other feminists have indicted liberalism for its conception of the individual as an atomistic entity, striving for autonomy, thus obliterating and devaluing women's social embeddedness and ethical orientation toward caring (Chodorow 1978; Gilligan 1993). Against the liberal view which claims that the state must and does stop at the threshold of the family, feminists have shown that the state has, in fact, shaped the unequal structure of roles inside the family and that the "separate" spheres are in fact solidly interconnected through patriarchy (Pateman 1989). This suspicion of the private sphere leads many feminists to accept the view offered by anthropologist Michelle Rosaldo that women's status "will be lowest in those societies where there is a firm differentiation between domestic and public spheres of activity and where women are isolated from one another and placed under a single man's authority in the home." Rosaldo further suggests that "perhaps the most egalitarian societies are those in which public and domestic spheres are [...] weakly differentiated" (quoted in Elshtain 1981, 338).

By this standard, the Israeli case should have offered us an example of gender relations more equalitarian than those found in a liberal polity. Indeed, not only is the ideology of romantic love far less prominent in Israel than in America, but Israeli women have been allowed to bear arms and to participate actively in the army. Furthermore, they have not been as essentialized and locked into a rigid ideology of femininity, they have entertained numerous informal relationships with men in positions of power, and they have not been as isolated from the public sphere as their American counterparts. All these characteristics should have yielded a more egalitarian gender structure and gender ideology than in the US. Yet, we would like to suggest, this is far from being the case, and this in turn should invite a reevaluation of the traditional feminist critiques of love. We suggest instead that an empirical comparative analysis evaluating love in the context of liberal and communitarian polities might yield new insights on the role of the private sphere in the constitution of women's autonomy.

When compared to the American case, the Israeli case disproves Rosaldo's claim that weakly differentiated private and public spheres generate greater equality between men and women. The contrary seems to be true: because masculinity is institutionalized in key state organizations (the army) and functions, symbolically, as if it were the collective body writ large, and because the private sphere is not opposed to the public sphere but rather subservient to it, Israeli women have had to align themselves more closely around hegemonic masculinity—which in the Israeli context defines and validates them primarily as mothers.

In this context, it may become clearer why we argue that liberal social organization gives more leeway to women: precisely because the nexus running from the state to the private sphere is looser than it is in a communitarian polity. That is to say, because the communitarian family embeds the family and the state more tightly as a single unit, it makes it more difficult to develop a sense of separateness from the body collective, to challenge its assumptions on the basis of claims to individual self-fulfillment. In this respect, romantic love opens up a cultural space to challenge, if not patriarchy itself, at least the family institution.

Acknowledgements

An earlier version of this chapter has appeared in Hebrew as Illouz and Wilf (2004).

References

Abu-Lughod, Lila (1986). *Veiled Sentiments: Honor and Poetry in a Bedouin Society.* Berkley: University of California Press.

Alberoni, F. (1983). *Falling in Love.* New York: Random House.

Arendt, Hannah (1958). *The Human Condition: A Study of the Central Dilemmas Facing Modern Man.* Chicago: The University of Chicago Press.

Bailey, B. L. (1993). *From Front Porch to Back Seat: Courtship in Twentieth-Century America.* Baltimore: Johns Hopkins University Press.

Barbalet, Jack M. (1998). *Emotion, Social Theory, and Social Structure: A Macrosociological Approach.* Cambridge: Cambridge University Press.

Beauvoir, Simone de (1970). *The Second Sex.* New York: Bantam Books.

Beck, Ulrich, and Elisabeth Beck-Gernsheim (1995). *The Normal Chaos of Love.* Cambridge: Polity Press.

Ben-Ari, Eyal (2001). Tests of Soldierhood, Trials of Manhood: Military Service and Male Ideals in Israel. In Daniel Maman, Eyal Ben-Ari, and Zeev Rosenhek (eds.). *Military, State, and Society in Israel: Theoretical and Comparative Perspectives,* 239–67. New Brunswick: Transaction Publishers.

Bernstein, D. (1987). *The Struggle for Equality: Women Workers in the Palestine "Yishuv."* Tel-Aviv: Hakibbutz Hameuchad. [in Hebrew]

Biale, D. (1992). *Eros and the Jews: From Biblical Israel to Contemporary America.* New York: Basic Books.

Cancian, Francesca M. (1987). *Love in America: Gender and Self-Development.* Cambridge: Cambridge University Press.

Chodorow, Nancy (1978). *The Reproduction of Mothering: Psychoanalysis and the Sociology of Gender.* Berkeley: University of California Press.

Cott, Nancy F. (1977). *The Bonds of Womanhood: "Woman's Sphere" in New-England, 1780–1835*. New Haven: Yale University Press.

— (1988). The Bonds of Womanhood. In Robert N. Bellah and Richard Madsen (eds.). *Individualism and Commitment in American Life: Readings on the Themes of Habits of the Heart*, 125–35. New York: Harper and Row.

D'Emillio, John, and Estelle B. Freedman (1988). *Intimate Matters: A History of Sexuality in America*. New York: Harper & Row.

Demos, J. (1997). Oedipus and America: Historical Perspectives on the Reception of Psychoanalysis in the United States. In J. Pfister and N. Schnog (eds.). *Inventing the Psychological: Toward a Cultural History of Emotional Life in America*, 63–78. New Haven: Yale University Press.

Douglas, A. (1978). *The Feminization of American Culture*. New York: A. A. Knopf.

Ehrenreich, Barbara, and Deirdre English (1978). *For Her own Good: 150 Years of the Experts' Advice to Women*. New York: Anchor Press.

Elshtain, Jean Bethke (1981). *Public Man, Private Woman: Women in Social and Political Thought*. Princeton: Princeton University Press.

— (1995). *Democracy on Trial*. New York: Basic Books.

Firestone, Shulamith (1979). *The Dialectic of Sex: The Case for Feminist Revolution*. New York: Bantam Books.

Geertz, Clifford (1973). The Impact of the Concept of Culture on the Concept of Man. In his *The Interpretation of Cultures*, 33–54. New York: Basic Books.

Giddens, Anthony (1992). *The Transformation of Intimacy: Sexuality, Love, and Eroticism in Modern Societies*. Cambridge: Polity Press.

Gilligan, C. (1993). *In a Different Voice: Psychological Theory and Women's Development*. Cambridge: Harvard University Press.

Gillis, J. (1988). From Ritual to Romance: Toward an Alternative History of Love. In Carol Zisowitz Stearns and Peter N. Stearns (eds.). *Emotion and Social Change: Toward a New Psychology*, 87–122. New York: Holmes and Meier.

Herzog, Hanna (1999). *Gendering Politics: Women in Israel*. Ann Arbor: The University of Michigan Press.

Illouz, Eva (1991). Reason Within Passion: Love in Women's Magazines. *Critical Studies in Mass Communication*, 8, 231–48.

— (1997). *Consuming the Romantic Utopia: Love and the Cultural Contradictions of Capitalism*. Berkley: University of California Press.

Illouz, Eva, and Eitan Wilf (2004). Hearts or Wombs? A Cultural Critique of Radical Feminist Critiques of Love. *Theory and Criticism*, 25 (Fall), 205–34. [in Hebrew]

Katriel, Tamar (1986). *Talking Straight: Dugri Speech in Israeli Sabra Culture*. Cambridge: Cambridge University Press.

Katz, Elihu, Hadassah Haas, and Michael Gurevitch (1997). 20 Years of Television in Israel: Are There Long-Run Effects on Values, Social Connectedness, and Cultural Practices? *Journal of Communication*, 47 (2), 3–20.

Kimmel, M. S. (1996). *Manhood in America: A Cultural History*. New York: The Free Press.

Kimmerling, Baruch (1982). *Zionism and Economy*. Cambridge: Schenkman.

— (1999). Religion, Nationalism, and Democracy in Israel. *Constellations*, 6 (3), 339–63.

Landes, Joan B. (ed.). (1998). *Feminism, the Public and the Private*. Oxford: Oxford University Press.

Lévinas, Emmanuel (1963). *Difficile Liberté: Essais sur le Judaïsme*. Paris: A. Michel.

Lissak, M. (1995). Immigration, Absorption and Society Building in the Jewish Community in Eretz-Israel (1918–1930). In M. Lissak (ed.). *The History of the Jewish Community in Eretz-Israel Since 1882 (The Period of the British Mandate, Part 2)*, 173–302. Jerusalem: The Bialik Institute.

Luhmann, Niklas (1986). *Love as Passion: The Codification of Intimacy*. Cambridge: Harvard University Press.

Lutz, C. A. (1988). Emotion, Thought and Estrangement: Western Discourses on Feeling. In her *Unnatural Emotions: Everyday Sentiments on a Micronesian Atoll and Their Challenge to Western Theory*, 53–80. Chicago: The University of Chicago Press.

Lystra, K. (1989). *Searching the Heart*. New York: Oxford University Press.

MacKinnon, Catherine A. (1989). Abortion: On Public and Private. In her *Toward a Feminist Theory of the State*, 184–94. Cambridge: Harvard University Press.

Martin, M. L., and E. S. McCrate (1984). *The Military, Militarism, and the Polity: Essays in Honor of Morris Janowitz*. New York: The Free Press.

Moller-Okin, S. (1991). *Justice, Gender, and the Family*. New York: Basic Books.

Nussbaum, Martha. C. (1999). *Sex and Social Justice*. New York: Oxford University Press.

Ozment, Steven (2001). *Ancestors: The Loving Family in Old Europe*. Cambridge: Harvard University Press.

Pateman, Carole (1989). *The Disorder of Women: Democracy, Feminism, and Political Theory*. Stanford: Stanford University Press.

Portuguese, J. (1998). *Fertility Policy in Israel: The Politics of Religion, Gender, and Nation*. Westport: Praeger.

Rapoport, Tamar, Anat Penso, and Yoni Garb (1995). Religious-Zionist Adolescent Girls Contribute to the Nation. *Te'orya ve-Bikoret*, 7, 223–34. [in Hebrew]

Rich, Adrienne (1995). *Of Woman Born: Motherhood as Experience and Institution*. New York, London: Norton and Company.

Rosaldo, Michelle Zimbalist (1980). *Knowledge and Passion: Ilongot Notions of Self and Social Life*. New York: Cambridge University Press.

Rosaldo, Renato (1980). *Ilongot Headhunting, 1883–1974: A Study in Society and History*. Stanford: Stanford University Press.

Rothman, E. (1984). *Hands and Hearts*. Cambridge: Harvard University Press.

Rousseau, Jean-Jacques (1911). *Emile*. London: Dent.

Rubin, S. (1987). *Patterns of Continuity and Change in Women's Magazines in Israel.* M.A. thesis, Hebrew University of Jerusalem. [in Hebrew]

Sasson-Levy, O. (2000). *Construction of Gender Identities Within the Israeli Army.* Ph.D diss., Hebrew University of Jerusalem. [in Hebrew]

Shorter, Edward (1975). *The Making of the Modern Family.* New York: Basic Books.

Silverman, Kaja (1983). *The Subject of Semiotics.* New York: Oxford University Press.

Simonds, W. (1992). *Women and Self-Help Culture: Reading Between the Lines.* New Brunswick: Rutgers University Press.

Smith-Rosenberg, Carroll (1986). *Disorderly Conduct: Visions of Gender in Victorian America.* New York: Oxford University Press.

Stearns, Carol Zisowitz, and Peter N. Stearns (eds.). (1988). *Emotion and Social Change: Toward a New Psychology.* New York: Holmes and Meier.

Stearns, Peter N. (1993). Girls, Boys, and Emotions: Redefinitions and Historical Change. *Journal of American History,* 80 (1), 36–73.

Sternhell, Z. (1997). *The Founding Myths of Israel: Nationalism, Socialism, and the Making of the Jewish State.* Princeton: Princeton University Press.

Stone, L. (1979). *The Family, Sex, and Marriage in England 1500–1800.* New York: Harper and Row.

Swidler, Ann (2001). *Talk of Love: How Culture Matters.* Chicago: University of Chicago Press.

Vincent-Buffault, A. (1991). *The History of Tears: Sensibility and Sensuality in France.* Hampshire: Macmillan Press.

Vogiel-Bijaoui, S. (1999). Families in Israel: Between Familism to Postmodernism. In D. Yizraeli (ed.). *Sex, Gender, Politics,* 107–66. Tel-Aviv: Hakibbutz Hameuchad.

Weitman, Sasha (1998). On the Elementary Forms of the Socioerotic Life. *Theory, Culture, and Society,* 15 (3): 71–110.

Winship, J. (1980). *Advertising in Women's Magazines, 1956–74.* Birmingham: Center for Contemporary Cultural Studies, University of Birmingham.

Zaretsky, Eli (1994). Identity Politics: Its Roots in Romanticism, Psychoanalysis, and the Enlightenment. In Craig Calhoun (ed.). *Social Theory and the Politics of Identity: From Persons to Nations,* 198–215. New York: Blackwell.

Mediatizing Traumas in the Risk Society: A Sociology of Emotions Approach

Nicolas Demertzis

Introduction

In mainstream clinical psychology the study of traumatization emerged at the end of the seventies and early eighties (Ehrenreich 2003). In cultural sociology and cultural studies at large, studying traumas is a relatively fresh social-scientific endeavor. It is without doubt attributable to the legacy of the Holocaust, the other atrocities of World War II, the numerous civil wars, the veterans' experience of the Vietnam War, the racial and ethnic conflicts, the crimes committed by military regimes and dictatorships, the gender inequalities and the concomitant politics of recognition that contributed to their formation. They have been also fueled by the more recent experiences of post communist nationalist conflicts and genocides (in Yugoslavia, Chechnya, Rwanda and elsewhere), the terrorist attacks in New York, Madrid and London as well as by the so called war against terrorism, the dramatic natural disasters and the abundance of hazardous environmental conditions due to human activity. In a way, from Japan and China to South Africa, and from Northern Ireland and Kosovo to Latin America, the contemporary world seems to be haunted by traumatic memories intrinsically related to the (re)construction of national and local histories, and the (re)formation of collective identities. It is not accidental, therefore, that a number of scholars talk about our times and culture as "trauma time" (Edkins 2003, xiv) and "the culture of trauma" (Miller and Tougaw 2002, 2). Nor is it accidental that the new sub-fields of memory studies, trauma studies and disaster studies have appeared in social science and humanities in tandem with the sociology of emotions.

Of course, national identities have been always constructed via the interplay of remembering and forgetting that forges the difference with the national Other, the reference to a national heartland, the testimonial of predecessors' blood, and the selective, as it were, definition of righteous victims and villain perpetrators. All these are old and familiar discursive strategies. What is new in the post-Cold War period is not only the perpetuation of wars and violence that produce new victims and traumas, as horrendous as they might be, but two additional elements: firstly, in the newly formed international environment almost everybody (states, groups, nationalities, ethnicities, movements, etc.) wants to take the position of the victim without currently being one; in a time when victimhood and survivor status have attained substantial symbolic value, they wish that they had been victims in the past, without wishing to be in the present (Todorov 1995; Koulouri 2002). This helps them to legitimize current acts of violence in the name of a discursively elaborated, in other words mythologized, past (e.g. the Israeli-Palestinian conflict). Secondly, the generalization of traumatic experiences of all sorts and, what is more, the global dissemination of their (tele)visualization calls for a newly, late modern, emerging politics of pity and moral stance, which is no less ambivalent than modern ethics.

The central purpose of this essay is to connect the cultural sociological notion of trauma with the notion of risk society and look at them through the perspective of the sociology of emotions. This is accomplished by exploring the links between memory and trauma studies, on the one hand, and delving into the moral consequences of the visualization of traumatic experiences, on the other.

Cultural-Social and Psychic Trauma

As a matter of fact, scholars engaged in trauma/memory studies, either directly and extensively or latently and minimally, refer to the concept of psychic trauma, as it has been originally outlined by Freud. Obviously, there is a huge time interval separating the concept of cultural-social trauma and the concept of psychic or psychological trauma and the vicissitudes of the traumatic in psychoanalytic literature. From his *Studies on Hysteria* (Freud and Breuer 1956) up to *Moses* (1986), Freud attributes a key position to the concept in order to understand the (dys)functions of the psychic organ. On the other side of the Atlantic, for twenty-five years now, under the pressure of the anti-war and feminist movements and also of the psychic diseases of the veterans of Vietnam, the American Psychiatric

Association in 1980 added a new category in its diagnostic guide: the Post Traumatic Stress Disorder (PTSD). Therefore, "trauma" either as a psychoanalytic or as a clinical psychological concept has been present for many decades (Edkins 2003, 2–3, 42–3).

On the contrary, "cultural-social trauma" is a much newer concept that taps a multitude of social phenomena which are related to the transgressing of the boundaries and terms of reproduction of social systems and subsystems (crises, wars, risks, ethnic cleansings, genocides, etc.). It is forwarded systematically as a distinct sociological concept referring to institutional changes, to the constitution of collective memory and to forms of collective action; doing that, it steers clear from similar notions advocated by psychologists ("mass trauma," "collective trauma," "historical trauma," etc.) which are quite un-theorized or treated deterministically according to applied psychosocial models (Ehrenreich 2003; Pupavac 2007). In this section I shall attempt to trace the elective affinities and the differences between the psychic-clinical and the cultural-social trauma, proposing thus a reflective intersection of the two which may give a more articulate frame of analysis.

Relating the Two Concepts

Transcribed to the semantic field of *cultural sociology*, the concept of cultural-social trauma has been elaborated by Alexander et al. (2004). This transcription was thought to be necessary since a significant amount of bibliography had already been published in the fields of psychology, psychoanalysis, social psychology and literary criticism, where "trauma" occupied a central position (Leys 2000; Kansteiner 2004). The authors wanted to differentiate themselves from previous uses of the term, especially from psychological/psychoanalytic ones, in order to point out its significance in the analysis of social (not personal) issues and phenomena. However, they did not discuss the way in which their theory is related to the newly-formed sociological "trauma" studies—or even to the destruction studies—, to the formation of which both psychology and psychoanalysis has notably contributed (Misztal 2003, 139). Had they demonstrated such a relation, the links between their cultural sociological approach of trauma would join ranks with the psychoanalytic point of view.

In any case, by establishing a locus of differentiation, the authors have come across to think that even when people experience simultaneously and massively a negative, harmful or catastrophic, event (such as, for example, a 9 Richter "global" earthquake), it is inadequate to outline a discourse of "cultural" or/and "social" trauma. This is because an event of massive proportions of catastrophes lacks subjective meaning; cultural-social trauma involves the realization (in both meanings of the word, that is as becoming conscious of something and as something becoming real) of a common plight. It has to be defined collectively as such in order to influence the systems of reference of a whole society or, at least, of a significant part of it and change established roles, norms, and narratives. In other words, it has to function as a total social event and not just as the aggregate of nume-rous individual experiences. A traumatogenic event (whether it is the result of a natural disaster or a social dislocation like, for example, a civil war) does not in itself constitute a "trauma." In order to become "trauma," it has to undergo a process of social signification; namely, it has to be signi-fied and become socially accepted and constructed as "trauma."[1]

However, the adoption of social constructionism cannot sustain the sharp differentiation of the cultural from the psychological trauma in the manner, as well as to the degree that the aforementioned authors argue—especially Alexander (2004; 2003, 85–107). To be more precise: when Alexander states that trauma does not draw "naturally" from the events themselves (as a commonplace understanding based on the positivism of the PTSD would have it, a position that he lingers over psychoanalysis as well), but from their representation and social-semantic definition, it would be arguable that such a position violates open doors. By mentioning, for instance, that cultural trauma occurs when members of a collectivity feel that they have suffered a horrendous event that leaves indelible marks upon their group consciousness, marking their memories for ever and changing their future identity in fundamental and irrevocable ways (2004, 1), Alexander doesn't only go beyond the Freudian conceptualization of trauma, but he positions himself as being outmoded, to a certain extent. This is because the trauma of the earlier, at least, childhood, according to Freud, may well be a crack of the protective shield (*Reizschutz*), but still it is

---

1 According to Sztompka's definition (2004, 165–6), "The cultural traumas generated by major social changes and triggered by traumatizing conditions and situations *interpreted* as threatening, unjust and improper, are expressed by complex social moods, characterized by a number of collective emotions, orientations and attitudes" (my emphasis).

always a retrospective experience, whose meaning is always constructed *a posteriori* (Laplanche and Pontalis 1986, 503–7).

Traumas are at first repressed, stay latent and are then retrieved if and when the right circumstances exist, acquiring thereof a meaning for the subject. So, psychic trauma does not follow automatically. Emerging as a symptom (neurosis of traumatic causation) at a latter time, when the subject faces circumstances which activate repressed negative feelings and when the defense mechanisms start to be loosened, psychic trauma is always a reconstruction.

Therefore, the psychic traumas as well as the cultural trauma are belated experiences, a memory and a reconstruction of a negative encounter. As a matter of fact, for Freud (1986, 317) the psychic trauma does not necessarily result from a bodily experience or a consequence of a specific event (as in the case of cultural trauma). It could well be a completion of an impression or a fantasy. From this point of view, Freud articulates a more radical constructionism than the one professed by Alexander, who nonetheless merely mentions (2004, 8–9) that sometimes events that are deeply traumatizing may not actually have occurred at all.

Another common characteristic of the two concepts is the intense and continuous impact of the traumatic experience: largely, cultural trauma brings about irreversible changes to collective memory and identity; psychic trauma brings about durable harmful effects to the psychic constitution of the subject. However, not all of the negative and hurtful circumstances lead to trauma (whether cultural-social or clinical-psychic). It is the process of social construction (e.g. cultures of revenge are conducive to trauma formation *vis-à-vis* cultures of forgiveness) that transforms selectively a risky and painful condition into "trauma" as a boundary mark of social memory and collective identity. Likewise, according to Freud (2003, 85–6), a traumatizing condition is converted into trauma when its "quantity" is such that the dynamics of the pleasure principle cannot master it any more. In both cases, the "pre-traumatic" conditions selectively determine to a high degree the very formation of trauma, as well as the post-traumatic stage. The experience of good motherhood, of a developed ego-ideal, the ability to work through and incorporate, are certain internal pre-traumatic factors that bound the formation of psychic trauma and allow for the individual's adjustment to the post-traumatic environment, reducing in that way the manifestation of symptoms. Correspondingly, cultural trauma always poses a question: "trauma for whom?" This is so because the inequality of economic, symbolic, social and political capital influences—if not determines altogether—the vulnerability of the particular social groups facing the traumatizing circumstances. Not everyone suffers from trauma in the same way nor does everyone adopt the same strategies for dealing with it (Sztompka 2004, 166–7). With regards to war traumas one could argue that there are manifold personal, political and social factors, as well as domestic and international circumstances, which mediate war experiences and influence whether an individual does or does not become traumatized (Pupavac 2007).

Neil Smelser tries to develop a more sophisticated articulation of psychic and cultural-social trauma. He makes extensive use of Freudian and other psychoanalytic and psychological texts and, by avoiding psychological reductionism, proposes a fourfold typology of the mechanisms for dealing with trauma—mainly psychic trauma (denial, projection, reaction formation, and depersonalization). Adopting the paradigm of social constructionism, Smelser (2004, 44) offers the most complete definition of cultural trauma:

"A memory accepted and publicly given credence by a relevant membership group and evoking an event or situation, which is (a) laden with negative affect, (b) represented as indelible, and (c) regarded as threatening a society's existence or violating one or more of its fundamental cultural presuppositions."

Drawing on empirical material from the American Civil War, Pearl Harbor, the internment of American citizens of Japanese descent in 1942, Vietnam and September 11th—and in accordance to the above definition—he shows that the study of cultural-social trauma should be articulated within the sphere of three interrelated levels: the cognitive, the emotive and the mnemonic. He argues (2004, 36–7) that a given historical event or situation may qualify as trauma at one moment in a society's history but not in another, and while that event may not be traumatic for other societies is more likely to constitute trauma in afflicted societies. Hence, "cultural traumas are for the most part historically made, not born." He also emphasizes the selective nature of memory, stressing the mediating role of intellectuals, social movements, the media, journalists, educational institutions and various other moral entrepreneurs. Cultural trauma has to be understood, explained and publicly represented through discourse. Since cultural traumas do not arise by themselves and *ex nihilo*, then, arguably, they are the historical products of discursive (re)constructions. A classic case in point is presented by the traumatic narratives of origin that deal with the (re)birth of the nation: mostly, this formation means wars, genocides, sacrifices and losses which are the cornerstones upon which nations, as imaginary political communities, are founded. Such shaping involves the interplay between memory and oblivion in the selective invention of a tradition on the base of which collective identities are constituted (Demertzis 1996, 95–100; Misztal 2003, 37–49, 139–45). In this process there are various interests fighting against each other, from the top (elite) as well as from the bottom (the people, the underdogs etc.), since the traumatic content of an event has to prevail retroactively and hegemonize the alternative conceptions. This process is a kind of "symbolic struggle," a "drama of trauma," and a "speech act" *à la* Austin, whose outcome leaves deep traces on collective identity, on the networks of social capital and on the personality structure.

Another elective affinity between the psychic and the cultural trauma, following Smelser's argumentation, is that both concepts give birth to, and are accompanied by, negative feelings and emotions. Terror, anxiety, fear, shame, humiliation, anger, disgust and guilt are some of the negative feelings stirred by the breaking of the social bond and the normative system of reference. Smelser is categorical as to the importance of affect in the analysis of cultural trauma: "if a potentially traumatizing event cannot be endowed with negative affect (e.g. a national tragedy, a national shame, a national catastrophe), then it cannot qualify as being traumatic" (2004, 40). One could argue that the "universal language" of the basic negative emotions as described by Ekman (1993) i.e. fear, anger, sadness, disgust, is necessary in the negotiation of the meaning of a traumatic event.[2] If the impetus of negative affects is not activated, an event cannot be defined and interjected as threatening, disastrous, harmful, and so on.

---

2 The "universal language" of the basic emotions does not imply a naturalist conception of emotion in general. To my mind, basic emotions provide a minimum of affective universals, a thin foundation whereby an infinite array of situationally formed emotions flourish. Between the strong cases of the organic and the extreme constructionist approach, I adopt an intermediate approach of mild constructionism, based on the idea that everything is not a construction or constructible with regard to emotions. A contemporary historian summarizes what Hume, James and other great thinkers of emotions took for granted: "nearly everyone agrees that there is a biological substratum to emotions that simply cannot be denied, but emotions themselves are extremely plastic" (Rosenwein 2001, 231). See also Kövecses' (2000) formulation of "body-based social constructionism," which he argues enables us to see anger and its counterparts as both universal and culture specific.

It could be argued, however, that affection also offers an additional account equally important to our argument: this account refers both to the phylogenetic and the ontogenetic bridge which connects the cultural and the psychic trauma. A cultural trauma may bring about dramatic changes and ruptures to the systems of reference and the politico-economic structures of a society or a wide social group (a civil war for example); yet, it is the individuals as individuals who interiorize and feel the impact of these societal changes, so that the trauma of the macro-level (cultural-social trauma) is retranslated in terms of the micro-level (psychic-personal and clinical trauma). As we know from the sociology of emotion, emotions[3] are links that join the collective and the individual, social structures and individual behavior; in addition, emotions are seen as intervening variables in the maintenance, modification, or disruption of society (Barbalet 1998, 27). This holds true for the psychology of emotions as well; for Oatley and Jenkins (1996, 122, 124, 130) emotions structure our relations with others in the sense that they establish, maintain, change, or terminate the relation between the person and the environment on matters of significance to the person.

Finally, Smelser insists on the analogy of the defense and working through mechanisms in both kinds of trauma, clinical and cultural. He underscores the "displacement" and "projection" with regards to the attribution of responsibility and the rationalization of trauma. In situations of cultural trauma, moral panics, the demonization of the other, scapegoats, expiatory victims, conspiratorial explanations of history, and so on, constitute defense mechanisms which belong to the same class as those concerning psychic trauma. Another similar defense mechanism is the double tendency of remembering and forgetting. For one and the same traumatic event, precisely because it constitutes a field of competing interpretations and significations, there is, on the one hand, the demand to "leave everything behind us," but there is also the injunction to "preserve our historical memory." By way of analogy, in clinical cases of psychic traumas we can observe in one and the same person denial and avoidance (amnesia, emo-

---

3 Often in the sociology of emotion the terms "emotion," "feeling," "affect," "sentiment" and "passion" are used interchangeably. This is not the place to raise the question of the definition of emotion which ultimately leads to an endless and counterintuitive argumentation. However, for the sake of the argument I offer hereby a working definition; by "emotion" (or feeling) I refer to the arousal of the human organism that takes place within a definite time context, involves awareness but not necessarily verbalization, and induces readiness for action and evaluations of objects, relations and situations.

tional paralysis, repression, etc.), but also the reliving of trauma through repetition compulsion.

Dismembering the Two Concepts

It is clear that there are a number of common elements between the social-cultural and the psychic trauma: they are both retroactive constructions, they are accompanied by negative feelings, they leave permanent traces and activate similar defense mechanisms. So, where lays their differences? It would be an outmoded mistake to point them at the micro *versus* macro pseudo-differentiation. Freud himself (1986; 1977) had from the very start relativized the distinction between individual and social psychology, and modern social theory has long ago aimed at the non-reductive bridging of the gap between the macro and the micro level (Giddens 1984, 139–44).

There are three fundamental differences between the two concepts. As Eyerman suggests (2001, 3; 2004, 61), we can still talk of cultural trauma without it having been necessarily felt by everyone, directly or indirectly. In order for a cultural trauma to exist it does not have to be felt directly by everyone, since some take it up indirectly from the selective social memory (as happens to the next generations of a civil war or a genocide), and it does not have to involve everyone. Obviously, not all Jews were equally affected by the Nazi's "final solution," plenty of them actually exempted it; yet it does not follow that they have not been affected by the Holocaust trauma (Lev-Wiesel 2007). Cultural-social trauma is not only grounded on group-specific communicative or social memories—i.e. commonly shared bad memories experienced personally and instigating a host of negative emotions—but on cultural or historical memories which are not necessarily lived first hand by everyone. In memory studies, "cultural" or "historical" memories are those which exist independent of their carriers, are institutionally shaped via a number of mnemotechniques and mediated by books, commemorating holidays, media, educational systems, popular culture and so on (Levy and Sznaider 2002). Of course, they elicit negative emotions as well. In both ways, therefore, traumas mark collective memory, thus molding the socialization mechanisms and the identity formation processes of the generations to come. Even if some or many people are exempt from this process, the cultural-social trauma does not stop existing and producing permanent effects. Something like that cannot be said, of course, not even by way of analogy, about the psychic-clinical trauma.

The second difference has to do with the mechanisms of instituting and sustaining trauma. Clinical trauma is constituted and administered by the inner-psychic mechanisms of repression, denial, adjustment and working through. On the contrary, cultural trauma results from discursive-authoritative mechanisms of defining (and therefore instituting) an event as being traumatic (Smelser 2004, 38–9; Edkins 2003, 44–5). Competing issue claimers, interest groups, the organic and traditional intellectuals of Gramsci or the free-floating intellectuals of Mannheim, and the media contest for: a) the very existence of the traumatic event itself (e.g. the dispute concerning the truth of the Holocaust); b) its interpretation (was the 1946–49 clash in Greece a "civil war" or an "insurgence of gangs?"); c) the proper accompanying emotions (anger, sadness, nostalgia, guilt, shame, disgust, pride, etc.).

The third difference is that the psychic trauma may well not be related to a particular event, but to be structured around a fantasy. On the contrary, cultural trauma is always formed by referring to an event, whose accuracy, memory and significance is negotiable. Cultural-social trauma is related to an event or events whose significance and meaning may be negotiated and constructed discursively; its meaning is not derived out of thin air, as there is a factual basis, whatever its exactness, prior to any symbolic mediation. Its "fate" (i.e. its characterization as trauma or not) depends on the specific "regime of signification." Two examples elucidate this argument: in early December 1938 the Japanese army invaded China and slaughtered 300,000 civilian Chinese in the Nanking area within a six week period. This extremity was known to the international public opinion from the start. However, it was never constituted as a national "trauma" for China itself, for Japan or even as a trauma for humanity as such, as it was with the case of the Jewish Holocaust (Alexander 2003, 106). It is well known that in 1995 a horrendous atrocity, perpetrated by the Serbs, took place in the Bosnian city of Srebrenica during the war in Yugoslavia; for more than a decade the Bosnians, as well as other constituents of the European public opinion, have been at pains to name that atrocity as genocide, while Serbia was denied it. At the end of the day, in 2007, it was The Hague International Court which characterized that atrocity as genocide without, however, putting the blame to Serbia as a state.

Traumas and Risk Society

Irrespective of the conceptual similarities and differences between cultural-social and clinical-psychic trauma, the theory of cultural trauma carries special weight for the analysis of contemporary societies. It has been put forward as a middle range theory (Alexander 2004, 24) in order to give answers to urgent conceptual and normative questions of "risk society." Therefore, it is not by chance that this theory (and memory and trauma studies for that matter) has achieved prominence within the late modern risk society (meaning the society of other-inflicted and involuntary risk), in which the state of emergency threatens to become the normal state (Beck 1992, 24, 79). This prominence has a double sense: a) there is a slow but undisputable spreading of the idea of the subject as "that-which-can-be-hurt;" and b) there is a loss of trust in institutions, systems, and reference groups.

As to the first property of prominence, it should come as no surprise that risk society is a traumatizing and traumatized society, a society whose self-image is no longer organized around the dominant and, in many ways, reassuring signifier "progress." But what is qualitatively different in risk society, such that it changes the experience of trauma? Arguably, in the past people were definitely running many risks and were exposed to hazardous conditions; but these were particular and isolated risks to be coped with separately and within the optimistic emotional climate of "progress," "development," "modernization," and so on. Nowadays, on the contrary, the very self is in danger; gradually, individuals feel unprotected and deprived of resilience (Furedi 2004). It is precisely because the discourse of progress and development has been more or less replaced by the discourse of crisis and fear that "trauma" tends to develop into one of the central imaginary significations of late modern societies. Here Cornelius Castoriadis' terminology is used on purpose in order to illustrate that nowadays reference to trauma, with all its cognitive and emotional implications, is *inter alia* a way in which society as a whole, as well as a particular social group, may think and speak of itself (Castoriades 1987). Somehow, it is a semiotic means for the self-representation and self-understanding of societies, groups, and individuals. More precisely, for Castoriadis' analysis—which of course cannot not be given herein the space it deserves—a central imaginative signification is not an image of something or someone, nor is it reduced to, or derivative of something "objective," external and non-imaginative. Rather, it constitutes and posits social being and social action by giving meaning to, and defining what is and what is not, what is worthwhile and what is not worthwhile. A central imaginative signification reorganizes, reforms, and re-determines retroactively the host of meanings and significances already available in a society or social group; in this way it can offer a new, and adversarial for that matter, interpretative frame of social reality(ies). It operates in the way a "master signifier" functions according to the advocates of Lacanian social theory, i.e. as a special signifier that quilts the chain of floating signifiers providing a nodal point in the production and circulation of discourse (Žižek 1989, 100–5; Laclau and Mouffe 1985, 105, 112; Stavrakakis 1999, 127–8). In this way discourses organized as particular and different entities; e.g. "nature," "terrorism," "freedom," and "the people" articulate the environmental discourse, the bellicose discourse of the Bush Administration, the neo-liberal economic discourse, and the populist political discourse, respectively. Thus the point is not that people did not have any traumatic experiences in the past. It is rather that the signifier "trauma" has become a nodal point, a central signification through which many individuals and social groups can imagine themselves retroactively as past, current, or virtual victims.

To be sure, the upgrading of "trauma" to the status of a central imaginative signification does not come out of thin air, nor is it a mere scheme of speech. It derives from the very dynamic of the late modern risk society itself which not only systematically produces threats about hazardous situations in the future (e.g. nuclear risks), but entails the politics of fear (Anselmi and Gouliamos 1998; Smith 2006; Richards 2007) which in effect makes for the description of contemporary society as "angst society" instead of "risk society" (Scott 2000).

As to the second sense of prominence, regarding the case of the signifier "crisis" (Koselleck 1988), trauma also originates in medical discourse and it is precisely as a metaphor that we use it in this context; it is a metaphor we live by. Yet, since it is not a dead metaphor and its metaphorical meaning is constantly under negotiation, the analysis of cultural trauma could give rise to an ambivalent attitude: on the one hand, trauma can activate the logic of self-fulfilling prophecy, victimizing the subject and cultivating a fatalistic culture of risk and helplessness (Žižek 1997, 136). This victimization is accompanied and supported by the breaking of bonds of social trust and confidence. As Edkins (2003, 4) notes, an event is called traumatic not only when it offends the subject's capabilities, but when at the same time it implies the betrayal and breaching of relations of trust. Similarly, Beck (1992, 28, 61) maintains that "risks experienced presume a normative horizon of lost security and broken trust" and that risk is lived nowadays as a condensation of "wounded images of a life worth living" and its side effects have "voices, faces, eyes and tears." Therefore, the insistence on cynicism, nihilism, anti-party sentiments, and distrust, apparent in social theory and political sociology literature of the last two decades (Sloterdijk 1988; Goldfarb 1991; Bewes 1997), should be appreciated in connection with the more recent sociology of trauma and emotions.

On the other hand, however, it is outlined that cultural traumas have the capacity to widen the field of social understanding and sympathy. Their institutionalization implies necessarily the designation of victims, the attribution of responsibility and the allocation of material and symbolic consequences. Earlier in this paper it was argued that, frequently, cultural-social trauma is *inter alia* constituted via historical memories in the articulation of which the media plays a crucial role. In the following section the media's influence is analyzed further by focusing on the possible moral consequences of the mediatization of traumas, i.e. the visualization of others' suffering.

Media, Trauma, and Morality

The strong feelings that accompany cultural-social trauma entail the identification with the victims, not only of those who suffer from it in the first place (inner group), but also of the wider public. Here, a crucial (although often ambivalent) role is played by the media since the extended availability of their messages about people's suffering allows forms of empathy with distant others (Thompson 1995, 258–65; Baer 2001). Observing the pain of others through the media does not always follow the logic of the spectacle and does not always give birth to "quasi-emotions;" namely, emotions which do not motivate, do not endure in time and which mortify our sensitivities (Meštrović 1997). A common wisdom in the critical media debate is that suffering is commodified chiefly by the electronic media and the audience becomes passive spectators of distant death and pain endowed with no moral commitment.

Nevertheless, the mediated participation in the pain of others (especially when the trauma is acute and hard to face) through the means of communication can lead to new forms of social interaction (Alexander 2004, 22, 24) and it may initiate what Luc Boltanski (1999, 3–19), drawing from Arendt, calls "the politics of pity." That is, the spectacle of suffering at a distance by people who do not suffer is possible to induce moral obligation and responsibility for the distant unfortunate. The politics of pity is premised on commitment, on strong moral sentiments like indignation, anger and denunciation, as well as on specific forms of individual and collective public action in favor of the unfortunates, such as accusation of the persecutors, petitions, demonstrations, humanitarian action, fund raising and so on. In contrast to Mestrovic's thesis on quasi-emotions and Baudrillard's analysis of simulacra, Boltanski discerns a strong possibility of effective political action in the present triggered by the spectacle of suffering, by carving out new public domains for the defense of the unfortunate victims (Chouliaraki 2004; 2006).

Boltanski differentiates (1999, 96–101) the presence of moral sentiments as a necessary condition for the articulation of the politics of pity, as distinct from sentimentalism, that is, an essentially aesthetic stance towards the pain of the other. The sentimental person seeks out the spectacle of suffering not in order to relieve it, but in order to get the pleasure that the aroused sensibility confirms his/her humanity. According to Boltanski (1999, 99) it becomes crucial "to separate real emotions, the externalization of the inner going back directly to the roots of the heart, from purely external, imitated or depicted emotions with no inner reference."

To be sure, participation in the pain of others, new forms of solidarity and the emotional armor of the politics of pity is a very complex issue that pinches with the essentials of moral philosophy. A whole array of phenomena of fellow-feeling is involved in the politics of pity and the visualization of others' suffering is similar to these analyzed insuperably by Max Scheler (1954, 8–36). Vicarious feelings of sympathy, pity, understanding, imitation and emotional identification are evoked and it is certainly too difficult, if not impossible, to separate pity from compassion, as Boltanski does. Compassion is supposed to be premised on a face-to-face basis, on immediacy and a community of feeling not conducive to political action proper, i.e. abstract and general goal attainment; pity is premised on the distance between the spectator and the sufferer and it is this distance that permits the development of political strategies and the enactment of impersonal rules (Boltanski 1999, 6). In Scheler's terms, to whom, incidentally Boltanski scarcely makes reference, pity is fellow-feeling which involves intentional reference to the other person's experience in the sense that "*my* commiseration and *his* suffering are phenomenologically *two different facts*" (1954, 13).

Yet, in actual postmodern, mediatized, politics it would be too much to expect crystal clear differences in the emotional responses to the visualization of the distant others' sufferings and traumas. Besides, the difference between compassion and pity is not self-evident for everyone in academic community. For instance, Sznaider (1998) speaks of "public compassion" which originates in an abstract, theoretical and rational idea of humanity rather than in a face-to-face encounter with suffering persons. According to his thesis, public compassion draws from the humanitarian movements that arose in the eighteenth and nineteenth centuries, such as movements to abolish slavery and child labor, rather than from the tradition of religious charity. For Nussbaum (2001, 301) compassion is "a painful emotion occasioned by the awareness of another person's undeserved misfortune," and it seems that in her account "awareness" does not necessarily entail physical proximity and interpersonal communication. I guess that Scheler himself would steer clear from Boltanski's "pity" to the extend that "modern humanitarianism" or "humanitarian love" is only interested in the sum total of human individuals, it is a quantitative equalitarian force that "does not command and value the personal act of love from man to man, but primarily the impersonal 'institution' of welfare" (Scheler 1961, 116, 120–1). Also we could take notice of Höijer's (2003, 20) point that "compassion has to do with perceiving the suffering and the needs of distant others through media images and reports. Global compassion is then a moral sensibility or concern for remote strangers from different continents, cultures and societies."

Nevertheless, in fairness to arguments *à la* Boltanski and Chouliaraki, it needs to be said that the crux of the matter is not of terminological nature; rather, the crucial moral question is whether the media's presentation of the others' traumas undermines the nature of sympathy in the human form as the "taking the attitude of the other when one is assisting the other" (Mead 1934, 299) or as "a function of the whole mind" according to which "what a person is and what he can understand" is accomplished "through the life of others" (Cooley 1964, 140). This question could be posited in another way as well, i.e. to what extent can the media of communication eradicate the natural disposition of the human being to empathize with other people, a disposition much praised by moral philosophers like Hume and Smith?

In any case, estimating the representation of others' traumas through the logic of the "culture industry," simulation and "hyper-reality" leads to quite different conclusions from those forwarded by Alexander, Boltanski, Chouliaraki, and Sontag. For the latter, exposure to traumatic images can function as a "challenge to turn our attention to, to think, to learn, to check the explanations invoked by those in power in order to justify collective pain" (Sontag 2003, 121–2). On the contrary, for "apocalyptic" followers of Adorno and Jameson the commodity aesthetics of the electronic media has blocked all possible critical reflection, as false accounts of collective memory and social-cultural traumas have colonized the audience's historical imagination instead of liberating and broadening it. A mediatized trauma is seen as mere entertainment and detached curiosity (Kansteiner 2004).

Needless to say that things are never or rarely "either-or" and it is not compulsory for someone to adopt either an ungrounded optimism, or an unnecessary pessimism in the debate under consideration (Chouliaraki 2004). It is true that media aesthetics and consumerism are sometimes detrimental to the development of vigorous solidarities and active trust and it would be naïve to undercut the legacy of the Frankfurt School altogether. In fact, following the beats of war journalism by offering dramatic coverage of civilian populations in pain (Luostarinen 2002), the media not only sell human tragedies in a global market place, but they cultivate the numbing effect, if only because "the spectacle of suffering becomes domesticated by the experience of watching television" (Chouliaraki 2004, 189). Journalists themselves become desensitized and the audience acquires a *blasé* and/or quasi emotional stance towards this spectacle. On top of this, one should take into account particular results of psychological research which point to the fact that mediatized and visualized traumas and the exposure to others' suffering bring about vicarious helplessness since the subject feels that control of his/her environment is out of hand (Johnson and Davey 1997).

On the other side, however, it would be too harsh to exclude moral sensibility from the mediated quasi-interaction (Thompson 1995, 87–118). The electronic mass media does help the politics of pity and global compassion to emerge as the immediate speed in the transmission of distant others' traumas and suffering facilitates recipients to identify somehow with the visualized victims. That was the case, for instance, with the so called "Kosovocaust," an aftermath of the "CNN effect;" i.e. footage and news photos articulated in reference to the "lessons of the Holocaust" provoked intense moral outcries among the western public opinion, thus affecting to a considerable degree international decision making. Yet, identification with the victims can be accomplished retroactively as well; for instance, the film *Schindler's List* and almost two decades earlier the TV drama *The Holocaust* (not to mention a host of other products of popular culture on Jew's cultural-social trauma) greatly contributed to the formation of a global awareness and a strong moral stance. Either through real time transmission or retroactively, or both, the media builds up a sort of "cosmopolitan memory" sustained by the visualization of others' pain— say, for instance, the Rwanda genocide, the atrocities in Somalia, the Khmer Rouge's extermination of one-third of Cambodia's population, the famine in Darfur, and September 11th—, triggers in the spectators the expression of some of the most basic emotions recognizable by everyone: disgust and anger for the perpetrators, sadness and fear for the victims. Willy-nilly, the spectator is addressed as a witness of the evil and while recording it she/he is interpellated as a moral subject; as long as this interpellation takes place, new *loci* of global solidarity and ethical universality are carved out (Levi and Sznaider 2002, 88), fueled by the above mentioned emotions. It is precisely through these emotions that television becomes "an agent of moral responsibility" (Chouliaraki 2004, 186) and, consequently, a facilitator of the "democratization of responsibility" (Thompson 1995, 263–4).

It can be argued that time-space compression is a sufficient condition for the rising of cosmopolitan memories and the global spreading of responsibility; the ultimate, though, necessary condition is the feeling of guilt. It is guilt that allows the spectators to engulf the suffering of the distant others and their traumatic history; but why is this so? Attempting an interpretation—and here I am roughly following a sort of psychoanalytic argumentation, though not so closely as it deserves—I would claim that this is so because every normal or average person is endowed with unconscious guilt due to Superego's imperatives (Freud 2001). The paradox Freud underscores is that the more ethical the subject is, the more guilty he/she feels. Ambivalence towards the father or everyone who assumes the role of the father, and the subsequent repressed aggression come back to the Ego through the Superego. This is so, because it is not only that the subject has repressed the forbidden drives before an external authority, i.e. the father; what counts more is that the subject feels anxious in front of the internal authority, the Superego. This internal authority monitors all forbidden desires so that intention becomes equivalent to wrongdoing. That is why many people feel guilty without prior wrongdoing.

Yet, it is not only the severe and punishing Superego that elicits guilt; it is also the symbolic Law underlying all social relations, i.e. the Law of the signifier, which according to Lacan commands that not everything is possible in human affairs. The prohibition of incest is an example of the symbolic Law which actually "superimposes the kingdom of culture on that of nature" (Lacan 1977, 66). It seems to me that somehow the Lacanian account of the Law, closely related to Kant's Categorical Imperative, is linked to the normative vulnerability of which Velleman (2003) speaks. Normative vulnerability is the sense of being unjustified and defenseless against negative reactions and responses aimed at one by the other(s) which appear to one to be warranted even though one has personally wielded no harm. Thus, even if one commits no wrongdoing one may feel guilty upon the imaginary anticipation that there is somewhere someone else suffering who resents or envies one's good fortune. So, whenever a spectator is in front of a horrendous mediatized event, e.g. the collapse of the Twin Towers on September 11th or the Rwanda genocide, not only she/he feels that the symbolic order, represented by the Law, is violated by the intrusion of pure negativity (or Evil one would say) evading any discursive intermediation; what is more, he/she experiences that his/her secure state and wellbeing is unacceptable and unjustified before the victims' tragic plight. In virtue of the unconscious guilt, the spectator feels that the violation of the Law is somehow her/his responsibility. Besides, I would also claim that the spectator of the pain of Third World distant others on Western television and the internet may also experience a preconscious guilt in line with the following logic: although I as a person have done nothing for their suffering, somehow I am guilty because I enjoy the goods of the capitalist center which exploits and dominates countries in the periphery.

In one way or another, therefore, guilt is an ontogenetic moral ground for the development of the politics of pity, precisely because it is rooted deep in the human psyche. It is not an accidental or contingent, rather than it is an immanent moral stance. Yet, the crucial point in the information age is the degree of its universalizability against the grammar of the media of communication; apart from redefining the interplay between distance and proximity, the latter systematically promotes particularity over universality through personalization, dramatization and episodic coverage of traumatic situations.

As ambivalent their moral impact might be, and irrespective of the compassion fatigue and the routinization of the others' traumas that they produce (Tester 2001, 13; Alexander 2003, 103), observing the pain of others through the media cannot totally shield spectators from moral interpellation, from their direct or indirect moralization. It is certainly true that media reporting on distant suffering serves cynical commercial interests; telethons dedicated to the alleviation of Third World suffering and misfortunes are part of the entertainment programming and offer ample opportunities for human sponsoring and image making. It is true that frequently the politics of pity or compassion is reduced in giving money for charity just in order to keep the distant other at an arm's length. It is also true that mediatized cosmopolitan memories buttress the ideological discourse on "human rights" which provides moral grounds to international interventions described euphemistically as "humanitarian interventions" which of course create new victims, as was in fact the case when NATO and the U.S. dropped bombs over Kosovo and Serbia in the spring of 1999.

All these are true, but they are not the whole truth. It seems to me that there is always a moral remainder, call it unconscious or preconscious guilt if you like, which escapes the commercial logic of the medium and under certain circumstances overwhelms quasi-emotions leading to autonomous public action. It is in these rare cases where the public media assumes the role of the "mediapolis," about which Silverstone (2006) spoke so passionately; i.e. as a space of socio-political dialogue and deliberation of moral significance with remote others, precisely because they contribute to keeping proper distance from the victims, bringing them neither too close nor keeping them too distant. Here I would claim that in virtue of "mediapolis," though fragile and precarious, the feelings of guilt, indignation and sadness aroused while watching the unpleasant plight of distant others can be a stimulating condition for alternative moral-practical thinking. Despite the reluctance people experience in interpreting their concerns and sentiments into determinate courses of action, the mediatized trauma of the distant other could give rise to a sense of responsibility for his/her life and dignity. It prompts what Hans Jonas (1984) regards to be the attribute that differentiates *par excellence* the humans as a species: the undertaking of substantive responsibility towards the entire Being and the other human being. Perhaps the mediatization of traumas is unable to mobilize the Levinasian ethics of being *for* the other instead of being simply *with* the other. The likelihood is that time-space compression is conducive to the moral stance of being with the other, due to the disguised proximity of the sufferers in the screen. Yet, as long as this takes place, it is already too much; one can maintain, therefore, that the media makes possible the enunciation of an ethics of care and responsibility in our age where care seems impossible. This is accomplished, *inter alia*, through the social construction of "moral universals," i.e. generalized symbols of human suffering and moral evil (Alexander 2003, 27–84). By the same token, I would even argue that the media may make our direct or indirect encounter with the suffering of others easier and mobilize that sort of moral minimalism that Walzer (1994) was writing about: a moral minimum, a "thin morality," which does not serve any particular interest but instead regulates everyone's behavior in a mutually beneficial way. Isn't this, after all, the meaning of the international mobilizations against the war in Iraq and the solidarity that was expressed for the people in South East Asia after the earthquake of the 26th of December, 2004? And isn't this a sample of a "morality of spatial and temporal distance" translated somehow into effective social interests and into tangible political forces (Bauman 1993, 222)?

Conclusion

What I have tried to achieve in this essay is to delineate the mutual links between cultural-social trauma, risk society, the mass media and the politics of pity. My route was marked by three signposts, not necessarily corresponding to the designated sections of the text. The first was a comparative reading of cultural-social and psychic-clinical traumas. It was argued that both types of traumas result retroactively from construction processes on personal and collective level respectively. Also, they bring about irreversible changes to identities, personal as well as collective, which, however, do not mark everybody exposed to a traumatogenic situation in the same way. As in the case of psychic trauma, cultural-social trauma is conveyed through multiple negative emotions on the basis of which collective memory is selectively organized. If the impetus of negative affect is not activated, an upsetting event cannot be experienced and codified as trauma. Accordingly, the task for the sociology of emotions is to identify particular emotions elicited in and through the trauma drama and analyze their confluence and interconnections.

The second signpost of this paper refers to the conditions under which the cultural sociological theory of trauma and the rise of trauma, memory and disaster studies gain currency. It was asserted that this has become possible by virtue of the dynamics of risk society; this society is self-defined as traumatic and traumatogenic in the sense that it promotes vulnerability as one of the main characteristics of the subject, both at the national and international level. It is not simply that individuals face a host of risks in their everyday life; the crucial difference is that the very idea of the self is permeated by risks and dangers. As a consequence, trauma becomes a central imaginative signification of our era changing social bonds and the terms of social remembering.

The third signpost of the paper deals with the articulation of traumatic historical memory via the media of communication. The latter are not the only means for the (re)construction of collective and historical memory in view of traumatic experiences; yet, they may be regarded as one of the most powerful mnemotechnical apparatuses because they stretch time and space, therefore redefining the interplay between distance and proximity. Effectively, they may make for the possibility of cultural-social trauma not to be experienced directly by anyone. Yet, even more important is the fact that the media conveys moral implications when they render traumas as part of the spectacle. A strong case is made as to the ambivalent role of the media as it is argued that the observation of others' suffering via the media may lead to two different stances: either to a routinized quasi-emotional experience which inhibits action or to a thin morality that may motivate a global politics of pity.

The theory of social-cultural trauma can contribute to the understanding of our own sufferings as well because the concept of trauma as such refers to a dynamic process which includes both the traumatic element itself *and* the process of its healing. Failure to mourn is the main reason for conceptualizing why the historical traumas keep arousing the population and instigating violence (Volkan 2004). As long as collective reflexivity on historical memory does not materialize, vindictiveness will be preserved, the blood of the ancestors will seek justice and shame will be lurking underneath anger and hate for the (national, tribal, ethnic, religious) other. Forgiveness is of utmost importance here; but to forgive is not to forget, nor is it denial or disavowal. Forgiveness entails transformation of negative emotions based on strong will, a will to start anew, a gesture quite opposite to vengeance. Forgiveness is never predicted, as it comes out of free will and frees both doer and sufferer from the relentless automatism of a vicious cycle (Arendt 1958, 236–41). What is more, forgiveness can be offered only by those (previous victims) who are able to punish (perpetrators) by all means (Ricoeur 2004, 469–70); otherwise it might be disguised *ressentiment* (Demertzis 2006).

However, who is exactly the one who forgives? Is it the persons, the sufferers, or the collectivities? Hannah Arendt is crystal-clear: "forgiving is [...] always an eminently personal [...] affair in which what was done is forgiven for the sake of who did it" (1958, 241). But is it just all? I do not think so. Alongside individual acts of forgiveness, social institutions of all sorts, the media included, should undertake the ethical task to reinterpret the traumatic past in order to break the process of perpetual victimization. A host of brave work has been done lately to this direction in the historiography of the Balkans (Koulouri 2002) and in the German civil society with regards the Nazi past and the Holocaust. Such endeavors may contribute to social and political change in the long run. At any rate, a theory of cultural-social trauma could offer better analyses incorporating collective healing processes, acquiring thereafter explicit qualities of a normative social theory of trauma.

Acknowledgements

Thanks to Ron Eyerman, Teresa Capelos, Costa Gouliamos, and Mirca Madianou for their helpful comments on earlier drafts of this essay.

References

Alexander, Jeffrey (2003). *The Meanings of Social Life. A Cultural Sociology*. Oxford: Oxford University Press.

— (2004). Toward a Theory of Cultural Trauma. In Jeffrey Alexander, Ron Eyerman, Bernhard Giesen, Neil J. Smelser, and Piotr Sztompka (eds.). *Cultural Trauma and Collective Identity*, 1–30. Berkeley: University of California Press.

Alexander, Jeffrey, Ron Eyerman, Bernhard Giesen, Neil J. Smelser, and Piotr Sztompka (2004). *Cultural Trauma and Collective Identity*. Berkeley: University of California Press.

Anselmi, W., and C. Gouliamos (1998). *Elusive Margins – Consuming Media, Ethnicity and Culture*. Toronto, Buffalo, Lancaster: Guernica Publications.

Arendt, Hannah (1958). *The Human Condition*. Chicago: The University of Chicago Press.

Baer, A. (2001). Consuming History and Memory Through Mass Media Products. *European Journal of Cultural Studies*, 4 (4), 491–501.

Barbalet, Jack M. (1998). *Emotion, Social Theory, and Social Structure. A Macrosociological Approach*. Cambridge: Cambridge University Press.

Bauman, Zygmunt (1993). *Postmodern Ethics*. Oxford: Blackwell.

Beck, Ulrich (1992). *Risk Society. Towards a New Modernity*. London: Sage Publications.

Bewes, T. (1997). *Cynicism and Postmodernity*. London: Verso.

Boltanski, L. (1999). *Distant Suffering. Morality, Media and Politics*. Cambridge: Cambridge University Press.

Castoriadis, C. (1987). *The Imaginary Institution of Society*. Cambridge: Polity Press.

Chouliaraki, L. (2004). Watching 11 September: The Politics of Pity. *Discourse and Society*, 15 (2–3), 185–98.

— (2006). *The Spectatorship of Suffering*. London: Sage Publications.

Cooley, Charles Horton (1964). *Human Nature and the Social Order*. New York: Schocken Books.

Demertzis, Nicolas (1996). *The Nationalist Discourse. Ambivalent Semantic Field and Contemporary Tendencies*. Athens: A. Sakkoulas Publications.

— (2006). Emotions and Populism. In S. Clarke, P. Hoggett, and S. Thompson (eds.). *Power, Passion and Politics*, 103–22. London: Palgrave/MacMillan.

Edkins, J. (2003). *Trauma and the Memory Politics*. Cambridge: Cambridge University Press.

Ehrenreich, J. (2003) Understanding PTSD: Forgetting "Trauma". *Journal of Social Issues*, 3 (1), 15–28.

Ekman, P. (1993). Facial Expression and Emotion. *American Psychologist*, 48, 384–92.

Eyerman, Ron (2001). *Cultural Trauma. Slavery and the Formation of African American Identity*. Cambridge: Cambridge University Press.

— (2004). Cultural Trauma. Slavery and the Formation of African American Identity. In Jeffrey Alexander, Ron Eyerman, Bernhard Giesen, Neil J. Smelser, Piotr Sztompka (eds.). *Cultural Trauma and Collective Identity*, 60–111. Berkeley: University of California Press.

Freud, Sigmund (1986). Moses and Monotheism: Three Essays. In *The Origins of Religion, The Pelican Freud Library*, vol. 13. London: Penguin Books. [first published in 1939]

— (1977). *Group Psychology and the Analysis of the Ego*. Athens: Epikouros. [first published in 1921]

— (2001). Civilization and its Discontents. In *The Standard Edition of the Complete Psychological Works*, Vol. XXI. London: Vintage, The Hogarth Press. [first published in 1930]

— (2003). *An Outline of Psychoanalysis*. London: Penguin Books. [first published in 1940]

Freud, Sigmund, and Joseph Breuer (1956). *Studies on Hysteria*. Pelican Freud Library, Standard Edition. London: Penguin Books. [first published in 1895]

Furedi, F. (2004). *Therapy Culture. Cultivating Vulnerability in an Uncertain Age*. London: Routledge.

Giddens, Anthony (1984). *The Constitution of Society*. Cambridge: Polity Press.

Goldfarb, J. (1991). *The Cynical Society*. Chicago, London: The University of Chicago Press.

Höijer, B. (2003). The Discourse of Global Compassion and the Media. In *Nordicom Review*, 24 (2), 19–29.

Johnson, W. M., and G. C. L. Davey (1997). The Psychological Impact of Negative TV News Bulletins: The Catastrophizing of Person Worries. *British Journal of Psychology*, 88, 85–91.

Jonas, H. (1984). *The Imperative of Responsibility: In Search of an Ethics for the Technological Age*. Chicago: University of Chicago Press.

Kansteiner, W. (2004). Genealogy of a Category Mistake: A Critical Intellectual History of the Cultural Trauma Metaphor. *Rethinking History*, 8 (2), 193–221.

Koselleck, R. (1988). *Critique and Crisis. Enlightenment and the Pathogenesis of Modern Society*. Cambridge, Massachusetts: MIT Press.

Koulouri, Ch. (ed.). (2002). *Clio in the Balkans. The Politics of History Education*. Thessaloniki: CDRSEE.

Kövecses, Zoltán (2000). The Concept of Anger: Universal or Culture Specific? *Psychopathology*, 33 (4), 159–170.

Lacan, Jacques (1977). *Ecrits. A Selection*. London: Tavistock/Routledge.

Laclau, Ernesto, and Chantal Mouffe (1985). *Hegemony and Socialist Strategy*. London: Verso.

Laplanche J., and J.-B. Pontalis (1986). *Vocabulaire de la Psychanalyse*. Athens: Kedros Publications.

Lev-Wiesel, R. (2007). Intergenerational Transmission of Trauma Across Three Generations. A Preliminary Study. *Qualitative Social Work*, 6 (1), 75–94.

Levy, D., and Sznaider, N. (2002). Memory Unbound. The Holocaust and the Formation of Cosmopolitan Memory. *European Journal of Social Theory*, 5 (1), 87–106.

Leys, R. (2000). *Trauma: A Genealogy*. Baltimore, MD: John Hopkins University Press.

Luostarinen, H. (2002). Journalism and the Cultural Preconditions of War. In W. Kempf and H. Luostarinen (eds.). *Journalism and the New World Order. Studying War and the Media*, Vol. 2, 273–83. Gothenburg: NORDICOM, Gothenburg University.

Mead, George Hebert (1934). *Mind, Self, and Society. From the Standpoint of a Social Behaviorist*. Chicago, London: The University of Chicago Press.

Meštrović, Stjepan G. (1997). *Postemotional Society*. London: Sage Publications.

Miller, N., and J. Tougaw (eds.). (2002). *Extremities. Trauma, Testimony and Community*. Urbana, Chicago: University of Illinois Press.

Misztal, B. (2003). *Theories of Social Remembering*. Maidenhead: Open University Press.

Nussbaum, Martha C. (2001). *Upheavals of Thought. The Intelligence of Emotion*. Cambridge: Cambridge University Press.

Oatley, K., and J. Jenkins (1996). *Understanding Emotions*. Oxford: Blackwell Publishing.

Pupavac, Vanessa (2007). *Therapeutic Governance: The Politics of Psychosocial Intervention and Trauma Risk Management*, accessed March 11, 2007, http://www.odi.org.uk/hpg/confpapers/pupavac.

Richards, B. (2007). *Emotional Governance: Politics, Media and Terror*. London: Palgrave Macmillan.

Ricoeur, Paul (2004). *Memory, History, Forgetting*. Chicago: University of Chicago Press.

Rosenwein, B. (2001). Writing Without Fear About Early Medieval Emotions. *Early Medieval Europe*, 10 (2), 229–34.

Scheler, Max (1954). *The Nature of Sympathy*. London: Routledge & Kegan Paul Ltd.

— (1961). *Ressentiment*. Glencoe: Free Press.

Scott, A. (2000). Risk Society or Angst Society? Two Views of Risk, Consciousness and Community. In B. Adam, U. Beck, and J. V. Loon (eds.). *The Risk Society and Beyond. Critical Issues for Social Theory*, 33–46. London: Sage Publications.

Silverstone, R. (2006). *Media and Morality. On the Rise of Mediapolis*. London: Polity Press.

Sloterdijk, Peter (1988). *Critique of Cynical Reason*. London: Verso.

Smelser, Neil J. (2004). Psychological Trauma and Cultural Trauma. In Jeffrey Alexander, Ron Eyerman, Bernhard Giesen, Neil J. Smelser, and Piotr Sztompka (eds.). *Cultural Trauma and Collective Identity*, 31–59. Berkeley: University of California Press.

Smith, D. (2006). *Globalization. The Hidden Agenda*. Cambridge: Polity.

Sontag, Susan (2003). *Regarding the Pain of Others*. New York: Farrar, Strauss and Giroux.

Stavrakakis, Y. (1999). *Lacan and the Political*. London: Routledge.

Sznaider, Natan (1998). The Sociology of Compassion: A Study in the Sociology of Morals. *Cultural Values*, 2 (1), 117–39.

Sztompka, Piotr (2004). The Trauma of Social Change. A Case of Postcommunist Societies. In Jeffrey Alexander, Ron Eyerman, Bernhard Giesen, Neil J. Smelser, and Piotr Sztompka (eds.). *Cultural Trauma and Collective Identity*, 155–95. Berkeley: University of California Press.

Tester, K. (2001). *Compassion, Morality and the Media*. Buckingham: Open University Press.

Thompson, J. (1995). *The Media and Modernity. A Social Theory of the Media*. London: Polity Press.

Todorov, Tzv. (1995). *Les abus de la mémoire*. Paris : Arléa.

Velleman, J. D. (2003). Don't Worry, Feel Guilty. In A. Hatzimoysis (ed.). *Philosophy and the Emotions*, 235–48. Cambridge: Cambridge University Press.

Volkan, V. (2004). *Blind Trust. Large Groups and Their Leaders in Times of Crisis and Terror*. Charlottesville, Virginia: Pitchstone Publishing.

Walzer, Michael (1994). *Thick and Thin. Moral Argument at Home and Abroad*. Notre Dame: University of Notre Dame Press.

Žižek, S. (1989). *The Sublime Object of Ideology*. London: Verso.

— (1997). *The Plague of Fantasies*. London: Verso.

The Civilizing of Emotions: Formalization and Informalization

Cas Wouters

On Good Societies and Regimes of Manners and Emotions

In the study of patterns of emotion regulation, a general starting point is that within the relations in which they grow up, all individuals are confronted with demands for self-regulation according to the regimes of manners and emotions prevalent in their particular group and society. All people develop emotional impulses and counter-impulses that are more or less attuned to the codes of these regimes. Regardless of the specific way and direction in which they develop, until their death people always remain emotional beings; they can never be *not* emotional. Nor is it possible for them *not* to behave. The intensity and complexity of emotions, as well as the degree and balance of individual and social control over them, is however, variable, and is displayed in their manners. Changes in manners open a window onto changes in the relations *between* people, as well as onto changes *in* people, that is, in their demands for emotion regulation. Therefore, the study of any regime of manners can reveal a corresponding regime of emotions. This paper aims at showing how overall trends in Western regimes of manners within the twentieth century, and in earlier centuries, have been connected to general trends in emotion regulation or self-regulation.

Another premise is that within each society, the code of manners and emotion regulation is derived from sociability within the centers of power and their "good society," that is, the circles of social acquaintance among people of families who belong to the centers of power, and who take part in their sociable gatherings. The codes of good societies serve as an example or model for other social groups and classes—they have a modeling function. Here, the dominant social definition of proper ways to establish and maintain relations is constructed. For all socially aspiring people, the manners of good society are decisive in making acquaintances and friends, for winning a desirable spouse, and for gaining influence and recognition. As increasing layers of society became emancipated and more socially integrated, the social codes of good societies came to represent these layers—they have a representational function. In order to avoid social conflict and maintain their elevated position, the people in the centers of power and good society increasingly had to take the presence of rising groups into account. As part of this, the former had to show more respect for the ideals, sentiments, morals, and manners of the latter. Therefore, the codes of a good society tended to spare the sensibilities of all groups represented in them.

Authors of manners books pretend to present the codes of behavior and emotion regulation of those who form the good society of every society. They try to capture those sensibilities and practices which reflect the dominant codes, and to sell this knowledge to insecure social climbers. These authors are not backed up by any profession, in academia or anywhere else, and they neither possess nor produce any expert knowledge other than that based upon participant observation in good society. This knowledge can only become profitably exploited (published and sold) if they know how to address people who aspire to acceptance in higher social circles, but who are insecure about how to achieve this. Every author of a manners book has to deal somehow with the difficulty of presenting the manners and sensibilities of higher-class people to lower-class people, or include the excluded, as it were, without ever making this (too) explicit. For these books to be sold, the readers have to be lifted up, not put down. Therefore, the codes expressed in manners books tend to reveal a mixture of actual and ideal behavior. However, it is important to realize that these ideals are *real* in the sense that they are not constructed by social scientists, and thus they are truly "unobtrusive measures."

The study of changes in manners books in particular provides evidence of changes in the way all kinds of emotions and relations are fashioned among the established. Such a study also reveals some advice as having become obsolete, and other advice as no longer being mentioned, because the corresponding regulation of behavior and emotions had become taken for granted. This is a reminder that the modeling function of good society operates only partly through the medium of social codes or rational individual choice, because differences in manners and sensibilities become ingrained into the personality of individuals—their *habitus*—as they grow up. The same goes for many external social constraints as they are transformed into habitual self-restraint. In this context, Norbert Elias described important connections between the formation of good societies, status motives, and the transformation of constraints by others into self-restraints:

"A compulsive desire for social prestige is to be found as the primary motive of action only among members of classes whose income under normal circumstances is substantial and perhaps even growing, and at any rate is appreciably over the hunger threshold. In such classes the impulse to engage in economic activity is no longer the simple necessity of satisfying hunger, but a desire to preserve a certain high, socially expected standard of living and prestige. This explains why, in such elevated classes, affect-control and self-constraint are generally more highly developed than in the lower classes: fear of loss or reduction of social prestige is one of the most powerful motive forces in the transformation of constraints by others into self-restraints" (Elias 2000, 395–6).

Once these external social constraints have been transformed into habitual, second-nature self-restraints, the social constraints from which they originate and which continue to back them up, are no longer experienced or perceived as such, nor are the powerful status motivations involved in their transformation.

The present paper is based upon a study of manners books. It is one of the results from a research project of many years, the purpose of which was to find, compare and interpret changes in American, Dutch, English and German manners books from the end of the nineteenth century to the end of the twentieth. My study of these books aimed at finding anything that would reveal something about the changing relations between people of different rank (or class) and sex, and that would imply a change in the demands being made on emotion regulation or self-regulation, as well as implying anything that seemed typical of a country or a time. In addition, I looked for general trends and national variations in comparing changes in social dividing lines between formal and informal, and public and private manners, in such matters as privacy, introductions, reserve, visiting hours, business manners, social kissing, dancing, dating, the use of superlatives, personal pronouns, and so on.

The project has resulted in two books, the first, *Sex and Manners* was published in 2004 and the second, *Informalization: Manners and Emotions since 1890* appeared at the end of 2007. In these books general trends are reported, as well as national variations. Among the overall trends reported was a declining social and psychic distance between social classes, sexes and generations, a mixing of codes and ideals, increasing interdependencies, an informalization of manners, expanding mutual identifications, and an *emancipation of emotions*: emotions that had been denied and repressed (re)gained access to consciousness and wider acceptance in social codes. All in all, these interrelated trends amounted to an informalization of manners, rising demands on emotion regulation, and increasing social and national integration.

A quite simple illustration of ongoing social integration processes exists in the fact that, in the course of the twentieth century, the public who read manners books expanded. Authors in the four societies under study increasingly came to direct themselves to wider middle-class and "respectable" working class circles, and thus manners books came to represent growing numbers of people from more and more layers of society. This expansion reflected the successive ascent of large middle-class groups, their ongoing partial social emancipation, as well as, of course, the growth and spread of wealth over broader social layers. The widening of the circles of readers of manners books reflected a widening of the circles who were directing themselves in terms of the dominant code, which, therefore, through the course of the century, increasingly became the *national* code. These integration processes were carried by the successive ascent of larger and larger groups and their representation in national centers of power and their good societies.

In contrast to individual social ascent, the ascent of an entire social group involves some form of mixing of the codes and ideals of the groups which have risen alongside those of the previously superior groups. In the twentieth century, the successive social ascent of larger and larger groups has been reflected in the dominant codes and habitus—being a shorthand expression for the mentality, the whole distinctive emotional make-up of the people who are thus bonded together. The sediments of this mixing process can be found in manners books: the patterns of self-regulation of increasingly wider social groups come to be reflected in the codes of manners. They can be perceived in such changes as in the ways in which authors of manners books address their readers, how they draw social dividing lines, such as between public and private, formal and informal, and what they have written about social introductions and forms of address. As a rule, any regime of manners and emotions symbolizes and reinforces ranking, hierarchy and other social dividing lines, while the same rule holds that changes in these regimes reflect changes in social dividing lines and in balances of power. This helps one to understand why the nineteenth century witnessed an *aristocratization* of the bourgeoisie alongside an *embourgeoisement* of nobility, to be partly succeeded and partly supplemented in the twentieth century by an *embourgeoisement* of the working classes and a *proletarianization* of the bourgeoisie: *informalization.*

This paper particularly focuses on the balance of controls in regulating emotions by seeking to answer the question: what overall changes in social codes can be interpreted as involving specific changes in the balance of external social controls and internal social controls or self-controls? I will try to interpret these changes by connecting them to social integration processes. In addition, I will explore connections between social integration and psychic integration.

The Disciplinary Forces of State Formation and Market Expansion

Until the end of the nineteenth century, in a long-term phase of formalizing manners and disciplining people, "dangerous" emotions such as those related to physical (including sexual) violence came to be avoided, repressed and denied in increasingly automatic ways, that is, increasingly regulated by the inner fears of a rather rigid and authoritarian conscience. Driven by the disciplinary forces of expanding interdependency networks, in particular by state formation and market expansion, a conscience-dominated type of personality was in the making, and became dominant.

Until the nineteenth century, courts had a modeling function. In comparison with court circles, later circles of good society were larger, and sociability in them was more *private*, the private sphere being more sharply distinguished from the public and occupational spheres. However, the novelties of occupational work and the division into professional and private spheres did not change the modeling function of good societies, nor the fact that entrance into them offered important power chances. What *was* affected, though, was the visibility of their functioning. The relegation of most forms of sociability to the sphere of private life made the modeling function almost invisible, and this may help to explain why its importance was (and remains) easily underestimated, and hardly, or not at all researched. Yet, professional success and success in good society remained strongly interdependent, as the rank and reputation of each individual member of the economic and political bourgeoisie continued to be made or broken in the circles of good society.

As occupational and political businesses depend on building trust, that is, on making friends and acquaintances in the field, all involved practiced the custom of inviting each other to dinner and to other sociable occasions, such as parties organized in private drawing rooms. Thus, they continued to seek the protection and reinforcement of their occupational and political interests in the formation and functioning of a good society (or a functional equivalent further down the social ladder, or in the country or provinces).

The life and career of the bourgeois classes both in business and in the professions depended heavily on keeping promises, and on the rather punctual and minute regulation of social traffic and behavior. Accordingly, nineteenth-century manners books placed great emphasis on acquiring the self-discipline necessary for living a "rational life;" they emphasized time-keeping and ordering activities routinely in a fixed sequence, and at a set pace. Thomas Haskell has pointed to the significance of the "disciplinary force of the market" in connection to the rising norm of promise keeping and the ascendancy of conscience. This "force of the market provided the intricate blend of ceaseless change, on the one hand, and predictability on the other, in which a preoccupation with remote consequences paid off most handsomely" (Haskell 1985, 561). An overall change in sensibility occurred via the expansion of the market, the intensification of market discipline, and the penetration of that discipline into spheres of life previously untouched by it. The expectation that everyone would live up to promises—as comprised in contracts made on "the market"—became a mutually expected self-restraint, which eventually became taken for granted to the extent that it came to function as part of people's conscience.

This type of conscience-formation presupposes state formation in the sense that the monopolization of the use of violence by the state, and ensuing pacification of larger territories, provided a necessary condition for the expectation of promise keeping and living up to contracts to become taken for granted, and engrained in the personality as conscience (Elias 2000). Taking the development of these conditions into consideration helps us to understand why it was not until the eighteenth century, in Western Europe, England, and North America, that societies first appeared whose economic systems "depended on the expectation that most people, most of the time, were sufficiently conscience-ridden (and certain of retribution) that they could be trusted to keep their promises. In other words, only then did promise keeping become so widespread that it could be elevated into a general social norm" (Haskell 1985, 353).

This argument adds to the one put forward by Durkheim in his writing about the order behind the contract: "For everything in the contract is not contractual." The order behind the contract, "in current parlance, is designated by the name, state" (1964, 211, 219). It was in the process of state formation that the commitment to live up to a contract came increasingly to be taken for granted. Without the whole system of sanctions, established after the use of violence was monopolized by the state, this commitment would not have become internalized. This internalization ran in tandem with, and depended upon, rising levels of mutually expected protection of people and their property.

The entrepreneurial bourgeoisie largely took this protection by the state, the order behind the contract, for granted. It was their point of departure. Their whole social existence depended heavily upon contracts, contracts regulating the conditions of such activities as buying, producing, transporting and selling. In turn, the making of these contracts, as well as the conditions stipulated in them, depended upon an individual's reputation for being financially solvent and morally solid. To a large extent this reputation was formed in the gossip channels of good society (or its functional equivalent among other social strata).

The Moral Solidity of Nineteenth-Century Bourgeois Men

A reputation for moral solidity referred to the self-discipline of orderliness, thrift, and responsibility as being the qualities needed for a firm grip on the proceedings of business transactions. Moral solidity also pertained to the social and sexual sphere: without demonstrable control over their wives and families, working bourgeois men would fail to create a solid impression of reliability, and ability to live up to the terms of their contracts. Therefore, bourgeois means of controlling potentially dangerous social and sexual competition depended to a substantial degree on the support of a wife for her husband. Her support and social charm could make a crucial difference, as is implied in the opinion that "nothing makes a man look more ridiculous in the eyes of the world than a socially helpless wife" (Klickman 1902, 25).

At the same time, these pressures offered specific opportunities for women. Whereas men dominated the eighteenth-century courtesy genre of manners books, in the nineteenth-century etiquette genre, women gained a prominent position, both as authors and as readers (Curtin 1987). As the social weight of the bourgeoisie increased, middle-class women enjoyed a widening sphere of opportunities. Although confined to the domain of their home and good society, upper- and middle-class women came, more or less, to run and organize the social sphere of good society. The workings of this social formation took place, in large part, in women's private drawing rooms. To some extent, women came to function as the gatekeepers of good society.

In developing the level of trust and respect within a relationship necessary for signing a contract, an invitation into the world of sociability was (and remains) an appreciated strategy. In their relations with friends and acquaintances, with women in general, and with their own wife in particular, men could demonstrate and prove their respectability and trustworthiness. They could show this to a potential client by inviting him and his wife into their home and into the rest of their secluded good society world. Hence, to be introduced, accepted and entertained in the drawing rooms and parlors of the respectable or, in other words, to be successful in the good society, was an important and sometimes even a necessary condition for success in business.

Entrance into good society was impossible without an introduction, and, particularly in England, any introduction required the previous permission of both parties. This regime of manners not only regulated sociability, but also functioned as a relatively refined system of inclusion and exclusion, as an instrument to screen newcomers seeking entry into social circles, thus helping to identify and exclude undesirables and ensuring that the newly introduced would assimilate to the prevailing regime of manners and self-regulation. Michael Curtin observed an "obsessive concern" among British etiquette writers: "to establish criteria by which to identify and to exclude undesirables" (1987, 420).

A basic rule of manners among those acknowledged as belonging to the circle was to treat each other on the basis of equality. Quite often this was expressed in what became known as the Golden Rule of manners: do unto others as you would have them do unto you. Some were treated with relative intimacy. Others were treated with reserve, and were thus kept at a social distance. Therefore, the questions, who was properly introduced or introducible, and who was not, were equally important. To spot undesirables and to keep one's distance from strangers was a matter of great concern. The prototypical stranger was someone who might have the manners of the respectable, but not the morals. Strangers personified the bad company that would endanger the self-control of the respectable, prompting loss of composure in response to repulsive behavior or, worse, the succumbing to temptation.

The Fear of the Slippery Slope: The Rise of a Second-Nature Type of Personality

In the nineteenth century, authors of manners books came to describe the fall of innocent young men as being instructive of lessons in moral virtue and vigilance. Their repeated warnings against strangers expressed a strong moral appeal, revealing a fear of the slippery slope towards giving in to immoral pleasures. The author of a study of a number of such American stories relates here, "these anecdotal dramas encompass many pitfalls— from seemingly harmless pleasures like dancing to the mortal dangers posed by alcohol—for conduct writers see young men's mistakes not just as individual dangers, but as part of a web of dangerous activity: one slip inevitably leads to the next" (Newton 1994, 58). These warnings were directed at young men in particular. Playing a single game of cards with strangers, for example, would "always end in trouble, often in despair, and sometimes in suicide," an early nineteenth-century advice book warned. In her study of Dutch books of this genre, the author concluded that, by its nature, any careless indulgence in pleasure would lead to "a lethal fall" (Tilburg 1998, 66–7). In a similar (American) study, Stuart Blumin also reports on a whole genre of

"purportedly true stories of individual drunkards, nearly all of whom were identified as wealthy, educated, or respectable, or by specific non-manual occupations before they took to drink. Moderate drinking invariably led to heavy drinking and drunkenness, and drunkenness to financial ruin and the destruction of family life. Often it led to the death of the drinker, his impoverished wife (the drunkard in these tales was almost always male), or his children. The loss of respectability, of the ability to pursue a respectable occupation, of wealth, and of family life in a well-appointed home (the forced sale of furniture is a common motif) was crucial to these tales, and spoke clearly and powerfully to the major preoccupations of the upper and middle classes" (1989, 200).

Newton concludes:

"Self-control, self-government, self-denial, self-restraint, and discipline of the will are all terms used repeatedly in the conduct book lexicon to reinforce the social construction of masculinity. The true man, then, is he who can discipline himself into qualities of character that lead to material and personal success. This discipline also extends to controlling and subjugating the passions as well. Control of anger, of sexual appetite, of impatience, even of emotion are instilled in the American male psyche as essential to the manly character. Thus the young man is set in competition with himself in the great battle of life" (1994, 58–9).

This strong moral advice was intended to teach young men the responsibilities needed not only for a successful career but also, because marriages were no longer arranged by parents, for choosing a marriage partner. Advice betrayed the fear that such choices would be determined mainly by sexual attraction.

Social censorship verged on psychic censorship: warnings expanded to the "treacherous effects" of fantasy, itself a demonstration of the prevailing conviction that dangerous thoughts would almost automatically lead to dangerous action. The rigorous and violent censorship in stricter and more authoritarian regimes demonstrates the extent to which authorities and others believed in the danger of thoughts, imagination or fantasy. Because of this direct connection between thoughts and actions, warnings against having dangerous thoughts were formulated as powerfully as possible. This kind of high-pitched moral pressure signaled the development of rather rigid ways of avoiding anything defined as dangerous or unacceptable via the formation of a rigorous conscience. It stimulated the rise of conflict-avoiding persons, obsessed with self-discipline, punctuality, orderliness, and the importance of living a rational life. For them, the view of emotions came to be associated predominantly with dangers and weaknesses. Giving in to emotions and impulses would lead either to the dangers of physical and/or sexual violence, or to the weaknesses of devastating addictions and afflictions. Thus the successive ascent of large middle-class groups and their increasing status and power relative to other groups was reflected in the regimes of manners and emotions. From the pressures of these growing interdependencies and intensified status competition, a particular type of self-regulation originated.

This particular type of personality was characterized by an "inner compass" of reflexes and rather fixed habits (Riesman et al. 1950). Impulses and emotions came to be controlled increasingly via the more or less automatically functioning counter-impulses of a rigorous conscience with a strong penchant for order and regularity, cleanliness and neatness. Negligence in these matters indicated an inclination towards dissoluteness. Such inclinations were to be nipped in the bud, particularly in children. Without rigorous control, "first nature" might run wild. This old conviction expresses a fear that is typical of rather authoritarian relations and social controls, as well as a relatively authoritarian conscience.

The long-term trend of formalization reached its peak in the Victorian era, from the mid-nineteenth century to its last decade; the metaphor of the stiff upper lip indicated ritualistic manners and a kind of ritualistic self-control, heavily based on a scrupulous conscience, and functioning more or less automatically as a "second nature," that second-nature type of personality which Riesman called inner-directed.

The Longing for Total Belonging and Control

It was particularly in the last decades of the nineteenth century, in the wake of expanding industrialization, that many new groups with new money demanded representation in the centers of power and their good societies. Facing mounting pressures arising from the necessities of social mixing, from increased interdependencies and its intensified competition and co-operation, the advantages of the stiff upper lip diminished. In that *fin de siècle* period, the "domestication of nature," including one's own (first) nature, increasingly came to trigger both the experience of an "alienation from nature" (one's own nature included) and a new romanticized longing for nature. The more nature was exploited and controlled, the more the image of an unexploited nature was valued. There was a new interest in mountains and seaside scenery, satisfying many of the new emotional longings: "The absolute stillness, the dying of the day, the open landscape, all gave a feeling of total belonging, of a quiet ecstasy. [...] It was like a ritual return to a mystical past and a real life." The connection with the rise of a second-nature type of personality seems obvious, for "the man who endures hardship and deprivations to conquer a mountain single-handed [...] masters both an inner and an outer nature" (Frykman and Löfgren 1987, 52, 55). These decades saw the genesis of sports as an important part of public life (Elias and Dunning 1986). It seems likely that most of them became fashionable and popular, at least partly, because practicing them could bring this feeling of total belonging and control. The same feeling was also projected through the romanticizing of a past, with an old harmonious peasant society, where each person knew his or her station in life.

Swedish sociologists Frykman and Löfgren describe a comparable development regarding "our animal friends:" when middle-class people "had mastered the animal within" and had developed a moral superiority to "the more bestial lower classes," they felt a growing intimacy with animals and at the same time distanced themselves from them. They developed "'an abhorrence for natural ways' together with a longing and fascination for 'the natural way of life'" (1987, 85–6). There was a quest for spontaneous, authentic, relaxed and informal conduct, which carried the spread of informalizing processes.

Throughout the twentieth century, however, that typical second-nature domestication of "first nature" survived, despite increasingly losing adherents and vitality, particularly since the sixties. Here is an example from an early-twentieth-century manners book, demonstrating a fear of the slippery slope that seems typical of a second-nature type of personality:

"Each lie breeds new lies; there is no end to it. Let no one begin to lie to members of the household or to cheat with customers, for no escape is possible: one has to continue! Each deceitful deed, each untruth, must be either frankly admitted—only few have the courage to do so—or propped up, overcome by new untruths again. [...] your whole life will be one chain of lies that, like the links in a chain mail, will cover you all over; it will be an entangled ball, from which neither beginning nor end can be found any longer. Disentangling it has become impossible, it can only be cut. [...] Therefore, beware of beginning. Do not take that first step. And if you have already turned into the wrong path, possibly have walked it a long way already—then turn around at once, avert yourself [...] It is better to die than to be false!" (Oort 1904, 10–1, 14).

A similar rigidity in dividing the world into black and white, right and wrong, is captured in the lyrics of a popular (USA) song of the fourties: "you've got to accentuate the positive, eliminate the negative, [...] don't mess with Mister In-Between." Mister In-Between is the personification of the slippery slope, of course. His presence would jeopardize all beauty and virtue, but "virginal purity" in particular. The following words, quoted from a Dutch translation of a German book published in the first half of the 1910s, are fairly typical of the ways of addressing young girls from "good families:"

"She must never forget that she is a woman, and never lose touch with that value. And what is that treasure a woman should guard ceaselessly? It is encapsulated deep in her heart, without her being conscious of its high value. Only when her virginal feeling is affected, in her awakens a force, which brings blood to her cheeks, makes her eyes flicker, and gives her the appearance of a supernatural being. This feeling of virginal purity is the highest good for every girl. As soon as it is offended, in her awakens the voice of virtue, and happy is the woman who listens to it. It is the noblest and purest gift of heaven to her, the most precious thing she can possess, because it is so closely connected to honor and virtue that these will be lacking forever if one loses it. Therefore, one may often observe that a woman who has taken that first step on the wrong path, cannot return and continues to sink deeper, until she is the most miserable creature possibly existing on earth. [...] The girl takes care not to allow the least of liberties for which she must feel ashamed later. From the very moment on, at which both no longer dare to look freely and frankly into each other's eyes, love has been poisoned and swiftly vanishes. How many, for whom the gates to happiness had opened already, have thus denied themselves access for ever" (Seidler c. 1911–15, 9, 11).

In these words, the authoritarian conscience of a second-nature type of personality comes vividly alive: "It" is called "a force" [in her] and "the voice of virtue" [in her], and if not obeyed, it poisons love and makes life miserable. The first step on this path of vice is the point of no return: the slippery slope is an omnipresent bogey of the second-nature type of personality. To even mention what it is, exactly, that the voice of virtue warns against, is considered too dangerous and delicate for words. And it would have sounded way too physical, of course. Therefore, the dangerous "it" can only be suggested, hinted at. On the one hand, "it" is a treasure that can be given only when she finds someone who is prepared to give his all, all his life. "It" is dressed up beautifully with feelings of honor, virtue, happiness, and even with the feeling of virginal purity. But on the other hand, "it" is scarcely dressed at all, merely wrapped in the rags of misery. "It" has two sides, divided by rigid social and psychic dividing lines, just like Jekyll and Hyde.

Rising Social and Psychic Control Over Superiority Feelings and Displays

At the end of the nineteenth century and in the first decades of the twentieth, old ways of keeping a distance had to be abandoned as many groups of nouveau riche were allowed into the centers of power and their good societies. Further industrialization, including new forms of public transport, demanded more social mixing, at work as well as in trams and trains. Growing interdependency implied that social and psychic dividing lines were opening up, and the new levels of social mixing made it more necessary to achieve greater mastery over the fear of being provoked, pulled down by losing one's self-control, and degraded. Social mixing obliged increasing numbers of people to accelerate, steadily, "down the slippery slope." Thus, the fear of degrading contact with lower classes and/or with lower impulses had to be brought under more flexible social and psychic control. This was a major incentive to control expressions of superiority.

In the thirties, some etiquette books, mainly Dutch and German, still contained separate sections on "good behavior" towards social superiors and inferiors. Later, these sections disappeared. In the introduction to an English manners book of the fifties, the change away from "best people" was retrospectively commented upon.

"One casualty of the new spreading wave of middle-class living is the old criterion of all etiquette writers—The Best People [...] Today, few people would care to go on record defining The Best People. [...] In place of the old hard and fast formulas there is a new, gentler code of manners [...] less cruel, less exacting, less censorious and much easier to live by" (Edwards and Beyfus 1956, x).

Ideals of good manners became dissociated from superior and inferior social position or rank. The trend tended towards drawing social dividing lines, less on the basis of people's belonging to certain groups—class, race, age, sex, or ethnicity—, but rather more on the basis of individual behavior. An example of this process is the use of references to "best Society" or "best sets," or even "the very best sets." Until the late thirties, these references had not been exceptional in American manners books. In the new edition of 1937, however, Emily Post had changed the title of her first chapter from "What is Best Society?" to "The True Meaning of Etiquette." By formulating the latter mostly in terms of individual qualification—that is, in terms of personal qualities such as charm, tranquility, taste, beauty, and so on—Mrs. Post had turned the perspective away from the social level to the psychic, or even the biological level. Formulations such as "In other words, the code of a thoroughbred [...] is the code of instinctive decency, ethical integrity, self-respect and loyalty" (1937, 2) are examples of social avoidance internalized: from avoiding lower-class people, to avoiding layers of superiority feelings.

Display of such feelings would not only humiliate and provoke social inferiors, but also grate on the senses of anyone in good society. Superiority feelings had come to be considered as a lower class of feelings, and to display them as betraying a flaw of the personality. As subordinate social groups were emancipated, references to hierarchical group differences, and to "better" and "inferior" kinds of people, were increasingly tabooed. Whereas at one time people of inferior status were avoided, later in the twentieth century behavior that betrayed feelings of superiority and inferiority came to be avoided: avoidance behavior was internalized, turning tensions *between* people into tensions *within* people. In the process, the once automatic equation that superiority in power equals superiority as a human being declined to the point of inviting embarrassment. As many types of "lofty grandeur" came to be viewed as insulting stiffness, a different pattern of self-control came to be demanded: a stronger and yet more flexible self-regulation in which these feelings of superiority were expected to be kept under control. This was a motor in the process of informalization.

The Slippery Slope Rejuvenated

According to Davidoff, "enlargement and segregation of various 'sets' within Society allowed a certain relaxation in the rigid codes of behavior that had been demanded at mid-century" (1973, 66). This process of informalization was observed by many authors of manners books. In 1899, for example, a German author wrote that "social relations have gradually become much more informal, that is, more natural" and added that "to strive after nature" was "a general trend in art, science, and living" (quoted in Krumrey 1984, 413). The trend was generally welcomed, until early in the twentieth century, when an English author also expressed a concern:

"The boy of early Victorian days was a ceremonious little creature. He called his parents 'Sir' and 'Madam,' and would never have dreamed of starting a conversation at table, and scarcely in joining in it [...] One would not wish to see the ceremoniousness of those times revived, but it is possible that we [...] err in the opposite direction" (Armstrong 1908, 187–8).

In this question "Do we err in the wrong direction?" the old fear of the slippery slope was rejuvenated and has accompanied the whole twentieth-century process of informalization. No longer was it that first step which needed to be avoided, but where *did* solid ground and confidence stop, and the slippery slope become unstoppable? These questions became pressing each time young people had escaped further from under the wings of their parents, the questions being revived in particular by each flow of emancipation of young women and their sexuality.

The Constraint to be Unconstrained

As interdependency networks expanded, status competition intensified, and the art of obliging and being obliged became more important as a power resource, demonstrations of being intimately trustworthy while perfectly at ease also gained importance. In this sense, processes of democratization, social integration, and informalization have run parallel with an increasing constraint towards developing "smooth manners." The expression "a constraint to be unconstrained" seems to capture this paradoxical development.

This expression resembles that used by Norbert Elias: the social constraint towards self-constraint. Indeed, in the process of informalization, the two constraints have become hardly distinguishable: the constraint towards becoming accustomed to self-constraint is at the same time a constraint to be unconstrained, to be confident and at ease. Almost every etiquette book contains passages that emphasize the importance of tactful behavior, rather than demonstrative deference, and of "natural" rather than mannered behavior. However, in processes of emancipation and informalization, some ways of behaving, experienced previously as tactful deference, came to be seen as too hierarchical and demonstrative, in the same way that what had once been defined and recommended as natural came to be experienced as more or less stiff and phony, and branded as mannered. It then became so obvious a "role" in which so many traces of constraint could be "discovered" that "playing" this role would provoke embarrassment. People who stuck to these old ways of relating were running the risk of being seen as bores, as lacking any talent for "the jazz of human exchange" (Hochschild 1983). Hence, new forms of relaxed, "loose," and "natural" behavior were developed.

All of this also helps one to understand changes in the practices and ideals in raising children. In the old and new middle classes, parents who themselves had learned to behave in a rather reserved, inhibited and indirect manner, and to conceal their "innermost feelings behind a restrained observance of conventional forms" (Goudsblom 1968, 30), became charmed and fascinated by the more outright, spontaneous, straightforward and direct behavior of children. This attractiveness of the (more) "natural" functioned as a catalyst to the emancipation of emotions.

As "ease" and "naturalness" gained importance, and demands for individual authenticity and a socially more meaningful personal identity rose, to behave according to a set of fixed rules of manners increasingly came to be experienced as rigid and stiff, and their performance as too obvious and predictable, as "insincere," even as "fraudulent" or as "deceit." In its wake, for example, the mourning ritual was minimized (Wouters 2002, 7). This means that traditional ways of behaving and regulating emotions have been losing part of their "defense" or "protective" function. The former formal codes had functioned as a defense against dangers and fears which were now diminished, or could be avoided or controlled in more varied and subtle ways—ways in which both social superiority and inferiority were less explicitly and less extremely expressed. Increasing numbers of people pressured each other to develop more differentiated and flexible patterns of self-regulation, triggering a further impetus towards higher levels of social knowledge, self-knowledge and reflexivity.

Emancipation of Emotions – Rise of a "Third-Nature" Personality

As most social codes have been becoming more flexible and differentiated, manners and emotion regulation have also been becoming more decisive criteria for status or reputation. People have been pressurizing each other to become more conscious of social and individual options and restrictions, and this has been putting social and self-knowledge in greater demand. The same goes for the ability to empathize and to take on others' roles. Respect and respectable behavior have been becoming more dependent upon self-regulation.

Between the fifties and eighties, these processes of social and psychic emancipation and integration accelerated dramatically. The old conviction that being open to such "dangerous" emotions would almost irrevocably be followed by acting upon them was destroyed. The dominant mode of emotion management had reached a strength and scope that increasingly enabled people to admit to themselves and to others to having "dangerous" emotions, without provoking shame, particularly the shame-fear of losing control, and of having to give in. This kind of self-regulation implies that emotions, even those which could provoke physical and sexual violence, have become more easily accessible, while their control is less strongly based upon a commanding conscience, functioning more or less automatically as a "second nature."

In the course of the integration of "lower" social groups within Western societies, and the subsequent emancipation and integration of "lower" impulses and emotions in personality, both psychic and social censorship declined. The fear and awe of fantasy or dissident imagination diminished together with the fear and awe of the authorities of state and conscience. There was a significant spread of more and more unconcealed expressions of insubordination, sex and violence, particularly in the realms of imagination and amusement. Ego functions came to dominate conscience, or Superego functions, and a more ego-dominated pattern of self-regulation spread. To the extent that it has become "natural" to perceive the pulls and pushes of both "first nature" and "second nature" as well as the dangers and chances, both short term and long term, of any particular situation or relation, a "third nature" has been developing. Increasing numbers of people have become aware of emotions and temptations in circumstances where shame-fears and dangers had been dominant before. This emancipation of emotions is also implied in the conclusion of a study subtitled "The struggle for self-control in Modern America:" "Americans were told to become less stiff but more cautious" (Stearns 1999, 154).

Obviously, this emancipation of emotion involves an attempt at reaching back to "first nature" without losing any of the control that was provided by "second nature." Thus, the rise of a "third-nature personality" demands and depends on an emancipation of "first nature" as well as "second nature." Of this development, the history of the corset may serve as a metaphor.

A Short History of the Corset

Wearing a corset spread from Spanish aristocratic women in the sixteenth century to other strata and other countries, and it flourished in the nineteenth century. The spread of the corset symbolizes the spread of increasing control over the body—loose clothes came to indicate loose morals. Towards the end of the nineteenth century, as for instance in the movement for reform of clothing, ideals of naturalness amalgamated with ideals of beauty. From that time onwards until the sixties, the boned corset came to be used only as an orthopedic gadget for female bodies gone out of control, ones that burst the bounds of the prevailing standard of beauty. This standard increasingly contained ideals of naturalness, but not without control: much female flesh that was not quantitatively excessive remained controlled by corset-like underwear, girdles, straps, corselets, and bras. Only at the end of the sixties did women succeed in liberating their bodies from this kind of control. However, it was not a full liberation. It was clearly a controlled decontrolling, while the control of the corset over the body was continued as self-control: women turned heavily to diets, sports, aerobics, fitness, home trainers, and other forms of "working the body" such as plastic surgery (Steele 2001). Since the eighties, a stylized visible corset has reappeared as a playfully provocative form of erotic display, but as it is taken for granted that the women who wear one do not need such a corset for controlling their bodies, the visible corset can also be taken as a symbol of how ideals of beauty, naturalness, and self-control have merged with each other—another indication of the spread of a third-nature personality.

From Guilt to Shame and Shaming

In the sixties and seventies, the *emancipation of emotions* and the shift from a second-nature towards a third-nature type of personality involved a different function for, and appreciation of guilt. In comparing the three types of persons that he distinguished—tradition-directed, inner-directed, and other-directed—Riesman et al. wrote about the inner-directed type:

"He goes through life less independent than he seems, obeying his inner piloting. Getting off course, whether in response to inner impulses or to the fluctuating voices of contemporaries, may lead to the feeling of guilt. [...] [In contrast,] the other-directed person, must be able to receive signals from far and near; the sources are many, the changes rapid. [...] As against guilt-and-shame controls, though of course these survive, one prime psychological lever of the other-directed person is a diffuse anxiety" (1950, 24–5).

These words can be read as a harbinger of the widespread attack on guilt and guilt feelings in the sixties and seventies, expressed through the widely used words "guilt trip" in exclamations like "Don't lay that guilt trip on me"! Ralph Turner observed that "guilt becomes an evil thing. It becomes the impediment to individual autonomy and to an individual sense of worth. Guilt is the invasion of the self by arbitrary and external standards" (1969, 402). This social movement was mirrored in changing opinions about guilt in criminal law and punishment, as well as in a critique of blame attribution as a means of orientation (Benthem van den Bergh 1986), and in the "self psychology" of Kohut (1977).

Guilt feelings came to be experienced more strongly as indicative of a conscience-ridden personality make-up and, therefore, as an anxiety to be mastered. They came to be seen as a symbol and a symptom of a commanding and rather automatically functioning conscience. Thus, in fact, guilt was rejected for being an internalized form of shame that functions as a form of rigid self-constraint. In comparison, shame feelings which have been less internalized and which, therefore, function less rigidly and automatically than do guilt feelings, are more strongly experienced as external constraints. They refer more directly to other people and also, of course, to the fact that one's conscience is at least partly in agreement with these others. This perspective opens a window on to the reasons why the shift from a superego-dominated personality in the direction of an ego-dominated personality has coincided with a decline in the status of guilt, both as a feeling and as a concept.

This seems to be a reversal of the direction of development from a shame-culture to a guilt-culture, as it has been represented in an extensive body of literature, especially in the "culture and personality" school of anthropology, of which Ruth Benedict's *The Chrysanthemum and the Sword* (1946) is a classic example. In the informalization process of the twentieth century, this development from a shame-culture to a guilt-culture seems to have been reversed: from a guilt-culture to a shame-culture. It would be absurd, however, to equate the pattern of shame in what has been described as shame-cultures with the pattern of shame in informalized societies. Obviously, a distinction between two types of shame mechanisms—or better, shaming mechanisms—corresponding to (at least) two types of external constraints is needed (see Schröter 1997, 102–4), just as much as is a distinction between two types of shame-culture.

Traditional Shame-Cultures, Inner-Directed Guilt-Cultures, Other-Directed Shame-Cultures

In traditional shame-cultures, shaming is a form of external social control exercised mainly to prevent people from engaging with opportunities to go against the codes. If they had done so anyway, shaming techniques such as the pillory, functioned to punish them. Continued shaming processes fuelled these external social controls to become transformed into habitual self-controls, resulting in the making of a guilt-ridden second-nature type of personality. In people with this inner-directed type of personality, the shame-fear of being unable to control emotions and affects in accordance with the prevailing regimes of manners and emotions was internalized, placed under the authority of a rigorous conscience, and experienced as guilt. The sociologist Johan Goudsblom has argued that the authorities of state and church were at the cradle of this process. Seen from a developmental sociological perspective, he writes,

"a process of differentiation has taken place, in the course of which a number of causes for shame were gradually brought under the control of more centralized institutions, the state and the church. Part of the burden of shame was converted into guilt by virtue of those institutions which developed special branches for meting out punishment. Other institutions, especially the family, adjusted to this penal pattern. In society at large, it was the state and the church that created guilt-generating forms of punishment. In doing so, both state and church have strengthened the processes of conscience formation. The confessional and the courtroom were the material reflections of the effort to replace shaming rituals by more rational forms of accusation, allowing the victims (be they 'culprits' or 'sinners') the possibility of appeal according to written rules" (2007, 15).

From this perspective, in which guilt appears mainly as the product of new forms of shaming, to conceptualize more recent changes as a transformation from a guilt-culture to a new shame-culture may not seem very illuminating. Yet, doing so might add to the meaningfulness of Riesman's concept "other-directedness." It draws attention to a change in the pattern of self-regulation in the direction of less inner-directedness—in the sense of bowing to the rules of a rigorous conscience—and greater awareness of others and of the pressures they exercise, or have exercised in the past. For the *emancipation of emotions* also implied that more and more people increasingly became conscious of emotions that, as a rule in the past, had been either ignored or concealed for fear of parents and others on whom they were dependent. In the informalization spurt of the sixties and seventies, many people discovered that self-restraints of all kinds were in fact constraints by others, or at least based upon such external constraints (Wouters 1990, 53). Thus, processes of psychologization and sociologization were tightly interwoven.

As the range of behavioral and emotional alternatives expanded in processes of informalization, avoiding shame and shaming became increasingly dependent upon the ways in which individuals control and regulate their manners and emotions. Self-regulation increasingly became both the focus *and* the locus of external social controls. The implied reading of the two shame cultures shows a markedly different balance of controls. The same goes for two other balances. Whereas the regime of emotions in the old shame-culture was characterized by a we-I balance that is strongly tilted to the side of the we, the we-I balance in the regime of the recent shame-culture is strongly tilted to the I. Likewise there is a commensurably strong tilting in the balance of involvement and detachment: emotion regulation in the old shame-culture was characterized by relatively low levels of detachment, while the new shame-culture has relatively high levels. Yet, no matter how the controlling of shame-fears in new shame-cultures of other-directed persons may differ from that of the old shame-culture of tradition-directed persons, their concern has remained the same: status degradation, loss of respect and self-respect, with total social expulsion and loss of all meaning in life as an extreme.

Sociogenesis and Psychogenesis

As national, continental, and global integration processes exert pressure towards increasingly differentiated regimes of manners, they also exert pressure towards increasingly reflexive and flexible regimes of regulating emotions and the self. The period after World War II was characterized by decolonization, global emancipation, and democratization. Cooperation between people and their organizations expanded and came to be more complex and multi-level, while competition intensified but was increasingly pacified and subtle, amounting to a further differentiation and integration of the balance between cooperation and competition. It was a period of expanding interdependencies and rising levels of mutual identification, in which ideals of equality and mutual consent spread and gained strength.

On this basis, avoidance behavior came to be less and less rigidly directed at "lower-class" people and "lower" emotions, and on the whole, in most Western countries, behavioral and emotional alternatives expanded and there was an emancipation of impulses and emotions, accompanied by a shift from conscience to consciousness (to use this shorthand expression). The term "third nature" refers to a level of consciousness and calculation in which all types of constraints and possibilities are taken into account. In this way, social processes in which relations and manners between social groups have become less rigid and hierarchical are connected with psychic processes in which relations between the psychic functions of people's emotions and impulses have become more open and fluent. A self-regulation via the rather automatically functioning counter-emotions and counter-impulses of conscience has lost out to a regulation via consciousness. As social and psychic dividing lines have opened up, social groups as well as psychic functions have become more integrated – that is, the communications and connections between both social groups and psychic functions have become more flowing and flexible. Lo and behold: the sociogenesis and psychogenesis of a "third-nature personality!"

There was, however, one important exception to the expansion of behavioral and emotional alternatives: the social codes increasingly came to dictate that overt expression of inferiority and superiority feelings be avoided. The avoidance of these feelings and of behavior that expressed them was a confirmation of social equalization and a necessary condition in order for informalization to occur. Thus, there was a further curbing of emotions in relation to the display of arrogance or self-aggrandizement, and "self-humiliation." These displays were either banished to the realm of imagination, games and sports, or compartmentalized behind the social and psychic scenes. The latter leads to hiding superiority and inferiority feelings, and this process can be interpreted as a countertrend or, at least partly, as a reversal of the direction of the main process.

From this perspective, a question of major importance concerns whether processes of an *emancipation of emotions* and *controlled decontrolling of emotional controls* will continue and eventually come to include more feelings of superiority and inferiority. Will feelings of inferiority and superiority be further admitted into consciousness, while, at the same time, they come under a stronger, a more comprehensive, more stable and subtle internal (ego) control, one that is sharply scrutinized and thus backed up by external social controls? The answer to these questions strongly depends, of course, on the future of integration processes and their inherent integration conflicts. Will these integration conflicts remain sufficiently controlled and contained? The opposite, however, is true also: the control and containment of social integration conflicts depends to a large extent on the degree of control over superiority feelings in the societies of the established; on their degree of informalization.

References

Armstrong, Lucie Heaton (1908). *Etiquette Up-To-Date*. London: Werner Laurie.
Benedict, Ruth (1946). *The Crysanthemum and the Sword*. Boston: Houghton Mifflin.
Benthem van den Berg, Godfried (1986). The Improvement of Human Means of Orientation: Towards Synthesis in the Social Sciences. In Raymond Apthorpe and Andreas Krahl (eds.). *Development Studies: Critique and Renewal*, 109-36. Leiden: Brill.
Blumin, Stuart M. (1989). *The Emergence of the Middle Class. Social Experience in the American City, 1760–1900*. Cambridge, New York, Melbourne: Cambridge University Press.
Curtin, Michael (1987). *Propriety and Position. A Study of Victorian Manners*. New York: Garland.
Davidoff, Leonore (1973). *The Best Circles. Society, Etiquette and the Season*. London: Croom Helm.
Durkheim, Emile (1964). *The Division of Labour in Society*. London: Glencoe. [first published in 1893]
Edwards, Anne, and Drusilla Beyfus (1956). *Lady Behave: A Guide to Modern Manners*. London: Boswell & Co.
Elias, Norbert (2000). *The Civilizing Process. Sociogenetic and Psychogenetic Investigations*. Cambridge, MA: Blackwell.
Elias, Norbert, and Eric Dunning (1986). *Quest for Excitement. Sport and Leisure in the Civilizing Process*. Oxford: Blackwell.

Frykman, Jonas, and Orvar Löfgren (1987). *Culture Builders. A Historical Anthropology of Middle-Class Life.* New Brunswick, London: Rutgers University Press.

Goudsblom, Johan (1968). *Dutch Society.* New York: Random House.

— (2007). Shame as Social Pain. *Sociology of Emotions Newsletter,* 21 (1), 6, 10–5.

Haskell, Thomas (1985). Capitalism and the Humanitarian Sensibility. *American Historical Review,* 90, 339–61, 547–66.

Hochschild, Arlie Russel (1983). *The Managed Heart. Commercialization of Human Feeling.* Berkeley: University of California Press.

Klickmann, Flora (1902). *The Etiquette of To-Day.* London.

Kohut, Heinz (1977). *The Restauration of the Self.* New York: International Universities Press.

Krumrey, Horst-Volker (1984). *Entwicklungsstrukturen von Verhaltensstandarden.* Frankfurt am Main: Suhrkamp.

Newton, Sarah E. (1994). *Learning to Behave: A Guide to American Conduct Books Before 1900.* Westport, Conn.: Greenwood Press.

Oort, Dr. H. L. (1904). *Goede Raad aan de Jonge Mannen en Jonge Meisjes der XXste Eeuw. By a Business Man.* Utrecht: Broese.

Post, Emily (1937). *Etiquette in Society, in Business, in Politics and at Home.* New York: Funk and Wagnalls. [first published in 1922]

Riesman, David, N. Glazer, and R. Denney (1950). *The Lonely Crowd.* New Haven: Yale University Press.

Schröter, Michael (1997). *Erfahrungen mit Norbert Elias.* Frankfurt am Main: Suhrkamp.

Seidler, Dr. H. J. (*circa* 1911–15). *Hoe Men Zich bij de Heeren het Best Bemind Kan Maken.* Rotterdam: Bolle.

Stearns, Peter N. (1999). *Battle Ground of Desire. The Struggle for Self-Control in Modern America.* New York: New York University Press.

Steele, Valerie (2001). *The Corset – A Cultural History.* New Haven: Yale University Press.

Tilburg, Marja van (1998). *Hoe Hoorde Het?* Amsterdam: Spinhuis.

Turner, Ralph H. (1969). The Theme of Contemporary Social Movements. *British Journal of Sociology,* 20 (4), 390–405.

Wouters, Cas (1990). *Van Minnen en Sterven. Informalisering van de Omgangsvormen Rond Seks en Dood.* Amsterdam: Bakker.

— (2002). The Quest for New Rituals in Dying and Mourning: Changes in the We-I Balance. *Body & Society,* 8, 1–27.

— (2004). *Sex and Manners: Female Emancipation in the West Since 1890.* London: Sage.

— (2007). *Informalization: Manners and Emotions Since 1890.* London: Sage.

What Makes Us Modern(s)? The Place of Emotions in Contemporary Society

Patrick Becker

> "A new paradigm is slowly gaining ground: you're lost if you rely on reason alone. Often enough, it's rather our feelings that unconsciously guide us through life—especially in situations where pure rationality seems to be the norm: be it in the context of political decision-making or global business strategies, or in the evaluation of international conflicts [...]. The 'Generation E' (E for Emotion) has realized that emotions are a world power, and they know when to better trust your emotions, and when not."
>
> *Christian Ankowitsch, Generation Emotion*

Whether we agree with Ankowitsch's (2002) characterization of contemporary society as *Generation Emotion* or not, his diagnosis of an increasing importance of emotion cannot be denied. Emotions are held in high esteem these days and this can be observed in all spheres of society:

In the business world, for example, professional knowledge is no longer considered to be sufficient for doing your job properly. Instead, "emotional competencies" are now seen as the real driving forces of a successful career. It is thus no wonder that the training of emotions has become part of the curriculum in many schools. Here, students are taught how best to identify and manage their feelings in all kinds of situations (Petermann et al. 1999). This "education of feeling" ranges from lessons on how to experience one's own sexuality up to the training of moral emotions.

Apart from the spheres of work and education, a new appreciation of emotionality can also be noticed in the sciences—especially within those disciplines that originally thought that feelings shouldn't matter to them: in economics, the role of emotions in economic processes is increasingly recognized (Bolle 2006). A case in point is the research on the role of trust for efficient market transactions, or on the affective bases for altruistic or collective action. In the neurosciences, the "emotional turn" has even put the classical dichotomy between passion and reason into question. Here, the notion of affect and cognition as two conflicting forces of human action makes way for concepts that try to integrate both sides: today, many neuroscientists no longer regard emotions and feelings as the antithesis of rationality, but as its very basis (Damasio 1999).

Concurrent with, and partly based on, the emotional turn in science is a similar one in many professional fields, especially in medical and therapeutic settings: Experts in psychology and psychiatry are convinced that most mental disorders are actually caused by emotional dysfunctions. And as a result new approaches for the definition, etiology and therapy of these newly named "emotional" disorders (Bradley 2000) are now emerging.

From a sociological point of view, Ankowitsch's diagnosis is therefore as irrefutable as it is irritating. The diagnosis is irrefutable because the many forms of this new appreciation of emotion cannot be overlooked, and it is irritating because it contradicts what most sociological thinkers understand to be the essence of modern culture—namely, its rational organization of both the public sphere and the private conduct of life. It is indeed this rational organization that led to a subduing and marginalization of emotions in society. But in contrast to the understanding of modern society as a rationalized social system, and its view of emotions as irrational impulses and sources of irritation that need to be controlled, emotions nowadays are considered to be highly valuable, if not indispensable resources for both the individual and society at large.

In the following I develop an interpretation of this new emotionalism from a cultural sociological point of view. I start with a discussion of modernity's self-understanding and its relationship to emotion, reason, and rationality. Here it will become apparent that conventionally, modernity is defined on the basis of its strict demarcation from, and control of what is generally conceived as an irrational and pre-modern remnant—the emotions. I then review classical and current sociological positions on the role of emotions in modern life, and illustrate how both are embedded in the modern vision of a rationalized society devoid of feelings (or its simple inversion, i.e. an emotionally "re-enchanted" society that lacks the modern imperative of instrumental reason).

In the subsequent parts of my article I propose an alternative understanding of the place of emotions in modernity that goes beyond such antagonistic conceptions. I first discuss some episodes in the cultural history of modernity that illustrate how a certain "romantic" conception of emotionality has, in fact, played a crucial role in the course of modernization, and thus suggest that, contrary to the modern self-image, emotionality (and waves of emotionalism) shouldn't be considered to be antithetical to modernity, but rather as an important and integral part of it. I then continue with an exploration of the emotional turn in current scientific and professional discourses on emotion, and the way they redefine what emotions "really" are. Based on these insights, my chapter concludes with an interpretation of the new emotionalism in contemporary society that construes the relationship between modern emotionality and rationality in a non-dichotomous way.

Emotions and the Self-Understanding of Modernity

For several decades the concept of modernity was applied rather unquestioningly to the social formations in the northwestern part of the world. A central topic of sociological thinking since the classical works of the founding fathers of sociology, it constitutes the Archimedean point for both the diagnosis and interpretation of contemporary society, and the genesis of its specifically "modern" character. Although its exact definition has always been contested, the concept gained increasing attention in the second half of the last century, where a certain understanding of a "modern society" and what constitutes "modernity" gained dominance both in scientific and public discourse.

According to this understanding, the social world attained its modern character between the second half of the 19th century up to the First World War. This process of modernization was driven by waves of industrialization and rationalization on the one hand, and parallel processes of urbanization and democratization on the other, which resulted in an increasing disciplining and civilizing of society. These processes of social and cultural change, which originated in Western Europe, were conceived of as striving for universal expansion. Moreover, they were considered to be of such a revolutionary and fundamental nature that they served to instigate and legitimate a strict demarcation of these modernized societies from all premodern ones. In explaining the driving force behind this great transformation, one usually posits the workings of new principles of rationality. As such, the relationship between modernity and rationality was taken not to be just a contingent, but rather an essential one (Imbusch 2005, 75).

The association of modernity with reason and rationality, however, had its price, as Jack Barbalet (1998, 33–4) pointed out:

"If there is a single aphorism or credo which summarizes the cultural formation of the modern Western world it would have to be Rene Descartes' *cogito ergo sum*. I think therefore I am [...]. If I am because I think, then I am undone if I feel. This is the other side of the *cogito*, namely that persons have no control of the emotions which subvert their thoughts and reason. The best thing to do with the emotion which subverts reason is suppress it."

Under the aegis of this understanding of modernity, modern society thus became equated not only with the establishment of rationalistic orientations in both the public sphere and in private life, but also with the development of a strict regime of emotion regulation.

Following a Foucaultian understanding of a "discourse" as a complex of interrelated ideas, assumptions and statements, as well as specific patterns of argumentation and classification which constitute and delimit what can be said on a given topic (Foucault 1981, 74), I want to analyze the discursive constitution of rationalist, unemotional modern society in more detail. In particular I wish to do so with regard to the above-mentioned equation of modernity and rationality on the one hand, and the corresponding depreciation of emotions as non-rational and pre-modern on the other. In the following, I therefore review this "discourse of modernity" and its constitutive ideas.[1]

The Discourse of Modernity

In its most condensed form, the discourse of modernity portrays modernity as the result of an encompassing process of disenchantment and ratio-

---

1 In this context, it is important to make a distinction between the "discourse of modernity" (which itself is object of historical changes and transformations and which can be analyzed from the point of view of a sociology and history of knowledge), and the actual practices, forms and institutions of modern society which have been erected in the name of modernity. Although both the discourse of modernity and its actual cultural and social forms strongly inform each other, their relationship is one of affinity, not of identity, and thus the one should not be reduced to the other. Despite this distinction, one has to acknowledge that there has been in fact, a crucial break and profound transformation in the dominant discourse on humans and society that occured at the end of the 18th century (Wagner 1995, 25). This discursive break established modern ideas as relevant for individuals and society as a whole and instituted new social and political topics and conflicts which shape the world up to this day. For a further discussion of this discourse and its role in the (self-)description and interpretation of the present state and the historic development of the western world, see Michel Foucault (1971), Reinhard Koselleck (1979), Jürgen Habermas (1985), Stephen Toulmin (1991), Peter Wagner (1995), and Armin Nassehi (2006).

nalization of the world view that was firstly implemented in economic contexts, but soon spilled over into all other spheres of life, thus gaining universal significance. This process of rationalization is based on the diffusion and establishment of new norms of reasonable and rational organization of human action in all kinds of contexts. This was achieved, for instance, via the re-orientation of one's private and public conduct of life on the basis of calculated means-ends-relationships, the establishment of scientific (i.e. objective and systematic) methods of knowledge production, the evolution of a rationalistic-utilitarian disposition in the economy, and finally the diffusion of bureaucratic organizations as the most rational form of exercising power. This large-scale rationalization of thought and action in all social contexts became the starting point for an increasing domination of nature on the one hand, and a rejection of all religious, mystical or other aspects of life that were not rationally explicable or justifiable on the other.

In particular, the latter development went hand in hand with a deep distrust of emotions, which were considered to lead to irrational and (thus) detrimental consequences. Or, as Stephen Toulmin (1991, 181) poignantly summed up the dominant modern view on emotions and rationality in his analysis of the "standard" account of modernity: "Emotions usually tamper with, and impede the workings of rationality, and therefore one should better trust and strengthen the human reason, but distrust and curb one's emotions."[2]

Quite in line with this idea of modernization as rationalization, the discourse of modernity also strongly enunciates the modernizing effects of a concurrent process of civilizing which since the middle ages, has successively set up and established increasing standards of self-control and self-discipline. This process has gone hand in hand with a further differentiation and specialization of society. In fact, it is considered to provide its very basis, as it has helped to make individual behavior consistent and predictable enough for the long and complex interaction chains that make up

---

2 It is important to note that this dominant discursive framing of rationalization and emotional discipline as societal progress was sometimes contrasted by a more pessimistic narrative: while still acknowledging the transformative effects of the process of rationalization, this critical version of the discourse of modernity portrayed it as being of a highly destructive nature and considered it to lead to an age characterized by pure instrumental reason. As such, it was made responsible for all the anomies of modernity—most of all, the loss of affective bonds and social solidarity in modern society, and the increasing alienation of the modern individual.

modern society. The disciplining effects of the civilizing process are said to work on two levels at once: first of all, the unrestrained expression of one's impulses and passions (especially the aggressive ones) became confined through the modern state which increasingly monopolized power and thus has been able to effectively control and sanction any act of violence or aggression. Apart from the evolution of these external forms of behavioral control, the individual has been put, simultaneously, under a second, "internal" regime of affect regulation and self-control: thus an ever-growing canon of social conventions, etiquette, and good manners has served to mediate between one's own spontaneous affects, drives, and bodily reactions on the one hand, and the socially acceptable forms of their expression on the other. Any violation of these norms would lead to severe social (i.e. loss of status) and psychological (i.e. feelings of shame) consequences for the wrongdoer.

Under this perspective of modernization as civilization, then, affect regulation becomes the pivotal point in the development of modernity: Controlling one's emotions and feelings is necessary not only because it safeguards us from its disruptive effects on the optimal working of reason and rationality, but also (or even more so) because it constitutes the basis for the stabilization and extension of the complex social interaction chains that make up a functionally differentiated society. As such, the continuing disciplining of emotions is considered to be crucial for the future of modern society, whose very existence depends on the effective control of our impulses and drives.[3]

While the discourse of modernity construes the twin processes of civilization and rationalization as the driving forces that gave rise to and formed the modern world, it has introduced a third element that confers upon these processes a deeper, (world) historic significance—namely, the idea that both have to be taken as manifestations of a unique evolutionary dynamic that, once started, inevitably leads to the development of a func-

---

3 Here also, the dominant view of modernization as the subjugation of man's destructive impulses and drives sometimes becomes countered by an alterative version of the "modernization as civilization" argument. It also stresses the importance of the civilizing process for the development of the modern world, but focuses on the negative aspects and psychic costs of this development. This critical framing of the civilizing process portrays the disciplining of emotions as a dangerous subjugation and deformation of human nature as well as a stupefaction of emotional life, which will ultimately make modern life not worth living anymore.

tionally differentiated and industrialized society of the Western sort (Wehling 1992, 20, 119). In the context of this teleological interpretation of the historical development of modernity, the evolution of the modern Western world becomes idealized as the "great narrative of occidental modernization" (Toulmin 1991, 21–33). It portrays the modern societies of the West as the outcome of an encompassing universalizing of reason and rationality, and further states that they constitute the culmination and final result of this historical process of social evolution. Based on this socio-evolutionary (and one could add, Eurocentric) conception of modernization, all non-modern societies were redefined as being both underdeveloped and outdated *vis-à-vis* the modern Western ones. In fact, one often identified their particularistic and non-rational orientations, norms and schemes of action as the ultimate causes of their underdevelopment. In consequence, all these so-called "pre-modern" or "traditional" societies would only be on a par with, and just as modern as, the societies of the West if they were to "catch up" by imitating the Western model of modernization.[4]

The differentiation between modern and traditional societies which underlies the evolutionary conception of modernization is the final and maybe most crucial aspect of the discursive construction of modernity, as it establishes a clear-cut demarcation and essential difference between the modern world and the pre-modern one. As a recurring leitmotif in modern self-definition, it can be found in many related differentiations and classifications that gained prominence in the course of modernization, and that were often taken to be concrete manifestations of the supposed "great divide" between tradition and modernity. Among these, the most well-known were the distinction between *Gemeinschaft* and *Gesellschaft*; the opposition between (uncivilized) nature and (human-made) culture; and of course, the dichotomy between body and mind, that is to say, between the forces of (subjective) passions and feeling, and the power of objective

---

4 Also, the view of modernization as a process of purposeful evolution and development has been contrasted by a critical framing of the evolutionary dynamics of modernity: here, the modernization process is described as effectuating an epochal socio-cultural change from a pre-modern *Gemeinschaft* (held together by affective bonds and non-instrumental orientations) into a modern *Gesellschaft* (constituted by unemotional, instrumental relationships). This transformation of pre-modern societies into modern ones, however, is not seen as a higher stage of social evolution, but as a dangerous step towards social disintegration, as it comes along with an erosion of most traditional forms of life, and an irretrievable loss of community and sense of solidarity.

reason.[5] What all these dichotomies have in common is that they construct and demarcate certain (non-modern) "others" from the moderns in terms of essential temporal, spatial or anthropological differences. This is so whether we refer to the "barbarians" of the past who lived in close-knit communities without any kind of modern functional differentiation, the "primitives" in the far off countries that live in harmony with nature but lack any sign of high culture and civilization, or the madmen, the lower classes and the women in modern times, who were excluded from participation in modern society because of their supposedly untempered passions and lack of reason and rationality.

Despite their apparently self-evident nature, most of these dichotomies should be seen as resulting from the modern self-conception, rather than being taken as its justification. Klaus Lichtblau (1998, 50–1, 67–8, 85–6) has pointed out that, without the construction of this "great divide" between tradition and modernity and its cognate dichotomies, modern society itself would loose its identity, for it is only through the application of these categories and the resulting differentiation and separation from a contrasting "other"—something that is exactly the opposite of what is modern—that modern society is able to define itself.[6]

In this context, a constitutive feature of the great divide and its concordant dichotomies needs to be mentioned: In each and every case, it seems to be that "the others" (on the non-modern side of the divide) are always defined and excluded because of their (supposed) lack of reason and civilizing achievements. Hence, what all these differentiations have in common is their ascription of reason to one side, and irrationality and lack of emotional self-control to the other side of the great modern/non-modern divide.

---

5 Talcott Parsons' (1951) conceptualization of the "pattern variables" (i.e., collective vs. self-interest, particularistic vs. universalistic orientations, affectivity vs. affective neutrality, etc.), which were used to categorize different social roles and social systems, also rests on some of these dichotomies.

6 As such, it isn't surprising that within the discourse of modernity, all "other" societies (i.e. all societies separated from the western ones in either time or space) became redefined as "traditional" and non-modern just because they lacked the specific ideals of rationality, civilization or development that modern societies attributed exclusively to themselves. In other words, "traditional" societies were thus constructed first and foremost to serve as a convenient foil against which the ideal "modern" society could be contrasted and described.

The discourse of modernity thus constructed emotions and emotionality as the necessary "other" against which modern society sets itself against.[7] As such, the discursive construction of modernity not only hinges on the establishment of a strong, "inner" relationship between rationality and modernity (see Imbusch 2005, 75), but likewise on the construction of an equally essential (but inverse) relationship between modernity and emotionality as the non-modern "opposition" to modern rationality and civilization.

In summary I claim here that the discourse of modernity revolves around four central ideas: firstly, the modern world is considered to be the result of an encompassing process of rationalization, which, secondly, went along with a process of civilization that increasingly tempered, disciplined and suppressed affective impulses and strong emotions. Thirdly, these interrelated processes constitute the driving forces of a great and epochal social transformation. Fourthly and maybe most crucially, based on this social evolutionary perspective, the discourse of modernity postulates a fundamental difference between modern societies and pre-modern ones—a "great divide"—which ultimately rests on the opposition between reason and rationality on the one hand, and between emotions and irrationality (as its inverse) on the other.[8]

Under the aegis of this discursive construction of what is modern, the idea of modernity became firmly grounded in a fundamental division between reason and civilized manners on the modern side of this divide, and its inverse (manifested in the form of tradition, emotionality or irrationality) on the other.

This is maybe no more apparent than in the prevailing social scientific reflections on the subject, as Jack Barbalet (1998) has pointed out with

---

7 In his historical analysis of the discourse of modernity, Peter Wagner (1995, 76) even argues that the differentiation and opposition of reason and irrationality is the point of origin of all modern efforts of self-understanding and (self-)definition.

8 As already mentioned, the discourse of modernity was always made up of two conflicting accounts, with the dominant one framing modernization as the engine of social progress and emancipation, and the heterodox other framing it as the origin of man's (emotional) deformation and social alienation. The opposition between modern reason and pre-modern emotionality, however, is crucial for the heterodox version of the modernity discourse as well: in deploring and comparing the ills of a cold and unemotional modernity *vis-à-vis* a pre-modern, more emotional society saturated with emotions, it obviously still follows the overall theme of a great divide between unemotional (and modern) rationality and irrational (and pre-modern) emotionality—it is just the respective evaluation of emotionality and rationality which has been switched.

regard to sociology's view on the role of emotions (or rather, the lack thereof) in modern life. According to Barbalet (1998, 16), sociology generally considers emotions to be rather incompatible with modernity:

"'Affective neutrality,' as an aspect of modern social development, insists that emotion is irrelevant to the secondary institutions and relations of modern society, indeed, is undermining of them [...]. Emotion was regarded as not only irrational but pre-modern: such views became sociological conventions."

The notion of a fundamental divide between unemotional rationality that characterizes (or even constitutes) the modern world on the one hand, and irrational and pre-modern emotionality on the other, is not only prominent in sociological thinking. It also underlies canonical historic and philosophical concepts of modernity, as Barbara Rosenwein (2002) and Stephen Toulmin (1991) have convincingly demonstrated.[9]

The following discussion, however, will focus on the sociological view on emotions and modern society. In reviewing classical and current sociological reflections on the role of emotions in modern society, it will become apparent that most sociological accounts of modern society oscillate between the vision of an unemotional, thoroughly rationalized society devoid of feelings, and that of the vision of a non-rational, emotionally re-enchanted society as its inverse. As such, both concepts remain deeply embedded in the conceptual framework of the discourse of modernity—a framework that might no longer be adequate to fully grasp the transformative effects of the current emotional turn on the understanding of emotions and their role in society.

Sociological Views on Emotions and Modern Life

Almost every prominent analyst of modern society has identified the rational organization of both the public sphere and private life as a characteristic feature of modernity. As a result of this encompassing process of

---

9 Rosenwein argues that the dominant historical conception of modernity as an epochal break in the evolution of mankind heavily relies on a differentiation of the modern epoch from earlier ones based on their completely different handling of emotions (Rosenwein 2002, 825). Toulmin identifies a similar line of thought in the common philosophical view on modernity as a "project" that aimed at the emancipation of the subject through the power of reason and further argues that the suppression and expulsion of emotions is the unavoidable flipside of the modern project (Toulmin 1991, 262).

rationalization, emotions and feelings became marginalized as irrational impulses and primitive drives, which in turn needed to be disciplined and controlled.

In his study on *The Protestant Ethic and the Spirit of Capitalism*, Max Weber (2007) presents the classical version of this argument: The Calvinistic asceticism encouraged protestants in the 17th and 18th century to cultivate a methodical and rational lifestyle, but at the same time it aimed at controlling and suppressing any disruptive desires and passions. For Weber, this Protestant asceticism constitutes the beginning of instrumental rationality that became the backbone of modern capitalism. However, this economically instrumental rationality came at the price of a conscious and continuous suppression of emotions. Over time, the process of rationalization spilled over from the economy into almost every other societal context. As a result, emotions and affects became largely excluded from modern life.

Of course, Weber is not the only one to characterize modernity's urge to discipline emotions as one of its defining features. Emotional self-discipline and affect control also play a prominent role in Norbert Elias' grand narrative of the civilizing process in Europe (Elias 2000). In his view, the increasing functional differentiation of society since the Renaissance has caused an ever-growing mutual dependence between its members. But the stronger their interdependence, the greater would be the potentially negative repercussions were they simply to follow their impulses and passions. Thus, it becomes a social necessity to be able to control one's affects instead of acting blindly on them. Even more than Weber, Elias highlights the importance of affect control as a constitutive element in the formation and stabilization of modern societies.

The often problematic and painful internalization of society's conventions and constraints, and their clashes with one's own desires, drives, and affects are also a cornerstone of Sigmund Freud's view of modern culture. Without going into the details of Freudian thought, it seems fair to say that he also viewed modern society as characterized by an elaborate system of affect control, affect suppression or affect sublimation. And as his deliberation on *Civilization and its Discontents* (Freud 1982) suggests, this civilizing process is not without its psychogenic cost.

Weber, Elias and Freud all concurrently described modern society as marked by a dual process of increasing rationalization and emotional self-restraint. Although they voiced their concerns over the future fate of emotions (which they feared would become increasingly undermined and marginalized), it was Max Horkheimer's and Theodor Adorno's *Dialectic of Enlightenment* (1977) which most empathically warned against the alienating effects of rationalist modernization. Based on a Marxist understanding of history, they claimed that the process of capitalist modernization and its imperative of instrumental reason would effectuate the reification of even the most intimate human reactions in relation to oneself and thus would inevitably lead to an emotional depletion and erosion of the self—until "personality scarcely signifies anything more than shining white teeth and freedom from body odor and emotions" (Horkheimer and Adorno 1977, 167).

In sum, then, all these classical concepts of modern society centered on the thoroughly formally-rationalistic organization of its social relations which effectuated a suppression or even expulsion from emotions in all spheres of life. As such, they mirror the key assumptions and arguments of the discourse of modernity, even if they alternate between the dominant framing of modernity as progress, and its heterodox counterpart which frames modernization as a disciplinary regime leading to estrangement.

Without denying the accuracy of these sociological descriptions of modern society for the 19th and early 20th century, many analysts of contemporary society now observe a new appreciation of emotions as valuable resources. This comes with a wider acceptance of expressive emotionality from the late 20th century onwards, an observation that puts into question the dominant conception of modern society as a rationalized social system that suppresses emotions.

Sociological theory has reacted to this new emotionalism: after decades of neglect, the topic of emotions reappeared on the sociological research agenda and soon led to the formation of the sociology of emotions as a proper and recognized sub-discipline. Its exponents have shown that modern societies and their actors can neither abolish emotions from the public or economic sphere, nor can they afford to renounce the use of emotions as a means for their ends.[10] Rather than being marked by "affective neutrality," as Talcott Parsons (Parsons and Shils 1951, 77–80) described the modern action orientation, the emotion theorists' works have demonstrated that almost all social processes in modern society are saturated with emotions, and are accompanied by specific forms of emotion management that actively shape the emotions of the actors involved.

---

10 See Shilling (2002), Barbalet (1998) and Flam (2002) for an introduction into the intellectual traditions, canonical contributions and current issues in the sociology of emotions.

Despite this apparent revalorization of emotions in current sociological analyses of contemporary society, I would argue that, like the classical positions they oppose, these accounts also build on an antagonism between the modern ideal of a perfectly unemotional rationality and that of a potentially subversive irrational emotionality, so that they thus still operate within the frame of thought which has been provided by the discourse of modernity. In the following, I want to illustrate this claim on the basis of two seemingly juxtaposing canonical perspectives in the sociology of emotions that particularly center around the role of emotions in current society:[11] the hypothesis of an informalization and emotional re-enchantment of society in the wake of an "expressive revolution" on the one hand and the hypothesis of a further domestication and instrumental objectification of emotions in late modern capitalism on the other.

Ironically, it was Talcott Parsons (1978) who, together with Daniel Bell (1976), first noticed that a major social change—an "affective-expressive revolution," as he termed it—was taking place. It was characterized by an increasing acceptance of expressive emotional patterns, and an informal and unconstrained handling of feelings and emotions in many different contexts: for instance, new social movements, from the women's liberation to the hippies, questioned the rational world-view and proclaimed their right to express themselves, be it politically, emotionally or otherwise. Moreover, in many educational settings, including the workplace, the traditional focus on unquestioned compliance with rules and authority was replaced by more sensitive and egalitarian forms of societal affect control (Wouters 1999). However, the most remarkable change in the emotional regime of contemporary society occurred in the relation between the genders, especially with regard to intimate relationships. In his studies on the changing rules on dating and sexuality in the 20th century, Cas Wouters (2004) illustrated how new options and liberties in shaping love relationships opened up for both genders in the wake of the sexual revolution.

For Wouters and others, all these changes are part of a widespread process of informalization, i.e. a general decline in the range, density, and rigidity of social control over emotions, which is now moving in the direction of comparatively less obligatory and more flexible forms of self-control. The thesis of an informalization of society has recently been taken further by writers such as Michel Maffesoli (1995; 1996), for whom waves

---

11 Here I follow a characterization made by Sighard Neckel (2005).

of informalization are merely part of a broader picture concerning the resurgence of Dionysian values (i.e. spontaneity, expressivity, and authenticity) in contemporary society. They induce a deep-rooted societal and cultural transformation from an individualized, rationalized society governed by the Protestant Ethic, to a new form of non-instrumental sociality based on a culture of sentiment and expressivity, and on new forms of collective effervescence.[12] With this in mind, Maffesoli claims that we are living at a decisive moment in the history of modernity, one in which the rationalization of the world is being displaced by its emotional "re-enchantment."

Although all exponents of the thesis of a re-emotionalization of modernity concede that this process represents a development opposite to that posited by classical modernization theory, they significantly differ in their judgments on the final consequences of the "expressive revolution:" Parsons and Wouters consider this development still congruent with the cultural and social texture of modernity and suggest that it might bring about a modern society that is more humane, less suppressive, and less alienating. Others have more radical views: while Maffesoli believes that the transformative effects of re-emotionalization will propel the modern world into a new, post-modern condition, Bell takes this development as a manifestation of the cultural contradictions inherent in modern capitalism and pessimistically states that the hyperbole of emotionality undermines the moral values of the modern project and thus signals the imminent demise of modern society.[13]

What all these interpretations of the new emotionalism have in common, however, is the assumption that unrestrained, authentic emotionality stands in opposition to the rational character of modernity and hence that any emancipation of emotion will inevitably change the very structure of modern society and culture. As in the classical sociological works mentioned above, emotions are still construed as the "other" of modernity and are set in stark opposition to modern principles and values.

---

12 For another analysis of the resurgence of such "post-traditional" communities based on strong sentiments of solidarity and empathy see Hitzler and Pfadenhauer (1998).

13 For Bell, the expressive revolution and its inherent hedonism stands in stark opposition to the "sprit" of capitalism and thus threatens to disrupt modern society: "The one emphasizes functional rationality and meritocratic rewards, the other, anti-rational modes of behaviour. It is this disjunction which is the historical cultural crisis of all Western bourgeois society" (Bell 1976, 84).

A similar antagonism also underlies the other dominant perspective in the sociology of emotions, which focuses on the conflict between the modern striving for an all-embracing rationality (that depletes emotional experiences), and the human need for unconstrained emotionality that disrupts the functioning of modern institutions. This line of thought is greatly influenced by the works of Arlie Hochschild (e.g. 1983), who took up central ideas of alienation critique and posited a domestication and commercialization of emotions in post-industrial capitalism, especially in the service industry. At the core of Hochschild's argument is the idea that today's employees are coerced to perform a kind of strategic self-manipulation that leads to emotional inauthenticity: here, the norms of customer orientation demand that employees outwardly express feelings that they do not really have. In addition, stressful work situations give rise to strategies of "deep acting," with which the actor must produce the required feelings. According to Hochschild, these requirements in emotion management result in a split between the expression of emotions and the experience of them and produce a strategic use of emotional inauthenticity which turns the emotional world of the individual external to him/herself.

Hochschild's critique of an alienation and instrumental objectification of emotions in (late) modern capitalism has recently been renewed and radicalized by Stjepan Mestrovic (1997). He claims that we are now living in a "post-emotional" society, a world of rationally ordered, "McDonaldized" emotions and mechanized feelings which leaves only little room for truly authentic or spontaneous emotional responses. Post-emotionalism is portrayed as a system designed to avoid disorder and "loose ends" in emotional exchange, to civilize wild arenas of emotional life, and, in general, to order emotions so that the social world "hums as smoothly as a well-maintained machine" (Mestrovic 1997, 150). Mestrovic argues that the incessant process of rationalization has led the way to a world of mechanized feelings and "quasi-emotional" responses; a world, in fact, where even the ways of escape—from leisure to therapy—have been rationalized and McDonaldized.

Despite their critical view of modernity, however, the analyses of Hochschild, Mestrovic and other exponents of this perspective also remain trapped in the conventional conception of emotions as the non-modern other: in objecting to the alienating effects of the modern imperative for instrumental reason which threatens to colonize emotions as the last bastion of human freedom, they renew the basic assumptions and demarcations of the modernity discourse, especially its view of emotions as anti-thetical to the rationalist texture of modern society and as disruptions of its perfect rational order.

An Alternative View on Emotions and Their Place in Modernity

The previous discussion has shown that the sociology of emotions provides us with two mutually exclusive repertoires of explanation. Either, the emotional turn is just the logical continuation of previous waves of rationalization, a rationalization of emotions that now aims at putting even feelings to instrumental use, or, quite to the contrary, that the return of emotions signals a decisive shift or even a reversal of the modern process of rationalization towards a non-rational emotionalization of our society.

Despite their differences, however, both perspectives share a common view on authentic emotions as forces that, for better or worse, undermine the effects of modern rationalization as well as the effects of a common understanding of modern society as being characterized by a fundamental tension between the desire for authentic and unconstrained emotions on the one hand and rationalist-capitalist needs to control and instrumentalize them on the other. The problem with these views on emotions in modernity is that they are based on an apodictic antagonism between (supposedly non-modern and irrational) emotionality and an essentially modern, un-emotional rationality. As such, both remain embedded in the conceptual framework of the discourse of modernity, especially its construction of a "great divide" between modern reason and emotions as its non-modern other. In consequence, they cannot but make us think of the historical and future development of modernity as a zero-sum game between rationalization and emotional expressivity—that is to say, whatever is gained in rationality is lost in emotional freedom and vice versa.

I think that the idea of such a "natural" antagonism between rationality and emotionality is problematic, as it ignores the historically changing nature of the relationship between emotionality and rationality. Hence, instead of taking the current dichotomous conceptualization as an a priori fact to account for the emotional turn, one has to make it part of the analysis. For if the dichotomy between emotionality and rationality itself has to be seen as a result of a specific discursive constitution of modernity, then it seems to be an open question whether the emotional turn only reaffirms this dichotomy (be it as a new wave of rationalization or emotionalization), or whether it eventually leads to a modernity that construes the relationship between emotions and rationality in a different, that is to say, non-antagonistic way.

Before looking at the effects of the emotional turn in more detail, however, I would like to substantiate my claim that this dichotomy is not at all nature-given, but rather the historical result of socio-cultural transformations in the course of modernization.

Emotions and the Development of Modernity

In short, my argument is that the development of modernity was driven by two visions: the one was based on the ideals of the Enlightenment, the other one on the ideals of the Romantic Movement. Although both actually aimed at emancipating and empowering the modern subject, they came to be seen as conflicting forces in the process of modernization. The historical connection between modernity and the Enlightenment has already been pointed out above, wherein I argue to consider it as a rather undisputed fact. As such I refrain from reviewing it here, but rather I turn my attention to another question:[14] why would one also have to consider the Romantic Movement and its historical successors as another driving force of modernization?

In fact, the Romantic Movement began as a reaction to the Enlightenment and its absolute belief in the power of reason. Romantic thinkers feared that a one-tracked, dogmatically rationalistic enlightenment wouldn't lead to the promised emancipation from all forms of subjugation, but rather install just another form of dominion—this time, the blind rule of universal laws and the objective forces of logic. In order to secure the enlightenment ideals of emancipation and self-determination, they argued for a pluralism of values and norms as well as a stronger appreciation of one's subjective experiences and feelings as an important source of self-knowledge.

---

14 Habermas (1985) and Toulmin (1991) offer a detailed discussion of this topic.

Far from being a reactionary "counter-enlightenment," the Romantic Movement therefore must be recognized as a critical self-reflection and radicalization of enlightenment ideas. It pointed out the blind spots and previously neglected areas of the enlightenment—the expressive, emotional, and bodily aspects the self—and tried to emancipate and further develop these aspects of the modern subject as well. As such, romantic ideas should be considered to be an important and integral part of the process of modernization.[15]

Since the age of romanticism, then, this dynamic tension between the enlightenment ideal of a rational subject (and a rationally ordered society) on the one hand and the romantic ideal of an expressive subject (and a pluralistic, non-reductionist world) on the other has strongly shaped and driven the modernization process.

For the most part of the 19th century, these two motives were actually considered to form a complementary relationship with each other. There was, however, a certain differentiation between the rationalistic and expressive forces of modernization: whereas enlightenment ideas strongly influenced the formation of the public sphere in capitalist society, romantic ideals were realized mostly in the private sphere and the arts, but both elements were of equal importance for the formation of the (early) modern society and its *bourgeois* subject.

Towards the end of the century, however, this balance became increasingly questioned by the negative effects of industrialization (rural exodus, pauperism, class conflicts, etc.) which profoundly disrupted society and provoked a cultural crisis. It also marked the birth of a new, "neo"-Romantic Movement. Its proponents claimed that the crisis of modernity was caused by the incessant rationalization of all spheres of life and argued for a renewed orientation towards the romantic ideals of spontaneity, emotionality, and self-expression so as to prevent the modern subject from their own alienation. The neo-romantic commitment to unconstrained vitality and emotionality became manifest not only in new artistic movements such as Expressionism or Art Nouveau, but also in such broad socio-cultural phenomena as the youth movement, naturism, and similar social reformatory movements. In this context, the birth of sociology has to be seen as another intellectual reaction to the cultural crisis of the fin de siècle. In fact, many works of Weber, Simmel, Tönnies, and Durkheim were first

---

15 For a more detailed analysis of the relationship between romanticism and modernity see Helduser and Weiß (1998).

and foremost attempts to understand the ambivalent transformative effects of modernization that they were witnessing. In contrast to the neo-romantic mainstream, however, these sociologists didn't believe in an alternative to the modern processes of rationalization and societalization—even if that meant that modern society would end up in a purely rational, emotionless culture of instrumental reason without room for emotions and feelings.

In the end, the sociological commentators seemed to be right with their predictions, even against their own wishes: after the First World War, the belief in a romantic renewal of modern society drastically lost its persuasion, and a new wave of rationalization touched all spheres of society, from *Neue Sachlichkeit* in the arts, to Taylorism in the economy. Concurrent to this social change were some profound changes in the dominant self-description of modern society. Not only in art and architecture, but also in the sciences, one now equated rationalization with socio-cultural progress. Partly based on the classical analyses of Weber and his contemporaries of modern society, yet ignoring their critical comments *vis-à-vis* the ambivalent effects of modernization, societies now self-consciously defined themselves as being "modern," and that precisely *because* of their independence from all traditional or affective types of orientation. This "great divide" between modern societies and pre-modern ones was further justified by the ascription of reason on the modern side and irrationality and lack of emotional self-control on the other, non-modern side of the great divide.

In the following decades, the new concept of modern society and what constitutes "modernity" increasingly gained dominance both in scientific and public discourse. In the context of this discursive construction of modernity, emotions thus became marginalized as not only irrational, but essentially pre-modern, and the old bourgeois ideal of emotionality and rationality as being complementary became replaced by a dichotomous understanding that pitted the one against the other.

As mentioned before, this antagonism remains as the Archimedean point in much sociological thinking about modern society. The historic development of modernity suggests another interpretation. Instead of being characterized by a uniform progression from pre-modern emotionality to modern rationality, the history of modernization should rather be understood as a dynamic interplay between rationalist and romantic-expressive aspects of modernization. As such, emotions and waves of emotionalism are not antithetical to modernity, but an integral part of its constitution. Moreover, this perspective also opens up a fresh view of the emotional turn that goes beyond its "zero-sum" interpretation as being either a process of re-emotionalization, or a rationalization of modernity.

In the following, I take a closer look at how emotionality and its relation to rationality have come to be redefined in the sciences and propose an alternative view of the new emotionalism in contemporary society.

Redefining Emotions in the Emotional Turn

I specifically focus here on a sub-area within the emotional turn: the interdisciplinary debate on emotions and their regulation, which links current discussions in psychology and neuroscience with those in medicine, education, and therapy.[16]

Especially in neuroscience and psychology, the idea of affect and cognition as two conflicting forces of human action has made way to the thesis that emotions are the very basis of cognitive processes. Antonio Damasio (1999), one of the main proponents of this perspective, characterizes emotions as indispensable evolutionary mechanisms that enable the human self to adapt to the everyday challenges of social life. For Damasio, emotional signals play a central role as guides and pathfinders for the best course of action in such challenges. In his theories, the bodily aspects of emotion act as "somatic markers" that provide us with important cues on how to decide on and act in a given situation. In other words, emotions are no longer only the target of cognitive regulatory efforts, but are considered as crucial regulators of cognitive processes themselves.[17]

In Damasio's idea of emotions as proto-rational phenomena, emotions are thus complemented by their framing as specific stimulus-response patterns, which is the second key element in the neuroscientific debates on emotion. Here, emotions and the capacity to emotionally self-regulate are construed as phenomena that can be explained on a purely biological basis. An exemplary case for such a naturalization of emotion is the current re-

---

16 I decicded to focus on this area of the emotional turn due to the crucial importance given to concepts of emotion regulation in contemporary scientific and professional discourses on emotions. Gross (2007) as well as Philippot and Feldman (2004) offer a comprehensive overview of this new field of research.

17 At the same time however, Damasio stresses the importance of a reflective regulation of one's own emotions, that is, one always has to check when to better trust your emotions and when not.

search on the newly discovered "mirror neurons,"[18] which led neuroscientists to advocate the view that mirror neurons are the "real" basis of empathy. On this basis, empathy became redefined as a naturally given, as opposed to a culturally acquired, aspect of human nature.

In medicine, emotions are thus reconsidered as both possible origins of psychological problems and as starting points for therapeutic intervention. Clinical psychiatrists argue that many behavioral disorders have to be reconceptualized as emotional disorders in general and as errors of emotion regulation in particular (Bradley 2000). In such a view, one's deficit or inability to manage distress and to regulate troubling emotional states becomes the real cause of many mental illnesses. In consequence, emotions and affective states that cannot be managed or coped with become easily stigmatized as being psychologically dysfunctional. The concept of the so-called "Attention Deficit/Hyperactivity Disorder" (ADHD) is a case in point. Previously thought of as a cognitive problem of perception and information processing, it is now construed as a dysfunction of impulse control. Here, emotional problems become redefined as a patient's problems with emotions and their regulation, whereas the events and circumstances that triggered the emotional problems in the first place are largely removed from sight.

Complementing the new role of emotion regulation in the definition and diagnosis of mental health problems, therapeutic practice sees the emergence of several new programs that focus on helping the client to *consciously regulate* his/her own emotions, and thus to *normalize his/her emotional reactions* and affective states (Greenberg 2002).

In the fields of education and developmental psychology, the debates focus mostly on the ethical qualities of feelings. Emotions are considered to be important factors in moral decision-making and pro-social behavior (Goschke and Bolte 2002). This "moralization" of emotionality becomes manifest in numerous educational and psycho-social programs which revolve around the training of specific emotions and affective orientations, such as empathy and compassion, or shame and guilt, for these emotions are seen as the foundations of society's values and norms. As a case in point, the so-called *Denkzeit*-program is a popular training program for

---

18 These are a special kind of neurons that are active whenever we perceive the affective state of others, and they do so by imitating or mirroring the neuronal activity patterns of the other person's brain. Joachim Bauer (2005) offers a popular (naturalistic) account of the workings of mirror neurons and their social effects.

juvenile delinquents which, according to its self-description, "specifically aims at fostering the juvenile's socio-cognitive competences. It focuses on such modalities as moral discernment, involving the ability to anticipate the consequences of one's action, to differentiate and control one's affects, and to be able to change perspectives and to empathize" (see www.denkzeit.com).

The underlying rationale of this view on emotions can thus be summed up as follows: if you've learned to feel morally "right," that is sympathetic in a given situation, you will also know how to best deal with it, that is to say, how to act in a socially responsible manner.

Apart from being conducive to a stable social order, emotions are also seen as important resources for one's personal development, as the popular concept of "Emotional Intelligence" (Mayer et al. 2004, Goleman 1995) illustrates. Its proponents in psychology, therapy, and education point out the crucial role of emotional factors in the development and formation of one's personality and consequently argue that the cultivation of emotional skills—especially the ability to identify and manage your own feelings—is the most important aspect of personal development as well as a key competence in coping with the complex demands of today's society.

In this context, it is important to note that the many concepts and programs that are proffered to foster moral emotionality or emotional competencies use quite different approaches to regulate and cultivate feelings. What they all have in common, however, is a new understanding of emotions as objects that can be *consciously influenced* and *deliberately formed*, irrespective of cultural settings or the situation that originally evoked them.

Conclusion

In sum, the different conceptualizations of emotions in the debates on emotion regulation seem to be neither indicative of a universal rationalization of emotions, nor of a general shift from rational to expressive-emotional orientations and values in society. Instead, one reckons that the emotional turn is characterized by a revival of romantic notions of emotions as valuable personal resources and unique forms of self-expression

on the one hand, and efforts (in the Enlightenment tradition) to scientifically disenchant and rationalize the emotional world on the other.

Speaking of the latter first, one especially notices a materialist-rational-
istic redefinition of emotions as proto-cognitive and purely neuronal phenomena, which, as such, became the object of systematic scientific scrutiny, as well as therapeutic and biomedical invention. In the course of this
(neuro-)scientific disenchantment of emotions, they are remade into phenomena that can be ordered, regulated and normalized, according to scientific standards, and thus turned into objects that can be handled and remo-
deled according to the wishes of a rationally enlightened mind.

Concurrent to this rationalist reconceptualization of emotions, however, emotions are also revaluated in a romantic sense as unique mental
and personal resources of the individual which—as a kind of pre-cognitive
and somatic complement to reason—guides his/her decision-making and
actually enables him/her to act in a socially responsible manner in the first
place. Here, emotions are seen as the expressive and moral side of the self,
which consequently have to be set free and cultivated so that they can be
put to good use for both personal development and societal progress.

In spite of what sociological theory suggests, these two views on emotions and emotionality are no longer incompatible, but converge in a new
understanding of emotions that conceives of them as states which can be
willfully regulated and *purposively shaped*. Emotional experiences are now being
redefined as phenomena which come into existence, and which can be
intentionally changed through inner reflection and the exercising of the
will.

As such this new idea of emotions deconstructs and rescinds the old
dichotomy between unemotional rationality and irrational emotionality,
upon which the discourse of modernity rested so far. For, if emotions are
considered to be intentionally evocable objects, they can be used for both
rational and non-rational purposes; at the same time, being rational no
longer means to be unemotional, but to optimally manage and use one's
own emotional resources to further one's goals.

Thus, the new emotionalism might indicate a new phase in the development of modernity and its emotional regime, which no longer pits emotional expressivity against instrumental rationality, but blends them together. What remains to be seen, however, is whether this new view of
emotions leads up to a new modern paradox: the understanding of feelings
as objects that can be freely chosen might give rise to the very kind of

affective neutrality and *blasé* attitude that Weber and his sociological contemporaries once saw as the trademark of modernity. Were this to be the case, however, it would not be as a result of an ever increasing emotional discipline, but, quite to the contrary, as a result of the fact that emotions would now come to be formed, and experienced, completely at will.

References

Ankowitsch, Christian (2002). *Generation Emotion.* Berlin: BTV.

Barbalet, Jack (1998). *Emotion, Social Theory, and Social Structure.* Cambrigde: Cambridge University Press.

Bauer, Joachim (2005). *Warum ich fühle, was du fühlst.* Hamburg: Hoffmann und Campe.

Bell, Daniel (1976). *The Cultural Contradictions of Capitalism.* New York: Basic Books.

Bolle, F. (2006). Gefühle in der ökonomischen Theorie. In R. Schützeichel (ed.). *Emotionen und Sozialtheorie,* 48–65. Frankfurt am Main: Campus.

Bradley, S. J. (2000) *Affect Regulation and the Development of Psychopathology.* New York: Guilford.

Damasio, Antonio R. (1999). *The Feeling of What Happens.* London: Heinemann.

Elias, Norbert (2000). *The Civilizing Process.* Oxford: Blackwell. [first published in 1939]

Flam, Helena (2002). *Soziologie der Emotionen.* Konstanz: UVK-Verlags-Gesellschaft.

Foucault, Michel (1971). *Die Ordnung der Dinge.* Frankfurt am Main: Suhrkamp.

— (1981). *Archäologie des Wissens.* Frankfurt am Main: Suhrkamp.

Freud, Sigmund (1982). *Civilization and its Discontents.* London: Hogarth Press. [first published in 1930]

Goleman, D. (1995). *Emotional Intelligence.* New York: Bantam.

Goschke, Thomas, and Annette Bolte (2002). Emotion, Kognition und Intuition. In Sabine A. Döring and Verena Meyer (eds.). *Die Moralität der Gefühle,* 39–57. Berlin: Akademie-Verlag.

Greenberg, L. (2002). *Emotion-Focused Therapy.* Washington, D.C.: APA.

Gross, J. J. (2007). *Handbook of Emotion Regulation.* New York: Guilford.

Habermas, Jürgen (1985). *Der philosophische Diskurs der Moderne.* Frankfurt am Main: Suhrkamp.

Helduser, U., and J. Weiß (eds.). (1998). *Die Modernität der Romantik.* Kassel University Press.

Hitzler, Ronald, and Michaela Pfadenhauer (1998). Eine posttraditionale Gemeinschaft. In F. Hillebrandt, G. Kneer, and K. Kraemer (eds.). *Verlust der Sicherheit?,* 83–102. Opladen: Westdeutscher Verlag.

Hochschild, Arlie R. (1983). *The Managed Heart*. Berkeley: University of California Press.

Horkheimer, Max, and Theodor W. Adorno (1977). *Dialectic of Enlightenment*. New York: Seabury.

Imbusch, Peter (2005). *Moderne und Gewalt*. Wiesbaden: Verlag für Sozialwissenschaften.

Koselleck, Reinhard (1979). *Vergangene Zukunft*. Frankfurt am Main: Suhrkamp.

Lichtblau, Klaus (1998). Die Selbstunterscheidungen der Moderne. In J. Weiß (ed.). *Mehrdeutigkeiten der Moderne*, 43–87. Kassel: Kassel University Press.

Maffesoli, Michel (1995). *The Time of Tribes*. London: Sage.

— (1996). *Ordinary Knowledge*. Cambridge: Polity Press.

Mayer, J. D., P. Salovey, and D. R. Caruso (2004). Emotional Intelligence. *Psychological Inquiry*, 15, 197–215.

Mestrovic, Stjepan (1997). *Postemotional Society*. London: Sage.

Nassehi, Armin (2006). *Der soziologische Diskurs der Moderne*. Frankfurt am Main: Suhrkamp.

Neckel, Sighard (2005). Emotion by Design. *Berliner Journal für Soziologie*, 15, 419–30.

Parsons, Talcott (1951). *The Social System*. London: Routledge.

— (1978). Durkheim on Religion Revisited. In Talcott Parsons. *Action Theory and the Human Condition*, 213–32. New York: The Free Press.

Parsons Talcott, and Edward A. Shils (eds.). (1951). *Towards a General Theory of Action*. New York: Evanston.

Petermann, F., G. Jugert, and A. Rehder (1999). *Sozialtraining in der Schule*. Weinheim: Beltz.

Philipot, P., and R. Feldman (2004). *The Regulation of Emotion*. Mahwah, NJ: Erlbaum.

Rosenwein, Barbara H. (2002). Worrying About Emotions in History. *The American Historical Review*, 107 (3), 821–45.

Shilling, Chris (2002). The Two Traditions in the Sociology of Emotions. In Jack Barbalet (ed.). *Emotions and Sociology*, 10–32 Oxford: Blackwell.

Toulmin, Stephen (1991). *Kosmopolis*. Frankfurt am Main: Suhrkamp.

Wagner, Peter (1995). *Soziologie der Moderne*. Frankfurt am Main: Campus.

Weber, Max (2007). *Die Protestantische Ethik und der "Geist" des Kapitalismus*. Erftstadt: Area-Verlag. [first published in 1920]

Wehling, P. (1992). *Die Moderne als Sozialmythos*. Frankfurt am Main: Campus.

Wouters, Cas (1999). *Informalisierung*. Wiesbaden: Westdeutscher Verlag.

— (2004). *Sex and Manners*. London: Sage.

Shame and Conformity: The Deference-Emotions System

Thomas J. Scheff

This chapter proposes a unitary explanation of conformity in terms of the interaction of deference with normal pride and shame. Darwin, Cooley, and others had suggested the social context for pride and shame: self's perception of the evaluation of self by other(s). The assumption that there is a continuous social monitoring of the self from the standpoint of others suggests a puzzle: if monitoring is continuous and causes either pride or shame, why are so few manifestations of either emotion visible in our lives? One possible explanation is that pride and shame usually are unnoticed. I call this the Cooley-Goffman conjecture. Goffman's work on "face" implies it and Lewis's discovery of unacknowledged shame documents it. Her analysis of hundreds of clinical interviews demonstrates that low-visibility shame was present in every session, though neither therapist nor patient seemed to be aware of it.

Drawing on Lewis's exact description of the markers of shame, and Goffman's analysis of the relation between deference and embarrassment, a deference-emotion system is described. Members perceive this system as compelling conformity to norms exterior to self by informal but pervasive rewards (outer deference and its reciprocal, inner pride) and punishments (lack of deference, and the inner shame). Asch's study of conformity illustrates the role of unacknowledged shame in compelling conformity to exterior norms.

The Basic Sociological Idea

Durkheim (1951) proposed that the force of social influence is experienced by individuals as exterior and constraining, but he only hinted at the causal sequence implied. What are the steps that lead individuals to experience social control as outer compulsion? This is an important question because exterior constraint has become a basic in modern sociology. Conformity poses a central problem for social science not only in its normal, but also in its pathological, form. What gives rise to excessive and rigid conformity? This is the question implied by many analyses of bureaucracy and authoritarian forms of social organization. This article outlines a model that speaks to both normal and rigid social control.

There is agreement that conformity is encouraged by a system of sanctions: we usually conform because we expect to be rewarded when we do so, and punished when we do not. However, conformity often occurs in the absence of sanctions. Durkheim's formulation refers to the ubiquity of conformity. The reward of public acclaim and the punishment of public disgrace rarely occur, yet the social system marches on. Formal sanctions are slow, unwieldy, and expensive. In addition to the formal system, there must be a complex and highly efficient system of informal sanctions.

A clue to this puzzle can be found in Goffman's treatment of interaction ritual (Goffman 1967). He notes that the emotion of embarrassment or anticipation of embarrassment plays a prominent role in social encounters. In presenting ourselves to others, we risk rejection. The form rejection takes may be flagrant, but it is much more frequently quite subtle, perhaps only a missed beat in the rhythm of conversation. Depending on its intensity and obviousness, rejection usually leads to the painful emotions of embarrassment, shame, or humiliation. By the same token, when we are accepted as we present ourselves, we usually feel rewarded by the pleasant emotions of genuine pride and fellow feeling.

I propose that the degree and type of deference and the attendant emotions of pride and shame make up a subtle and pervasive system of social sanctions. This system leads to experiencing social influence as compelling. Our thoughts and perceptions of social expectations only set the stage for social control. We experience the system as so compelling because of emotions—the pleasure of justified pride on the one hand, and the punishment of embarrassment, shame, or humiliation on the other.

The deference-emotion system may take formal and public forms: the ceremony for awarding the Congressional Medal of Honor confers the highest degree of deference, and we assume that it arouses pride in the recipient. At the other extreme, an impeachment proceeding takes away deference and presumably would arouse shame in the defendant. Disgrace subsumes both public and private sides—outer demotion and inner shame.

However, formal rewards and punishments are infrequent, even rare. The deference-emotion system functions virtually continuously, even when we are alone, since we can imagine and anticipate its motions in vivid detail. Systematic research has been unable to document this system; it is too subtle and ubiquitous for laboratory experiment or social survey. Since it often functions outside of awareness, qualitative fieldworkers seldom catch the details.

Unlike the system of formal sanctions, the deference-emotion system is virtually instantaneous and invisible. Its invisibility makes it difficult to describe. Durkheim implies shame and pride in his writing about social influence, although he never named them. Shame appears to be profoundly taboo (Scheff 1984); it is not mentioned even when it is being used as an explanation. Asch's discussion of his findings (see below) illustrates this evasiveness in a well-known study of conformity.

Although he pointed to the ubiquity of embarrassment in social encounters, Goffman confuses the reader because he also claimed that he restricts his purview to the social aspects of embarrassment, to what is going on between interactants (1967, 108). Goffman actually strayed from this claim, especially in his many treatments of facework: the harried individual trying to stave off embarrassment, or failing that, attempting to manage it.[1]

Goffman's attempt to deal only with outer behavior pays rich dividends in certain areas, e.g. the contagion of embarrassment between interactants. His treatment of social embarrassment is subtle and evocative but does not convey the explosive force the deference-emotion system may have. One difficulty is that his analysis completely separates embarrassment ("the social organization of embarrassment") from anger and hostility, which he treated as properties of "character contests" such as duels and vendettas (*Where the Action Is*, Chapter 7 in Goffman 1967, 149–270).

It is constructive to contrast Lewis' (1971) treatment of shame with Goffman's attempt. She emphasized the inner process. In analogy to his use of the metaphor of contagion between persons, she pointed to what she called a feeling trap, i.e., inner contagion. In Goffman's analysis, one becomes ashamed that the other is ashamed, who in turn becomes ashamed, which increases the first person's shame, and so on: an interpersonal feeling trap develops. In Lewis's analysis, one becomes ashamed that

---

1 For a later treatment of this issue see Scheff (2006, chapter 3).

one is ashamed, an inner loop which feeds on itself, an intrapersonal trap. Unlike Goffman, however, she did not separate her analysis of shame from her analysis of anger. She postulated an affinity between the two, with shame sometimes followed by anger directed at other(s). This loop, which can go on indefinitely, may be experienced as though it were a single affect, "helpless anger," or, in a more intense form, "humiliated fury." She proposed that more frequently, however, shame is followed by anger directed at self, which results in guilt, depression, and or withdrawal.

By combining Goffman's social analysis with Lewis' psychological one, it is possible to convey the power of the deference-emotion system. This system occurs both between and within interactants. Ordinarily it functions so efficiently and invisibly that it guarantees the alignment of the thoughts, feelings, and actions of individuals. Mutual conformity and respect lead to pride, which leads to further conformity, which leads to further positive feeling, in a system that seems virtually automatic.

However, when there is a real or imagined rejection (withdrawal, criticism, insult, defeat, etc.) the deference-emotion system may show a malign form, a chain reaction of shame and anger, or shame about shame between and within the interactants. This explosion is usually brief, perhaps a few seconds, although it can also take the form of bitter hatred or withdrawal (shame-shame spirals) that can last a lifetime. It can occur not only between individuals, but also between groups, or even nations. Such explosions I will call triple spirals of shame and anger, or shame/shame (one spiral within each party and one between them). A chain reaction between and within groups can last longer than a lifetime, handed down from generation to generation; I interpret Franco-German relations (1870–1945) as an extended spiral of this kind (Scheff 1987; 1994).

Spirals of shame without anger can be illustrated by self-conscious blushing. One blushes from embarrassment, and consciousness of blushing leads to further blushing, and so on further. Shame-shame spirals lead to withdrawal rather than conflict, and seem to be much more prevalent than shame-anger. Otherwise, humankind would probably have ended itself long ago.

For all its brilliance, Goffman's analysis of interaction ritual usually implies that such matters may be fateful, at most, only to individuals, but not within larger arenas. Embarrassment, he seemed to imply, can be exquisitely painful, but it is personal and transitory and not relevant to larger social institutions. Goffman's attempts to exclude the psychological domain and separate embarrassment from anger delivered a behavioral analysis that is too specialized to capture the larger implications of his vision.

Lewis' specialization, equal but opposite of Goffman's, also precluded her from drawing out the social implications of her work. Although she is aware that her concept of the feeling trap has implications beyond neurosis, there is little development in this direction in her written work. Only by combining the two partial analyses can we see their respective implications.

Because of the ubiquity of shame and shame/anger sequences, social and societal interaction can instantly become what Goffman called a character contest. When chain reactions of shame or shame/anger occur between and within interacting persons or groups, there is no natural limit to the intensity and duration of arousal. The unlimited fury of shame/rage in a triple spiral may explain why social influence can be experienced as absolutely compelling. The emotion-deference system, as represented in the sequence of honor, insult, and revenge, may decide the fate, not only of individuals, but also of nations, civilizations, and, in our era, of all life on earth.

Analysis of sequences of interaction ritual and emotion in concrete episodes may enlarge on Durkheim's (1951) investigation of suicide. In another, co-authored article, we applied this analysis to a classic work of fiction, whereby we outlined a model of the way in which a class-based insult led to suicide (Scheff and Mahlendorf 1988). As mentioned above, we can see the bizarre and highly self-destructive behavior of France and Germany during the period spanning 1870–1945 in terms of the interaction ritual between the two countries (Scheff 1994). French and German politics and diplomacy in this period was extremely irrational, to the extent that we can best understand the situation as a character contest that engaged the two sides, even at the risk of respective self-destruction. With analyses of the interaction between deference and emotion, it may be possible to develop Durkheimian ideas of social influence into a comprehensive study of interaction at both the interpersonal and institutional levels.

A recent analysis of the politics of dignity by Fuller (2003; 2006; Fuller and Gerloff 2008) offers a parallel treatment of emotion dynamics as leading to inequality and violence. His treatment is much clearer than Goffman's, and much more accessible than mine. In his terminology, what I call pride is termed dignity, and what I call shame he terms humiliation. For various reasons, this terminology seems to make his work understandable both to academics and to the public at large; a huge step forward. To expand on this, in vernacular usage, we understand the term shame to be a very narrow individual emotion of utter disgrace, confusing normal shame, a mere bodily signal, with shame spirals that are consciously felt. Similarly, my use of genuine pride is hard for readers to understand because vernacular usage usually implies a shadow of vanity or egotism—the pride that goes before the fall. Fuller's terminology avoids this problem by using vernacular terms that are unequivocal and unshadowed: instead of pride, dignity; and instead of shame, humiliation. In the vernacular, humiliation is seen as coming from the outside, and therefore unshadowed by blame of self and utter, irrevocable disgrace. Embarrassment is seen not only as lighter in weight, but as also coming from outside. For these and other reasons, humiliation and embarrassment are speakable, but shame is unspeakable.

The Source of Shame: Biological and Social

In modern societies, shame is considered rare among adults. This belief is reflected in the division made in anthropology between shame cultures and guilt cultures, with traditional societies relying on shame for social control, and with modern societies relying on guilt. A matching premise is found in orthodox psychoanalytic theory, which places almost total emphasis on guilt as the adult emotion of self-control, with shame thought of as "regressive," that is, childish.[2]

For many years, however, there has been a continuing suggestion in the literature that shame is the primary social emotion, generated by the virtually constant monitoring of the self in relation to others. Such monitoring, as suggested by Goffman, is not rare but almost continuous in social interaction, and, more covertly, in solitary thought. If this line of thought were correct, shame would be the most frequent and possibly the most important of emotions, even though it is usually invisible. Threads of this idea can be found in Darwin (1872), Cooley (1922), MacDougall (1908), Lynd (1958), Lewis (1971), and as already mentioned, Goffman (1967).

---

2 An early attempt to break away from both restrictive premises can be found in Piers and
   Singer (1953).

In his 1872 volume, Darwin devoted a whole chapter to blushing and its relation to shame. He stated his thesis quite simply: blushing is caused by "shyness, shame, and modesty, the essential element in all being self-attention." For my purposes here, the important proposition comes next in his text, where he explained what he meant by self-attention: "It is not the simple act of reflecting on our own appearance, but the thinking *what others think of us, which excites a blush*" (325, emphasis added). His discussion suggests that it is perceptions of other people's evaluation of the self, whether positive or negative, that causes blushing.

Darwin's argument about the relationship between blushing and self-attention can be restated as two propositions connecting blushing with what might be called, in current terms, emotions on the one hand, and social perception on the other. First, blushing is caused by shame (as discussed below, "shyness" and "modesty," can be considered, following Lewis (1971), shame variants; or following Wurmser (1981), cognates). Second, and more importantly, it is the perception of negative evaluations of the self that causes shame. Blushing is only one of several visible markers of overt shame, and is, therefore, not a primary concept for a theory of social influence. The second statement, however, contains the basic proposition for the whole theory: shame is the social emotion, arising as it does out of the monitoring of one's own actions by viewing one's self from the standpoint of others.

Shame as a crucial emotion is prominent in the work of William Mac-Dougall (1908). He thought of shame as one of the "self-regarding sentiments," perhaps the most important one: "Shame is the emotion second to none in the extent of its influence upon social behavior" (1908, 124). Like Darwin, he seems to have understood that it arises as a result of self-monitoring. He also made another important point, that, although shame undoubtedly has a biological basis that we share with the higher mammals, the human emotion of shame in adults is considerably more elaborate and complex (1908, 56).

The Cooley-Goffman Conjecture

We next turn to Cooley (1922), who considered pride and shame as the crucial "social self-feelings." At some points he seems to have regarded as a self-feeling any feeling that the self directs toward itself. This passage about the extraordinary importance of self-feelings in human behavior is in that key: "with all normal and human people, (social self-feeling) remains, in one form or another, the mainspring of endeavor and a chief interest of the imagination throughout life" (1922, 208). Cooley continued:

"As is the case with other feelings, we do not think much of it (that is, of social self-feeling) so long as it is moderately and regularly gratified. Many people of balanced mind and congenial activity scarcely know that they care what others think of them, and will deny, perhaps with indignation, that such care is an important factor in what they are and do. But this is illusion. If failure or disgrace arrives, if one suddenly finds that the faces of men show coldness or contempt instead of the kindliness and deference that he is used to, he will perceive from the shock, the fear, the sense of being outcast and helpless, that he was living in the minds of others without knowing it, just as we daily walk the solid ground without thinking how it bears us up" (Cooley 1922, 208).

Although neither pride nor shame is mentioned by name in this passage, they are implied, especially the almost continuous presence of low-visibility pride in ordinary discourse. Cooley thought of pride and shame as the crucial self-feelings. This idea is continued in the concept of "the looking-glass self," his description of the social nature of the self. He thought self-monitoring has three steps:

"As we see our face, figure, and dress in the glass, and are interested in them because they are ours, and pleased or otherwise with them according as they do or do not answer to what we should like them to be; so in imagination we perceive in another's mind some thought of our appearance, manners, aims, deeds, character, friends, and so on, and are variously affected by it. A self-idea of this sort seems to have three principal elements: the imagination of our appearance to the other person; the imagination of his judgment of that appearance, and some sort of self-feeling, such as pride or mortification" (1922, 184).

In this passage he restricted self-feelings to the two he seemed to think are the most significant, pride and shame (considering mortification to be a shame variant). He mentioned shame three more times in the passage that follows:

"The comparison with a looking-glass hardly suggests the second element, the imagined judgment, which is quite essential. The thing that moves us to pride or *shame* is not the mere mechanical reflection of ourselves, but an imputed sentiment, the imagined effect of this reflection upon another's mind. This is evident from the fact that the character and weight of that other, in whose mind we see ourselves, makes all the difference with our feeling. We are *ashamed* to seem evasive in the presence of a straightforward man, cowardly in the presence of a brave one, gross in the eyes of a refined one, and so on. We always imagine, and in imagining share, the judgments of the other mind. A man will boast to one person of an action—say some sharp transaction in trade—which he would be *ashamed* to own to another" (1922, 184–5, emphasis added).

What is unfamiliar about the looking-glass self, perhaps shockingly so, is that Cooley implyed that society rests on a foundation of pride and shame. His analysis of the social nature of the self can be summarized in two propositions:

1. In adults, social monitoring of self is virtually continuous, even in solitude. (We are, as he put it, "living in the minds of others without knowing it.") (1922, 208).
2. Social monitoring always has an evaluative component, and gives rise, therefore, to either pride or shame.

Together these propositions suggest a puzzle. If social monitoring of self is almost continuous, and if it gives rise to pride or shame, why do we see so few manifestations of either emotion in adult life? Among possible answers is that the pride or shame is there, but has such low visibility that we do not notice it. This answer gives rise to a third proposition, the Cooley-Goffman conjecture:

3. Adults are virtually always in a state of either pride or shame, usually of a quite unostentatious kind.

This proposition is a step toward an exact definition of a concept that has been so far undefined: level of self-esteem. Such a definition would concern the balance between pride and shame states in a person's life, taking into account both duration and intensity.[3]

---

3 This issue was the topic of an earlier article (Scheff and Fearon 2005).

In his discussion of grief (he calls it distress-anguish), Tomkins (1963) notes a parallel puzzle:

"The reader must be puzzled at our earlier affirmation that distress is suffered daily by all human beings. Nothing seems less common than to see an adult cry. And yet we are persuaded that the cry, and the awareness of the cry, as distress and suffering, is ubiquitous" (1963, 56).

His answer also parallels the one I have suggested: "The adult has learned to cry as an adult. It is a brief cry, or a part of a cry or a miniature cry, or a substitute cry, or an active defense against the cry, that we see in place of the infant's cry for help" (1963, 56). He went on to discuss various substitutes for, or defenses against, crying that adults employ. For example, an adult suffering in the dental chair might, instead of crying, substitute muscular contractions: clamping the jaw, tightly contracting the muscles in the abdomen, and rigidly gripping the arms of the chair (1963, 59). As an example of defending against the cry, Tomkins suggested masking the facial expression of sadness with one of anger, becoming angry as well as sad (1963, 64–5). Most men in our society use this transformation, but many women do the opposite, masking anger with grief.

One way of summarizing the gambits that adults use when they are suffering is that most adults' grief is of a type with low visibility because its manifestations have been disguised or ignored. Tomkins' question and answer with respect to adult grief are exactly parallel to the ones I have derived from Cooley's treatment of adult shame.

What may be the most dramatic of Cooley's views on shame, and the one that brings him closest to my position, is his use of an autobiographical excerpt to illustrate the power of what he calls "social fear:"

"Social fear, of a sort-perhaps somewhat morbid, is vividly depicted by Rousseau in the passage of his Confessions where he describes the feeling that led him falsely to accuse a maid-servant of a theft which he had himself committed. 'When she appeared my heart was agonized, but the presence of so many people was more powerful than my compunction. I did not fear punishment, but I dreaded shame: *I dreaded it more than death, more than the crime, more than all the world.* I would have buried, hid myself in the center of the earth: invincible shame bore down every other sentiment; shame alone caused all my impudence, and in proportion as I became criminal the fear of discovery rendered me intrepid. I felt no dread but that of being detected, of being publicly and to my face declared a thief, liar, and calumniator'" (1922, 291, emphasis added).

Rousseau's phrase, "invincible shame," will stand us in good stead in the reinterpretation of the Asch study that I undertake below. Notice also that Cooley suggested this instance is an example of "morbid" (i.e., pathological), rather than normal, shame. This is a key point also. Normal shame is not at all invincible, since it is a mere signal (of threat to the bond). I use a similar distinction in my discussion of the Asch experiment.

Cooley's discussion of the social self in terms of self-monitoring (the movement now called "role-taking") clearly invokes pride and shame as the basic social emotions. At this point, intellectual history takes a surprising turn. George Herbert Mead and John Dewey based virtually their entire social psychology on the process of role-taking, the ability of humans to continuously monitor their own selves from the point of view of others. Yet neither Mead nor Dewey ever mentioned what was so obvious to Darwin, MacDougall, and Cooley: social monitoring gives rise to feelings of pride or shame. Mead and Dewey treated role-taking, their basic building block of human behavior, as a cognitive process. Neither had anything to say about pride and shame, as if Darwin, MacDougall, and Cooley never existed. Social psychology has yet to recover from this oversight.[4]

In modern societies, adults seem to be uncomfortable manifesting either pride or shame. The emotions of shame and pride often seem themselves to arouse shame. (This proposition explains Darwin's observation that both positive and negative evaluations can give rise to blushing.) It seems likely, as both Darwin and MacDougall suggested, that shame has a biological basis and is genetically programmed. It may also be true, as recent infant-caretaker studies suggest, that for infants and very young children, the arousal of shame is largely biological. For adults, however, it also seems certain that shame is not only a biological process, but also a social and cultural phenomenon. The discussion so far has suggested that adult shame is doubly social: shame arises in social monitoring of the self, and shame itself often becomes a further source of shame, depending on the particular situation and culture. The second social aspect of shame, its recursiveness, can give rise to pathological shame, a potentially limitless spiral (Scheff 1987). As will be suggested below, the concept of pathological shame may explain the Asch effect, and more broadly, excessive or rigid conformity.

---

4 A prior attempt to rectify Mead and Dewey's oversight can be found in Shibutani (1961), particularly chap. 13, *Self-esteem and Social Control*, which implies, in part, the thesis of the present article.

Low-Visibility Shame

If, as I have suggested, shame is strongly recursive in modem societies, we would expect most shame and pride to have very low visibility. Even if shame and pride were widely prevalent, persons who were proud or ashamed would be ashamed of their state and attempt to hide it from others and from themselves. If this were the case, how could one study pride and shame, if they are usually hidden?

A beginning method for detecting low-visibility shame and other emotions was developed by Gottschalk and Gleser (1969). Their procedure for extracting emotions from verbal texts includes a long list of sentences containing words they considered to be shame markers. These sentences are listed under five categories (I provide a few of their examples under each category.):

"1. Shame, embarrassment: 'I feel funny [...]' '[...] I had behaved improperly [...]' (and other sentences using terms such as disconcerting, discredit, or unworthy).
2. Humiliation: 'I don't know what was wrong with me letting myself go like that [...]' (other sentences involve such terms as humbling, degrading, or little self-respect).
3. Ridicule: 'He twitted me about being fat [...]' '[...] I really feel utterly ridiculous in a situation like that [...]' '[...] They stared at me and laughed [...]'
4. Inadequacy: 'Where was I when brains were passed out? I feel stupid [...]'
5. Overexposure of deficiencies or private details: 'I don't even know how to wipe my ass. I didn't want to talk about such personal things'" (1969, 49–52).

Although Gottschalk and Gleser did not discuss the matter or refer to any of the shame theorists discussed above, few of the sentences contain explicit references to shame. Instead, most of their examples assume what shame theorists posited to be the basic context for shame—a perception of negative evaluation of the self by self or others, even if the negative evaluation is somewhat indirect. Nor did the authors attempt to include nonverbal markers of shame.

In her pioneering analysis of clinical dialogues, Lewis (1971) took up the issue of shame markers much more explicitly and broadly than did Gottschalk and Gleser. Her work is both theoretical and empirical, tying broad concepts and hypotheses to concrete episodes of behavior. In this capacity, she is the heir of Darwin, MacDougall, and Cooley. She advances our knowledge of shame, however, because, unlike either the original theorists or the more recent advocates (Lynd 1958; Tomkins 1963; Goffman

1967) who used carefully selected examples only in an illustrative way, she conducted a systematic analysis of shame content in complete episodes of real social interaction: entire clinical sessions. Her laborious, word-for-word analysis of these sessions led her to the discovery of what she called "unacknowledged" shame, the low-visibility shame predicated here.

Lewis first distinguished acknowledged and unacknowledged shame. She showed that in hundreds of clinical sessions, most of the shame episodes were virtually invisible to the participants, unacknowledged by either the patient or the therapist. She divided these episodes into two basic types: *overt, undifferentiated* shame and *bypassed* shame. Overt, undifferentiated shame involves painful feelings that are not identified as shame by the person experiencing them. These feelings are instead referred to by a wide variety of terms that disguise the shame experience: feeling foolish, stupid, ridiculous, inadequate, defective, incompetent, awkward, exposed, vulnerable, insecure, having low self-esteem and so on.

Lewis classified all these terms as shame markers because each occurred in conjunction with (1) contexts in which the patient appeared to perceive self as negatively evaluated, either by self or other(s), the central context for shame; and (2) a change in the patient's manner, characterized by non-verbal markers such as speech disruption (stammering, repetition of words, speech "static" like "well," "uhhhh," long pauses, etc.), lowered or averted gaze, blushing, and, especially noticeable, a sharp drop in volume, often resulting in near inaudibility.

Both the verbal and nonverbal markers of overt shame can be characterized as forms of hiding behavior. The verbal terms disguise shame, and the nonverbal forms suggest physical hiding: averting or lowering the gaze to escape the gaze of the other, hiding behind a mask-like blush, and hiding the meaning of speech and thoughts behind speech disruption and inaudible speech.

To summarize, overt, undifferentiated shame occurs when a person (1) feels the self negatively evaluated, either by self or other; (2) manifests hiding behavior (speech disruption, lowered or averted gaze, blushing, or barely audible speech); and (3) labels or associates the painful feeling with undifferentiated terms such as those listed above. In these instances, although the negative evaluation of self appears so painful so as to interfere with the fluent production of thought and/or speech, the pain is mislabeled.

In addition to the overt, undifferentiated pattern, Lewis described the second pattern, bypassed shame. Like the overt pattern, bypassed shame always begins with a perception of the negative evaluation of self. Where the markers of undifferentiated shame are flagrant and overt, those of bypassed shame are subtle and covert. Although thought and speech are not obviously disrupted, they take on a speeded-up, repetitive quality that Lewis refered to as obsessive.

Typically, patients repeated a story or series of stories, talking rapidly and fluently, but not quite to the point. They appeared to be unable to make decisions because of seemingly balanced pros and cons ("insoluble dilemmas"). Patients complained of endless internal replaying of a scene in which they felt criticized or in error. Often they reported that when they first realized the error, they winced or groaned, then immediately became obsessed with the incident. The mind seems to be so taken up with the unresolved scene that one is unable to become adequately involved in the present, even though there is no obvious disruption. One is subtly distracted.

The two patterns of shame appear to involve opposite responses. In overt, undifferentiated shame, victims feel emotional pain to the point that it obviously retards or disrupts thought and speech. They seem to be trying to hide the painful state from themselves as well as from others. In bypassed shame, the victim appears to avoid the pain through hyperactive thought, speech, or actions. These two types appear to correspond to my own distinction between under- and over-distanced emotion (Scheff 1979). Overt, undifferentiated shame is under-distanced, since the intense pain of embarrassment or humiliation is experienced. What Mead (1934) called the "I" phase of the self, the "biologic individual," predominates in consciousness. Bypassed shame is over-distanced; one avoids the pain by stepping outside of self, into the "me" phase of the self, as if the pain were not happening.

Adler's (1956) theory of human development anticipated Lewis discovery of the two basic types of unacknowledged shame. Although he did not use the term, what he called "the feeling of inferiority," i.e., shame, played a central role in his theory. He argued that developing children's greatest desire is for love. If love is not available at the crucial points, the development of their personality can proceed along one of two paths. Either they develop "inferiority complexes," i.e., they become prone to overt, undifferentiated shame, or they compensate by seeking power, i.e., they avoid feeling shame by bypassing it, through what I have termed hyperactive thought, speech, or actions.

Both the slowed-down pattern of overt shame and the speeded-up pattern of bypassed shame are disruptive, however, because both involve the victim in rigid and distorted reactions to reality. Both kinds of shame are equally invisible; one is misnamed, the other ignored. These two basic patterns explain how shame might be ubiquitous, yet usually unnoticed.

The respective works of Tomkins and Lewis converge with, and extend Freud's early work on repression. In his first book (1966, with Breuer), he argued that hysteria was caused by repressed emotion, "strangulated affect," as he called it. He observed that patients improved when they expressed forgotten emotions, e.g., by crying, a rudimentary theory of catharsis (Scheff 1979).

Tomkins (1963) approached repression from a very different direction, through deduction about the fate of grief that did not result in catharsis (crying). This approach led him to describe the outer signs of low-visibility grief, an affect that overlaps with, but is not identical with, that of repressed grief (some low-visibility grief is a result of conscious or partly conscious masking or avoidance).

Lewis extended the concept of repression both theoretically and empirically. Using the kind of shuttling back and forth between deductive and inductive methods that Peirce (1955) called abduction, she laid the groundwork for the shame construct, the description of the context and markers for unacknowledged shame, and its role in the genesis and maintenance of neurotic symptoms. Most of the shame episodes she reported seem to be not only unperceived but also not available to consciousness. Her work therefore confirms not only the Cooley-Goffman conjecture (the part about shame), but also confirms and expands on Freud's original hypothesis that neurosis is caused by strangulated affect (Freud and Breuer 1966).[5] I will now turn to the re-analysis of a study that points to the role of shame in rigid or excessive conformity, which I think is a much more widely prevalent form of pathological behavior than conventional psychopathology allows.

---

5 In a parallel finding, Volkan (see Volkan and Josephthal 1979 for a list of citations) discovered the syndrome of pathological grief, and its cure, a cathartic treatment, called "regrief therapy."

The Asch Conformity Studies

Asch's (1956) study of conformity illustrates the way in which emotions may lead to social control. In this classic laboratory study, single subjects found themselves alone, facing what seemed to be a unified majority. Since the task was a simple comparison of the lengths of lines, the naive subjects must have been baffled by the completely erroneous responses of the other subjects. Unknown to the naive subject, the others were confederates of the investigator, instructed to give erroneous responses. A high proportion of conforming behavior resulted: three-quarters of the subjects were swayed at least once by the majority responses, only one-quarter remained completely independent.

In this study, Asch followed the inductive design that characterizes modern experimental social psychology; it is not a test of a hypothesis derived from theory. In retrospect, however, the study comes close to testing a basic aspect of Durkheimian theory by holding constant one element, social influence (exteriority), while allowing the other element (constraint) to vary. All of the naive subjects perceived the judgment of the majority to be different from, and therefore exterior to, their own judgment. Asch's study demonstrates the exteriority of group standards by showing that naive subjects who were allowed to make judgments alone, without an erring majority, made no errors at all.

The study tests the hypothesis, that given the kind of task demanded, a majority of the subjects will find group standards compelling, even though they are exterior and contradictory to their own individual standards. This formulation suggests a key question: what is the difference between those subjects who maintained their independence from the group and those who yielded? I will suggest that the answer involves the part played by emotions: subjects who yielded to the majority were attempting to avoid the embarrassment (shame) of appearing different from the group.

Although Asch did not design the study to show the effects of emotion or to ask questions about emotions, many of the post-study interview responses suggest that emotions played an important part in the results. It is clear from both Asch's observations and from direct analysis of the subjects' responses that many of them found the experience of being in the minority extremely painful. Asch reported that as the division between the majority and the individual continued, the individual became more tense, flustered, nervous, and anxious. A reaction that occurred both in independent and yielding subjects indicated the fear that they were suffering from a defect, and that the study would disclose this defect: "I felt like a silly fool [...] A question of being a misfit. [...] they'd think I was queer. It made me seem weak-eyed or weak-headed, like a black sheep" (1956, 31).

Many of the comments show negative viewing of self from the point of view of the others: "You have the idea that the attention of the group is focused on you. I didn't want to seem different. I didn't want to seem an imbecile. They might feel I was just trying to be out of the ordinary. [...] They probably think I'm crazy or something" (Asch 1956, 31). These comments are all markers of overt shame (see the earlier discussion of markers).

Asch made an important point, however, in differentiating the post-study interview responses of those who remained independent from those who yielded to the majority. He noted, first, that both independent and yielding subjects were troubled by disagreeing with the majority:

"As the disagreement persisted many began to wonder whether it signified a defect in themselves. They found it painful to be (as they imagined) the focus of attention, in addition to which they feared exposure of their weakness, which they suspected the group would disapprove of [sic]" (1956, 32).

Asch pointed out that though these feelings were all but universal, not everyone who experienced them yielded. Those who maintained their independence responded to their own perceptions of the lines despite their strong feelings. Asch characterizes the responses of those who yielded in a different way:

"They were dominated by their exclusion from the group which they took to be a reflection on themselves. Essentially, they were unable to face a conflict which threatened, in some undefined way, to expose a deficiency in themselves. They were consequently trying to merge in the group in order not to feel peculiar" (1956, 45).

There are several key ideas in this passage. First, there are two markers of overt, undifferentiated shame: "feel peculiar," and "expose a deficiency in themselves." A second point is implied by the first sentence, the subjects' perception of "exclusion from the group," which they took to be a "reflection on themselves" rather than on the group. Because the group took no action to exclude the naive subjects, the perception of exclusion must have been solely in the subjects' imagination, implying the basic shame context: perceiving one's self negatively evaluated.

Finally, the entire passage can be summarized by translating it into the language of emotions. The subjects who yielded to the group were those who not only felt overt shame, but also whose perceptions, cognitions, and/or actions were controlled by the attempt to avoid it. Conversely, many of the subjects who maintained independence from the group appeared to feel conflict, i.e., overt shame, but elected to hold their ground in spite of this feeling.

So far, the discussion of the role of emotion in compelling conformity has been entirely in terms of overt, undifferentiated shame. There is also scattered evidence in the subjects' post-study remarks, and in Asch's summaries of these remarks, of bypassed shame as a causal element in compelling conformity. In the summary by Asch cited above, he refers to those subjects who acknowledged conflict between themselves and the group. There is another group of subjects, however, all of whom yielded to the influence of the group, in which there is little or no acknowledgement of conflict, and no markers of overt shame. The emotion markers in this group suggest the presence of bypassed shame.

After stating that the interview responses of the independent subjects were apt to be frank and forthright, he noted that those of the yielding subjects were different:

"[Their] reactions were more often evasive and shallow, and some revealed a lack of appreciation of the situation and of the possible significance of their action [...] When asked to describe his experiences at the outset of the interview, one subject (who yielded completely) inquired: 'Exactly what do you mean by experiences?' Another remarked: 'I didn't have any experiences, I felt normal'" (1956, 33).

These two responses, especially the latter, suggest a complete denial of conflict and the feelings resulting from that conflict. The comments of two other yielding subjects also suggest denial, but in a different form; they reduced their experience of the study to ponderous or obfuscating generalizations: "People perceive things differently [...]" and "How do we know who is right?" Another group of yielding subjects, according to Asch, "granted to the majority the power to see correctly [...] allowed themselves to become confused, and at the critical point adopted the majority judgments *without permitting themselves to know of their activity*" (1956, 42, emphasis added).

This is a very strong statement about avoidance of conflict and denial of feelings through self-deception. Asch found among the yielding subjects another frequent form of self-deception: considerable underestimation of the number of times each had yielded. He showed that the amount of underestimation was proportional to the amount of yielding (the greater the yielding, the greater the underestimation) (1956, 34–5). Many of these subjects acted as if there were only a few such incidents, even those who had yielded at every opportunity. By denying reality, perhaps they sought to avoid painful feelings.

One of Asch's summaries of the interview responses emphasizes both types of shame responses-the pain of overt shame and what I have called here the obsessive quality of bypassed shame:

"Our observations suggest that independence requires the capacity to accept the fact of opposition without a lowered sense of personal worth. The independent person has to organize his overt actions on the basis of experience for which he finds no support; this he can do only if he respects his experiences and is capable of claiming respect for them. The compliant person cannot face this ordeal because he translates social opposition into a reflection of his personal worth. Because he does so the social conflict plunges him into pervasive and incapacitating doubt" (1956, 51).

Most of this passage is commensurate with both forms of shame, but the last sentence seems to focus on the obsessive form, the insoluble dilemma characteristic of bypassed shame. On the whole, Asch's report inadvertently suggests that unacknowledged shame plays a central role in causing subjects to yield to group influence, even when it contradicts their own direct perceptions of reality.

To conclude this section, I will return to a still unresolved issue in my interpretation. Recall that many of the subjects who remained independent, as well as some of those who yielded, manifested markers of overt, undifferentiated shame. (All of those cited above who showed bypassed shame had yielded.) In this case, the presence of bypassed shame may adequately explain yielding; however, overt, differentiated shame does not, because it seemed to be present in both those who yielded and those who did not. For this latter group, at least, some further explanation is needed.

One possible formulation is in terms of self-esteem. The subjects who remained independent, although they experienced shame, had sufficiently high self-esteem to act on their judgments despite their feelings of shame. Those who yielded had low self-esteem and sought to avoid further feelings of shame by acting contrary to their own judgment. Asch came close to stating it in these very terms. Such a formulation, a causal explanation based on the personalities of the subjects, could be tested in future studies.

Although this formulation could mark an advance in understanding, the advance would probably be very slight. The concept of low self-esteem can be seen as a gloss, implying a person who habitually feels shame rather than pride. Perhaps the concept of pathological shame, as already indicated, would specify the causal process more precisely. Low self-esteem might be conceptualized as a tendency toward endlessly recursive shame, spirals of potentially limitless intensity and duration. As suggested in other articles (Scheff 1987; Scheff and Fearon 2004), in such persons, shame alone, or in combination with other emotions such as anger, might be recursive to the point of chain reaction. Such a dynamic sequence could explain explosive episodes of acute panic (a shame-fear alternation), resentment (shame-anger alternation, with the anger directed out), and guilt (shame-anger sequences with the anger directed in).

Using this model, persons with high self-esteem would be those with the experience of managing most shame so that it is acknowledged and discharged. Although shame is a painful emotion for them, as for everyone else, it is not overwhelming. Persons with low-self esteem would be those who have been unable to manage shame. For such persons, a situation that threatened to be shaming would be perceived as overwhelmingly painful, since it might involve them in an unending spiral of shame. Such a person might do anything to avoid the pain, to "turn the world upside down, rather than turn themselves inside out," to use one of Helen Lewis's favorite phrases. One example is the episode in which Rousseau's conscience lost the battle with what he called "invincible shame." Another is a troublesome and otherwise baffling remark that one of the yielding subjects made to Asch in the post-study interview. He said that he voted for Dewey in the election of 1948, even though he preferred Truman, because he thought Dewey would win and that he was preferred by most (1956, 48). Apparently, unacknowledged shame is not only invincible, but also insidious.

This formulation does not imply that social control is dependent entirely on individual personality, only that individuals have differing susceptibilities to shame. The situational component in conformity is equally important in the deference-emotion model (the deference awarded to individuals in a situation). The Asch experiment was almost diabolical with respect to shame because it was arranged to rob, in a covert way, the individual of her own view of reality. As the deference-emotion model suggests, conformity results from the interaction of individual and situational components. This interaction is also a cultural phenomenon because status arrangements consist, at the microscopic level of analysis, of the blend of awarding and withholding deference.[6]

Summary

I have proposed that Durkheim's analysis of social influence implies a deference-emotion system in which conformity to exterior norms is rewarded by deference and feelings of genuine pride, and nonconformity is punished by lack of deference and feelings of shame. In this analysis, social control involves a biosocial system that functions silently, continuously, and virtually invisibly, occurring within and between members of a society. Cultural taboos on the acknowledgement of pride and shame seem to lead to pathological states of shame, which give rise to rigid or excessive conformity. Asch's study of independence and conformity may be reinterpreted in these terms. If the deference-emotion system were universal, the theory would provide a unitary explanation of conforming behavior, a central problem in social science.

Acknowledgements

S. M. Retzinger and T. D. Kemper gave helpful advice on earlier drafts of that article. This chapter is an updating of Scheff (1988). A longer version can be found as chapter 5 in Scheff (1990).

---

6 For an earlier formulation, which suggests a link between status and emotion, see Kemper (1977).

References

Adler, Alfred (1956). *The Individual Psychology of Alfred Adler*. New York: Basic Books.

Asch, Solomon (1956). Studies of Independence and Conformity: 1. A Minority of One Against a Unanimous Majority. *Psychological Monographs*, 70, 1–70.

Cooley, Charles H. (1922). *Human Nature and the Social Order*. New York: Scribners.

Darwin, Charles (1872). *The Expression of Emotion in Men and Animals*. London: John Murray.

Durkheim, Emile (1951). *Suicide*. New York: Free Press. [first published in 1897]

Freud, Sigmund, and Josef Breuer (1966). *Studies of Hysteria*. New York: Avon. [first published in 1897]

Fuller, Robert (2003). *Somebodies and Nobodies*. Gabriola Island, Canada: New Society Publishers.

— 2006. *All Rise*. San Francisco: Berrett-Koehler Publishers.

Fuller, Robert, and Pamela A. Gerloff (2008). *Dignity for All*. San Francisco: Berrett-Koehler Publishers.

Goffman, Erving (1967). *Interaction Ritual*. New York: Anchor.

Gottschalk, Lewis A., and Goldine C. Gleser (1969). *Manual of Instruction for Using the Gottschalk-Gleser Content Analysis Scales*. Berkeley: University of California Press.

Kemper, Theodore D. (1977). *A Social Interactional Theory of Emotions*. New York: Wiley.

Lewis, Helen B. (1971). *Shame and Guilt in Neurosis*. New York: International Universities Press.

Lynd, Helen M. (1958). *Shame and the Search for Identity*. New York: Harcourt Brace.

MacDougall, William (1908). *An Introduction to Social Psychology*. London: Metheun.

Mead, George Herbert (1934). *Mind, Self and Society*. Chicago: University of Chicago Press.

Peirce, Charles Sanders (1955). Abduction and Induction. In J. Buchler (ed.). *Philosophical Writings of Peirce*, 150–6. New York: Dover. [first published in 1896–1908]

Piers, Gerhart, and Milton B. Singer (1953). *Shame and Guilt: A Psychoanalytic and Cultural Study*. New York: Norton.

Scheff, Thomas J. (1979). *Catharsis and Healing in Healing, Ritual, and Drama*. Berkeley: University of California Press.

— (1984). The Taboo on Coarse Emotions. *Review of Personality and Social Psychology*, 5, 146–69.

— (1987). The Shame/Rage Spiral: Case Study of an Interminable Quarrel. In H. B. Lewis (ed.). *The Role of Shame in Symptom Formation*, 109–50. Hillsdale, NJ: Lawrence Erlbaum.

— (1988). Shame and Conformity: The Deference-Emotion System. *American Sociological Review*, 53, 395–406.

— (1990). *Microsociology: Discourse, Emotion, and Social Structure*. Chicago: University of Chicago Press.

— (1994). *Bloody Revenge: Emotion, Nationalism and War*. Lincoln, NE: iUniverse.

— (2006). *Goffman Unbound: A New Paradigm for Social Science*. Boulder: Paradigm Publishers.

Scheff, Thomas J., and David Fearon (2004). Cognition and Emotion? The Dead End in Self-Esteem Research. *Journal for the Theory of Social Behavior*, 34, 73–90.

Scheff, Thomas J., and Ursula Mahlendorf (1988). Emotion and False Consciousness: Analysis of an Incident from Werther. *Theory, Culture, and Society*, 5, 57–79.

Shibutani, Tamotsu (1961). *Society and Personality*. Englewood Cliffs, NJ: Prentice-Hall.

Tomkins, Silvan S. (1963). *Affect/Imagery/Consciousness*. New York: Springer.

Volkan, Vladimir, and Daniel Josephthal (1979). Brief Psychotherapy in Pathological Grief: Regrief Therapy. In T. B. Karasu and L. Bellak (eds.). *Specialized Techniques in Psychotherapy*, 102–52. New York: Brenner/Mazel.

Wurmser, Leon (1981). *The Masks of Shame*. Baltimore: Johns Hopkins University Press.

A "Neurosociology" of Emotion? Progress, Problems and Prospects

Simon J. Williams

Introduction

This chapter is premised on a simple yet for some perhaps controversial claim, namely, that despite important advances and developments in recent decades, the sociology of emotion may benefit from a fuller or more generous engagement with the biological aspects of emotion. This, of course, begs the obvious next question as to why sociologists should engage "more fully" with these matters, whatever that means, assuming they have not done so already. Surely, one might justifiably argue, sociology can get by quite happily without recourse to the biological dimensions of emotion given the primary emphasis is upon their social and cultural dimensions and dynamics. This, to be sure, is a reasonable retort, but only *to a point*. To the extent that the biological or neurobiological aspects of emotion are neglected or downplayed within sociological accounts of emotion, if not dismissed altogether, then they remain at best *partial* accounts given the complexity of emotion. Or to put it in more positively, incorporating aspects of the neurobiology of emotion may add further *depth* and *detail* to existing sociological accounts of emotion, in much the same way that neurobiological accounts of emotion may benefit from greater sociological inputs regarding their social and cultural dimensions and dynamics.

A "neurosociology" of emotion, I argue, may go someway toward meeting this goal or fulfilling this promise.[1] This moreover is no lone call on my part. Neurosociological work of this kind, as we shall see, is already underway, whilst other strands of biologically or neurobiologically minded work within the sociology of emotions may also profitably be drawn up in

---

1 The term "neurosociology" in fact, as both Smith and Franks (1999), and TenHouten (1999) note, dates back to the early seventies where the term was first introduced in a paper by Bogin et al. (1972). See the final section of this chapter, however, for some further cautious comments and reflections on the merits of any such title or moniker.

this vein. In part then, this chapter considers progress to date on these neurosociological fronts or frontiers. In doing so, however, the problems and prospects of current and future work in this area are also considered and discussed, given the considerable challenges as well as opportunities any such work poses.

What, then, are the core issues which a "neurosociology" of emotion involves or entails? What contribution, in particular, can the neurosciences make to the sociology of emotion, and reciprocally, what contribution can the sociology of emotion make to the neurosciences, and in particular to the affective neuroscience? What problems and pitfalls, moreover, lie ahead in any such venture or undertaking? It is to these very questions and issues that we now turn in the remainder of this chapter.

Border Crossings and Interdisciplinary Conversations: Lessons from/for Neuroscience

At stake here, I suggest, are at least five key themes or issues which a neurosociology of emotion may profitably engage with or address.

Evolution: The "Deep Sociality" of Emotion

Perhaps the first key issue to tackle here head on, given its foundational importance for the sociology of emotion, concerns what Wentworth (1999) has usefully termed the "deep sociality" of emotion: a notion which, at one and the same time, signals *both* the socially constructed character of emotions, and their biological basis as the product of natural selection (see also Wentworth and Yardley 1994). Emotions, Wentworth stresses, were the original means of communication amongst our hominid ancestors, particularly through facial expression, the reading of which *preceded* spoken language but also served two further *enhancing* functions given their *alerting* role and, through their ability to promote reciprocal emotions, their social bonding role. Emotion systems then, from this perspective, are best viewed as "evolved products" of natural selection, which make complex patterns of sociality and social organization possible and hence are "fitness enhancing" (Wentworth 1999), at the same time that they are culture enhancing. Natural selection, in this respect, pushed our ancestors via emotions toward "deep sociality" as a means of adaptation to the environment. For Wentworth nonetheless, the number of so-called innate, primary or hard-wired emotions are thought to be few (e.g. anger, fear, disgust, hatred, sadness), compared to other more complex emotions that, despite being *dependent on the expanded neurobiology of humans as a product of evolution*, are nonetheless primarily a product or expression of culture rather than of neurology (see also Elias 1991). Complex social or secondary emotions, in other words, depend on this evolved neuroanatomy yet are irreducible to it.

Turner (2007; 2000; 1999; Turner and Stets 2005), sheds further valuable light on these evolutionary issues, particularly through his emphasis on the selection pressures that expanded humans' emotional repertoires and capacities (i.e. the *how* and *why* of selection pressures for emotions themselves in human evolution). These selection pressures, it is argued, were primarily *sociological*, given that they effectively rewired the brain in ways that enabled a "low sociality animal to generate emotional bonds necessary for stable social structures" (Turner and Stets 2005, 269). Six key dimensions or domains of selection pressures, in this respect, are identified by Turner: (i) the mobilization of the appropriate amount and type of *emotional energy* to produce social bonds (cf. Goffman 1983; Collins 2004); (ii) the capacity to *attune* responses on the basis of fine grained emotional dispositions; (iii) the use of positive and negative *social sanctions* for social control; (iv) the provision of *moral codes* with emotional force or content to make them binding or compelling; (v) attaching emotions for *exchange* purposes or the valuing of exchange, and finally; (vi) the ability to attach *emotional valences to cognition* to enable *rational* decision making (the latter, an issue we shall return to shortly in this chapter). Each of these capacities, Turner stresses, promoted fitness and enabled our ancestors to become better organized on the African savanna. Natural selection in this respect, whilst blind of course, "contrived" to rewire the brain for enhanced sociality, solidarity and social organization. Thus, rather than sociology "having to accept a purely biological explanation for the emergence of emotions," the "biology of brain structures generating emotions" can itself in part be explained by reference to the selection pressures identified above, which themselves revolve around core sociological issues regarding the wiring and channeling of emotions to promote social bonds (Turner and Stets 2005, 269; Turner 2007, 39–43).

A number of important points for the sociology of emotion follow from this evolutionary viewpoint, not least regarding the strengths and weakness of social constructionist perspectives on emotion and associated debates regarding biology and culture, primary and secondary emotions and so forth. In particular, recourse to this evolutionary perspective provides a powerful reminder if not corrective to a wholly or strongly constructionist view of emotions. Whilst constructionists in this respect, strong or weak, are undoubtedly right to stress the fact that emotions are always channeled and constrained by culture and social structure—including the important role of cultural norms, values, beliefs and ideologies in the very experience and expression of emotion (Gordon 1990; 1989; 1981; Hochschild 1983; Lutz 1988; Stearns 1994)—the biological dimensions of emotion are significantly underplayed here not simply in terms of our evolved biological capacity for emotion, but also by virtue of the fact that these biological dimensions or drivers of emotion remain critical to the nature and intensity of emotion yet are not wholly constrained or channeled by culture. McNay (2008) argues that one of the weaknesses of the sociology of emotions is that the constructionist perspective tends to dominate the area and does so in a way that over valorizes the management of emotions to the extent that it appears like mere social role playing. Whilst constructionists, moreover, rightly stress that emotions are culturally labeled, thereby giving rise to an emotional culture, an evolutionary perspective suggests an alternative conclusion, namely, that "culture is emotionally constructed by humans' neurological capacity to produce a complex array of emotional states" (Turner 2007, 42), or rather on the basis of this capacity. Culture and social structure, in other words, "cannot exist without humans' evolved capacities." These capacities, moreover, are "not neocortical. They are subcortical and evolved long before humans' unique cognitive abilities." Our capacity to generate emotion, and to use it in the service of culture and social structure, in short, is not a "constructed" capacity, so much as it is part of our evolved biology "to a far greater extent than most sociologists are willing to admit" (Turner 2007, 42). What appears to emerge from this discussion is that a characteristic of the area is that it is social researchers' various renditions on how the *sociological* significance of emotions should be apprehended, as much as neuroscientific insights themselves, that determines the way in which neuroemotions will be taken up by sociologists.

A profitable basis nonetheless, as we have seen, is still provided here for the reconciliation of these perspectives or positions. Whilst there is likely to be a greater degree of "wiring" (of a "hard" or "soft" kind[2]) for a wider array of emotions than is currently acknowledged or accepted for example, it is nonetheless important to remember here that it is only the "neurological capacity to generate these emotions which is essential, with socialization and experience in a culture determining just how this generalized capacity is activated" (Turner and Stets 2005, 285). Some emotions, in other words are probably:

> "wired into body systems responsible for emotions, but their activation, expression and use are highly constrained by the emotion culture of a society, and the structure of those situations that call for individuals to experience and express particular emotions" (Turner and Stets 2005, 286).

In this way then, social construction and evolutionary accounts of emotion may be profitably (or at least partially) reconciled. To the extent, moreover, that socio-cultural emotional experience affects, alters or shapes neural processes or mechanisms, including the brain's morphology and physiology—see for example Doidge (2007) on these reciprocal relations in terms of "neuroplasticity" and the "culturally modified brain"[3]—then this further underlines the need to appreciate the inextricability of sociological or socio-cultural and neurobiological orientations if we are to more fully understanding the complexities and indeed the contradictions of emotions in social life.

Emotion and Feeling: One and the Same?

Here we encounter a second critical issue to do with emotion and feeling and their relationship to one another. This distinction, to be sure, is not news or unknown in the social sciences. Nor indeed is the idea that some emotions remain unconscious and remain unacknowledged or unnamed. Barbalet (1998; and in this volume), for example, acknowledges emotions as physiological states that sometimes become conscious feelings and at

---

2 A variety of recent neuroscientific research points in this direction in terms of the neuroplasticity of the brain—see, for example, Doidge (2007).

3 A "neuroplastically informed view of culture and the brain," as Doidge puts it, "implies a two-way street" in which "the brain shapes culture" and "culture shapes the brain" (2007, 287).

other times remain subliminal, semi-conscious or unconscious. Scheff's (1997) work is also, of course, instructive here, particularly regarding the role of acknowledged and unacknowledged, overt or bypassed, shame— see also Theodosius (2006), Clarke (2007), and Craib (1995) on the unconscious dimensions and dynamics of emotion, and Katz (1999) on *How Emotions Work*. Emotion moreover, as Flam's account (in this volume) of "extreme emotion" reminds us, may also "overwhelm" us at times in both positive and negative ways.

Again however, recourse to neuroscientific work on emotion and feeling may deepen and enrich our sociological theorizing of these matters, including those elements of emotion and feeling which personally as well as professionally, puzzle, perplex or just plain surprise us.

Damasio (2003), for example, draws the familiar distinction (discussed above) between "primary" emotions such as fear, anger, disgust, surprise, sadness (read, innate, pre-organized, consistent across cultures and species), which depend on "limbic system" circuitry (especially the amygdala and anterior cingulate), and "secondary" or "social" emotions such as sympathy, embarrassment, shame, pride, jealousy, envy, admiration, gratitude, indignation and contempt. He also, however, in doing so, points to the interesting and intriguing role of "background" emotions which, he claims, are not especially prominent in one's behavior but are nonetheless "remarkably important," given the continuous yet variable sense of our bodies they provide—see also Barbalet (1998) and Heller (1990) on background and foreground emotions.

These three types of emotion then make up what is, for Damasio, "emotion-proper," which in turn relate to one another, he argues, in a "nested" or "tiered" fashion. Thus social emotions, for example, incorporate responses that are part of primary and background emotions. These emotions-proper in turn are nested in a complex structure of regulatory and homeostatic processes which Damasio claims are best thought of or pictured as a tree with multiple branches, some higher and some lower. In the lowest branches of the organism, we have basic processes such as metabolism, reflexes, and immune system functioning. In the middle branches lie behaviors normally associated with pleasure (and reward) and pain (and punishment). In the next level up we have a number of basic drives and motivations such as hunger, thirst, curiosity, exploration, play and sex. Near the top lie emotions-proper as described above, but right at the top Damasio places *feeling* which, he claims involve *conscious* or *felt* elements or aspects of emotion. Emotion, on this account, echoing LeDoux (1998), *precede* feelings; we have *emotions first* and *feelings afterwards* because "evolution," quite simply, "came up with emotion first and feelings later" (Damasio 2003, 30)—see also Pankseep (1998).

Much of what we conventionally think of or refer to as emotion then, according to this neurobiological evidence, does not in fact surface at a conscious or cognitive level at all. When it does register as feeling, moreover, a lot has already happened in our brains and in our bodies, which we are unaware of (LeDoux 1998; Damasio 2003). The possibility of a "disconnection" between emotion-feeling also arises here, as when an emotional impulse such as anger for example is experienced as feelings of shame (cf. Scheff 1997; Freund 1990). This, of course, is not necessarily news for sociologists of emotion. Some if not many sociologists of emotion, as already noted, are indeed ready and willing to acknowledge if not incorporate these distinctions and dynamics into their theorizing. These neurobiological findings, nonetheless, add further valuable evidence and insights into these relationships, which are important to consider in our theorizing of emotion and feeling.

Consider, for example, the strengths and weaknesses of Hochschild's (1983) hugely influential emotion management perspective in this light. Despite its widespread adoption within the sociology of emotion and cognate fields of inquiry, a number of criticisms have nonetheless been leveled at this perspective over the years, including the fact that emotions management does not involve objects or outcomes but is best conceived in processual terms (Barbalet 1998), and that the unconscious dimensions and dynamics of emotion are significantly underplayed in favor of conscious processes of cognitive management (Theodosius 2006; Craib 1995). Recourse to the neurobiology of emotions lends further support to these critiques. Not only does much of this emotion management in fact turn out to be feeling management, for instance, but further neurobiological light is also shed on the very nature and dynamics of emotions themselves which again points to limits of emotion management, conceived as a sociological process of conscious, cognitive control. Two key points in particular are worth stressing here. First, whilst conscious cognitive control or modification of emotion clearly remains important (see for example Ochsner 2007), emotion is not necessarily dependent on conscious processes of evaluation. Indeed, in order for emotion to occur, as Damasio states, "there is no need to analyze the causative object consciously let alone evaluate the situation in which it happens" (Damasio 2003, 55). Secondly, emotions may "flood" or "bump" other more mundane aspects of conscious awareness out of "the mental spotlight" by virtue of the fact that "the wiring of the brain at this point in our evolutionary history is such that the connections from the emotional systems to the cognitive systems are stronger than the connections from the cognitive systems to the emotional systems" (LeDoux 1998, 19). This in other words, sheds further valuable neurobiological light on "how" and "why" questions regarding emotions, especially those that seem to come from "nowhere," "overwhelm" us, or "catch" us by "surprise," which in turn, once again, underlines the limits of a purely or strictly constructionist approach to emotion.

Thus, the sociological significance of the qualitative character of emotions and feelings, and the social significance that they are not always one and the same, testifies once again to the potentially profitable relays between neuroscientific and sociological perspectives.

Rationality and Emotion: The Neurobiology of Decision-Making

A third, closely related issue concerns the valuable linkages and contribution which neuroscience can make to ongoing sociological debates about rationality, decision-making and associated issues regarding the role emotions play in social and ethical behavior.

Assaults on, or problematizations of, the separation of reason and emotion, of course, have come from many quarters over the years and are in fact constitutive of the sociology of emotions (e.g. Flam 1990a; 1990b). The counterpositions in this respect, come from so-called "oppositional" viewpoints through more "critical" viewpoints in which emotions are shown to *support* rationality, to more "radical" viewpoints in which emotions are seen to be *constitutive* of or *synonymous* with rationality—see, for example Barbalet (1998), who draws on longer lines of theorizing in the social sciences and humanities going back to e.g. William James, Robert Franks and Ronald de Sousa, and Williams (2001; 2000).

Again, Damasio's work can be important here to the advancement of these arguments and issues, particularly his much cited book *Descartes' Error: Reason, Emotion and the Human Brain* (1994)—see also Lehrer (2009) on *The Decisive Moment*. To the extent that emotion, for Damasio, may be subversive as well as supportive of rationality, he clearly falls into the "critical" rather than "radical" camp or viewpoint above. This work, nevertheless, has been extremely valuable in providing further neurobiological evidence of these reason-emotion relations, including powerful illustrations of the effects of brain damage on our decision-making capacities.

The critical part of the brain here, it appears, is the ventromedial prefrontal region, which is crucial for normal decision-making and which may, when damaged—as the classic case of Phineas Gage, the brain damaged railroad worker attests—adversely affects the ability to: (i) plan for the future; (ii) decide on the most advantageous course of action, and; (iii) conduct ourselves with respect social rules previously learnt. "Somatic markers" or "gut feelings," in this respect, guide our decision making in more or less rational ways through the positive and negative valences they provide. These emotions and feelings, through learning over time, come to be connected to predicted future outcomes of certain scenarios, such that "when a negative somatic marker is juxtaposed to a particular future outcome the combination functions us an alarm bell." When, instead, a positive somatic marker is juxtaposed to future outcome, it becomes a "beacon of incentive" (Damasio 1994, 174).

Far from being peripheral, subversive or simply sand in the machinery of rationality then, *emotion*, from this neurobiological perspective, plays a *crucial role in decision making*, the absence of which (as case studies such as Gage and his modern day counterparts clearly attest) leave us endlessly dithering between various options or courses of action, and affect in numerous other ways our social and ethical capacities, capabilities and behaviors. To the extent, moreover, that: (i) emotions are crucial to rational decision-making, and (ii) thinking, reasoning and decision-making "comes to mind in the form of images" in this body-minded anti-Cartesian fashion (Damasio 1994, 96), then two "cornerstones" of general sociological conceptions of thinking and acting, as rightly Turner comments, appear problematic:

"rational choice theories present calculations in too simplistic terms, ignoring the emotions involved, whereas symbolic interactionists, in particular, are likely to view thought in purely verbal terms. Thinking is really images, ordered by the association cortex and subordinated to the dominant visual sense modality that can be assembled and reassembled with incredible speed, and without being tagged by emotions generated in subcortical regions of the brain, these images have less substance and cannot be used to plan and make decisions" (Turner 1999, 102).

That rational choice theorists indeed are themselves now incorporating emotion into their work (Elster 2004), not merely as objects but shapers of rational choice, is testimony indeed to the combined and compelling force of these neurobiological and sociological critiques of the reason-emotion distinction. Applications of this work moreover, extend far beyond the confines of sociology, to such diverse fields of enquiry as neuroeconomics, law, politics, psychology, personality theory, psychopathology, art and ethics. While the neurological renditions of emotions have great therapeutic and practical application in the psych professions, for example, it is in the critical social sciences where the "prereflexive emotional substratum is not explained through the idea of intra-psychic dilemmas but is related to the complexities of social position" (McNay 2008, 187) that serves to remind us of the importance of not reducing individual decision making to individual neurochemistry.

Recourse to the neurobiology of emotion nonetheless, as noted earlier, provides an important reminder of the potentially subversive elements of emotion in relation to rationality and decision making, including normal decision making processes in the absence of brain damage. In this sense, they can provide additional input into ongoing theorizing within the social sciences and humanities, which has, however, advanced even more complex conceptions of the relationship between emotion and rationality (Barbalet 1998, 45–54). The sociology of emotion reminds us of the complexity of "normal" everyday decision-making, and the complexities of decision making involved in contexts in which rationality and emotion may *appear* at first take as antagonists rather than as co-constituents of social relations, such as in intimate relations. The emotional registers of patterns of co-dependency (which doubtless involve a complex mixture of both positive and negative somatic markers) would provide a good example here, in serving the important sociological fact that differing emotions and the same emotion in differing contexts have different relations to rationality (cf. Barbalet 1998; Crossley 1998). In the highly rationalized register of psychodynamic language, codependencies as "passionate attachments" (McNay 2008) are conceived of as mainly or solely erroneous intra psychic dynamics of desire gone array, rather than as connected to the internal logic of patriarchic capitalism and wider structures of power. Again then we see here the potential instructive and productive relations or relays, both ways, between sociological and neurobiological accounts of reason, emotion and decision-making.

The Self and Social Interaction: Bringing the (Neuro)Biological Back in?

Here we arrive at a fourth potential point of interchange between the sociology of emotion and the neurosciences, namely, the question or problem of selfhood or personhood. As with notions of mind, consciousness, subjectivity, will or intentionality, appeals to identity, selfhood or personhood, are subject to multiple interpretations and definitions, thereby making this, to say the very least, contested terrain—see, for example, Taylor (1989), Rose (1990) and Damasio (2000).

Again however, I venture, neurobiology has important things to say here which, whilst in no way eclipsing or overshadowing current sociological renditions of these matters, may nonetheless be profitably and productively engaged with if not incorporated into our theorizing of emotions, selfhood and social interaction. Turner (1999), for example, once again flags a number of important and instructive sociological points and issues here. For example, consider that: (i) the very ways we come to view ourselves as "objects"[4] in social situations is primarily the product of the right side of the brain; (ii) self-cognitions are tagged with emotion and triggered through emotion and memory systems that enhance self-feelings, and; (iii) much emotion remains subcortical and does not therefore register as self-feeling at all, yet contributes greatly to communication and interaction with others, including critical issues of "tracking, rhythm and attunement," through the mobilization of various body systems (Turner 1999, 102–3). Others indeed, as Turner rightly stresses, can often do a better job of assessing ourselves than we can thanks to the mobilization of these emotion body-systems (1999, 103). To these observations, of course, we may add the recent discovery of so-called "mirror neurons" in primate brains—i.e. neurons which "fire" when an individual performs an action and when the same individual observes another performing the same action (Gallese and Goldman 1998)—which itself is fuelling much current speculation about the neurological bases of learning, empathy, trust and awareness of other minds. Self therefore, from this viewpoint, is:

"not so much a cognitive construct as an architecture of the emotion systems implicated in strong memories in the frontal lobe, in thought processes couched in the 'brain's way of thinking,' in subcortical emotional memory systems, and in the

---

4 We are also, of course, subjects, who are actively engaged in social action, social situations and social meaning making.

reactivation of emotional body systems" (Turner 1999, 103; see also Damasio 2000 on the "proto," "core" and "autobiographical" self[5]).

Similarly, much of what passes within conventional sociology as role taking and role occurs subcortically, with consciousness awareness of these processes arising less frequently, "typically when emotions are at a relatively high level of mobilization" (1999, 104)—see also Franks (1999) on convergences and divergences between symbolic interactionism and neuroscience.

A return to the likes of Phineas Gage and his modern day counterpart is also instructive at this juncture for what it tells us about the neurobiological basis or grounding of the self. What we see here indeed, in such cases, are the profound assaults on the self these injuries or lesions involve and the frequently heroic attempts people make in the face of them to rescue or recover some semblance or sense of their (former) selves—see for example Sacks (1985). The role of psychopharmaceuticals too of course provides another powerful reminder of the *neurochemistry of emotion* and feeling, if not "neurochemical" selfhood (Rose 2007)[6]—relations albeit, which are complex and cannot simply be read or mapped on to one another in any neat or tidy one-to-one fashion.

Stratification and Inequalities: The Sociobiological Translation

A final set of issues, in this chapter at least, has to do with the promise or potential of a neurosociology of emotion, broadly conceived, in relation to questions of social structure and social inequality. There has of course, as is well known, been a long tradition of structural work within the sociology on emotions, including important contributions from Kemper (1990; 1978), Collins (1984) and Barbalet (1998). Kemper's work is particularly valuable in this respect, resting as it does on both a sociological and bio-

---

5 The "proto-self," for Damasio, is based on neural patterns which represent the "state of the organism, moment by moment," but which remains unconscious or nonconscious; the "core self" in contrast, which we are conscious of, inheres in "the second-order nonverbal account that occurs whenever an object modifies the proto-self;" whilst the "autobiographical self" is based on "autobiographical memory" and the "anticipated future" (2000, 174).

6 Rose's line here indeed is altogether more neo-Foucauldian in tone: an emphasis, that is to say, on who we "think we are" and who we "take our selves to be" rather than what we "are" (2007, 25). For other recent work in this vein on new forms and configurations of "biosociality," see for example Gibbon and Novas (2008).

logical appreciation of emotion. Changes in relations of power (authority) and status (prestige, honor) of individuals within social structures, Kemper argues, have significant effects on the arousal of positive (e.g. satisfaction, confidence, security) or negative (e.g. anxiety, loss of confidence, fear) emotions—relations which themselves are mediated through individual expectations. Social solidarity, from this viewpoint, emerges from power and status dynamics and their emotional correlates. If individuals, for example, fail to maintain or lose status relative to their expectations, this may result in feelings of shame or embarrassment (if they blame themselves) or anger and aggression (if they blame others). Similarly, power dynamics can erode social solidarity when over used or abused. It is not simply a case of the emotional correlates of social structure, however, but their role in the very maintenance or transformation of social structures over time; what Barbalet (1998) usefully refers to as the social *responsiveness* and the social *efficacy* of emotion.

This work in turn links, in more or less promising ways, to other research on health inequalities, particularly work that addresses the so-called "sociobiological" translation of these broader aspects of social structure into the health and illness of the emotionally expressive body. Wilkinson's (2005; 1996) on-going work on "unhealthy" societies and income inequalities, for instance, is a case in point. The corrosive effect of income inequalities on health he shows, based on international comparative data, occur primarily through psychosocial rather than material pathways, once a certain standard of living has been reached. It is not so much material standards of living in affluent societies which make the difference, in other words, but our social status or social standing relative to others, and associated issues to do with stress, insecurity, lack of control in the workplace and so on. In terms of health status, these psychosocial pathways, Wilkinson suggests, include both direct neurohormonal or neurophysiological effects on the body and indirect effects through health risking forms of behavior. Feelings of stress, anxiety, insecurity in this respect may result in neurohormonal/neurophysiological arousal or perturbation of various kinds, which if prolonged or sustained, may have detrimental effects on health. Cortisol, for instance, a key "stress hormone" with a range of biological and physiological effects on the body, may have health damaging consequences if levels remain raised over a significant period of time so that, in effect, this resets our bodily "thermostat." Sustained stress may also damage the mechanisms by which insulin controls glucose levels in the blood and/or disrupts or compromises aspects of immune system functioning, thereby rendering individuals susceptible or prone to illness or disease (Wilkinson 2005; 1996; Marmot 2006). Alternatively, these psychosocial stressors may be expressed through health damaging behaviors of various kinds such as excessive alcohol consumption, smoking, accident-prone behavior, self-destructive or self-abusing acts, violence or aggressive behavior.

Emotions again, as I have argued elsewhere (Williams 2003; 1998), provide a critical link here in these psychosocial pathways and their "sociobiological" translation into bodily matters of health and illness. Freund's (1998; 1990) too of course, sheds further valuable light on these issues through his work on the "expressive" body, demonstrating through concepts such as dramaturgical stress and emotional false consciousness how one's position in any social hierarchy and the manner in which social relationships are managed both *affect*, and are *affected* by, biochemical states and other aspects of "bodylines." Since the body, indeed, as Freund reminds us, is a key means of expression, it is not unreasonable to suppose that people express somatically the conditions of their existence. Social conditions that create depression, for instance, may "construct an emotional mode of being in which the motivation to resist is blunted" (1990, 470). People's capacity to resist, in this respect, depends very much on the social relations and the social space in which they find themselves. Resistance, for example, may also be somatically expressed in various forms of political engagement or activism. Alternatively, the ebb and flow, cut and thrust, of daily social life may give rise to somatic expression (feeling tired, worn out or contemplative, for instance) in which the capacity to resist is blunted in the absence of depression—see also Sayer (2005) on the moral significance of class and some albeit tentative thoughts, via sociological notions such as habitus, on somatics, emotions and health inequalities.

Here again then, in these ways and countless others, we glimpse something of the promise and potential of a "neurosociology" of emotion, this time albeit in terms of the "expressive body" as a common ground for the sociology of emotions, health and illness. Perhaps most importantly of all, however, this points to the "socially pliable" nature of the (neuro)biological body itself (and associated notions such as "neuroplasticity"), which in turn underlines the importance of thinking both ways, so to speak, not simply from the neuro- to the social but from the social to the neuro.

Remaining Problems and Pitfalls: The Challenges Ahead

Despite the many important insights and potential points of contact, collaboration or communication between the sociology of emotions and contemporary neuroscience, problems remain of course, as they do in any such inter-disciplinary exchanges, if not trans-disciplinary ventures, which themselves are important to acknowledge and address if further progress is to be made on these fronts.

First, as touched on earlier, one of the key problems or stumbling blocks is a mutual skepticism, distrust, dismissal or disdain for each other, amongst both sociologists and neuroscientists, including unhelpful caricatures of one another or flat charges of reductionism. On the one hand, of course, this should not be overplayed. There are, as we have seen, both bio- or neuro-friendly sociologists and socially minded or at least socially aware neuroscientists. Social neuroscience moreover, is another new branch of neuroscience, albeit one with little sociological input to date (see, for example, Harmon-Jones and Winkielman 2007; Cacioppo and Berntson 2005; 1992). Yet the standoff remains in many respects. This perhaps is not surprising given that different disciplines have their own cultures, frames of reference, language, journals, methods and preferred ways of working (Cromby 2007), and that even within disciplinary boundaries there is often considerable "diversity of opinion" if not "in-house fighting," which may or may not be healthy, depending on your perspective. It does, nonetheless, point to some enduring obstacles which signify both now and in the foreseeable future in terms of allowing genuine interdisciplinary conversations or exchanges between neuroscience and sociology.

Other problems, however, are equally important to bear in mind in any such undertaking. Cromby (2007), for example, usefully flags a number of pertinent issues here pertaining to language, conceptual and methodological problems respectively. Terms such as the "self" for instance, as already noted, mean many different things both within and between disciplines and as such are open to contestation and dispute. These problems of language, in turn, are closely bound up with problems of a conceptual kind. Social scientists for example, as Cromby rightly notes, frequently (though not always of course) deploy a "meaningful," "normative" or "rule-based" metaphysic with respect to the social world, whilst neuroscientists instead tend to favor a "causal" or "deterministic" metaphysic in relation to the brain and brain based mechanisms, which in turn (to the extent that the social is addressed at all) frequently carries over in their conceptualization of the social world too (2007, 158). The social and natural realms, moreover, as Newton (2007) warns, cannot and should not be collapsed too readily or easily, given clear *temporal* differences between these realms which make it difficult if not impossible to apply uniform modes of inquiry across them. Difference, as such, between the natural and the social domain may have to be respected at the epistemological level even if, at the ontological level, they remain intimately entwined or related.

Another important conceptual issue here, which rightly Cromby (2007) raises, occurs when neuroscientists use metaphors to describe the brain: something which leaves them open to the charge of misattributing psychological predicates to the brain (i.e. the "thinking," "feeling," or even "ethical" brain) which rightly and properly only belong to people. As the eminent hermeneutic philosopher Ricoeur appositely puts it in his conversations with the neuroscientist Changeux: "I do not understand what it means to say 'consciousness occurs in the brain' [...] The brain does not 'think' in the sense that thought conceives of itself" (Changeux and Ricoeur 2000, 52). Problems of "mutant Cartesianism," as this suggests, frequently haunt contemporary neuroscience—i.e. the driving of the mind-body problem deeper inside the brain to questions of brain-mind or brain-consciousness relations (Cromby 2007; Bennett and Hacker 2003). The neurosciences in this respect, despite important strides or developments over the past two decades, are still, as Rose (2006, 4) appositely puts it, "data rich" but "theory poor." Whilst we now, indeed, have a wealth of data about the brain, putting it all together into something like a coherent theory of the brain, let alone consciousness or behavior, continues to elude even the best brains on the planet. On the very question of consciousness therefore, Rose boldly ventures, neuroscientists (like himself) "don't have anything very much useful to say" and would therefore, recalling Wittgenstein, "do better to keep silent" (2006, 4)!

The reference to Wittgenstein is indeed apposite here. Bennett and Hacker (2003) for example, as Cromby (2007) notes, raise a number of important philosophical issues regarding contemporary strands of neuroscience including the fact, from a Wittgensteinian perspective, that emotions and feelings (contra Damasio and his colleagues) are not "inside" or "within us"—i.e. are not, or need not, involve mental "images," neural "maps," "somatic markers" etc.—but are instead *public* events, generated by or emergent from dynamic social situations, from which they derive their meaning and character in an open, ongoing fashion (2007, 162)[7]—see also Burkitt (1997). In all these ways then, *potential* problems of misattribution, misunderstanding if not misplaced reductionism, loom large in neurobiological encounters or ventures of this kind (see also Newton 2007).

Finally, at a methodological level, problems remain in trying to work across disciplinary boundaries, not least given the difficulties of translating let alone transporting the experimental methods and findings of neuroscience, including its presumption of *methodological individualism* and its cumbersome technologies such as brain imaging and like, into the live or lived everyday contexts sociologists are familiar with (Cromby 2007, 163–4). There may, moreover, be in-built selection pressures here in terms of hierarchies of knowledge production which militate against any such genuinely collaborative endeavors on this neuro-social front, given: (i) neuroscientific research has huge resources behind it, compared to the social sciences, and; (ii) neuroscience is experimental in nature, with findings which are demonstrable, quantifiable and indeed highly visible through powerful if not seductive or misleading technologies such as fMRI (Crawford 2008) which readily capture both the public imagination and the public purse strings (Hopkins 2009). To the extent, nonetheless, that profitable or productive methodological alliances may be forged here, then they may allow sociologists access to aspects of emotion which hitherto have proved difficult to research.

None of this, I hasten to add, should discourage us. There are moreover some already potentially useful perspectives or positions to draw upon here as an "under-laboring" philosophy. A realist stance for example, has much to offer here, based as it is on robust philosophical principles and premises, which avoid the potential traps or pitfalls of misplaced reductionism of a sociological or biological kind. Many of the foregoing issues discussed in this chapter, indeed, can be happily or readily incorporated within a realist or "corporeal realist" (Shilling 2005) framework: a position which; (i) recognizes the ontologically stratified nature of the social and natural domains; (ii) respects important differences between these domains (cf. Newton's 2007 point above) and; (iii) resolves these issues through

---

7 Bennett and Hacker's (2003) philosophical critique of cognitive neuroscience is wide ranging in scope, and logical-conceptual in content, including a critique of the aforementioned emotion-feeling distinction. At heart, nonetheless, lies the charge that emotions "do not apply to brain structures at all, but to creatures who feel emotions and exhibit them in their behavior" (2003, 209).

principles of irreducibility and emergence—see, for example, Sayer (2000), Archer et al. (1998) and Shilling (2005). The social, in this respect, is emergent from yet irreducible to the biological, in much the same way as mind arises from or emerges in a "brain situated within a body-proper" (Damasio 2003, 191); a mindful body, that is to say. Biology, in this way, may be profitably and productively brought back into sociological forms of understanding and explanation without the fear or specter of reductionism.[8]

Whatever one's preferred theoretical or philosophical stance however, future progress on these complex interdisciplinary matters, as Cromby (2007) rightly notes, clearly depends in no small measure on a readiness and willingness for mutually informed and sustained dialogue and debate across these disciplinary divides: conversations moreover which remain realistic rather than romantic or naïve as to what can and cannot be achieved, both now and in the foreseeable future.

Suggestive questions, in this respect, for further work and future study include the following:

- How can remaining epistemological and ontological problems pertaining to the social and biological domains, and associated issues concerning mind, brain, body relations, best be addressed if not overcome?
- What happens when complexity is treated as a *resource* rather than a problem in traversing this terrain and thinking through the neurosociology of emotions?
- How generalized is the "hardwiring" of emotion and what further light can sociology shed on evolutionary selection pressures and the "deep sociality" of emotion? Can further progress be made here, moreover, in reconciling these evolutionary or biological and constructionist accounts of emotion?
- What further potential is there for inputs to/from the neuroscience regarding such key sociological matters as selfhood and social interaction, subjectivity and inter-subjectivity, individual and collective social behavior? How useful, furthermore, are concepts such as biosociality here?
- Can the neurosociology of emotion shed any further light on "deviations" in "normal" decision-making processes in complex situations such as intimacy and co-dependency?

---

8 Smith and Frank's (1999) call for a neurosociology of emotion that is (sic) "both *reductionist and emergentist*" (1999, 5), strikes me as strange and unnecessary on this count, despite their insistence that these positions are "not necessarily opposed" (1999, 5).

- To what extent are concepts such as habitus helpful, in neurosociological terms, for thinking through relations between social structure, emotions and the body? What other sociological or neuroscientific concepts (e.g. pliability, (neuro)plasticity, "soft" rather than "hard" wiring) might be helpful here for integrating the social and the neural and exploring relations "both ways"?
- What methodological challenges does work of this kind pose and how best might they be addressed? To what extent, for example, are case studies and mixed methodologies a profitable and productive way forward here in helping trace, track and unravel these complex, contingent, multi-level and multi-layered neurosociological processes and relations (Hopkins 2009)?

This it seems is a fitting place to stop, given the many important challenges ahead for work of this kind. At the very least, I suggest, sociologists of emotion may profitably and productively engage with neuroscience, particularly affective neuroscience, regarding the neurobiological aspects and dimensions of emotion. Doing so may indeed provide a more complete or comprehensive perspective on emotion: one that integrates the biological, cultural and social dimensions of emotion in a *non-reductionist* fashion whilst still nonetheless respecting the discrete analytical power and potential of a sociological perspective on these matters. Whether or not, of course, returning full circle to the very title and introduction to this chapter, this is best regarded or referred to as a "neurosociology" of emotion—i.e. a distinct strand within the sociology of emotion—is a moot point. To the extent indeed that the call here is for more widespread engagement with the biological or neurobiological dimension of emotion within the sociology of emotion as a whole, then any such title or moniker may be unnecessarily restrictive, or just plain unnecessary! To the extent nonetheless that it caters to particular or specific interests in these "neurosociological" matters, whilst still leaving plenty of room for the pursuit of other more familiar sociological topics or interests pertaining to emotions, then it clearly has its merits (as well as its drawbacks). This itself then, remains an open question, or further topic for debate. What is clear nonetheless is that the sociology of emotions is well placed to be one of the leading edges of any such robust and constructive sociological engagement with the neurosciences. Herein then, to conclude, lie the challenges and opportunities, problems and prospects of these sociological ventures or adventures in the decades to come. Watch this space…

Acknowledgements

Thanks to Debra Hopkins and Jochen Kleres, the editors of this volume, for their very sterling services and useful comments on this chapter.

References

Archer, M., R. Bhaskar, A. Collier, T. Lawson, and A. Norrie (1998). *Critical Realism: A Reader.* London: Routldge.

Barbalet, Jack M. (1998). *Emotion, Social Structure, and Social Theory.* Cambridge: Cambridge University Press.

Bennett, M. R., and P. M. S. Hacker (2003). *Philosophical Foundations of Neuroscience.* Oxford: Blackwell.

Bogin, J. E., R. DeZure, W. D. TenHouten, and J. F. Marsh, Jr. (1972). The Other Side of the Brain: The A/P Ratio. *Bulletin of the Los Angeles Neurological Societies,* 37, 49–61.

Burkitt, Ian (1997). Social Relationships and Emotions. *Sociology,* 31 (1), 37–55.

Cacioppo, John T., and Gery Berntson (1992). Social Psychological Contributions to the Decade of the Brain. *American Psychologist,* 40, 1019–28

— (2005). *Social Neuroscience.* Hove: Psychology Press.

Changeux, Jean-Pierre, and Paul Ricoeur (2000). *What Makes Us Think?* Princeton: Princeton University Press.

Clarke, S. (2007). Theory and Practice: Psychoanalytic Sociology as Psycho-Social Studies. *Sociology,* 40 (6): 1153–69.

Collins, Randall (2004). *Interaction Ritual Chains.* Princeton, NJ: Princeton University Press.

Craib, Ian (1995). Some Comments on the Sociology of Emotions. *Sociology,* 29 (1), 151–8.

Crawford, Matthew B. (2008). The Limits of Neuro-Talk. *The New Atlantis. A Journal of Technology and Society.* Winter, 65–78.

Cromby, John (2007). Integrating Social Science and Neuroscience: Potentials and Problems. *BioSocieties,* 2 (2), 149–69.

Crossley, Nick (1998). Emotions and Communicative Action. In Gillian Bendelow and Simon J. Williams (eds.). *Emotions in Social Life,* 17–38. London: Routledge.

Damasio, Antonio (1994) *Descartes' Error: Emotion, Reason, and the Human Brain.* London: Picador.

— (2000). *The Feeling of What Happens: Body and Emotion in the Making of Consciousness.* London: Vintage.

— (2003). *Looking for Spinoza: Joy, Sorrow, and the Feeling Brain.* London: Vintage.

Doidge, Norman (2007). *The Brain that Changes Itself.* London: Penguin.

Elias, Norbert (1991). On Human Beings and Their Emotions: A Process Sociological Essay. In Mike Featherstone, Mike Hepworth and Bryan S. Turner (eds.). *The Body: Social Process, Cultural Theory*, 103–125. London: Sage.

Elster, Jon (2004). *Alchemies of the Mind*. Cambridge: Cambridge University Press.

Flam, Helena (1990a). Emotional Man: I. The Emotional Man and the Problem of Collective Action. *International Sociology*, 5 (1), 39–45.

— (1990b) Emotional Man: II. Corporate Actors as Emotion-Motivated Managers. *International Sociology*, 5 (2), 225–34.

Franks, David D. (1999). Some Convergences and Divergences Between Neuroscience and Symbolic Interactionism. In David D. Franks and Thomas S. Smith (eds.). *Mind, Brain and Society: Toward a Neurosociology of Emotion*, 157–81. Stamford, Conn.: JAI Press.

Franks, David D., and Thomas S. Smith (1999). Summaries of Chapters. In David D. Franks and Thomas S. Smith (eds.). *Mind, Brain and Society: Toward a Neurosociology of Emotion*, 19–40. Stamford, Conn.: JAI Press.

Freund, Peter E. S. (1990). The Expressive Body: A Common Ground for the Sociology of Emotions and the Sociology of Health and Illness. *Sociology of Health and Illness*, 12 (4), 452–77.

— (1998). Social Performances and Their Discontents; Reflection on the Biosocial Psychology of Role Playing. In Gillian A. Bendelow and Simon J. Williams (eds.). *Emotions in Social Life*, 265–90. London: Routledge.

Gallese, V., and A. Goldman (1998). Mirror Neurons and the Simulation Theory of Mind Reading. *Trends in Cognitive Sciences*, 12, 493–501.

Gibbon, Sahra, and Carlos Novas (eds.). (2008). *Biosocialities, Genetics and the Social Sciences*. London: Routledge.

Goffman, Erving (1983). Presidential Address: The Interaction Order. *American Sociological Review*, 48: 1–17.

Gordon, S. (1981). The Sociology of Sentiments and Emotion. In Morris Rosenberg and Ralph H. Turner (eds.). *Social Psychology: Sociological Perspectives*, 562–92. New York: Basic Books.

— (1989). Institutional and Impulsive Orientation in Selectively Appropriating Emotions to Self. In D. D. Franks and E. D. McCarthy (eds.). *The Sociology of Emotions: Original Essays and Research Papers*, 115–35. Greenwich, Conn.: JAI Press.

— (1990). Social Structural Effects on Emotions. In Theodore D. Kemper (ed.). *Research Agendas in the Sociology of Emotions*, 145–79. Albany: State University of New York Press.

Harmon-Jones, Eddie, and Piotr Winkielman (eds.). (2007). *Social Neuroscience: Integrating Psychological Explanations of Social Behavior*. New York, London: The Guilford Press.

Heller, Agnes (1990). *Can Modernity Survive?* Cambridge: Polity Press.

Hochschild, Arlie R. (1983). *The Managed Heart: The Commercialization of Human Feeling*. Berkeley: University of California Press.

Hopkins, Debra (2009). Personal Communication.

Katz, Jack (1999). *How Emotion Works*. Chicago: Chicago University Press.

Kemper, Theodore D. (1978). Toward a Sociology of Emotions: Some Problems and Solutions. *The American Sociologist*, 13, 30–41.

— (1990). Social Relations and Emotion: A Structural Approach. In Theodore D. Kemper (ed.). *Research Agendas in the Sociology of Emotion*, 207–37. Albany: State University of New York Press.

LeDoux, Joseph (1998). *The Emotional Brain: The Mysterious Underpinnings of Emotional Life*. New York: Simon and Schuster.

Lehrer, Jonah (2009). *The Decisive Moment*. Edinburgh: Canongate.

Lutz, Catherine A. (1988). *Unnatural Emotions*. Chicago: University of Chicago Press.

Marmot, M. (2006). *The Status Syndrome: How Social Standing Affects our Health and Longevity*. London: Bloomsbury.

McNay, Lois (2008). *Against Recognition*. Cambridge: Polity Press.

Newton, Tim (2007). *Nature and Sociology*. London: Routledge.

Ochsner, Kevin O. (2007). How Thinking Controls Feeling. In Eddie Harmon-Jones and Piotr Winkielman (eds.). *Social Neuroscience*, 106–36. New York, London: The Guilford Press.

Pankseep, Jaak (1998). *Affective Neuroscience: The Foundations of Human and Animal Emotions*. New York: Oxford University Press.

Rose, Nikolas (1990). *Governing the Soul*. London: Routledge.

— (2007). *The Politics of Life Itself: Biomedicine, Power and Subjectivity in the Twenty-First Century*. Princeton: Princeton University Press.

Rose, Steven (2006). *The 21st Century Brain: Explaining, Mending and Manipulating the Mind*. London: Vintage.

Sacks, Oliver (1985). *The Man Who Mistook his Wife for a Hat*. London: Picador.

Sayer, Andrew (2000). *Realism and Social Science*. London: Sage.

— (2005). *The Moral Significance of Class*. Cambridge: Cambridge University Press.

Scheff, Thomas J. (1997). *Emotion, the Social Bond, and Human Reality: Part/Whole Analysis*. Cambridge: Cambridge University Press.

Shilling, Chris (2005). *The Body in Culture, Technology and Society*. London: Sage.

Smith, Thomas S., and David D. Franks (1999). Introduction. In David D. Franks and Thomas S. Smith (eds.). *Mind, Brain and Society. Towards a Neurosociology of Emotion*, 3–18. Stamford, Conn.: JAI Press.

Stearns, Peter (1994). *American Cool: Constructing a Twentieth Century Emotional Style*. New York: New York University Press.

Taylor, Charles (1989). *Sources of the Self*. Cambridge: Cambridge University Press.

TenHouten, W. D. (1999). Explorations in Neurosociological Theory: From the Spectrum of Affect to Time Consciousness. In David D. Franks and Thomas S. Smith (eds.). *Mind, Brain and Society*, 41–80. Stamford, Conn.: JAI Press.

Theodosius, Catherine (2006). Recovering Emotion From Emotion Management. *Sociology*, 40 (5), 893–910.

Turner, Jonathan H. (1999). The Neurology of Emotions: Implications for Sociological Theories of Interpersonal Behavior. In David D. Franks and Thomas S. Smith (eds.). *Mind, Brain and Society: Toward a Neurosociology of Emotion*, 81–108. Stamford, Conn.: JAI Press.

— (2000). *On the Origins of Human Emotions: A Sociological Inquiry Into the Evolution of Human Affect*. Stanford, CA: Stanford University Press.

— (2007). *Human Emotions: A Sociological Theory*. London: Routledge.

Turner, Jonathan H., and Jan E. Stets (2005). *The Sociology of Emotions*. Cambridge: Cambridge University Press.

Wentworth, W. M. (1999). Consciousness and the Potential for Contributions From Brain Science to the Sociology of Emotion. In David D. Franks and Thomas S. Smith (eds.). *Mind, Brain and Society*, 183–212. Stamford, Conn.: JAI Press.

Wentworth, W. M., and D. Yardley (1994). Deep Sociality: A Bioevolutionary Perspective on the Sociology of Human Emotion. In D. D. Franks, W. M. Wentworth and J. Ryan (eds.). *Social Perspectives on Emotion*, 21–55. Greenwich, CT: JAI Press.

Wilkinson, Richard, G. (1996). *The Afflictions of Inequality*. London: Routledge.

— (2005). *The Impact of Inequality: How to Make Sick Societies Healthier*. London: Routledge.

Williams, Simon J. (1998). Capitalising on Emotions? Rethinking the Inequalities Debate. *Sociology*, 32 (1), 121–39.

— (2000). Is Rational Choice Theory "Unreasonable"? The Neglected Emotions. In Margaret S. Archer and Jonathan Q. Tritter (eds.). *Rational Choice Theory: Resisting Colonisation*, 57–72. London: Routledge.

— (2001). *Emotion and Social Theory*. London: Sage.

— (2003). *Medicine and the Body*. London: Sage.

Refugee Solidarity: Between National Shame and Global Outrage

James Goodman

Introduction

Action by national citizens to assist humanitarian migrants has become a key issue in many high-income countries. Refugee solidarity of this sort is a realm of mobilization where cross-cultural and transnational imperatives are keenly felt—it is the place where national sentiment encounters global injustice, where worldwide human suffering is personalized and asserted in the face of national exclusion. Solidarity with refugees may be seen as the embodiment of reaching across global divides, as the crucible of transnational solidarity, where an inter-subjective impulse forces a move to a shared humanity. A key issue for such movements is how they relate with the national-level affiliations. In addressing refugee rights, movements have found themselves at a crossroads between humanitarian norms and national identity, between global passion and national sentiment, between borderless cosmopolitanism and reconstituted nationalism. Movements enacting refugee solidarity thus directly engage with what is perhaps the key issue facing transnational social movements—how to bridge levels of emotion and action, and how to embed cosmopolitanism.

This chapter focuses on the Refugee Rights Movement that intensified in Australia between 2000 and 2003, and it discusses solidarity between national citizens of Australia and refugees detained by the Australian government. The discussion is not so much centered on the diasporic linking amongst refugees or migrants, as analyzed for instance by Peteet (2000). Neither is it on the formation of transnational networks of migrant advocacy organizations, as, for instance, addressed by Piper (2003). Rather, the focus is on the relationship between nationals and refugee non-nationals, and the emergence of social movements around such relationships, as an instance of transnational mobilization. Such analysis immediately revolves around border politics, a key political theme of the current period, and on the passionate "hot cognitions" of cross-border humanitarianism (Amin-zade and McAdam 2001). Border politics is a highly-charged realm where narratives of national belonging are both imposed and exposed. Belonging is a key nexus-point between political power and public emotion, and counter-struggles at the borders of belonging conjure especially deep-seated emotive dynamics (Yuval-Davis et al. 2006).

Indeed, the emotional power of refugee solidarity can be overwhelm-ing, and can impel people to do remarkable things. One example is the Woomera 2002 demonstration in Australia, when a large protest helped refugees escape from a detention camp in the central Australian desert. At one moment during the filming of the breakout, by SKA-TV, a woman is captured on film expressing her solidarity with refugees at the fence of the camp, lost for words, unable to express the power of the personal contact with refugee detainees, reaching out across the border between them (SKA-TV 2002). There are similar moments of high emotion at other demonstrations outside detention camps, for instance in Sydney in 2002 where detainees waved from an exercise yard in full view of the demon-strators, making symbolic contact across the border—across three metal fences, a line of security guards, a line of police horses and two lines of riot police. The demonstrators responded by waving hands, many in silence, and many in tears. The symbolic power of these moments of inter-subjec-tive solidarity is perhaps most clearly demonstrated by the capacity to break down the brutalizing effects of state power. At Woomera several participants reported that a number of riot police, male and female, began to cry while carrying out their duties. Another illustration is in the breaking of ranks in the Australian Navy, which saw some senior naval officers refusing to take on the role of repelling and expelling refugee arrivals (Tip-pett 2001).

With these accounts, refugee solidarity movements' intense dilemmas of how to act across the border, at the crossroads of "domestic" and "for-eign" realm, are forced into view. Dilemmas are played out in movement schisms and conflicts, and in the divergent emotional life of movements. The crossroads effectively bifurcate refugee solidarity, between nationally-focused and global approaches. In both approaches, the movement elabo-rates normative structures and literally produces public emotions (Calhoun 2001). The first approach is broadly instrumental, geared to national policy change, effectively to remaking "the nation," and reclaiming national pride against the shame of refugee detention; the second is more expressive, in demonstrating anger and outrage in the name of human empathy and dignity, geared to the cosmopolitan aspiration of "breaking the borders." This paper unfolds in two main parts. After outlining some of the dynamics of transnational solidarity in section 1, section 2 outlines the contrasting policy positions, expressions of solidarity, modes of action and emotional registers.

Embedded Solidarities and Emotional Registers

Globalism heralds a new era of corporate globalization, and generates powerful responses. Just as the globalizing forces of classical imperialism generated anti-colonial nationalisms, so today's globalization creates new frameworks for mobilization. Reflecting this, in recent decades a range of transnationally-organized social movements have emerged to contest corporate globalism, and in the process prefigure new cosmopolitanisms. In response, mainstream social movement studies have been extended. With the "shift from nation states to transnational actors," Smith argues in her introduction to the *Mobilization* special issue on the topic, that the "future of social movements [...] is increasingly global" (Smith 2001, 16–7). Movements, it is argued, develop new repertoires and organizational forms to exploit the emergent international opportunity structures, and in the process become, *themselves*, transnationalized (Tarrow 1998; McCarthy 1999; Lahusen 1999).

Often the assumption is that these "transnational advocacy networks" can relatively smoothly extend the politics of national social movements into transnational spheres (Keck and Sikkink 1999). The national social movement is reframed or translated into a transnational context. Such arguments can underestimate the difficulties of transnational mobilization that have intensified with the recent promotion of anti-terrorism and border security, and have resulted in radicalization of statist nationalism. Refugee solidarity sits at the center of this reassertion—refugees have been targeted as threatening national security, and in several contexts, including in Australia, strong-arm detention regimes have become a popular electioneering tool. Refugee solidarity confronts nationalist prejudice and exclusion, and directly addresses the challenge of how to mobilize national publics in the name of cross-national norms. In microcosm, it demonstrates the difficulties movements face when encountering globalism, namely those of demonstrating the immediacy and urgency of seemingly abstract or distant social forces, and of the necessity to act on humanitarian norms. Across a range of fields, this process of embedding and domesticating universality has been prioritized as movements seek ways of working between abstract principles and immediate commitments. Increasingly, political action rests in a dynamic interaction across levels of identification, within political communities caught in the "dyad of global—local" (Marchand et al. 1999, 899). The nexus with territory and place is central, where the political infrastructures of globalism confront the multifarious instances of local action. The result is a form of reflexive counter-globalism—which some characterize as "globalization from below" (Falk 1999). Here the dynamics of culture, nationality and territory flow through the social movements, patterning responses. Feminist, environmental, human rights and labor movements, for instance, all in their own ways dominated by Western perspectives, are forced to construct such transnational strategies. Feminist unity is balanced with gender difference, human rights with cultural rights, eco-globality with living environments, and worker solidarity with differing development priorities. In the process, political community is rebuilt around situated universals, designed to reconcile polarities between cultural positions.

In these more fluid contexts, the process of embedding claims becomes central to political traction. Embedding is achieved in a variety of ways—through ideology, through actions, and, a key focus for this book, through emotions. Affective embedding, one may say, is a precondition for sustained mobilization. The aim here is to evoke an emotional response to an issue, one that then elicits cognitive reflection and action. This involves the mobilization of moral emotions, arising from, or in reference to an experience or situation, an affective value appeal or normative judgment, and which then generates moral evaluations and social expectations, and thus actions. There must be a means of turning an emotive response (for instance outrage) into an intellectual response (understanding cause and solution) and into action (creating or enacting the solution) (Cadena-Roa 2002). The movement must become adept at deploying the "vocabulary" or "grammar" of emotion that they learn, draw on and contribute to.

Such capacity to mobilize public emotions, in the pursuit of humanitarian goals, is at the core of refugee solidarity, and we may say, of transnational solidarity generally. Given the relatively fluid contexts, we may speculate that the emotional work of transnational solidarity is greatly magnified. The emotional appeal may need to be deeper where the unit of affiliation is unstable, and far from immediate. This can mean stronger, perhaps more strident constructions of emotional belonging, along with clearer boundary work. Furthermore, given that globalizing pressures apply across-the-board, the imperative to ground movements emotionally applies as much to nationally-focused movements as it does to global movements (see Aminzade and McAdam 2001).

Yet the affective dimensions of embedding should not be over-emphasized. The specific emotional register of a movement may be important, but emotional responses only gather traction in relation to other dimensions of the movement. Emotional connotations must be consonant with ideological, organizational and action frameworks, and thereby reinforce the overall message of the movement. Collective identity and emotion are integrated within that process of movement participation which generates expressions of public emotion. Emotion is thus not simply a tool of mobilization—it emerges in dynamic interaction with other aspects of the movement, with emotions existing as "both a cause and an outcome of participation" (Bayard de Volo 2006, 471).

This understanding of the specific place of emotion, as integrated with aspirations, structures and action, contrasts with the model of "new emotional movements," where public emotion dominates the movement. As outlined by Walgrave and Verhulst, such movements are highly episodic, rely on elite and media support, are anti-political in the sense of rejecting goals, and lack organizational form (Walgrave and Verhulst 2006). As outlined here, refugee solidarity movements share some of these features, but it would be a misrepresentation to identify them as "emotional movements." Certainly, the movement plays a key role in generating and sustaining what may be seen as "moral emotions" (Cadena-Roa 2002). Indeed, the symbolic power of movement actions rests with these emotions. Emotional engagement mediates cognition and action to stimulate reflexive engagement amongst wider publics and forces a public process of moral deliberation. The Woomera breakout is one example of this process—an action that deliberately sought to provoke moral emotions and polarize public debate, in order to force a process of collective self-reflection on the question of refugee detention.

Refugee Solidarity

Refugee solidarity emerges at the nexus-point between nationalism and cosmopolitanism. From a national perspective, acts of refugee solidarity suggest, as a "Free the Refugees" poster put it in Australia, "not all Aussies are heartless bastards;" from a global perspective they suggest that humanity takes precedence over nationality, that for humanity there are "no borders." What follows is a discussion of these themes within the refugee solidarity movement in Australia. National and global forms of solidarity produce contrasting ideological agendas and action frameworks, and mobilize quite different public emotions. Jasper argues that solidarity itself should be seen as a form of emotion, but under its ambit there is clearly a wide array of emotional resonances and inflexions (Jasper 1998). As argued here, expressions of shame, mercy and pride are common in national refugee solidarity, while quite different registers of anger, outrage and empathy are prevalent in more global modes. The two themes are inseparable, bound one into the other, reaching across national borders but at the same time, and in the same instance, affirming national frameworks for identity and action.

National Refugee Solidarity

A strong theme, perhaps the dominant theme in refugee solidarity is the process of making a claim on the nation. Like multiculturalism, refugee solidarity expresses an impulse to humanitarian values, which feeds into and drives a contest for national identity. This is the hand of national hospitality which says, "'we' welcome 'you' because we are people who are inclusive and caring." By offering that hand we affirm our own (positive) self-image, and reproduce our national identity. Groups taking this approach argue for a "just" refugee program that reflects international humanitarian principles, arguing that the boundary between a deserving "legal" refugee and an undeserving "illegal" arrival has to be shifted to more accurately reflect the 1951 United Nations Convention Relating to the Status of Refugees. The Convention defines a refugee as:

"A person who is outside his/her country of nationality or habitual residence; has a well-founded fear of persecution because of his/her race, religion, nationality, membership in a particular social group or political opinion; and is unable or unwilling to avail himself/herself of the protection of that country, or to return there, for fear of persecution" (United Nations 1951, Article 1).

As such the Convention is ultimately an instrument of exclusion, and those who argue for it are claiming the right to deport. This particular welcome to refugee arrivals, then, is a conditional welcome.

Themes of national hospitality have a long history in settler Australia. In 1990 Nancy Viviani wrote about the 2,000 refugees who arrived in Australia in the late seventies from Indo-China, highlighting how they forced a reassessment and re-grounding of Australian cultural values. Referring to migrants who had earlier fled persecution and poverty in South and Eastern Europe to arrive in Australia in the fifties, Viviani argued, "we got more than pasta and polka from this; we got, most importantly a chance at self-examination, the mirror held up to a smug, inward-looking, culturally narrow people" (Viviani 1990, 113–4). The "self" here is the Australian people, and the values that change are national values. National shaming of this sort signals a process of reorienting and reproducing the nation, and one that is often invoked in the name of national interest.

A more recent example is the mass solidarity network that emerged in support of East Timorese refugees in the mid-nineties in Australia. Here, again, the treatment of East Timorese people fleeing military oppression in East Timor—in particular the 1991 Dili massacre—was seen as an affront to Australian national values. Solidarity with East Timorese refugees was embedded within Australian political culture through the language of national betrayal of a wartime ally, of a friend in need. Australia, it was argued, had played a key role in the denial of self-determination in East Timor, and was attempting to deport people who had fled the results of this policy. These arguments bolstered and embedded the abstract appeal to refugee rights and self-determination, defining these commitments as a core Australian responsibility, albeit only in relation to East Timor (Goodman 2000). The effect was powerful: the Sanctuary Network, a group of people offering their homes as sanctuary to Timorese in hiding from deportation orders, swelled to over 10,000 households (O'Connor 1998). Again, the national mirror had been held up, and many people did not like what they saw.

Mandatory detention of refugees—a policy officially in place in Australia since 1992—stimulated a similar process of shaming and self-examination. With the increase, from 2001, in unofficial refugee arrivals to Australia, primarily due to the war in Afghanistan, the Australian government increasingly sought to mobilize popular prejudice in a national crusade for border security. The crusade culminated in the 2002 Federal election campaign which saw the government send armed troops to commandeer and repel a Norwegian freighter, the Tampa, which had rescued refugees in Australian waters. The fear campaign played a key role in ensuring the incumbent government was returned, but it also inspired a counter-movement that grew over the ensuing years and eventually forced reform of the refugee policy regime.

In the first instance, as previously, appeals for refugee rights were couched in terms of national responsibility, reflecting conscious efforts at embedding humanitarian norms in the national context. A proud tradition of Australian inclusivity was asserted against the aberration of mandatory detention. The campaign group "Australians for Just Refugee Programs," for instance, stated:

"We aim for policies which show respect, decency and traditional Australian generosity to those in need, while advancing Australia's international standing and national interest. Working together with prominent Australians and community groups, A Just Australia aims to achieve just and compassionate treatment of refugees, consistent with the human rights standards which Australia has developed and endorsed" (A Just Australia 2002).

Likewise, the pro-refugee "Show Mercy" concert held in April 2002 at Sydney Town Hall explicitly claimed a positive tradition of inclusivity—as the promotional poster by the pop-artist Reg Mombassa stated, "Australians welcome boat people." The concert launched the "Show Mercy Citizens' Statement," which argued:

"A new policy should [...] reflect the best in Australian traditions of tolerance and understanding. [...] This Citizens' Statement points a way for Australia to regain a reputation within the international community as a fair-minded and democratic society which respects human rights" (Show Mercy 2002).

The Adelaide-based group, "Australians Against Racism," mounted a similar intervention during the 2002 Federal election campaign, with a TV advertisement called "Faces in the Crowd" that appealed "to all Australians for understanding and compassion with a statement invoking our history and community." The thirty-seconds long video showed people in a city street, speculating as to who had fled and from where, asking viewers whether they too would have fled (Australians Against Racism 2001). The group's secondary school art project, "Australia Is Refugees," echoed this sentiment in calling for pupils to interview and write-up the story of a former refugee living in Australia, stating: "many famous and successful Australians were refugees [...] they became part of everything that is Australia now." In 2003 the group funded the creation of two billboards, the text of one referred to "Australia, a fair go for all. [...] Unless you are a refugee;" the second asserted "Freedom, safety, life, hope, equality. Refugees deserve nothing less."

Public figures have spoken out in a similar vein. Former Chief Justice, Marcus Einfield referred to a "brutality [in the refugee detention camps] of a kind Australians only ever read as happening overseas" (Banham 2002). The political commentator, Robert Manne, accused the Australian government of having "recklessly endangered, as if it were a matter of no account, one of Australia's most precious assets—its good name" (Manne 2002). The historian, David Day, asserted that it was "too late to prevent this whole sorry episode from overshadowing our otherwise proud postwar story of embracing ethnic diversity and being relatively generous to outsiders;" Day argued that the Australian government should preserve Woomera as a national memorial, much like holocaust memorials in Germany, to remind the Australian people what they were capable of (Day 2002).

For groups taking this approach, a key focus for action was the provision of direct support for detained refugees. Informal voluntary visitor programs were created for all of the detention camps within relatively easy reach of urban centers. These programs centered on the provision of day-to-day needs of refugees, including consumer items, such as toys and phone-cards, and some educational and medical services. The focus here was on the welfare of existing detainees, and on trying to make existence in the camps more bearable. Groups lobbied for a more limited form of detention and for a formalized role for support agencies in processing asylum seekers, for instance in the form of "An Alternative Reception System," promoted by the "Justice for Asylum Seekers Network" (Justice for Asylum Seekers Network 2002). A similar initiative emerged with "Spare Rooms for Refugees," where people were put in direct contact with detainees and encouraged to approach the authorities, offering their home as an alternative to detention. This initiative and others like it were highly successful, with networks of welfare organizations established to coordinate transfers from detention when refugees were released under "Temporary Protection," and to organize translators and lawyers as well as accommodation. The government failed to embrace the "community release" program promoted by these groups, but some detainees were released on an ad hoc basis.

Direct humanitarian relief of this kind was combined with various actions embedded in Australian political traditions. Actions deliberately drew on existing national repertoires of Australian social movements, placing refugee solidarity in the mainstream of Australian political culture. One example is the "Welcome Book" organized by "Rural Australians for Refugees," which explicitly drew on the "Sorry Book" initiative of the indigenous solidarity movement in the nineties. Their "Welcome Towns" initiative took this a stage further, with rural settlements declaring themselves willing to accommodate a specified number of refugees, as a community-led alternative to the detention regime. This, again, had an historical precedent in the "Good Neighbour Councils" established by localities to welcome refugees to Australia from post-1945 Europe. A further example was the award given in 2003 by "A Just Australia" to the "Just Australian of the Year," on Anzac Day, the yearly Australian homage to the War Dead.

From this perspective, organizations were sometimes at pains to set limits on their solidarity, and to assert this as a measure of their reasonableness. Following protests in detention camps in 2002 and 2003, Amnesty International Australia issued a press release titled "Recent events in Immigration Detention Centres in Australia," that began "It is important to note that Amnesty International does not support or condone any violent or illegal activities in Australia's detention centres" (Amnesty International Australia 2003). In early 2003, a range of groups distanced themselves from what were seen as "detrimental" protests planned for Easter 2003 at the Baxter detention center in South Australia. The groups—Justice for Refugees, Amnesty International, Australians for a Just Refugee Program, and some sections of Rural Australians for Refugees—argued against "counter-productive" protest, such as had occurred at Woomera the previous year, stating it was "likely to be detrimental to those unfortunate people who are still in Baxter detention centre" (Williams 2003).

More generally, these aspects of national refugee solidarity reflect the primary objective of re-embedding national norms in humanitarianism. This objective shapes the range—or repertoire—of interventions that are employed. National refugee solidarity requires national interventions that engage with national traditions and amnesias. Such amnesias, or "historical errors," as Ernest Renan put it, are central to the national project, and thus to national refugee solidarity, of which it is a part (Renan 1996, 17). Underlying this national forgetting is a faith in the capacity of the "nation" and its state to express and implement humanitarian norms. Bound into it is an assertion of national pride against fear, of national mercy against shame.

Global Refugee Solidarity

Such faith in the "nation" is flatly rejected by advocates of global refugee solidarity. Here there is no appeal to national inclusivity—there is rejection of it. Instead of insisting that there can be a "just" refugee program that opens doors only to particular categories of people, the demand is to open the borders. While national refugee solidarity appeals to the nation, global refugee solidarity appeals to shared humankind and to shared freedom. The aspiration and assertion of this freedom, as a direct and inherent right—not as a conditional offer—shapes the emotional register, the ideological rhetoric, and the forms of action. The challenge is uncompromising and grounded in uncivil outrage, an unsubjugated will posed both inside and outside the camps (Hage 1998). This direct action deliberately and uncompromisingly offends national "civil society," mobilizing emotions that express extreme outrage, and engage in actions that break the codes of acceptable political behavior.

Under Australia's detention regime refugees are non-citizens: the refugee detention camps (which in 2008 remained in place) are physically inside Australia, with detainees excluded from Australian "civil society" (Abood 2002). The camps have a similar status to that of the 3,000 islands to the North of Australia, which from 2001 became an officially "excised offshore place." Only on the continental mainland and in Tasmania, dubbed Australia's "migration zone," have intending migrants been able to make an application for entry. As clarified by the Department of Immigration and Multicultural Affairs, "The migration zone is not the same as 'Australia'" (DIMA 2002a). This official "excision" also applied to "unauthorized" entrants who had nonetheless been found to be "genuine" refugees and had been released from detention: leaving the camp they became holders of three-year Temporary Protection Visas (TPVs), with no right to family reunion or to state benefits. Of the 13,000 boat arrivals from the period 1989–2001, 8,000 were granted TPVs, 3,500 were deported and 700 remained in detention (DIMA 2001). The regime—from excision, to camp, to TPV—was designed to deter "unauthorized" entry, as the Department of Immigration put it, to "remove the additional benefits that had been encouraging misuse of the protection process by unauthorized arrivals" (DIMA 2002b). Two categories of refugee were thus created, and which one applied in practice depended not on the conditions existing in a person's country of origin, but rather on the mode of entry into Australia.

The deterrence regime established in Australia from the mid-nineties was designed to punish "unauthorized" refugees, and thereby deter others. Importantly, almost anything could be justified as effective deterrence, including conditions of deprivation, humiliation and isolation in the camps themselves. The regime, one could argue, cannot be understood as in any sense "civil," and this had direct implications for solidarity. If deterrence were the objective, then the regime would have to be unreasonable, and reasoned challenges would necessarily "fall on deaf ears." Appeals to respect human rights were rejected by the government as being naive, and more often condemned as manipulative (Leach 2003). In this context, global "No Borders" campaigners argued that the only option was deliberately uncivil protest, with the protest directly aimed at breaking the border that divides "legal" from "illegal." These Australian "insiders," campaigning for "No Borders" sought to break the border between them and the refugee "outsiders," whether symbolically by throwing flowers into camps or flying a colorful kite over sites of detention, or literally by tearing down fences (Perera 2002).

In this sense, "No Borders" politics is expressive, not instrumental. There is no self-censoring or taming of the challenge—it is deliberately designed to express outrage. The goal is to be deliberately "un-Australian," and thereby to wake people up to the illegitimacy of the camps. Such solidarity is seen as action in empathy "with" rather than "for" refugees, and thus demonstrates "a commitment with those affected rather than to self-congratulatory displays of liberal tolerance" (Hoh 2002, 2). To genuinely act with refugees, protesters must break the political rules and be deliberately "uncivil:" the Woomera 2002 *Call to Action* stated "The people inside resist with the only thing they have left: their bodies. It is time to say enough! We propose to join their struggle with our bodies" (No One is Illegal 2002a).

Built into this position is the celebration of refugee identity as a disobedient identity—one that refuses to tolerate state oppression and insists on the right to move in the name of a common humanity. Here the refugee, and refugee solidarity, becomes the personification of unruly cosmopolitanism, of unsubjugated humanity. Fiedler sees this as a double refusal—a refusal to live under oppression and a refusal to accept limits on the human right to refuge (Fiedler 2002). Global refugee solidarity celebrates this refusal, with border-breaking, assisted breakouts and the creation of underground sanctuary networks for escapees. It also highlights, and legitimizes, various forms of self-harm by refugees, including attempts to set fire to detention camps, mass hunger strikes, attempted suicides and mutilation by lip-sewing, all defined as forms of uncivil protest that express the uncivil caging of refugees. Such acts, organized in the detention camps by refugees themselves, played a central role in bringing attention to their plight. They attracted condemnation from the government, which accused refugees of trying to manipulate Australian public opinion, demonstrating how unreasonable and thus unsuited they were for Australian society (Leach 2003). For "No Borders" campaigners, the government's response demonstrated the barbarity of the Australian state.

Open borders campaigns ground this mode of solidarity in cosmopolitan anti-nationalism. Advocates are radically anti-statist, arguing that we are all in some way "caged" by state power. In Australia, as in many countries, governments have been "more concerned with drawing people into the idea of 'nation' rather than with real concern with the idea of social rights" (Vasta 1993, 222). Hage draws a direct parallel between the boundaries of tolerance in an officially "multicultural nation," and the fences and cages at detention camps. He argues that people only have to press against the boundaries of acceptability in the Australian context, and very quickly, they will encounter state power. In this way, running "wild" can highlight how Australians are "caged" by their own state, and what they share with refugee detainees (Hage 1998). The later hardening of the "internal" boundary of tolerance through anti-terrorism legislation demonstrated again that civil freedoms in Australia were only ever conditional. Indeed, these measures, introduced during a (peacetime) "War on Terror," parallel restrictions imposed on migrants in the Second World War, when many were interned as threats to "public safety." The 1939 *Principles to Be Observed With Internment*, issued by the Department of Defence, stated "any persons who are reasonably suspected of being likely to act in a manner prejudicial to the public safety or defense of the Commonwealth [...] are regarded as suitable subjects for internment;" in 2002, with the "War on Terror," not dissimilar measures were introduced (Saunders 1994).

The "No Borders" position, then, asserts there is no essential distinction between "us" and "them," and denies "our" right to exclude. This position is defined against the historical amnesia of those who would claim the mantle of inclusivity, while excluding unauthorized arrivals. "No Borders" displays are designed to challenge the assumption that it is "we" who have the right to tolerate. Rather than extending mercy and affirming national pride, the "No Borders" position expresses anger at the violation of human dignity. The effort to destabilize national fictions extends to culture jamming. For example, the group "We are all Boat People," used guerilla projections to make their point: they projected an image of the first British ship to arrive in Australia, the Endeavour, onto public buildings in Sydney, and above it the simple statement "Boat People." The sentiment, "We are all Illegal—We are all Boat People," asserts a common humanity, that "we" have no right to impose conditions of access to "our" society. There were numerous other initiatives from this and other artists' collectives, expressing the sentiment, as one artist, Deborah Kelly, put it, "The only difference between 'us' and 'them' is circumstance" (Dean 2002).

In ideological terms, from this perspective, borders are seen as serving the powerful, and should everywhere be rejected. As "No One Is Illegal" put it in 2002 at one of their forums: "Do we need nations? Is a global community possible? How can we remove the barriers between us?" (No One is Illegal 2002b). The Melbourne-based group XBorders put it thus: "borders between workers are the key ingredients in the power of global capital [...] as capital moves ever more freely around the world, we are locked up, confined, enclosed" (XBorders 2002). A world without borders though, as corporate advocates recognize, is a world for the powerful. Ironically, the "No Borders" approach bolsters this position—as a global approach, in direct tension with efforts to limit the exercise of private power in local, national or regional contexts.

Some of these tensions were illustrated at May Day demonstrations held in Sydney in 2002. These began with a blockade of the offices of Australian Correctional Management (ACM), a company that held the contract for managing refugee detention camps. Here, protesters threw-up a cordon across the entrances to the company offices. The action thus suggested support for some borders, but not for others. As if to underline this point, the ACM blockade was immediately followed by an anti-World

Bank protest in a public square nearby. Here, campaigners performed a comedy routine on the theme "World Bank: This if Your Life," centering on the Bank's continued insistence on marketization and refusal to respect local peoples' priorities. Both events were attended by approximately 500 protesters, a significant number for a weekday demonstration in Sydney; the cordon was broken up by police horses, resulting in a number of injuries. The first action promoted "No Borders," but created a cordon; the second action promoted the right of peoples to assert their own borders against inter-state institutions. Both actions, ironically, demonstrated the need for barriers and the regulations they enable, to counter globalizing elites. Indeed, it is difficult to see how concepts of self-determination and self-government could have much meaning without such powers. The "No Borders" position, taken to this logical conclusion, starts to look more like a posture than a coherent position. Like its partner—national refugee solidarity—it is full of tensions and contradictions, not easily resolved on its own terms.

National and Global Solidarity?

The bifurcation in refugee solidarity outlined here, between a national and a global approach is not something to be avoided, or played down. The two approaches are in conflict but they are also complementary, offering alternative possibilities for dialogue, consciousness and action. Clearly, the two approaches generate contrasting policy positions. One asserts the need for a "just" refugee program, principally by revising the ways in which distinctions between "genuine" and "non-genuine" refugees are implemented, and thereby invoking and retaining the right to deport. The other demands no borders, and the free movement of people, arguing that borders only benefit the powerful and require and entail terror. The two positions also generate very different forms of solidarity. National refugee solidarity needs images of relatively passive victims of Australian intolerance—of people who are worthy of "our" generosity or tolerance. Global refugee solidarity needs images of refugees engaged in resistance, in forms of action that may offend Australian sensibilities, and that express suffering and the aspiration for freedom. The two approaches are also in conflict at the level of action. Where one seeks to embed its modes of action in Australian traditions of civil protest, the other deliberately steps outside civil protest, engaging in forms of uncivil action. The contrast is between in-strumental and expressive action—between action as a means to an end, and action as an expression of outrage, as an end in itself.

More broadly there are contrasting understandings of Australia's society and history. National refugee solidarity engages in national forgetting, as part of a process of re-imagining and re-making the "nation." Global ap-proaches assert the bankruptcy of a settler people who exclude others from the national framework. Where one constructs a new national amnesia grounded in cosmopolitan values, the other rejects the nation as negating those values. While national refugee solidarity is driven by the process of (re)claiming the "nation-state," global refugee solidarity is driven by anti-statist globalism "from below." The resulting emotional counterpoints are in tension: for advocates of national refugee solidarity, national shame is counter posed with national pride; for adherents of global refugee solidar-ity, anger and outrage is counter posed with empathy and the aspiration to universal dignity.

More controversially, the two approaches also have much in common. For both, refugee solidarity is the vehicle for the transformation of political community and identification. National approaches seek to embed cosmo-politan norms in a national context, while global approaches seek to de-mystify the nation, shocking people into humanitarian consciousness. Where the first recruits the refugee to the task of nation-(re)building, the second recruits the refugee to the task of transforming globality. Strategi-cally, the two approaches are not by necessity in conflict, as they share the same humanitarian objectives. Although they differ as to the vehicle re-quired to achieve these objectives, it is possible to view humanitarian na-tions and humanitarian globality as mutually reinforcing. There are also tactical complementarities with expressive politics creating the agenda, and instrumental politics carrying it forward. There is some evidence of this in Australia, with the shock value of expressive "No Borders" actions in 2002–2003, stimulating a wave of more instrumental national refugee soli-darity actions, which gradually forced an attenuation of the regime, through to 2007 when the conservative federal government was finally defeated at the polls. The movement, though, cannot be said to have won the day: the policy of mandatory detention of refugees, in violation of the UN Convention, remains in place, and while some of the harsher aspects have been removed, the regime for unofficial arrivals remains, in large part, in place.

Taken as a whole, the Australian refugee solidarity movement in the early 2000s was situated across the boundaries between national and cosmopolitan spaces, and expressed the imaginations of both national and cosmopolitan realms. It created a dialogue between these realms, posing alternative foundations for action. Within the refugee solidarity movement, as in other movements, critics of abstract cosmopolitanism entered into dialogue with critics of national amnesia, each informing the other. As noted at the outset, the possibilities this opened up have parallels with other social movements. Many movements are meeting the challenges of transnationality—the refugee solidarity movement throws these challenges into stark relief, posing dilemmas but simultaneously offering grounds for transcending them.

Conclusions

Transnational social movements constitute a range of dialogues across national differences, with respect to defining and pursuing common aspirations. Such dialogues, essential to the process of contesting globalism, are generating new forms of political community. These are grounded in national differences, and often deploy those differences to challenge globalizing projects. At the same time, such movements deliberately transcend national contexts, embedding them in broader cosmopolitan frameworks. In the emerging political frameworks, national political cultures and nationalist identification remain a key foundation for mobilization, a political resource that is being harnessed, not sidestepped. The emergent transnationalized modes of politics are thus fought both within and across national contexts. Clearly there is no leap into a world of pluralist difference; but at the same time there is no possibility of vacating politics beyond the national. These twin pressures are producing a form of politics not enclosed in the zero-sum logic of national and global. This form of "movement politics" resists institutional containers; it is a politics of ideological "flows" that cannot be tied-down into a hierarchy of levels (Walker 1994). Rather than setting levels against one another, this form of politics balances levels of identification. There is no absolute spatial fix—levels are relativized.

Refugee solidarity offers a powerful illustration of the issues faced by such movements. The division of political culture into "insiders" and "outsiders" has a hold over the logic of mobilization, and is reflected in the bifurcation of solidarity. The approaches are deeply contradictory, and exemplify the difficult process of building and extending transnational possibilities for transformation. At the same time though, there is a fluidity and a complementarity that allows positions to be held, and pursued in tandem. When taken together, the national and global strands of refugee solidarity prefigure a reconstituted political community embedded in national frameworks, but paradoxically reaching out beyond them, into transnational communities of conscience. Dialogue across positions drives new agendas and "visions of global change" (Smith 2002, 521), forcing new ideological and political programs into view. New realms of social life are contested and politicized, and new social agents come into view (Doucet 2001).

In pursuing solidarity with refugees, one may say that these movements are quintessentially emotive movements. Solidarity, when read as an emotional affect, signals a positive value of connectivity, rather than an emotional response or reaction (Jasper 1998). Solidarity suggests and requires emotive engagement, whilst at the same time invoking questions of purpose and direction. What is the basis for solidarity? How is it embedded, what is its driving force? Questioning the content of solidarity forces attention to its inner dynamics, to how it generates moral emotions, and positions them in the process of contestation. Whilst the register of emotions influences movement agendas, such emotions are themselves integrated within the ideological, organizational and action frameworks of the movement. In this respect, the emotional landscape of refugee solidarity itself exemplifies the practical dilemmas of constituting solidarity under globalism. Standing between shame and outrage, mercy and empathy, pride and dignity, refugee solidarity movements are themselves subject to the emotional challenges of countering globalism.

References

A Just Australia (2002). *What Is a Just Australia?* [pamphlet]. Sydney.

Abood, P. (2002). *Safe Spaces for Dissent.* Unpublished paper delivered to a forum at Civil Disobedience Today, 8 November 2002. Sydney: Research Initiative on International Activism.

Aminzade, Ron, and Doug McAdam (2001). Emotions and Contentious Politics. In Ronald Aminzade et al. (eds.). *Silence and Voice in the Study of Contentious Politics,* 14–50. Cambridge: Cambridge University Press.

Amnesty International Australia (2003). *Recent Events in Immigration Detention Centres in Australia.* [press release, 8 January 2003]. Sydney.

Australians Against Racism (2001). *Faces in the Crowd.* [television advertisement]. Adelaide.

Banham, C. (2002). Woomera Conditions Likened to Nazi Days. *Sydney Morning Herald,* 20 September 2002.

Bayard de Volo, L. (2006). The Dynamics of Emotion and Activism: Grief, Gender, and Collective Identity in Revolutionary Nicaragua. *Mobilization,* 11 (4), 461–74.

Cadena-Roa, J. (2002). Strategic Framing, Emotions and Superbarrio – Mexico City's Masked Crusader. *Mobilization,* 7 (2), 201–16.

Calhoun, Craig (2001). Putting Emotions in Their Place. In Jeff Goodwin, James M. Jasper, and Francesca Polletta (eds.). *Passionate Politics: Emotions and Social Movements,* 45–57. Chicago: University of Chicago Press.

Day, D. (2002) Howard's Razor-Wire Legacy. *The Age,* 20 July 2002.

Dean, B. (2002). The Artist and the Refugee: Tooling up for Action. *Real Time Arts,* 49, 5–8.

DIMA (2001). *Factsheet: Boat Arrival Details.* Canberra: DIMA.

— (2002a). *Factsheet, Australia's Excised Offshore Places.* Canberra: DIMA.

— (2002b). *Factsheet, Temporary Protection Visas.* Canberra: DIMA.

Doucet, M. (2001). The Possibility of Deterritorializing Democracy: Agonistic Democratic Politics and the APEC NGO Forums. *Alternatives: Global, Local, Political,* 26 (3), 283–314.

Falk, R. (1999). *Predatory Globalization: A Critique.* Cambridge: Polity.

Fiedler, S. (2002). *Reflections on Civil Disobedience.* Unpublished paper. Sydney: University of Technology Sydney.

Goodman, James (2000). Marginalisation and Empowerment: East Timorese Diaspora Politics in Australia. *Communal/Plural: Journal of Transnational and Cross-cultural Studies,* 8 (1), 25–47.

Hage, Ghassan (1998). *White Nation: Fantasies of White Supremacy in a Multicultural Society.* Sydney: Pluto Press.

Hoh, B. (2002). We Are all Barbarians: Racism, Civility and the "War on Terror". *Borderlands,* 1 (1), 5–12.

Jasper, James M. (1998). The Emotions of Protests: Affective and Reactive Emotions in and Around Social Movements. *Sociological Forum*, 13 (3), 397–424.

Justice for Asylum Seekers Network (2002). *Asylum Seekers: There Is a Better Way. An Alternative Reception System*. Melbourne: Justice for Asylum Seekers Network.

Keck, M., and K. Sikkink (1999). Transnational Advocacy Networks in the Movement Society. In David S. Meyer and Sidney Tarrow (eds.). *The Social Movement Society*, 217–39. London: Rowan and Littlefield.

Lahusen, Christian (1999). International Campaigns in Context: Collective Action Between the Local and the Global. In Donatella Della Porta, Hanspeter Kriesi, and Dieter Rucht (eds.). *Social Movements in a Globalizing World*, 59–77. London: Macmillan.

Leach, M. (2003). "Disturbing Practices": Dehumanizing Asylum Seekers in the Refugee "Crisis" in Australia, 2001–2002. *Refuge*, 21 (3), 121–55.

Manne, R. (2002). Howard Squanders our Good Name. *The Age*, 4 February 2002.

Marchand, Marianne, Morten Boas, and Timothy M. Shaw (1999). The Political Economy of New Regionalisms. *Third World Quarterly*, 20 (5), 897–910.

McCarthy, J. (1999). The Globalization of Social Movement Theory. In Jackie Smith, Charles Chatfield, and Ron Pagnucco (eds.). *Transnational Social Movements and Global Politics*, 243–59. New York: Syracuse University Press.

No One is Illegal (2002a). *Woomera Call to Action*. [statement]. Melbourne.

— (2002b). *A Dialogue on Borders and the Movements Against Them*. Unpublished paper, Melbourne: University of Melbourne.

O'Connor, K. (1998). The Sanctuary Network. In J. Aubrey (ed.). *Free East Timor: Australia's Culpability in East Timor's Genocide*, 48–62. Sydney: Vintage.

Perera, S. (2002). What Is a Camp? *Borderlands*, 1 (1), 14–21.

Peteet, Julie (2000). Refugees, Resistance and Identity. In John Guidry, Michael D. Kennedy, and Mayer N. Zald (eds.). *Globalizations and Social Movements*, 301–17. Ann Arbor: University of Michigan Press.

Piper, N. (2003). Global Norms, Advocacy Networks and Female Migrant Labor in Asia. In T. Scrase, T. Joseph, M. Holden, and S. Baum (eds.). *Globalization, Culture and Inequality in Asia*, 48–67. Melbourne: Trans Pacific Press.

Renan, Ernest (1996). What Is a Nation? In Geoff Eley and Ronald Grigor Suny (eds.). *Becoming National: A Reader*, 42–56. New York and Oxford: Oxford University Press. [first published in 1882]

Saunders, K. (1994). The Dark Shadow of White Australia: Racial Anxieties in Australia in World War II. *Ethnic and Racial Studies*, 17 (2), 325–41.

Show Mercy (2002). *Citizens Statement*. [pamphlet]. Sydney.

SKA-TV (2002). *Woomera 2002*. [video recording]. Melbourne.

Smith, Jackie (2001). The Battle of Seattle and the Future of Social Movements. *Mobilization*, 6 (1), 1–21.

— (2002). Bridging Global Divides? Strategic Framing and Solidarity in Transnational Social Movement Organizations. *International Sociology*, 17 (4), 505–28.

Tarrow, Sidney (1998). Transnational Contention. In Marco G. Giugni, Doug McAdam, and Charles Tilly (eds.). *From Contention to Democracy*, 31–57. London: Rowan and Littlefield.

Tippett, G. (2001). Navy Office Condemns "Despicable Treatment of Boat People". *Sydney Morning Herald*, 7 November 2001.

United Nations (1951). *Convention Relating to the Status of Refugees*. New York: UN.

Vasta, E. (1993). Multiculturalism and Ethnic Identity: The Relationship Between Racism and Resistance. *Australia and New Zealand Journal of Sociology*, 29 (2), 209–25.

Viviani, N. (1990). Australia's Future in Asia: People, Politics and Culture. *Australian Cultural History*, 9, 93–103.

Walgrave, S., and J. Verhulst (2006). Towards "New Emotional Movements"? A Comparative Exploration Into a Specific Movement Type. *Social Movement Studies*, 5 (3), 275–304.

Walker, R. (1994). Social Movements/World Politics. *Millennium*, 23 (3), 669–700.

Williams, T. (2003). Baxter Protest Rethink Urged. *Australian*, 2 April 2003.

XBorders (2002). *Globalisation? Our Struggles Are as Global as Capital*. [statement]. Melbourne.

Yuval-Davis, N., K. Kannabiran, and U. Vieten (eds.). (2006). *The Situated Politics of Belonging*, London: Sage.

Just Being There: Buddies and the Emotionality of Volunteerism

Jochen Kleres

This chapter explores the nature of volunteerism in novel ways by adopting an emotion-focused sociological perspective. As I will show, this proves particularly useful for overcoming the confines of existing theorizing. These confines become especially visible against the backdrop of a related theoretical field—social movement research. The latter can also inspire a sociologically richer take on volunteering, while the theoretical crossover, at the same time, can help us develop a clearer distinction between volunteerism and activism.

Social movement research has undergone diverse theoretical developments that have produced a broad array of analytical concepts, including cultural dimensions such as identity, emotions, framing, rituals, discourses and so on (see e.g. Taylor and Whittier 1995), as well as such concepts as resources and political opportunities. Theories of volunteerism, in contrast, remain largely uninformed by these developments and analytical tools. This may in part be due to the assumption that there is some kind of difference between the two phenomena. This difference, however, remains highly under-theorized as both fields of research have developed largely independent of each other despite their related objects of inquiry. Partly because of this lack of theoretical crossover dominant theories of volunteerism are marked by a rationalist bias as they focus mainly on its socio-technical aspects (see Smith 1994; Musick and Wilson 2008; Wilson 2000). As Wilson (2000) summarized, some theories look at how human capital (education, workload, income) acts as a mechanism with which to handle the burdens of voluntary work. Others add a focus on benefits and rewards received in exchange for investing into voluntary work. Finally, there is a focus on social capital (networks, family status, social status, etc.) conducive to the production of trust, the spreading of information, the improvement of one's chances of being asked to volunteer, and other facilitating conditions. While these dominant theories may or may not elucidate conditions of volunteering, little attention is paid to the richness in cultural meaning and the emotions involved in volunteering. Meaningfulness is conceptualized away by "explaining" volunteerism with altruistic attitudes and sympathy for a certain cause ("purposive incentive") (Smith 1994, 251), rather than taking altruism and sympathy with certain goals as something to be explained. Instead, rather general social conditions are taken as explanations and it thus appears as if people volunteer *because* e.g. they are married, have children, earn a certain amount of income, are employed (part-time) and are white men(!).

Contrasting this dominant rationalist take on volunteerism, there is, however, a limited body of research which shows that volunteerism is in fact embedded in culture (e.g. Wuthnow 1991; 1995; Jakob 1993; Eliasoph 1998; Stirling 2007; see also Wilson 2000). Wolfe (2001) takes up some of this research to develop, on a more abstract level, an analytical frame that focuses on motives and emotions as embedded in social contexts. One of these contexts is culture, which provides meaning systems to volunteerism. Another context involves organizations as transforming the raw material of pre-existing motives and meanings into concrete volunteer behavior. This organizational aspect of volunteering is, in fact, most often ignored in research (see also Stirling 2007, 10; for other exceptions see Grube and Piliavin 2000, 10; Perrin 2005; Nadai et al. 2005; Haski-Leventhal and Bargal 2008; Wuthnow 1995). Also a sociological perspective on emotions in volunteerism has been wanting. Indeed, this aspect has been addressed mainly by psychologists. Wolfe's theory (2001) also does not imply a *sociological* understanding of emotions and hence falls short of analyzing emotions' social and, specifically, organizational conditions.

The goal of this chapter is to analyze the dimensions of meanings, emotions and their organizational and cultural contexts in volunteerism by focusing on one form of volunteer work: so-called buddies, i.e. volunteers who care for a person with HIV or AIDS individually and personally. While Wolfe's (2001) theory remains somewhat abstract, a focus on cultural dimensions like identity, discourses and emotions, as inspired by social movement research, can help develop a more concrete framework. To this end, buddying is first analyzed as an emotional response to AIDS as a social issue and to its emotional regime. Next, by looking at the extent and the limits of the buddy relationship, two dimensions of the emotional salience in buddy-volunteerism will be brought into closer relief: what emotions signify in the emergence and the emergent morphology of the relationship, and how specific meanings and identities (as embedded into organizations and professional and other discourses) shape buddy care.

This chapter is based on eight semi-structured interviews with buddies, and two semi-structured interviews with professional buddy coordinators. They describe experiences from a large and a mid-size German city.[1] Interviews were recorded, paraphrased/selectively transcribed and analyzed using computer-aided coding techniques (see e.g. Kleres 2007). The average duration of each interview was nearly two hours. The fieldwork was conducted in 2005. In both cities, buddy coordinators recruited interview partners. Unfortunately, no clients could or wanted to participate. Thus, the chapter only reflects the experiences and discourses of buddies and professionals.

Buddy Work – Volunteering as Emotional Care

The concept of buddying is rooted in the hospice movement. It was first adapted for AIDS work by American AIDS organizations (Shanti, GMHC) and was subsequently imported by German AIDS organizations (Aue 1999). Buddies can be briefly defined as volunteers who are assigned to individuals with HIV or AIDS to support them on a personal level, both practically (groceries, visits to a doctor, leisure activities, etc.) and emotionally (companionship, being an alter ego, etc.). The process of interviewing revealed that emotional care was in fact paramount to buddying. This may be because practical care is often provided by specialized care institutions in Germany,[2] but presented in such a detached way that it is distinguishable and distinct from emotional care. From the buddying perspective then, this would signify as anticipating what feminist care theorists argue is central to care work; that *caring for* and *caring about* overlap considerably (Hopkins et

---

1 Arguably, buddying may take on quite a different significance in other countries, for instance because the "social face" of AIDS or because institutional contexts of AIDS work differ considerably. This could be expected to be the case e.g. in the US where the magnitude of HIV-infection has been higher, especially among ethnic minorities, and where there is no encompassing welfare state in the European sense. In other countries, the principle of self-help as embodied in voluntary AIDS-organizations and specifically buddying may have a much weaker standing or be largely absent in dominant approaches to AIDS-politics.

2 See footnote 1.

al. 2005), as caring for is often expressive of caring about (cf. Burrage and Demi 2003, 53–4). The personal nature of care work also inspires emotions such as loyalty, trust and intimacy (Hopkins et al. 2005, 130). However, specific contexts call for and often evoke different types of emotional care. These contexts will be analyzed in the following pages, after a description of the main ways in which interviewed buddies cared for their clients.

Interview partners most often constructed typical clients as lonely or isolated, without anyone with whom they could openly share their situation. Not being able to share complex feelings related to being HIV-positive created this sense of loneliness: stigmatization, shame about the situation, fear of social consequences of disclosing one's condition to others. Peers may have turned away, and their empathy may have been limited (e.g. because of stigma, shying away from problems, fear of the disease). Frustrations around this may lead a person with HIV or AIDS to withdraw. Family bonds may have been broken even before the infection started, or may be conflict-ridden because of the clients' lifestyle (gay, drugs, homeless, poverty), thus arguably causing feelings of anger but also guilt or shame. Friends of the client may also have succumbed to AIDS. Finally, colonization of the client's life by multiple caring-systems (Merkenich 1999), or poor health may also hinder participation in normal life. As shame theorists have argued (Katz 1999, 150–2; Scheff 2000, 95), loneliness and abandonment are in themselves a powerful source of shame. A person with HIV or AIDS might become deeply apathetic.

Hence, interviewed buddies constructed a number of recurring emotional issues of clients and their peers. Crucially, buddying works as a counterbalance to loneliness and abandonment, and it is in this context that emotional care takes shape and attains its significance in buddy-work, as the following section on forms of emotional buddy-care demonstrates:

1. *Sharing Emotions.* Loneliness and abandonment leave clients alone with their feelings. Buddies mirror clients' emotions and thus share them. Relying on empathy and compassion, buddies can understand, and indeed in some ways feel their clients' emotions (cf. Shott 1979). Such sharing may include, for instance, sharing in the relief and happiness about good news or developments; or hope, expressed in dreams, aspirations and plans for the future. It may also invoke sharing more burdensome feelings like shock, grief, sadness or fear related to the prospect of possibly declining health and impending death, or the fear

of negative social consequences, like social insecurity, ostracism, deportation (of immigrants), or anger about the infection and one's situation.

2. *Emotional Affirmation.* Sharing emotions involves caring about the client and showing her/him sympathetic and compassionate interest: interest in how the client is doing, interest in positive developments (the excitement about good prospects, the happiness about good news, etc.), or not shying away from negative experiences, moods and feelings. This involves expressions of solidarity, compassion, trust, loyalty, friendship and intimacy, as well as showing the client appreciation and validation by respecting and acknowledging the client's experience as legitimate rather than treating it as dismissible.

3. *Offering Trust, Intimacy.* These modalities of caring address clients' feelings of loneliness and abandonment. Buddying tackles the emotional aspects of isolation in more ways than through merely the establishment of a social relation with the buddy. Clients can share emotions that are otherwise held back from the outside world. Emotions like fear, shame and frustration are directly countered by caring about, that is through extending compassionate interest, solidarity, validation, trust, friendship and intimacy.

4. *Countering Fear, Inspiring Hope.* Fear is another recurring emotional issue in buddy work, be it in the form of social fears (e.g. stigmatization, ostracism) or health-related fears. Buddies may intervene in the escalation of spiraling fears by helping to order thoughts and pointing to more realistic or optimistic assessments of situations, by allowing the client to voice and vent fears, or by encouraging clients to view death as an integral part of life. Buddies' solidarity and the sharing of fears may enable clients to take respite from a sometimes overwhelming experience. Solidarity, that is sharing feelings and standing by the client, also helps to counter other fears like fear of loosing one's job, not being able to care for one's child, or in the case of immigrants, of being deported. As buddies act as counter-balances to a broad array of fears, they inspire feelings of hope, in itself an antidote to persisting fears.

6. *Inspiring Confidence, Jois de Vivre, Playfulness.* Related to hope, buddies try to instill strength and self-confidence in the client, and to provide relief by bringing in a sense of joy and pleasure. Apart from being a reassuring peer, this may also be a matter of distracting the client from problems and troubling emotions. Playfulness, jesting, humor and gestures, such as giving small treats, may also provide relief and distraction.

7. *Normality and Keeping Emotions at Bay.* The last aspect of emotional buddy-work discussed here is the creation of some sense of normality for the client. This may be understood as an aspect of countering institutionalization with its relative absence of everyday-life emotionality. This normality may be a matter of developing friendship, trust and closeness/intimacy. In particular, normal, routine interactions with their lack of emotional uncertainty have an emotionally calming quality (see Flam, in this volume).

Linking Volunteering and the Emotionality of Social Issues

How can this emotionality of buddy-volunteerism be conceptualized? Dominant theories of volunteerism sometimes tend to explain volunteerism as a matter of rather abstract values and attitudes, like humanitarianism, altruism, reciprocity, etc. with an implicit image of pure "doing good" in the background (see e.g. Musick and Wilson 2008; Wuthnow 1995). The issues addressed through volunteerism sometimes appear as though they matter only in the abstract, as seemingly undifferentiated, almost exchangeable occasions, where these attitudes and dispositions may be put into practice. In contrast to this perspective I will argue that volunteerism as a meaningful, emotional activity can only be fully understood within the context of the socially constructed social problems it addresses and the specific emotional regimes inscribed into them. In particular, buddies' emotionality is linked to the personal experience of the emotional matrix of AIDS, which buddies (re)construct via the prism of their interactions with clients.

In interviews buddies implicitly refer to conditions of fear, stigma, resulting isolation and complex concomitant feelings, as underlying the recurring emotional issues they address through their work. They refer to conditions of being HIV-positive that can be traced to larger socio-cultural contexts, that is to the discourses that constitute AIDS as a social reality and with this, specific emotional matrices. Crucially, AIDS has operated as a dreaded and stigmatized disease (Sontag 1990; see also Treichler 1988; Bleibtreu-Ehrenberg 1989). It is by being confronted with the reverberations of AIDS discourses in the lives of clients that buddying becomes related to these larger discursive contexts. This applies most of all to those

AIDS discourses that pre-date the introduction of combination therapies in 1996. A few selective points will have to suffice here in order to demonstrate the link between discourses on AIDS and recurring emotional issues. One crucial aspect pertains to fear, as AIDS has been constituted as a "dreaded disease" (e.g. Doka 1997). In many ways, this extends beyond the fear of imminent death. AIDS-related fears have been greatly magnified by the discursive equation of HIV with death (the terror of an inevitable, difficult, dehumanizing death) and the contrasting of AIDS with life and hope (Sontag 1990, 112, 126; Wießner 2003, 57; Jones 1992, 442). The attribution of AIDS to social others (marginalized "risk-groups" or distant global regions, like the "dark"(!) continent Africa) has also cast AIDS as an outside threat to the collective body (Weingart 2002, 31; Wießner 2003; Jones 1992, 442). Fears of these—deviant—groups have been attached to AIDS, and AIDS in turn—though not invariably—has increased the fears and stigmatization of these groups at least for certain periods (Weingart 2002, 24; Devine et al. 1999, 1213; Wießner 2003). The image of AIDS as a polluting invasion (Sontag 1990, 134) has also attributed fault, guilt and shame to the polluter, that is the HIV-infected persons themselves, and conversely assumes that polluting people are in turn wrong (Sontag 1990, 136). Guilt and shame are further induced, as AIDS is "linked to an imputation of guilt" (Sontag 1990, 112–3; see also e.g. Devine et al. 1999, 1218; Wießner 2003, 35, 47, 51; Jones 1992): infection is readily explained in common view through group identity and concomitant deviant behaviors, casting AIDS as the tangible sign of intrinsic sickness (Weingart 2002, 58).

As this brief and cursory outline shows, AIDS discourses constitute an emotional matrix inscribed into the social reality of AIDS: they define objects, subjectivities, characters and their relations in the AIDS-narrative and thus calibrate how one can or indeed does feel about it (see e.g. Neckel 1991 on the nexus between subjectivities and shame). To the extent that they are subscribed to, these discourses constitute AIDS as a social reality and thus impact upon how HIV-infection or AIDS can be experienced. They help explain many aspects of the emotional experience of being HIV-positive, as well as the social conditions that buddy clients have to cope with. In its specific forms of emotional care, buddying is a response to some of the facets of this emotional experience. Thus buddy-volunteerism is strongly embedded into the socio-cultural phenomenon of AIDS. It is only within these larger discursive contexts, and the social realities they constitute, that buddy-volunteerism takes shape. However, this link is not abstract. Rather, the personal consequences of AIDS-discourses are continually experienced and (re)constructed in the course of ongoing interactions between client and buddy.

Significantly, there are no definite (or only vague and abstract) prescriptions of what buddying should be. In this sense, whatever preconceptions volunteers may initially bring along, the cause volunteerism is addressing is "not discovered but accessible only within the possibilities to experiment, reflect, understand, revisit" including the possibility to feel (Debra Hopkins in litt. May 2008). Nonetheless, and however indirect or loose connections to larger discourses may be, buddy-volunteerism cannot be understood as being *only* a matter of abstract altruistic attitudes, or as explainable through socio-structural variables. Systems of subjective meaning attached to AIDS and their emotional consequences must be included as they are key contexts in which this kind of volunteerism unfolds.

The process of finding a response to the client's situation is illustrated by a buddy whose client is an immigrant. Her deportation was to be decided on only days after the interview. With lawyers and social workers failing to accompany the client to a decisive appointment with the immigration authorities, the buddy had to decide if she was going to go along:

"and I was strictly determined not to go there because last time I was so shocked and because I was scared about what would happen there I cannot change the decision to be taken there I can only stand by her but I can't do anything […] also talked about this in supervision that that's nothing I have to do and also I shouldn't do it because people are being paid so that they do it and then I switched so I announced nope I won't be there and then there were two options that she goes alone or I go with her and then I wasn't able and actually not willing to draw the limit but rather I'll go along then […] I just wouldn't want to leave her alone even if I can't do anything" (B6)

Excursus

The links to older AIDS discourses are in themselves interesting, as in wealthy countries dominant meanings of AIDS have shifted in the wake of combination therapies, towards the normalizing paradigm of AIDS as a chronic disease (Rosenbrock et al. 2000; Dannecker 2006a; 2006b; curiously a much older discourse, see Beaudin and Chambré 1996). While this paradigm may certainly ring true for many people with HIV or AIDS in rich countries, interviewed buddies and their clients' stories testify to the continuing power of older meaning systems and their emotional regimes on some HIV-positive people. This is also in line with scant empirical research on contemporary psycho-social conditions of living with HIV, that points to continuing issues of fear, uncertainty, stigma, shame, depression, etc. (Siegel and Lekas 2002; Tiamson 2002; Dodds et al. 2004; Siegel and Schrimshaw 2005). In contrast to the dominant AIDS narrative as a story of uni-directional progress, therapeutic advances may arguably rather have diversified and re-shuffled personal experience of HIV-infection and AIDS: while previously AIDS-related identities and modes of experience may have been organized much more dominantly along lines of antibody status (being HIV-positive vs. HIV-negative), relevant distinctions may now also include, for example, treatment efficacy, financial resources, and the ability or the willingness to take treatments (Rofes 1998, 108–12). Having been HIV-positive or having progressed to AIDS before the introduction of combination therapies may continue to entail different identities and experience than it does for people who first experienced/contracted the virus later (Dannecker 2006b, 258). Even under the older paradigm, there was diversity as counter-discourses existed (Jones 1992) allowing, in particular, for anger as an alternative and politically mobilizing reaction (e.g. Gould 2001). In sum, HIV and AIDS need not entail the problems that buddying addresses. However, and all of this notwithstanding, a case can be made that there are also sub-groups of HIV-positive people today who continue to experience HIV and AIDS in ways that were perhaps more characteristic of earlier phases of the epidemic. It is the needs of these people that buddying caters to.

Emotion Work in Buddying

Buddying and its emotionality is not simply a matter of responding to the needs of clients. As argued above, this response involves careful negotiations: in facing their clients' situation, buddies need to determine the concrete form and scope of their (emotional) care. The emotionality of buddying thus depends on the outcomes of this—socially contingent—process. This can be conceptualized in terms of Hochschild's (1979; 1990) theory of emotion management. This pertains, for one, to buddies' own, potentially disruptive emotions like fear and grief. However, more frequently, interviewed buddies talked about the need to set limits for their work—an equally emotional issue (see below). Hochschild's concept also provides the analytical tools for investigating the nexus between volunteering and social contexts like discourses and organizations. In particular, Hochschild (1979, 566–8) addressed the interconnectedness of framing rules, which apply definitions and meanings to situations, and feeling rules, both of which mutually imply each other. Organizations are key contexts, in her analysis, that provide both of these rules.

As it turned out, assuming a helper[3] identity, as mediated by the organizational context, is in this sense a crucial tool for buddies' emotion work. The following section analyzes typical forms of emotion management among buddies. It is followed by a section exploring some of the social conditions of emotion management.

Dealing With Fear and Grief

Regarding the management of disruptive emotions, buddies recurrently talked about managing fears of disease and dying, and resultant shying away, as potential obstacles to their work. Grief and sadness are other, related issues. Training and supervision are instrumental as a shielded space for approaching the issues of death and disease, admitting fears, grief and sadness, and processing them, as well as for adopting a frame of death as part of life. What is more, this is a crucial context for forging a specific identity as a buddy involving, for instance, an emotionally more distanced, i.e. professional attitude, or counter-feelings of pride in being a helper/volunteer competent in dealing with death.

Limits

Emotional care was not an unquestioned and taken-for-granted activity for buddies. Rather, they put much thought into the scope of their care, and the role and extent of emotions in it. What emerged was the need to hold back one's own emotions and impulses, and the boredom that may some-

---

3 The terms "help" and "care" are used interchangeably throughout this chapter.

times come from giving priority to the client's interests, but also negative emotions from one's own life (stress, anger, moods). Other emotions that are deemed problematic may emerge in the interactions with the client, such as getting angry with, or annoyed by the client, or feeling frustrated, impatient and disappointed with the clients' pace of or lack of progress. Feeling ashamed and embarrassed because of their clients'—demented or disruptive—public appearance may be another issue. As the following quote indicates, a key to managing these emotions is the assumption of an identity as a helper/volunteer.

"but when he prefers to watch Star Wars II then watching Star Wars II is what he likes, I don't mind adapting to that I can also enjoy that [...] yes basically I see myself as an assistance so that he can do things that he likes to do because I say I can do my things all the time whenever I want and that is actually quite easy/simple for me." (B3)

Unlike friendship, which can be an end in itself, interviewees saw buddying as serving an instrumental goal, "being there for somebody," a goal that they reminded themselves of during difficult situations. The helper-identity also inspires a number of strategies, such as formulating a psychological analysis of the deeper reasons for the client's difficult behavior, or for their own annoyance (e.g. resonances with their own family conflicts, etc.). Another strategy is to take delight and pride in the benefit that clients receive from their work—emotions that are intimately linked to a helper identity. Equally connected to this identity is the strategy of excusing the client because of his/her condition or disease. As all these strategies show, a crucial aspect of the emotional substratum of this helper identity is empathy. Helper-identity also involves greater distance than in private relations, which also helps mediate certain emotions. Finally, helper-identity and the goal-orientation implicit in it may induce buddies to simply endure these emotions.

Some of the emotions, that can be perceived as problematic in the buddy relationship, are themselves linked to a helper/volunteer-identity. Frustration, disappointment or anger regarding the clients' slow progress or lack of co-operation etc. are instances where self-efficacy (see Weick 1995, 20–1) in terms of helper-identity is threatened, and taking pride in it may be limited. One buddy described his work as an "un-conceited" activity requiring a certain amount of humbleness/humility. Another interviewee talked about the impossibility of missionary zeal, considering his client's physical limitations.

This also relates to the second, equally important aspect of emotion management, the management of helpers' impulses. Buddies extensively discussed their wish to help their clients more, their ability to do so, and the need for restraint. Typically, this was about giving money, about devoting more time, or about allowing the client to enter the buddy's private sphere (e.g. family gatherings, the buddy's apartment, birthday party or circle of friends, etc.). Other instances of impulses requiring restraint were related to taking over aspects of the client's life, such as pushing clients to take medications against their expressed decision, imposing advice about child rearing on parenting clients or, more mundanely, insisting on changing clients' habits e.g. pushing for cleaning, or even renovating the client's apartment.

This desire to help more is grounded in buddies' emotional reactions to their clients' situation, invoking such emotions and emotional dispositions as compassion, sympathy, empathy, pity, attachment, friendship and love. But it may also engender feelings of guilt, shame and moral obligation. One dimension of this involves emotional evaluation, such as comparing one's own good living conditions and survival with those of the client (see Stolinski et al. 2004; Odets 1995; see also Demertzis, in this volume):

"to say we don't see each other tomorrow we see each other next week and such, then was accepted [by the client] but I realized that I kept walking around with such a guilt feeling, […] the drawing of limits was difficult, so the guilt feeling said abandon your life sacrifice yourself totally the other needs it much more and so on, this can't work of course." (B5)

Their helper-identity may also foster feelings of responsibility for the client's well-being, as well as pride and enthusiasm about one's own role, which can equally induce helping impulses. The emotional nature of these issues is also expressed in buddies' talk in terms of the danger to "slip," "rush" or "run blindly" into something they might later regret.

Several discourses legitimize this setting of limits. One normative argument demands respecting the client's autonomy against the urges mentioned above, so as not to take over aspects of her/his life. However, most arguments are related to assumptions of the nature of buddy work. This is particularly true when it comes to supporting clients financially, but also to performing household chores. Both are construed as being the opposite of buddying, that is, as a responsibility of other caring institutions. Other arguments are also related to the helper-identity. Pity would not help anyone and hence would not serve instrumental goals. Similarly, over-engagement would be counter-productive, so one needs to hold oneself back in order to protect oneself from strain and exhaustion. For example, one buddy said that she needed to hold herself back, because if she didn't, she would need a buddy herself. Reversing an increased but exhausting level of support would also disappoint the client, and thus threaten the relationship. Respecting the client's autonomy, it was argued, also serves to protect the client from strain stemming from buddies' colonization of their private spheres.

In sum, adopting a helper-identity is a key element in buddies' emotion management, as it allows buddies to hold back their own desires and neutralize negative emotions. It functions this way both as a set of cognitive frames, as well as a source of positive (counter-) emotions like pride and empathetic joy, but also as a source of negative emotions like anger. Buddies' helper-identity is both a source of helper impulses, and, by defining the nature and goals of buddy work, a basis for managing them. The following section examines social conditions necessary for this kind of emotion management.

Mediating Contexts of Volunteer Emotionality: Sources of Emotion Management

As indicated above, buddies' emotion management does not evolve in a social vacuum, but is rather embedded in social contexts. This relates most notably to AIDS-organizations, because buddying is typically carried out through such organizations, which provide structures explicitly aimed at its governance. However, buddies and their organizations are in turn embedded in larger contexts and meaning systems that are equally important for giving shape to buddying, like discourses on private relations, professionalism and volunteerism. These aspects will be analyzed next.

Training and Supervision

Constitutive for the adoption and ongoing construction of helper-identities and related emotion management are organizational contexts such as regular and compulsory supervision groups, along with initial trainings.

Significantly, buddies get few explicit guidelines. Instead, a key feature is self-experience: regarding one's own relation to death, illness, sexuality, addictions, interpersonal matters, or concrete situations in buddy work. This takes place, for instance, through role-playing, or mirroring by other participants. These practices of self-experience create awareness of one's emotions, and thus allow for the possibility that they be managed. Without this awareness buddies might, as they pointed out in interviews, just follow their impulses and—in their words—"run blindly," "slip" or "rush head on into something." One buddy, for instance, was annoyed by one of her clients' pessimism, which, she came to realize, somewhat painfully reminded her of herself at an earlier stage in her life. Significantly, however:

"I first didn't realize it at all that I find her unsympathetic only when somebody asked me in the group, tell me when you talk about her, you don't like her do you, then I thought about it, yes it's true, I find her totally unsympathetic, quite peculiar, which I couldn't have pinned down by myself." (B3)

Another buddy said:

"a framework like supervision etc. is simply given that that that people think about also what they are doing [...] and to have also people who say look after yourself now as well and don't run blindly into something" (B6)

Secondly, and building on this, supervision groups are more than simply a forum of reflection that allows for awareness and conscious decisions about one's emotions. Interviewees repeatedly talked in explicit terms about how they drew on discourses from supervisions in their emotion management:

"But then regarding the setting of limits, hello! that still isn't your task, keep out of there, so that was also difficult for me, so I think the big issue in supervision is setting limits" (B6)

Referring to a client's effort to get money from her, another buddy said:

"and if you realize that he's trying something that way you are alert already [through prior training] and then you can act with clear conscience and say why don't you go to the AIDS-Help organization because they are there for this and we volunteers simply aren't because we, let's say, contribute our time and our interest" (A1)

As both quotes indicate, it is in training and supervision groups where ideas about the nature and appropriate scope of buddying are forged and negotiated, and thus where a helper identity is shaped and modeled. Given the centrality of this identity to the management of buddies' emotions, the organizational context in which it emerges is crucial for how buddies feel about their clients, and how their volunteerism takes shape.

Buddies as Amorphous Actors

Brown (1997) theorized buddies as amorphous actors situated in between the semi-public sphere of (typically state-subsidized/contracted) AIDS-organizations, and the private sphere of clients. Interestingly, buddies pondered this dual character explicitly in interviews. They talked about buddying as being personal but not private, or as being semi-private. Particularly with respect to emotions, they likened buddying to family (parent-child dyads) or friendship. Additionally, they talked about how buddying is different, often regarding the limits of buddying. Here they drew on their location as a buddy, and as an organizational representative, and how this duality signified the artificial creation of the buddy relationship through an organization (as opposed to emerging out of life-world interactions), the instrumental character of buddying, the goal of helping someone in need, and concomitant asymmetries (helper vs. needy). In comparison to professionals, buddies referred to employees' greater skills, but mostly to professionals' different, less authentic interactions with clients (more methodical, therapeutic, pedagogical, guiding, more factual than emotional). They assume that professionals just "do a job" (routine, duties), partly motivated by the need to make a living.

Both models of relations, that is private and professional, carry specific normative implications for how, and on what levels, to interact. In particular, they come with distinct sets of feeling rules. Buddying constitutes itself as volunteerism in the concrete mix of these models. On the one hand, emotional care draws on notions of private relations, emotionality and authenticity. On the other hand, strategies of distancing oneself, setting limits and the careful and conscious management of relationships and emotions are clearly derived from professional discourses, as expressed by the very term "supervision" group, reminding of the professional context of psychotherapy and social work. This in a way introduces professional meaning systems and normative standards into volunteer work, even though there is very little supervision in the sense of teaching done.

While organizations and their organizational fields pre-define legitimate forms of these mixes (as for buddying see Aue 1999, 25), they are also constantly renegotiated by buddies in their interactions with clients and within intra-organizational forums. However, it is the mix of feeling rule systems, and the state of flux, which gives buddies some degree of autonomy and allows them to deviate. While supervision functions to contain orientations that are too private, these occasionally do inspire deviations from implicit guidelines. One buddy, for instance, talked about how she swiftly ignored many of the precautions she learned in training after she first met her client. Mutual feelings of friendship were crucial for not setting limits:

"for me, my first time buddying, and I was packed with information as a guideline for how to act more or less and that was is one side and, but the other was my immediate sympathy for [client name] and his his at the same time for me […] those were two levels, like I said this new thing and what we have learned how to try and put it into practice uhm and the other was uhm […] we did these group plays […] and then I said, so if one gets along fine, well I would also say oh just come out with us [i.e. with her family] or to the summer party and and and and then another participant, what for heaven's sake, don't, and we shouldn't so close […] because probably I'm the type who doesn't set limits, who, if one say he's sympathetic to me then he will be integrated in my my life" (B4)

Larger Discourses

Constructing helper-identities is not simply an intra-organizational matter. Rather, it also relies on larger discourses beyond the control of a single organization or volunteer. It comprises not only the blending of discourses of professional conduct and private relationships, but also, and more fundamentally, it involves the concept of volunteerism, which is socially constructed on a societal level, a consideration that is often ignored by research (Stirling 2007; see also Wilson 2000, 217). While this construct deserves a separate, more detailed analysis, some of its features are readily discernible: crucially, it is about individualistic support on a personal level. Arguably, the discursive models of the Good Samaritan (Wuthnow 1991) or humanitarianism (Wuthnow 1995; see also Sznaider 1998) are paradigmatic here. Individuals share their personal resources with someone in need (along their way, as it were, like in the biblical story) in order to relieve pain and suffering. At the core is individual, compassionate help based on fellow-humanness, but not on political discontent. Its central feeling rule then is altruistic, individual compassion (cf. Musick and Wilson 2008, 422). This is indeed similar to how some buddies and their coordinators have described their work (significantly despite dis-identifying with Christianity):

"like helping neighbors, practical neighborly help in a Christian sense, like ecclesiastical organizations would call it, to say I have possibilities, can give money or time, or whatever, and to provide that for people who need that" (B1)

"that is something that I donate to him so to speak a bit of my time, that is actually, and that is something totally different as if I as a social worker, professionally so to speak [...] then I see my role differently it is somehow more of a friendship service also." (B2)

"I am not a Christian but I hear myself talking, for the second time now, about the Christian, that is also something simply something very human I think that is to help others and such in times of general brutalization [laughs] that is how I feel it, then I find it also something really worth to live out, to say I decide to help someone because I find that that is something something good and I don't mean all of that religiously of course, but I do mean it in the sense of a certain morality that one stands for, that, it's simply better to help someone than not to help someone, so that is a very simply calculation." (B5)

In line with the Good Samaritan/humanitarianism paradigm, helping is understood here to be a matter of generosity, and of compassion and empathy (cf. Wuthnow 1991; 1995). It is about private-individual help first and foremost, driven by individual-level, personal emotions of compassion and empathy based on fellow-humanness (cf. Sznaider 1998), the most abstract and general basis for compassion.[4] Although individualized, volunteerism is nevertheless also relatively institutionalized (cf. Musick and Wilson 2008, 420), particularly as it is increasingly utilized by public policies.[5]

In all these ways, volunteerism can be contrasted with political activism and protest, which arguably may be defined as more than individualistic, as they assume a broader, political perspective transcending the immediate individual situation, and ultimately strive for political, rather than merely

---

4 In contrast, compassion could have also more collective underpinnings where it is concerned with the fate of members of certain groups or categories of people rather than with other individuals.

5 Volunteerism is thus also embedded into discourses of the good national/citizen or gender (Eliasoph 1998; Nadai et al. 2005, 158–62; Musick and Wilson 2008).

individual solutions. Activism is also driven by emotions (e.g. Flam and King 2005), yet other, oppositional emotions (Flam 2005), specifically anger (see Flam 2004 for a nuanced view of this), may be more central to it. Political activism is also less institutionalized as it is predicated on emotional liberation (Flam 2005), that is to say, detachment from emotions cementing structures of domination.

The Good Samaritan does not act, for instance, out of discontent with sharp social group alienation and anger about the unjust consequences this produces—emotions related to some kind of political frame. "He" is simply moved by compassion, based on fellow-humanness, for an individual in distress. From this perspective, volunteering and activism can be viewed as related, contrasting constructions (see also Wilson 2000, 217; Eliasoph 1998). While both may or may not look formally similar, what distinguishes them from each other are the meanings and emotions attached to them.[6]

It is significant from this perspective that buddies did not talk about their commitment in terms of activism. None offered some kind of political understanding of the epidemic.

Selection

The individualizing, de-politicized bent of volunteering neatly dovetails with equally individualizing professional approaches to social problems: solving these is considered to require the professional's expert knowledge and skill, put into effect in a (individual) professional relation (James 1992, 491; see also Patton 1990, ch. 1). It is this commensurability that allows for the intertwining of professional and private sphere orientations. However, the resulting proto-professionalism also rests on a careful selection of volunteer candidates by the organization (Nadai et al. 2005, 129–32), which searches for compatible motivations and skills among prospective volunteers. A buddy-coordinator said:

"One advantage I have [is that] I do the training here in house, I know them all, that is mostly I know them through the interview and then through the training [...] thus I see the buddies also in extreme situations uhm through the training, most of them engage themselves in it quite intensively, I do see there a bit how they deal with fear and death and thus I see them being very emotional, that is I often have a very precise feeling about [them]." (B1)

---

6 This distinction is likely to be blurred in reality, where hybrid forms exist.

Conclusion

Buddying, as an example of volunteerism, turns out to call for much emotion labor, emotion management and para-professional skills. However, rather than being taught to volunteers, the concrete shape and scope of volunteerism is negotiated in personal encounters between clients and buddies. These negotiations in turn are conditioned by various discourses and concrete organizational structures that constitute and govern buddying as a volunteer activity. A "compassionate," "Good Samaritan" helper-identity is the result. This means that volunteer organizations form "political microcultures" (Perrin 2005) the effects of which, however, go beyond the rules of political talk that Eliasoph (1998) and Perrin (2005) have analyzed. Rather, the discursive elements of organizational microcultures extend to the very constitution of the volunteer identities themselves. In addition, by constituting identities, microcultures frame the emotionality of concrete instances of volunteerism. As I have shown, it is only through the lens of the organizational context that we can understand how volunteers feel about their clients and their volunteer work more generally.

The way volunteerism is constituted through organizations—as volunteerism rather than, for example, political activism—is of fundamental significance for volunteers' citizenship. The concrete shape of volunteerism involves very specific ways of relating to, thinking about and feeling about what one does and the people affected by it. As Ilcan and Bazok (2004, 133) state:

"Voluntary agencies not only assume the responsibility for service provision; they also train other citizens, namely the volunteers they employ, to become responsible for service provision to disadvantaged people in 'the community' and therefore to have little or no opportunity to engage in social justice-oriented advocacy activities."

The authors coin the term community government for this, i.e. government through community. This draws our attention to the larger political processes that volunteerism is embedded in and that condition its limited civic potential. Ilcan and Bazok (2004) make us aware of the fact that volunteerism may be part of an overarching approach to dealing with social problems—one that is relatively apolitical. This perspective dovetails with research that describes state-sponsored nonprofits as a means of conducting merely symbolic politics—letting them act as "problem non-solvers" (Seibel 1989). However, both perspectives fail to pay attention to the discourses, organizations and processes which turn individual citizens into compliant volunteers. It is my argument that distinguishing different modes of civic action from each other, and developing a keen eye for their specific organizational, discursive and emotional dimensions allows us to assess and understand their respective civic potential and also to analyze how and by which means they are outcomes of a politics of volunteerism. To the extent that volunteerism is predominant in AIDS-organizations, these organizations emerge from my research as relatively depoliticized and depoliticizing entities of civil society.

In sum, this chapter demonstrates the possibility and potential of an approach that moves beyond simplistic rationalist perspectives and acknowledges the sociological richness of volunteerism. An in-depth analysis of concrete instances of volunteerism quickly brings to the fore the limited scope of any theorizing that views volunteerism as explainable exclusively through correlating variables such as education, income, status or reified values. In fact, the complexity of volunteerism, as demonstrated here using buddies as examples, requires an approach that can capture a whole array of its constitutive dimensions. This approach should not only investigate cognitive aspects of volunteerism but also emotions and their embeddedness into social contexts. These should then be compared to those involved in (political) activism and also to any pertinent form of professionalism. Their respective civic potentials and, ultimately, the micro- and macro-politics behind them should be linked to discussions about their merits for civil society. In all these respects most existing theories of volunteerism are found lacking. They blind themselves to—and make themselves compliant with—the larger social and political processes that shape acquiescent volunteerism.

Acknowledgements

I would like to thank Helena Flam, Debra Hopkins, and Christine Stirling for their attentive and instructive readings of the manuscript. I am indebted to Michael Bochow for challenging me on several grounds. I hope I have managed to convince him better now. I would also like to thank Eron Witzel for correcting my English.

References

Aue, Michael (1999). Wie alles anfing. In Thomas Biniasz, Dirk Hetzel, Karl Lemmen, Grit Mattke, and Kai-Uwe Merkenich (eds.). *Zwischen Selbstbezug und solidarischem Engagement*, 17–28. Berlin: Deutsche AIDS-Hilfe.

Beaudin, Christy L., and Susan M. Chambré (1996). HIV/AIDS as a Chronic Disease: Emergence From the Plague Model. *American Behavioral Scientist*, 39 (6), 684–706.

Bleibtreu-Ehrenberg, Gisela (1989). *Angst und Vorurteil. AIDS-Ängste als Gegenstand der Vorurteilsforschung*. Reinbek bei Hamburg: Rowohlt Taschenbuch Verlag.

Brown, Michael P. (1997). *RePlacing Citizenship. AIDS Activism & Radical Democracy*. New York, London: The Guilford Press.

Burrage, Joe, and Alice Demi (2003). Buddy Programs for People Infected with HIV. *Journal of the Association of Nurses in AIDS Care*, 14 (1), 52–62.

Dannecker, Martin (2006a). Abschied von AIDS. *Zeitschrift für Sexualforschung*, 19 (1), 63–70.

— 2006b. Zur Transformation von AIDS in eine behandelbare Krankheit. In Volkmar Sigusch (ed.). *Sexuelle Störungen und ihre Behandlung*, 257–62. Stuttgart: Thieme.

Devine, Patricia, E. Ashby Plant, and Kristen Harrison (1999). The Problem of "Us" Versus "Them" and AIDS Stigma. *American Behavioral Scientist*, 42 (7), 1212–28.

Dodds, Catherine et al. (2004). *Outsider Status. Stigma and Discrimination Experienced by Gay Men and African People With HIV*. London: Sigma Research.

Doka, Kenneth J. (1997). *AIDS, Fear, and Society: Challenging the Dreaded Disease*. Washington, London: Taylor and Francis.

Eliasoph, Nina (1998). *Avoiding Politics: How Americans Produce Apathy in Everyday Life*. Cambridge, New York, Melbourne, Madrid: Cambridge University Press.

Flam, Helena (2004). Anger in Repressive Regimes. A Footnote to Domination and the Arts of Resistance by James Scott. *European Journal of Social Theory*, 7 (2), 171–88.

— 2005. Emotions' Map. A Research Agenda. In Helena Flam and Debra King (eds.). *Emotions and Social Movements*, 19–40. London, New York: Routledge.

Flam, Helena, and Debra King (eds.). (2005). *Emotions and Social Movements*. London, New York: Routledge.

Gould, Deborah (2001). Rock the Boat, Don't Rock the Boat, Baby: Ambivalence and the Emergence of Militant AIDS Activism. In Jeff Goodwin, James M. Jasper, and Francesca Polletta (eds.). *Passionate Politics. Emotions and Social Movements*, 135–57. Chicago, London: The University of Chicago Press.

Grube, Jean A., and Jane Allyn Piliavin (2000). Role Identity, Organizational Experiences, and Volunteer Performance. *Personality and Social Psychology Bulletin*, 26 (9), 1108–19.

Haski-Leventhal, Debbie, and David Bargal (2008). The Volunteer Stages and Transitions Model: Organizational Socialization of Volunteers. *Human Relations*, 61 (1), 67–102.

Hochschild, Arlie R. (1990). *Das gekaufte Herz. Zur Kommerzialisierung der Gefühle.* Frankfurt am Main: Campus Verlag.

— (1979). Emotion Work, Feeling Rules, and Social Structure. *American Journal of Sociology*, 85 (3), 551–75.

Hopkins, Debra, Linda McKie, Nick Watson, and Bill Hughes (2005). The Problem of Emotion in Care. Contested Meaning From the Disabled People's Movement and the Feminist Movement. In Helena Flam and Debra King (eds.). *Emotions and Social Movements*, 119–34. London, New York: Routledge.

Ilcan, Suzan, and Tanya Basok. 2004. Community Government: Voluntary Agencies, Social Justice, and the Responsibilization of Citizens. *Citizenship Studies*, 8 (2), 129–41.

Jakob, Gisela (1993). *Zwischen Dienst und Selbstbezug: Eine biographieanalytische Untersuchung ehrenamtlichen Engagements.* Opladen: Leske+Budrich.

James, Nicky (1992). Care = Organisation + Physical Labour + Emotional Labour. *Sociology of Health & Illness*, 14 (4), 488–509.

Jones, James W. (1992). Discourses on and of AIDS in West Germany, 1986–90. *Journal of the History of Sexuality*, 2 (3), 439–68.

Katz, Jack (1999). *How Emotions Work.* Chicago: Chicago University Press.

Kleres, Jochen (2007). Experteninterviews: Die Methode und ihre Durchführung im Projekt XENOPHOB. In Helena Flam and Leipziger Forschungsteam (eds.). *Migranten in Deutschland. Statistiken – Fakten – Diskurse*, 282–92. Konstanz: UVK Verlagsgesellschaft.

Merkenich, Kai-Uwe. (1999). Verlaufsmanagement der HIV-Infektion – systemische Perspektiven. In Thomas Biniasz, Dirk Hetzel, Karl Lemmen, Grit Mattke, and Kai-Uwe Merkenich (eds.). *Zwischen Selbstbezug und solidarischem Engagement. Ehrenamtliche Begleitung von Menschen mit AIDS*, 51–9. Berlin: Deutsche AIDS-Hilfe.

Musick, Marc A., and John Wilson (2008). *Volunteers: A Social Profile.* Bloomington, Indianapolis: Indiana University Press.

Nadai, Eva, Peter Sommerfeld, Felix Bühlmann, and Barbara Krattiger (2005). *Fürsorgliche Verstrickung: Soziale Arbeit zwischen Profession und Freiwilligenarbeit.* Wiesbaden: VS Verlag für Sozialwissenschaften.

Neckel, Sieghard (1991). *Status und Scham. Zur symbolischen Reproduktion sozialer Ungleichheit.* Frankfurt am Main, New York: Campus Verlag.

Odets, Walt (1995). *In the Shadow of the Epidemic: Being HIV-Negative in the Age of AIDS.* Durham: Duke University Press.

Patton, Cindy (1990). *Inventing AIDS.* New York, London: Routledge.

Perrin, Andrew J. (2005). Political Microcultures: Linking Civic Life and Democratic Discourse. *Social Forces*, 84 (2), 1049–82.

Rofes, Eric (1998). *Dry Bones Breathe. Gay Men Creating Post-AIDS Identities and Cultures*. New York, London: Harrington Park Press.

Rosenbrock, Rolf et al. (2000). The Normalization of AIDS in Western European Countries. *Social Science & Medicine*, 50 (11), 1607–29.

Scheff, Thomas J. (2000). Shame and the Social Bond: A Sociological Theory. *Sociological Theory*, 18 (1), 84–99.

Seibel, Wolfgang. (1989). The Function of Mellow Weakness: Nonprofit Organizations as Problem Nonsolvers in Germany. In Estelle James (ed.). *The Nonprofit Sector in International Perspective. Studies in Comparative Culture and Policy*, 177–92. New York, Oxford: Oxford University Press.

Shott, Susan (1979). Emotion and Social Life: A Symbolic Interactionist Analysis. *American Journal of Sociology*, 84 (6), 1317–34.

Siegel, Karolynn, and Helen-Maria Lekas (2002). AIDS as a Chronic Illness: Psychosocial Implications. *AIDS*, 16 (suppl. 4), 69–76.

Siegel, Karolynn, and Eric W. Schrimshaw (2005). Stress, Appraisal, and Coping: A Comparison of HIV-infected Women in the pre-HAART and HAART Eras. *Journal of Psychosomatic Research*, 58 (3), 225–33.

Smith, David Horton (1994). Determinants of Voluntary Association Participation and Volunteering: A Literature Review. *Nonprofit and Voluntary Sector Quarterly*, 23 (3), 243–63.

Sontag, Susan (1990). *Illness as Metaphor and AIDS and its Metaphors*. New York: Picador.

Stirling, Christine (2007). The Volunteer Citizen, Health Services and Agency: The Identity Work of Australian and New Zealand Ambulance Volunteers. PhD diss., University of Tasmania.

Stolinski, Amy M., Carey S. Ryan, Leslie R. M. Hausmann, and Molly A. Wernli (2004). Empathy, Guilt, Volunteer Experiences, and Intentions to Continue Volunteering Among Buddy Volunteers in an AIDS Organization. *Journal of Applied Biobehavioral Research*, 9 (1), 1–22.

Sznaider, Natan (1998). The Sociology of Compassion: A Study in the Sociology of Morals. *Cultural Values*, 2 (1), 117–39.

Taylor, Verta, and Nancy Whittier (1995). Analytical Approaches to Social Movement Culture: The Culture of the Women's Movement. In Hank Johnston and Bert Klandermans (eds.). *Social Movements and Culture*, 163–87. Minneapolis: University of Minnesota Press.

Tiamson, Maria L. A. (2002). Challenges in the Management of the HIV Patient in the Third Decade of AIDS. *Psychiatric Quarterly*, 73 (1), 51–8.

Treichler, Paula A. (1988). AIDS, Homophobia, and Biomedical Discourse: An Epidemic of Signification. In Douglas Crimp (ed.). *AIDS: Cultural Analysis/ Cultural Activism*, 31–70. Cambridge (Mass.), London: The MIT Press.

Weick, Karl E. (1995). *Sensemaking in Organizations*. Thousand Oaks, London, New Delhi: Sage Publications.

Weingart, Brigitte (2002). *Ansteckende Wörter. Repräsentationen von AIDS.* Frankfurt am Main: Suhrkamp.

Wießner, Peter (2003). AIDS als moderner Mythos. In Deutsche AIDS Hilfe (ed.). *AIDS Im Wandel der Zeiten. Teil 1,* 19–71. Berlin: Deutsche AIDS Hilfe.

Wilson, John (2000). Volunteering. *Annual Review of Sociology,* 26, 215–40.

Wolfe, Alan (2001). What is Altruism? In J. Steven Ott (ed.). *The Nature of the Non-profit-Sector,* 320–30. Boulder, Oxford: Westview Press.

Wuthnow, Robert (1991). *Acts of Compassion. Caring for Others and Helping Ourselves.* Princeton: Princeton University Press.

— (1995). *Learning to Care: Elementary Kindness in an Age of Indifference.* New York, Oxford: Oxford University Press.

Mediated Parasocial Emotions and Community: How Media May Strengthen or Weaken Social Communities

Katrin Döveling

Introduction

Focal events portrayed in the mass media and the reactions to their portrayal clearly demonstrate the cohesive impacts of emotions in mass media, as a few examples such as Lady Diana's death, the September 11th attacks, the 2004 Tsunami catastrophe, and the recent election campaign in the US illustrate. This fact is increasingly recognized by communication analysts. To take one example: the death of Pope John Paul II was a media event "of global proportions" (Meinert 2005), and ultimately, it was a global media network which engendered the mourning that manifested itself in the wake of the Pope's death. Having a "worldwide reach," it brought people around the globe together in a *media(ted) community*—similar to the one formed on the occasion of Lady Diana's death (Döveling 2005b). As the cultural theorist Thomas Macho (2005) asserted:

"There is, so to speak, a dissolution into a mass, in that [...] in front of our television sets [...] we have the feeling [...] as was the case at the time of Lady Di's funeral—that we are now part of a group made up of many millions all over the world, a worldwide community of mourning."

Despite the differences between the cases of Lady Diana and John Paul II, there are notable similarities with respect to the mediatized role of emotions: emotions were shown, channeled, and thus reinforced through the permanent media coverage, thus allowing mourners to perceive themselves as an emotional community. In theorizing this emotionality, media reception needs to go beyond imperative psychological spheres. As this chapter demonstrates, an integration of perspectives from other disciplines, notably sociology of emotions and communication analysis, proves particularly fruitful in conceptualizing the emotional spectrum within the media in order to understand the cohesive power of the media. This paper scrutinizes these lines of research and considers their fruitfulness for an analysis incorporating both perspectives in an interdisciplinary way.

In the first part of this paper I briefly outline pertinent theoretical perspectives and merits in sociology, focusing on emotions and social cohesiveness. Relevant perspectives in communication studies are then laid out, followed by the presentation of an integrative model that offers potential to facilitate a deeper understanding of media's role in "collective emotionalization." Finally, the aforementioned components within the model are illustrated by means of a case study, which reveals the interrelation of emotions, social system, and media coverage. This explorative case study will examine how the religious media—in this case, newspapers—covered the Pope's visit to the US in 1995 and Germany in 1996 (for greater detail, see Döveling 2005a).

The Social Functions of Emotions: Sociological Perspectives

What happens when emotions are shared in medially induced collective emotional processes and how can this impact community building? To answer this, we first need to elaborate on the role of emotions in group formation and social cohesion. Here, classical sociology provides valuable analytical tools. Both Emile Durkheim and Georg Simmel emphasize a constructive character of emotions as being constitutive of social reality. For Durkheim, collective emotions play a central function as they entail an emotional differentiation between a collectivity and its environment, which simultaneously bestows meaning on the social context and creates social cohesion within the group (see Gerhards 1988, 40). In this sense, social groups are founded on an emotional basis. According to Durkheim, formation of a group, or rather of a collective state, involves a process of increased emotional intensity:

1. Within a gathering of people, this process is started when individuals feel drawn together by a common circumstance or occasion (such as a media event). There is likely to be at least partial awareness of this collective attraction as members use "identical signs through which each individual feeling is expressed" (Durkheim 1951, 125).
2. As images of other's reactions are formed in "the minds of all" there is thus a growing realization of this commonality among group members

(Durkheim 1951, 125); however, a collective emotional reaction to these common circumstances has not yet formed.

3. Individual emotional (and initially independent) reactions to these circumstances then combine with the realization of commonalities, and a new state manifests itself, one: "less my own than its predecessor, less tainted with individuality and more and more freed, by a series of repeated elaborations analogous to the foregoing, from all excessive particularity" (Durkheim 1951, 125).

It is through this process that group cohesion arises: as soon as a certain number of individuals have the same ideas, interests, feelings, and operations, they inevitably feel mutually drawn together under the influence of these congruencies. Thus, a group is formed (see Durkheim 1999, 40–2). Crucially, Durkheim conceptualized this process as one driven by emotions. For the analysis of emotional media events such as the Pope's visit to foreign countries, it is also vital to keep in mind the central role of collectively shared emotional events—not only for the formation of communities, but also for already existing collectivities which reproduce themselves in part through such events and the revitalization of collective emotions (see Döveling 2005a, 134).

In a similar vein the classical sociologist Georg Simmel also treated emotions as constituting factors of social reality. Simmel demonstrated that it is only as a part of the mass that the individual can express strong feelings in public (see Nassauer 1949/1950, 6). Much like Durkheim, Simmel pointed out that formation of the mass results from the merging of fractions of personalities and forces, the one-sided impulses, and the interests of the individuals (Simmel 1968, 115). Moreover, and importantly, Simmel also focused on how social relations effect emotional states. Specifically, he noted that an opposition to a third party, with its emotional substrate of aversion (hatred, anger, etc.), strengthens internal solidarity, that is, social cohesion, within a community (Simmel 1968, 457; see figure 1).

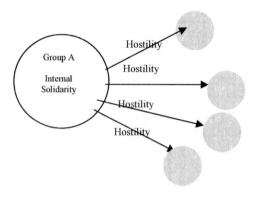

Figure 1: Emotional Solidarity in Groups and Hostility Towards Others (source: Döveling 2005a, 144)

Like Simmel and Durkheim, contemporary sociologist Randall Collins also views emotions as constitutive of social realities and, in particular, groups. Additionally, he stresses that social reality is based on social structures (Collins 1984, 386); as such, it is emotions that provide orientation in the world. Hence, for Collins, the basis of all social constellations is that they are *emotionally* structured. As Collins (2004) writes:

"A theory of interaction ritual (IR) and interaction ritual chains is above all a theory of situations. It is a theory of momentary encounters among human bodies charged up with emotions and consciousness because they have gone through chains of previous encounters" (Collins 2004, 3).[1]

Here, emotions fulfill various functions; for example, they provide structure to social situations. This is relevant because emotions such as love, hate, and fear lead to a social categorization of people and establish ranking in social encounters. Thus, they contribute not only to the constitution of the group-environment difference, but also to vertical differentiations and

---

1 For further details, illustrating how Collins combines Goffman's "presentational rituals" (referring to Goffman's *The Presentation of Self in Everyday Life*) with Durkheim's concept of ritual to restore the sense of social order, see Collins (2004, 22–5). Further on, he writes: "IR theory, as an intellectual enterprise, is a set of symbolic representations riding on its surge of emotional energy; it is the intellectual version of effervescence that gave élan to Durkheim and his research group, to Goffman and his followers, and to today's sociologists of emotion and process in everyday life" (Collins 2004, 46).

hierarchies (Collins 1984). At the same time, emotions themselves are re-sources of exchange. Social interactions, in this respect, are viewed as emo-tional exchanges directed at attaining the best emotional exchange of re-sources (Collins 1981; 1984).[2] As groups are prime contexts for any social exchange, this makes emotions particularly relevant for understanding group formation and perpetuation—as well as the role of the media in this process.

Collins adds a vertical dimension to Simmel's argument on cohesion and outside opponents. Interactions are, as Collins points out, above all, acts within group membership. Symbols are used to represent this membership with its concomitant emotions, such as group-internal joy, enthusiasm, warmth, and empathy, or, and externally, envy, anger, etc. This development can be linked to the (re)production of internal hierarchies, through which "emotional energy" (Collins 1984, 385–96) is produced or consumed in interactions, depending on whether solidarity and inclusion vs. exclusion is engendered, i.e., whether status is obtained or diminished. Here, the necessary (emotional) resources stem from previous interactions, and thus a series of interactions leads to the establishment of "interaction ritual chains," which engage individuals through, and in, *inclusion* and *exclusion* (Collins 1987, 198). Hence, social structures within groups are not only perpetuated but also created by emotions. Collins describes the role of mass media, focusing on television, in his work on *Interaction Rituals* as follows:

"It is possible to watch a funeral or a wedding on television, usually that of a public figure. During the fall of 2001, for example there were sometimes moving TV memorials for 9/11 victims. These long distance rituals can give a sense of a shared emotion, solidarity, and respect for symbolism. […] Television here ap-proximates bodily feedback, in effect allowing members of the remote audience to see others like themselves, picked out in the moments when they are displaying the most emotion and the most engrossment in the ceremony" (Collins 2004, 55).

He also differentiates between "large-scale, relatively formal rituals" (Collins 2004, 62) and "small-scale natural rituals" (Collins 2004, 62). He points out that large-scale rituals "come off better by remote communica-tion than do small-scale natural rituals. This seems to be so because large-

---

2 As Collins remarks: "These emotional energies are transmitted by contagion among members of a group, in flows that operate very much like the set of negotiations that produce prices within a market" (Collins 1984, 386).

scale rituals are working with established symbols, already build up through previous iteration of an IR chain" (Collins 2004, 62).[3]

Thus, Collins' understanding of emotions as resources in group contexts is of particular relevance for the analysis of media coverage and its role in community building, as he links ongoing interactions and their emotional dimension in group cohesion. This can serve as a broader theoretical framework for the analysis of "virtual" interactions between recipients and media figures (see below: parasocial interactions).

Emotions can also be rightly considered to be the product of direct social interactions, as analyzed by sociologists such as Theodore D. Kemper, Thomas J. Scheff, and Sighard Neckel, who focus on the social conditions of emotions. They argue that social gatherings of humans and their emotional outcome are determined by status and power. These are factors that enable reciprocal orientations of actions in social interactions; through them, i.e., through the emotions that result from the negotiations of these social and political asymmetries, the social order is maintained (Kemper 1978, 30–41; Scheff 1988, 395–406; Neckel 1991). Like Collins, these theorists also address issues of *inclusion* and *exclusion*, and their emotional substrate. In the context of the study of emotions and group-specific media coverage, the question thus arises: does the sharing of emotions through the media within a community transcend status differences and strengthen the community, or is emotional experience instead structured (by the media) in a way that reinforces preexisting hierarchies and patterns of exclusion? Either way, media can variously effect group formation and perpetuation processes through the portrayal of emotions.

The social-structural perspective characterized in the preceding, however, has been intensely criticized by those sociologists who focus on the actors' interpretations within emotional processes. From this perspective, it is only through reciprocal reference and interpretation (e.g., within power and status structures) in a social interaction that emotions result (Hochschild 1979, 555; Shott 1979, 1318; Zurcher 1982, 1–2). It is this emphasis on a culturally embedded interpretation in the emergence of emotions that distinguishes these theorists from those discussed previously. This is particularly relevant in group and community contexts (and the media's portrayal), as specific group cultures exist in terms of cultural

---

3 He stresses that the "remote broadcast must convey the audience's participation, not merely its leaders or performers" (Collins 2004, 62). This is crucial in the analysis which gives proof for his statement, as illustrated later.

codes and thus emotions. This process of reciprocal referencing and interpretation of social interactions gives rise to Hochschild's renowned concept of *feeling rules* (Hochschild 1989), which argues that people feel emotions according to culturally normative prescriptions. Such rules specifically
mold group processes and "reflect patterns of social membership." Some
"may be nearly universal [...] [others] are unique to particular social groups
and can be used to distinguish among them as alternate governments or
colonizers of individual internal events" (Hochschild 1979, 566). Feeling
rules are thus a part of the group culture. Hochschild (1989) has looked
most closely at how corporate actors attempt to establish feeling rules via
organizational hierarchies. The media can thus be viewed as conveyors of
feeling rules to their audiences, and hence can be analyzed in a similar fashion. However, this premise needs to be conceptualized in more interdependent terms. While feeling rules are already a part of preexisting group cultures, the crucial empirical question is how group-specific corporate (media) and emotional strategies interrelate with reception and, potentially and
ultimately: emotional cohesion processes.

It is on this basis that the argument is laid out: Media can convey, harness, and indeed produce "community relevant emotions," emotions of
belongingness, in a social community as they constitute and structure social
meanings of events for, and with their recipients. Thus, emotions are considered to be resources in medially portrayed interactions at the same time
that they are considered to be results of interactions that are engendered in
media portrayals through inclusion and exclusion, portrayal of group
membership, and corresponding feeling rules. This leads one to consider
how the mass media portray emotions in collective media processes and
how communications analysts explain the relevant variables involved in
such processes. These issues are considered in the following section.

The Social Functions of Media: Communication Studies Perspectives

Functions of the Media in Setting an Emotional Agenda

Within communication studies it has been suggested that the agenda setting function of the media "may not be successful much of the time in
telling people what to think, but it is stunningly successful much of the

time in telling its readers what to think about" (Cohen 1963, 13). The approach "refers to the idea that there is a strong correlation between the
emphasis that mass media place on certain issues (e.g., based on placement
or amount of coverage) and the importance attributed to these issues by
mass audiences" (Scheufele and Tewksbury 2007, 11). However, we need
to add the emotional aspect to this: The media "may not be successful
much of the time in telling people what to think, but they are stunningly
successful much of the time in telling its readers what to have feelings
about" (Döveling 2005a, 68). By *selecting* and *structuring* aspects of reality
(*priming*), the mass media influence not only the cognitive perception of
reality, but simultaneously the emotional one, as they promote topics and
objects the audience has feelings about. Through media's portrayal of
events such as those mentioned in the beginning of this article, an explicit
as well as an implicit "emotional agenda" (Döveling 2005a) becomes evident.

However, this emotional agenda extends beyond priming; the manner
in which they are framed also affects, to some extent, how recipients think
and feel about highlighted objects and issues. Like priming, *framing* is centered around the consideration "that mass media [have] potentially strong
attitudinal effects, but that these effects also depend [...] heavily on pre-
dispositions, schema, and other characteristics of the audience that influence [...] how they process [...] messages in the mass media" (Scheufele
and Tewksbury 2007, 11). This perspective has roots in both psychology
and sociology (Goffman 1974; see also Scheufele and Tewksbury 2007;
Pan and Kosicki, 1993). As noted by Entman,

"To frame is to select some aspects of a perceived reality and make them more
salient in a communicating text, in such a way as to promote a particular problem
definition, causal interpretation, moral evaluation, and/or treatment recommenda-
tion for the item described" (1993, 52).

It signifies that "the strongest effects are on the *affective* dimension"
(McCombs et al. 1997, 715–6; my emphasis). Media frame and prime not
only cognitive information, but also emotion, by selecting events and objects, giving them a color, and thereby making some stand out more than
others for any given piece of information.[4] Here, it is relevant to note, as

_____

4 Lang and Lang (1981) emphasize that media do not set the agenda alone, but the selection is the result of a complex inter-relational process between media organizations and
their surroundings.

Hochschild argues (1979, 566), that framing and feeling rules reciprocally imply each other.

In order to answer questions about how an emotional media event was portrayed in the emotional agenda of the print media examined—how it was structured in an interpretational frame and which emotions were primed—we need to understand the emotional response of recipients to people they will likely never meet in person, e.g. the Pope. Thus, before turning to the case study, it is important to first introduce the concept of "parasocial interaction" (Horton and Wohl 1956).

Mediated Parasocial Interaction and Relationships: "Intimacy at a Distance"[5]

The link that we experience between the medially portrayed world and our own perception of and engagement with the world is described as "parasocial *interaction*." Repeated exposure to these "felt as apparently real" contacts with media figures may lead to what Horton and Wohl referred to as *parasocial relationships*: "One of the striking characteristics of the new mass media—radio, television, and the movies—is that they give the illusion of face-to-face relationship with the performer [...] We propose to call this [...] a para-social relationship" (1956, 215).

The media recipient thus perceives people in the media as "social partners." The process of mass communication is conceptualized as "social action" and media reception is framed into daily actions of the recipient who behaves and reacts to the people on the screen in a way similar to that within interpersonal interactions in his or her own immediate world. In the case of the TV media, the recipient behaves as if the person on the screen were speaking directly to him or her.[6] The person on the screen—the "persona" (Horton and Wohl 1956, 216)—is known to the recipient through the observations of behavior, resulting in a mediated contact. Horton and Wohl characterized this as "intimacy at a distance" (1956, 215). According to this concept, media use can lead to "unilateral interactions" between the recipient and the persona on the screen; the emotional "intimacy at a dis-

5 This term was coined by Horton and Wohl (1956, 215).

6 Until now, research in this domain has mainly addressed parasocial interactions with TV protagonists. As my analysis shows, however, this concept can be fruitfully applied to print media as well.

tance" is created through the illusion of a "face-to-face relationship" with the performer (Horton and Wohl 1956, 215–29).

Among the various elaborations of this concept (see Döveling 2005a, 87), those from the perspective of symbolic interactionist communication analysis are particularly relevant here (see Krotz 1996, 79).[7] As these theorists point out, the recipient may take over roles of the "persona," without the pressure for action normally linked with role-taking in direct interactions (see Krotz 1996, 73–90). Although lacking reciprocity, it is noteworthy that parasocial interactions are active achievements of the recipient, as, indeed, through role-taking with the "persona," media recipients leave their passive roles. The recipients are not victims but rather active partners in a parasocial reception and interaction process. This implies direct consequences for the analysis of emotions in community-specific newspapers. The essential point is that (mass) media may create an *emotional proximity* and thus allow for the entire spectrum of quite personal emotions so characteristic of interpersonal relations, even though the actual partners in this communicative process are not known personally through face-to-face interactions. The recipient becomes engaged in a parasocial communication through his or her active emotional role taking: the recipient follows the media coverage when it occurs, and with time seemingly gets to "know" the medial persona through repeated parasocial interaction. In this manner, the recipient becomes involved in a parasocial relationship, involving emotion management—feels "with them," "for them,"—and takes over their roles. In a sense, then, the original concept of symbolic interactionism is expanded through the consideration of mediated symbolic interactions. Hence, parasocial interaction is another mechanism by which media as communication networks spread not only cognitive information, but also—and above all—engender feelings.[8] With this, they lead to parasocial emotionalization in which the recipient becomes involved as an active partner. Through the media's interpretation and portrayal of various figures, parasocial relationships are emotionally framed, in newspapers as well as in television (Döveling 2005a, 87). It is this link that is relevant in under-

---

7 Donald Horton and Anselm Strauss explicated already in 1957 an integration of the concept into symbolic interactionism (See Horton and Strauss 1957, 579–87, especially 587).

8 See, for example, Wettergren's (2005) analysis of emotions in social movements. Media substantially "co-design" feelings and become influential factors in the interaction of the designation of information and its reception.

standing emotions engendered by media: through a connection of the potential community-building function of the media's agenda settings, and the crucial interpretation of the recipient as part of a (mediated) social community.

In the following, I show that through a specific "media-emotion culture" (Saxer and Märki-Koepp 1992; Döveling 2005a) community-relevant emotions may be engendered, reinforced, and channeled in a parasocial exchange process that involves active role taking on both sides: by the recipient as well as by the communicator.

Mediated Emotion-Culture

Media systems constitute themselves with the objective of enduring as social systems (Saxer and Märki-Koepp 1992, 43). Thus, group-specific media in particular, such as the two Catholic newspapers[9] that were studied, need to produce a profile that leads to continuous demand for, consumption of, attachment to the media product on the part of the recipients (see Saxer and Märki-Koepp 1992, 42).[10] In this way, group-specific media not only bear on emotions within that group, but simultaneously depend on and respond to them. This intricate intertwining of media's emotional agenda and the group members' preexisting emotionality (e.g. desires for emotional gratification, belonging or parasociability) constitutes a complex system of media-emotion culture, as summarized in figure 2.

Media-emotion cultures form the larger context within which group-specific cultural signs are interdependently interpreted—a cultural sign system allowing for reciprocal interpretation as a basis for collective emotional experience (this from the above discussion of Hochschild). It is only on the basis of such mutually compatible understandings that emotions can function as resources within the collective process (this from the above discussion of Collins). Moreover, this establishes the basis for emotions to emerge from social constellations in group-specific ways (this from the above discussion of Simmel).

---

9 *Catholic Standard* and *Kirchenzeitung für das Erzbistum Köln.*

10 This requires the addressing of system-immanent demands as well as the simultaneous tackling of external environment conditions (see Saxer and Märki-Koepp 1992, 51; Luhmann 1987, 22–3, 31).

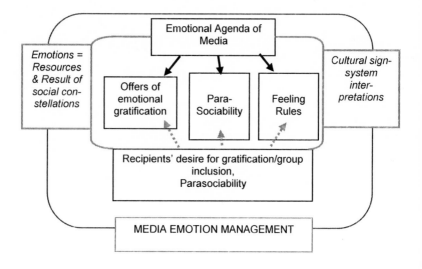

Figure 2: Powered by Emotions: Media – Emotion – Culture (see also Döveling 2005a: 186)

As a "systemic process" (Vester 1991, 194), this is based on preexisting collective identities, or rather on what Durkheim called the "collective state", i.e. the fact that group participants view their group peers not as alien, but as similar, in contrast to outside others (see above, Simmel). Simultaneously, media's emotional agenda functions to reinforce this sense of collectivity. The common frame of a media-emotion culture allows the media to display an emotional agenda so that cultural signs are signaled that can foster—by means of culturally specific encoding and decoding—an understanding of an offer of *gratification* and/or *parasociability* as well as group-relevant feeling rules, and this representing the three core mechanisms through which media and communities are intertwined. Emotions then function as *resources* exchanged in mediated parasocial interactions. Finally, this common interpretive framework enables the presentation of emotions as resulting from social constellations in a way that buttresses social order.

In sum, through interpretation and exchange of emotional resources in parasocial interactions, reception of media and their emotional agenda may lead to a strengthening of the recipient's identity as part of a social community. The portrayal of emotions may, in this sense, channel cohesion within a social process that, in the course of continual reception and use of the media, subsequently leads to *mediated emotion management* (see figure 2). The cohesive power of emotions, both on the side of the media and on the side of the recipient, can be regarded as a constituting, central link between the recipient's own world and the illustrated, mediated world. Thus, media fulfill a central function in society and within communities, and are therefore worthy of further interdisciplinary research.

Case Study: Mediated Socio-Emotional Community

The following section presents a case study that elucidates the above model of group-specific media-emotion cultures by analyzing the emotionally framed agenda of two community-relevant Catholic media organs. It summarizes the results of an extensive qualitative analysis of two diocese newspapers covering Pope John Paul II's travels to the U.S. in 1995, Germany in 1996, (for more detail, see Döveling 2005a). The two newspapers were selected on the basis of both the similarities of their communities (Catholic dioceses) *and* their differences. As Rodney Stark (1997, 184) remarks, the Catholic Church in the U.S. is embedded in a "free religious market," which leads to competition and creates a need to practice what he calls "religious mobilization." Contrary to this, the Catholic Church in Germany is financed to a substantial degree by a church tax and thus has a different institutionalized basis. Group-specific media may thus play a different role in the American Catholic Church as a means to religious mobilization. Parasocial-emotional media events are important in the recruitment and stabilization of a community, because media, as stressed previously, may create a sense of emotional proximity and engender processes of attachment towards people and organizations.[11] While this is vital

---

11 "Thus, media have power not only to insert messages into social networks themselves—to atomize, to integrate, or otherwise to design social structure—at least momentarily. We have seen that media events may create their own constituencies" (Dayan and Katz 1994a: 17). Dayan and Katz noted elsewhere: "We think of media events as holidays that spotlight some central value [...] Often such events portray an idealized version of society, reminding society of what it aspires to be rather than what it is" (1994b: ix). Yet, media events may not only trigger or reinforce common values but remind members of

in the U.S., the German Catholic Church does not need to mobilize and engender cohesion to the same extent. A different emotional agenda can thus be expected to surface in church media coverage. Based on the outlined perspectives, the questions guiding the analysis were:

1. Do the newspapers show differences or similarities in the cultural coding of emotions?
2. How and with which emotions do the group-specific newspapers of the different organizational forms reveal potential community strengthening?
3. How do the examined papers contextualize parasocial emotions?

To this end, the two newspapers, the *Catholic Standard* and the *Kirchenzeitung für das Erzbistum Köln* were selected. Relevant emotions were categorized theoretically into *emotions of inclusion* (such as unity, joy, and uplifting pride) and *exclusion* (such as aversion and anger); these emotions were then traced in the diocesan newspapers both before and after the visit of the Pope by means of qualitative content analysis (Mayring 1993, 85–90). In order to capture the process character of emotional agendas, i.e., their temporal dimension, the analysis focused on media coverage both before and after the Pope's visit.[12]

Emotional Agenda Before the Pope's Visit

While both papers portrayed the role of the Pope as head of the church and the joy of group members before his visit, they also demonstrated clear and noteworthy differences in the *framing* of emotions in terms of inclusion and exclusion, as well as in their offers of *parasociability*. The emo-

---

a cultural group such as a Catholic community of their common identity (see Dayan and Katz 1996: 239–57).

12 Presenting the entire analysis is beyond the scope of this paper, but see Döveling (2005a). Besides textual representations, visuals were equally included as they arguably have distinct emotional salience (see Wettergren 2005: 115), see Döveling (2005a) for example images. Content analysis strategies were adapted for this. Content analysis (Mayring 1993: 85–90) involved an exploratory phase in which emotions were categorized as inclusive or exclusionary in the light of existing theories. Next, these categories were applied to the empirical material through interpretation, explication and structuring. Finally, a synopsis summarized the main outcomes in each phase of media coverage before and after the visit, thus defining the respective emotional agendas within group-specific media-emotion cultures.

tional agenda of the German paper revolved around joy, but did so by formulating a call for joy and emphasizing its necessity. Significantly, this feeling was thus communicated as a feeling rule. This stipulation for joy as a requirement was indicative of internal aversion and hostility against certain group members, most notably critics of the Pope and the church as an institution. In the newspaper, church officials were quoted saying that there is a "rupture" that divides the church. Through this framing, a second, parallel feeling rule was communicated, which fostered feelings of resentment, aversion and, to some extent, even anger against what was construed to be a threatening faction opposing the "true" community of Catholics.

In contrast, the American paper conveyed emotions in an inclusive way focusing not only on joy, but also on pride, thankfulness, empathy, enthusiasm, and feelings of unity and togetherness as well as hope and even love etc. This inclusiveness was accomplished by framing these emotions clearly and notably as offers for emotional gratification that were not only highlighted in the texts, but equally in the pictures (see Döveling 2005a; 2007) showing the Pope together with group members, especially children. They described "the man who is Pope John Paul II" thus:

"In his youth, Wojtyla was an actor in dramas celebrating the cult of Polishness, an experience he fondly remembers to this day [...] And like no other Pope, Karol Wojtyla had to work for years as a poverty-stricken manual laborer under the wartime German occupation of his country. The Pope's philosophical and theological thoughts, his reaction to international occurrences, and his interpretation of history must therefore be examined in the light of his personal background, along with his familiarity with world problems and politics" (Szulc 1995, 9).

Instead of rejecting dissenting voices and trying to instill appropriate emotions about them through feeling rules, the American paper displayed neither critique nor aversion against group members. Quite to the contrary, the American paper quoted group members who revealed pride about the Pope's achievements as spiritual leader. Moreover, the American paper covered the upcoming visit of the Pope in great detail and in a way rather in accord with the pastoral care ethos of the charitable work of religious organizations, i.e., "taking care" of all who wanted to see him during his visit and who would have therefore needed to know where he was and when.

The American paper thus took a positive, inclusive, and optimistic stand rather than exposing any negative emotions within the community, and thus pursued to a much greater extent an agenda of parasocial emotional gratification offers. In the German paper, in contrast, such offers of emotional gratification were colored by a distinct reliance on feeling rules, revealing a negative, problem-centered position and disclosing *aversion* within the community.

Above all, the two papers differed significantly in their offers of parasocial interactions. The American paper elaborated on the "human" touch in depth, presenting the person Karol Wojtyla in pictures and, in an extensive analysis of his youth and his development from a young boy to the head of the Catholic Church, as one who learned how "to suffer in silence and dignity" (Szulc 1995, 9).

"This [experience of suffering] had the merit of exposing him directly to hardships and experiences in human relationships few other priests had known. It taught him how to suffer in silence and dignity, and instilled in him a habit of absolute discipline" (Szulc 1995, 9).

The interpretation of the human emotional bond—in short, "intimacy at a distance," (Horton and Wohl 1956, 215)—together with the display not only of unity, but also of mutuality and feelings of togetherness, was emphasized not only in the text but also in the pictures, as there were numerous visual presentations of the Pope in close situations, e.g., embracing a child, riding a bike, and as being in contact with "average" people. Additionally, photos showed children writing letters to the Pope. One letter is presented as an example: "Your holiness. I love you so much" (see Döveling 2005a for example images).

By contrast, there were no pictures of the Pope or of community members in the German newspaper before his visit. Rather than emphasizing the human touch and associated positive parasocial interaction, offers so prevalent in the American representation, the German paper exposed the authority of the Pope, and his role and function in uniting his church. The parasocial element thus played only a minor role in the German case. It is also worth taking into account that the German paper published very few, namely five articles only, before the Pope's visit, while the American paper covered the upcoming visit in length and extensively with twenty-three articles. In sum, the emotion-media culture differed notably between the two papers before the visit, specifically in terms of the interpretation of this visit, the framing of emotions of inclusion and exclusion, and feeling rules, as well as in their offers of parasocial interaction, gratification and participation, and in the amount of coverage.

While this emotion-media culture can be described as largely inclusive in the American case, the German newspaper coverage was much more characterized by an exclusionary bent. The analysis that I have outlined above, I claim, suggests that this difference can be attributed to the differing institutional environments of the papers, characterized in the American case by a need for broad religious mobilization versus a relatively secure financial base of the German paper. In accordance with these differences, both emotion-media cultures aim at fostering community in different ways: broad inclusion versus delineating a dissenting community. Corresponding to Durkheim's analysis of emotions in rituals, it is through this mediated emotional differentiation that social contexts achieve emotional value and meaning, i.e., that group boundaries are drawn. Hence, before his visit, while there were indicators of internal group instability in the German paper, in the American paper a process of inclusive parasocial emotional intensity, of *parasocial* "interaction ritual chains" (Collins 1987, 198) was revealed. The next section discloses that this had an enduring potential, which extends and increases after his visit.

Emotional Agenda After the Pope's Visit

The emotional agenda in the aftermath of the Pope's visit continued to be characterized by these central differences between both newspapers. Regarding the external exclusion, i.e. the exclusion of dissenters, the German paper continued to openly demonstrate aversion against those who criticized the Pope and the institutional practices of the church (Gerhardt 1996, 3). In framing his role as "shepherd—and not top-sheep" [*"Hirte— und nicht Oberschaf"*] (Läufer 1996, 11)—the German paper took a critical stance. Instead of pointing out the relevance for dialogue, those who blew a whistle were harshly criticized. The emotional agenda, which clearly had a divisive and exclusionary function, revealed this feeling of aversion as directed against dissenters. Following Simmel's argument discussed earlier in this chapter about the link between social cohesion and external opposition, this media's interpretation of positioning certain individuals in relation and opposition to an established emotional agenda in the media might have served to strengthen internal solidarity among those members who engaged with the emotional agenda. In this context, presentation of visual material that showed people dancing and celebrating the Pope's visit seconded this kind of exclusionary integration.

The American paper likewise demonstrated that the visit was a unique event and an occasion to celebrate, but the contextual framing of emotions took a different direction: in particular, the emotional framing and priming of joy, feeling of belongingness, hope, and pride became paramount as this focused on a strong emotional and religious mobilization within the mediated emotional culture. The American paper thus also continued to emphasize the human touch and offered parasocial interaction opportunities. There was greater emphasis on the "normal" group members, whereas the German paper highlighted the Pope's function, and showed pictures of him with priests and high officials in the church. Interviews with lay people in the American paper, for instance, expressed feelings of joy, devotion, adoration, admiration, and togetherness. This thrust was further buttressed by numerous accompanying pictures of the Pope in close contact with "average" people, including young and old, non-religious people, and Protestants. In a similar vein, the Pope was also described as a human being, and he was compared with "much younger journalists" and thus he was framed as entirely human and deeply caring about people:

"That was really why Pope John Paul II had come, to bring Christ to the people of America. It is why he keeps up the tireless schedule he does at the age of 75. While much younger journalists were ready to collapse from fatigue after several days of trying to keep up with the Pope, the Holy Father appeared robust throughout the trip" (Zimmermann 1995, 2).

The celebration was called the "papal parade," the Holy Father became "Uncle Pope," and the people seeing him became the "fans in the stands" (Burnim and Leonard 1995, 6–7). Moreover, the reader was directly addressed in parasocial interaction through visuals and texts. Whereas in the German coverage, the analysis revealed a pattern of mediated distance, the American newspaper offered (emotional) "intimacy at a distance" (Horton and Wohl 1956, 215—29). Such parasocial interaction offers continued to be largely absent in the German paper, where, instead, a sense of mediated distance, which was in parts joyful, yet still not as enthusiastic prevailed. The Pope was framed as the "creator of German unity" ["*Baumeister der neu gewonnenen Einheit des deutschen Volkes*"] (Gerhardt 1996) and Ex-chancellor Schroeder and President Herzog thanked him for Germany's unity.

In sum, coverage in both media following the visit continued the same pattern as in the Pope's advent. The American paper pursued a clear, emotionally inclusive agenda through framing and priming of positive emotions, whereas the German paper highlighted joy and enthusiasm (especially among young adults), while at the same time framing exclusive elements in the community, and invoking an agenda of external exclusion of dissenters.

Conclusion: Mediated Emotional Community – Like Shepherd, Like Sheep?

After laying the theoretical groundwork for the analysis of mediated parasocial emotions and their social functions within a community, including relevant perspectives from sociology and communication studies, the case study explored the media-emotion culture of two different newspapers in the portrayal of a religious media event. Through the mediated display of emotional reactions, a series of emotional endorsements was revealed (see Döveling 2005a). At the same time, group-specific feeling rules, together with the emotional portrayal of relevant characters, demonstrated feelings of belonging as sociological cohesive factors (Döveling 2005a; 2005b). It equally demonstrated the different elucidations of emotional energy as well as parasocial emotional interaction chains in the examined papers. In such a way, media's potential impact on the development of mutual emotional perceptions and potentially group-stabilizing function was analyzed.

To conclude: Humans as social beings are embedded in cultural contexts. Within a mediated emotion culture, recipients are influenced by emotions conveyed in the media, yet, at the same time the active recipient engages in a parasocial emotional interaction through his or her interpretation of the text. Thus, when looking at a group-specific newspaper such as that of a diocese, it is vital to take into account that cultural sign-systems and feeling rules are understood through interpretations on both sides. It is on this basis that I propose an analysis of emotions as specific, direct, socio-culturally coded resources in parasocial interactions as essential and furthermore necessary components to be integrated into research in sociology and communication studies. Hopefully, a first starting point has been made in this article.

In an increasingly functionalistic-individualistic society, media fulfill a central function in the creation and stabilization of *Vergemeinschaftung*, group cohesiveness, be it in a religious context, in a sports event such as the Football World Cup, or in the uniting sharing of grief as occurred in the wake of Princess Diana's death. Media as channels of communication convey relations of closeness and distance, intimacy, inclusion, and exclusion, and reveal emotions as resources and as results of social constellations; such a media-emotion culture can strengthen, or weaken, emotional integration. The key is that through the mediation of emotion management, the media fulfill a societal function. They convey emotion rules and can substantially influence the emotional climate within social groups (e.g., the religious groups examined here) and in society; this is achieved through emotional dramaturgy and parasocial experience. Group-specific media-culture, in particular, should not be overlooked here as it mediates norms and values within the respective groups and thus influences the group-relevant socialization of its recipients. By taking these factors into account, we, as analysts of media's interrelation with, and broader role in society, can reveal basic and necessary underlying conditions within emotional reception processes and clarify the potentially cohesive processes engendered by mass media. Attention is thus given to the potential role of media as a source of shared conceptions and also, in particular, of *shared emotions*. Emotions as resources are understood through an interpretative process on *both* sides, and the community-building and stabilizing function of the media occurs when the number of recipients who understand these signs increases, and they feel emotionally included and thus gratified (see Döveling 2003). In this process, media reveal not only a purely cognitively based agenda of subjects, but also increasingly an emotional agenda (Döveling, 2005a) which becomes relevant in the interpretation by the recipient. It is of vital significance that through the portrayal of an emotional agenda, cultural signs are signaled that may lead to an understanding of an offer of gratification, culturally coded feeling rules, and emotional para-sociability.

Acknowledgements

The constructive and fruitful feedback of Jochen Kleres and Debra Hopkins is gratefully acknowledged.

References

Burnim, Cinnamon, and Maureen Leonard (1995). Papal Parade. *Catholic Standard*, 6 October 1995, 12.

Cohen, Bernard C. (1963). *The Press, the Public and Foreign Policy*. Princeton: Princeton University Press.

Collins, Randall (1981). *Sociology Since Midcentury. Essays in Theory Cumulation*. New York, London, Toronto, Sydney, San Francisco: Academic Press.

— (1984). The Role of Emotion in Social Structure. In Klaus Scherer and Paul Ekman (eds.). *Approaches to Emotion*, 385–96. Hillsdale, New Jersey, London: Lawrence Erlbaum Associates.

— (1987). Interaction Ritual Chains, Power and Property. The Micro-Macro Connection as an Empirically Based Theoretical Problem. In Jeffrey C. Alexander, Bernhard Giesen, Richard Münch, and Neil J. Smelser (eds.). *The Micro-Macro-Link*, 193–206. Berkeley, Los Angeles, London: University of California Press.

— (2004). *Interaction Ritual Chains*. Princeton: Princeton University Press.

Dayan, Daniel, and Elihu Katz (1994a). Defining Media Events. High Holidays of Mass Communication. In Horace Newcomb (ed.). *Television. The Critical View*, 5th edition, 332–51. New York, Oxford: Oxford University Press.

— (1994b). *Media Events. The Live Broadcasting of History*. Cambridge, Mass., London: Harvard University Press.

— (1996). Political Ceremony and Instant History. In Tore Slaatta (ed.). *Media and the Transition of Collective Identities*. Papers From Research Symposium in Oslo 12–14 January 1995, IMK-Report No. 18, 239-57. Oslo: Department of Media and Communication.

Döveling, Katrin (2003). Emotions and the Community Building Function of the Media. *SPIEL. Siegener Periodikum für Empirische Literaturwissenschaft*, special issue, 22 (2), 339–51.

— (2005a). *Emotionen – Medien – Gemeinschaft. Eine kommunikationssoziologische Analyse*. Wiesbaden: Westdeutscher Verlag.

— (2005b). Feel the Pain. Eine Analyse der medial vermittelten Trauer anlässlich des Todes von Johannes Paul II. *Ästhetik und Kommunikation*, 36 (131), 95–8.

— (2007). Visuelles Trauer-Management. Zum Tod von Johannes Paul II. in der modernen Mediengesellschaft. In Helga Mitterbauer and Katharina Scherke (eds.). *Moderne. Kulturwissenschaftliches Jahrbuch*, 158–78. Innsbruck: Studienverlag.

Durkheim, Emile (1951). *Suicide*. New York: The Free Press. [first published in 1897]

— (1999). *Physik der Sitten und des Rechts. Vorlesungen zur Soziologie der Moral*. Ed. Hans-Peter Müller. Frankfurt am Main: Suhrkamp. [lectures originally held in 1890–1900 and 1902–1915]

Entman, Robert M. (1993). Framing. Toward Clarification of a Fractured Paradigm. *Journal of Communication*, 43 (4), 51–8.

Gerhards, Jürgen (1988). *Soziologie der Emotionen. Fragestellungen, Systematik und Perspektiven*. Weinheim, München: Juventa.

Gerhardt, Michael (1996). Botschaften für die Zukunft, Papst Johannes Paul II. besuchte zum drittenmal Deutschland. *Kirchenzeitung für das Erzbistum Köln*, 28 June 1996, 3.

Goffman, Erving (1974). *Frame Analysis. An Essay on the Organization of Experience*. New York: Northeastern University Press.

Hochschild, Arlie Russell (1989). *Das gekaufte Herz*, Frankfurt am Main: Campus.

— (1979). Emotion Work, Feeling Rules, and Social Structure. *American Journal of Sociology*, 85 (3), 551–75.

Horton, Donald, and Richard R. Wohl (1956). Mass Communication and Para-Social Interaction. Observations on Intimacy at a Distance. *Psychiatry*, 19, 215–29.

Horton, Donald, and Anselm Strauss (1957). Interaction in Audience-Participation Shows. *The American Journal of Sociology*, 57, 579–87.

Kemper, Theodore D. (1978). Toward a Sociology of Emotions. Some Problems and Some Solutions. *The American Sociologist*, 13 (1), 30–41.

Krotz, Friedrich (1996). Parasoziale Interaktion und Identität im elektronisch mediatisierten Kommunikationsraum. In Peter Vorderer (ed.). *Fernsehen als "Beziehungskiste". Parasoziale Beziehungen und Interaktionen mit TV-Personen*, 73–90. Opladen: Westdeutscher Verlag.

Lang, Gladys Engel, and Kurt Lang (1981). Mass Communications and Public Opinion: Strategies for Research. In Morris Rosenberg and Ralph H. Turner (eds.). *Social Psychology, Sociological Perspectives*, 653-83. New York: Transaction Publishers.

Läufer, Erich (1996). Hirte – und nicht Oberschaf. *Kirchenzeitung für das Erzbistum Köln*, 28 June 1996, 11.

Luhmann, Niklas (1987). *Soziale Systeme. Grundriß einer allgemeinen Theorie*. Frankfurt am Main: Suhrkamp.

Macho, Thomas (2005). Von der Sehnsucht nach Gemeinschaft. Interview, moderator Jürgen König. Available online: http://www.dradio.de/dkultur/ sendungen/kulturinterview/364479.

Mayring, Philipp (1993). *Einführung in die qualitative Sozialforschung. Eine Anleitung zu qualitativem Denken*. Weinheim: Beltz Psychologie-Verlags-Union.

McCombs, Maxwell E., Juan Pablo Llamas, Esteban Lopez-Escobar, and Frederico Rey (1997). Candidate Images in Spanish Elections. Second-Level Agenda-Setting Effects. *Journalism and Mass Communication Quarterly*, 74 (4), 703–17.

Meinert, Peer (2005). *Der große Kommunikator ist verstummt*. Available online: http://www.pnp.de/nachrichten/artikel.php?cid=29-8062861&Ressort=pol& Map=%C2%A7(MAP)&BNR=0.

Nassauer, Kurt (1949/1950). Zur Soziologie der Masse. *Kölner Zeitschrift für Soziologie*, 2 (4), 391–7.

Neckel, Sighard (1991). *Status und Scham*. Frankfurt am Main, New York: Campus.

Pan, Zhongang, and Gerald M. Kosicki (1993). Framing Analysis. An Approach to News Discourse. *Political Communication*, 10 (1), 55–75.

Saxer, Ulrich, and Martina Märki-Koepp (1992). *Medien-Gefühlskultur. Zielgruppenspezifische Gefühlsdramaturgie als journalistische Produktionsroutine.* München: Verlag Olschlager.

Scheff, Thomas (1988). Shame and Conformity. The Deference-Emotion System. *American Sociological Review*, 53, 395–406.

Scheufele, Dietram A., and David Tewksbury (2007). Framing, Agenda Setting, and Priming. The Evolution of Three Media Effects Models. *Journal of Communication*, 57, 9–20.

Shott, Susan (1979). Emotion and Social Life. A Symbolic Interactionist Analysis. *American Journal of Sociology*, 84 (6), 1317–34.

Simmel, Georg (1968). *Soziologie. Untersuchung über die Formen der Vergesellschaftung*, Berlin: Duncker & Humblot. [first published in 1908]

Stark, Rodney (1997). German and German-American Religiousness. *Journal for the Scientific Study of Religion*, 36, 182–93.

Szulc, Tad (1995). The Man Who Is Pope John Paul II. Papal Welcome. *Catholic Standard*, 28 September 1995, 9.

Vester, Heinz-Günter (1991). *Emotion, Gesellschaft und Kultur. Grundzüge einer soziologischen Theorie der Emotionen*. Opladen: Westdeutscher Verlag.

Wettergren, Åsa (2005). *Mobilization and the Moral Shock. Adbusters Media Foundation.* In Helena Flam and Debra King (eds.). Emotions and Social Movements, 99–118. London, New York: Routledge.

Zimmermann, Mark (1995). Chasing the Pope. *Catholic Standard*, 12 October 1995, 2.

Zurcher, Louis (1982). The Staging of Emotion. *Symbolic Interaction*, 5 (1), 1–22.

Notes on Contributors

Jack Barbalet is Professor of Sociology at the University of Western Sydney. He previously held positions in sociology at the University of Leicester and the Australian National University, in political science at the University of Adelaide, and economics at the University of Papua New Guinea. Among his recent publications are *Emotion, Social Theory, and Social Structure: A Macrosociological Approach* (Cambridge University Press 1998 and 2001), *Emotions and Sociology* (Blackwell 2002), and *Weber, Passion and Profits: "The Protestant Ethic and the Spirit of Capitalism" in Context* (Cambridge University Press 2008). He is presently writing another book, *The Constitution of Markets: Rationality, Power and Interests*, to be published by Oxford University Press.

Patrick Becker is a research fellow at the Institute of Science and Technology Studies at the University of Bielefeld, Germany. After receiving his Diploma in Social Sciences from the University of Mannheim and a M.A.-degree in Science Studies from the University of Maastricht, he is now working on his Ph.D. on the current emotional turn in the sciences and professions. His main areas of interest are science studies, cultural sociology, and the sociology of emotions. He has published contributions to journals and collected volumes in all three of these.

Nicolas Demertzis is Professor at the Faculty of Communication and Media Studies, Athens University. He studied political science and in 1986 received his Ph.D. degree in Sociology from the University of Lund, Sweden. His current academic and research interests include political sociology, political communication, and the sociology of emotions. His major works are: *Cultural Theory and Political Culture. New Directions and Proposals* (Lund, 1985), *Culture, Modernity, Political Culture* (Athens, 1989), *Essay on Ideology. A Dialogue between Social Theory and Psychoanalysis* (with Thanos Lipowatz, Athens, 1994), *Local Publicity and the Press in Greece* (Athens, 1996), *The Nationalist*

Discourse. Ambivalent Semantic Field and Contemporary Tendencies (Athens, 1996) *Political Communication. Risk, Publicity and the Internet* (2002), *Envy, Ressentiment. The Passions of the Soul and the Closed Society* (with Thanos Lipowatz, 2006). He edited the book *The Greek Political Culture Today* (1994), the collected volume *Political Communication in Greece* (2002), and he co-edited the book *Religions and Politics in Modernity* (2002).

Katrin Döveling completed her M.A. in Sociology, Psychology and Communication Studies at Heinrich-Heine-University, Duesseldorf in Germany, and received her doctoral degree from the University of Erfurt, Germany. She was a doctoral research scholar at the University of California, Berkeley, USA. She has had several research stays in the US and France, including a Visiting Professorship at the University Val de Marne Paris. She is currently Assistant Professor at the Department of Communication Studies at the Free University in Berlin. Her research interests include the analysis of emotions in media psychology and media sociology, communication studies, Reality TV, infotainment, identity and religion, mass media, visual and intercultural communication. She teaches media psychology and media analysis with a special focus on emotional media reception, interpersonal communication and media entertainment. Publications include: *Emotions – Media – Community* (VS Verlag, 2005). She is co-editor of *Im Namen des Fernsehvolkes [In the Name of the TV Audience. New formats for orientation and evaluation]* (with Mikos/Nieland, UVK, 2007) and of the upcoming *Handbook of Emotions and the Mass Media* (with v. Scheve, Routledge, 2009)

Helena Flam received her Fil. Kand. in Sweden and her Ph.D. at Columbia University. She has been Professor of Sociology in Leipzig, Germany since 1993. She has brought out many articles, monographs and collected volumes in the sociology of emotions, including *Soziologie der Emotionen* (2002) and *Emotions and Social Movements* (2005)—each was since reprinted once. She was a co-founder of the Emotions Network at the European Sociological Association.

James Goodman researches social movements and globalization at the University of Technology Sydney. He is a founding member of the Cosmopolitan Civil Societies Research Centre and co-editor of *Nationalism and Global Solidarities* (Routledge 2007). He is on the Editorial Board of *Globalizations*, and leads projects charting ideologies of justice globalism, and examining political communities and informational disorder. He is currently investigating collective action and climate change.

Arlie Russell Hochschild, Professor at the University of California, Berkeley, is the author of *The Managed Heart: Commercialization of Human Feeling; The Commercialization of Intimate Life: Notes from Home and Work;* and co-editor of *Global Woman: Nannies, Maids and Sex Workers in the New Economy,* among other books. Her 1975 essay, *The Sociology of Feeling and Emotion: Selected Possibilities* (in *Sociological Inquiry*) and her 1979 essay *Emotion Work, Feeling Rules and Social Structure* (in *American Journal of Sociology*) have been credited with inspiring the establishment of a sociology of emotion.

Debra Hopkins is a researcher at the Health Services Research Unit at the University of Aberdeen, and Associate Research Fellow at the University of Copenhagen. She completed her Ph.D. at the University of Melbourne, has held teaching and research posts in Melbourne and at the University of Glasgow, and a visiting scholar post at Karlstad University in Sweden. She is a vice-coordinator of the Sociology of Emotions Research Network within the ESA. She has published articles on the role of emotion in public policy, gender, contested conceptualizations of care, and disability and chronic illness.

Eva Illouz is the author of five books: *Consuming the Romantic Utopia: Love and the Cultural Contradictions of Capitalism* published in 1997 with the University of California Press (which won an award from the American Sociological Association in 2000); in 2002 *The Culture of Capitalism* (in Hebrew); in 2003 *Oprah Winfrey and the Glamour of Misery: An Essay on Popular Culture* (Best Book Award, American Sociological Association, 2005); *Cold Intimacies* (Polity Press, 2007); and *Saving the Modern Soul: Therapy, Emotions, and the Culture of Self-Help* (University of California Press, 2008). In 2004 she delivered the Adorno Lectures in Germany. Her work has been translated in ten languages. Eva Illouz has been a Visiting Professor at the EHESS in Paris and at Princeton University. In 2008–2009, she was a member of the Wissenschaftskolleg in Berlin.

Jochen Kleres is conducting his Ph.D.-research at the University of Leipzig (Germany) on dissolution processes in AIDS-organizations. Between 2003 and 2004 he was involved in an EU-funded comparative project on institutional discrimination against migrants (XENOPHOB). His fields of interests are social movements, NGOs and civil society, AIDS, migration and the role of emotions in these fields. He has published several contributions to journals and collected volumes on social movements, migration, and emotions.

Helmut Kuzmics, born 1949, is Professor of Sociology at the University of Graz/Austria and held teaching and research posts at the Universities of Vienna, Hannover, Innsbruck, and Cambridge, UK. He is a member of the section for Sociology of Culture within the German Sociological Association, a vice-coordinator of the Sociology of Emotions Research Network within the ESA, a member of the Advisory Board of the Centre for the Study of Culture and Politics, University of Swansea, UK, and of the Science Committee of the Austrian Federal Ministry of Defense. His publications include *Literatur als Soziologie. Zum Verhältnis von literarischer und gesellschaftlicher Wirklichkeit* (with Gerald Mozetic, 2003), *Authority, State and National Character. The Civilizing Process in Austria and England, 1700–1900* (with Roland Axtmann, 2007), and other books and articles on civilization theory, historical sociology, and sociology of emotions.

Thomas J. Scheff is Professor Emeritus at the University of California, Santa Barbara. He is past president of the Pacific Sociological Association, and past chair of the Emotions Section of the ASA. Some of his publications are *Being Mentally Ill; Microsociology; Bloody Revenge; Emotions, The Social Bond and Human Reality.* His latest is *Goffman Unbound!: A New Paradigm* (Paradigm Publishers, 2006), and *Easy Rider* (iUniverse, 2007).

Simon J. Williams is a Professor of Sociology, in the Department of Sociology, University of Warwick, UK. He has published widely in the sociology of health, the sociology of the body and the sociology of emotions. One of his current research interests concerns relations between the social sciences and neurosciences. To this end he recently established an interdisciplinary neuroscience and society research group at the University of Warwick, details of which can be found at http://www2.warwick.ac.uk/fac/soc/nsw. He is also currently co-editing a special issue of the new interdisciplinary journal *Subjectivities* on *Neuroscience and Subjectivities* and co-writing a book (with P. Martin) provisionally entitled *Neurofutures in the Making.*